Africans in Colonial Mexico

Blacks in the Diaspora

Herman L. Bennett

Africans in Colonial Mexico

Absolutism,

Christianity, and

Afro-Creole

Consciousness,

1570–1640

INDIANA
University Press
Bloomington & Indianapolis

Publication of this book is made possible in part with the
assistance of a Challenge Grant from the National Endowment
for the Humanities, a federal agency that supports research,
education, and public programming in the humanities.

This book is a publication of

Indiana University Press
601 North Morton Street
Bloomington, IN 47404-3797 USA

http://iupress.indiana.edu

Telephone orders   800-842-6796
Fax orders   812-855-7931
Orders by e-mail   iuporder@indiana.edu
First paperback edition 2005
© 2003 by Herman L. Bennett

The paper used in this publication meets the minimum
requirements of American National Standard for
Information Sciences—Permanence of Paper for Printed
Library Materials, ANSI Z39.48-1984.

Library of Congress Cataloging-in-Publication Data

Bennett, Herman L. (Herman Lee), date
Africans in Colonial Mexico : absolutism, Christianity, and Afro-Creole consciousness, 1570–1640 /
Herman L. Bennett.
p.   cm. — (Blacks in the diaspora)
Includes bibliographical references and index.
ISBN 0-253-34236-8 (cloth : alk. paper)
1. Blacks—Mexico—Mexico City—Social conditions. 2. Blacks—Marriage customs and
rites—Mexico—Mexico City. 3. Mexico—History—Spanish colony, 1540–1810. 4.
Acculturation—Mexico—History. 5. Church and state—Mexico—History. 6. Slavery and the
church—Mexico—History. 7. Ecclesiastical law—Mexico—History. I. Title. II. Series.
F1386.9.B55 B46 2003
972′.00496—dc21
ISBN 0-253-21775-X (pbk.)   2002152282

2 3 4 5 6 10 09 08 07 06 05

For my loved ones
Mutti, Pops, Jenna, Carlinho, & Emmazinha

Contents

Acknowledgments

This book began with what I thought were two simple but related questions: In what ways did Catholicism shape the African experience in colonial Mexico? and Why did Spaniards subject Africans and their New World descendants to the jurisdiction of the Inquisition? In seeking to answer these questions I have incurred numerous debts that I happily acknowledge. Friends who have shaped this project from the outset with their questions and companionship include Barbara Balliet, Lee Baker, Mia Bay, Peter Bergman, Nick Biddle, Antoinette Burton, Cheryl Clarke, Shelly Eversley, Kristin GoldMansour, Adib GoldMansour, Tera Hunter, Alex Juhasz, Mary Esther Malloy, Harry Marks, Zachary Morgan, Jennifer L. Morgan, Sharon Frances Moore, Robert Reid-Pharr, Tim Tyson, Lisa Waller, Sidney Whelan, and Keith Yazmir. This book is as much theirs as it is mine.

Institutional support in the form of course relief and the occasional semester-long leave from The Johns Hopkins University and Rutgers—The State University of New Jersey enabled the writing of this book. Without this institutional beneficence I would had opted for a more conventional trajectory—publishing my revised dissertation first. I am also very grateful to the staff at the Archivo General de la Nación, especially Sra. Clara González Melchor and the wonderful individuals who presided over what was then Galeria Quatro. The Duke Endowment, Shell International Studies, and Tinker Fellowships supported the research of this project, while a generous library acquisition grant from Deborah Jakubs at Duke University facilitated much-needed copying.

Over the years, I have had the fortune to be associated with some wonderful colleagues at The Johns Hopkins University, where the writing of this project began, and Rutgers—The State University of New Jersey. I wish to thank the following colleagues in particular for their support and, even more important, their exemplary scholarship: Sara Berry, Antoinette Burton, Richard Kagan, Harry Marks, A. J. R. Russell-Wood, Gabrielle Spiegel, Orest Ranum, Walter Benn Michaels, Neil Hertz, Mary Poovey, Robert Reid-Pharr, Donald Carter, and Rolph-Michel Trouillot. At Rutgers I owe a tremendous debt to Michael Adas, Barbara Balliet, Emily Bartells, Mia Bay, Rudy Bell, Carolyn Brown, Chris Brown, Wesley Brown, Kim Butler, Cheryl Clarke, Paul Clemens, Brent Edwards, John Gillis, Allen Howard, Donald Kelley, Nancy Hewitt, Will Jones, Temma Kaplan, Daphne LaMothe, Steven Lawson, T. J. Jackson-Lears, Jennifer L. Morgan, Ben Sifuentes-Jarequi, Tom Slaughter, Bonnie Smith, and Deborah Gray White. I also extend my sincere appreciation to wonderful individuals that make up the staff of the History Department both at Rutgers and The Johns

Hopkins University. In laughing and crying, celebrating and commemorating with them, I drew needed sustenance. Participants in the Carolinas-Virginia-Georgia Colonial Latin American Seminar offered much-needed encouragement. I am very appreciative to the following individuals for comments, lecture invitations, interest, and support: Ira Berlin, Stephan Palmie, Vera Kutzinski, Nancy Farriss, Ann Farnsworth-Alvear, Tom Skidmore, R. Douglas Cope, Norman Fiering, Manning Marable, Lee Baker, Peter Kolchin, Anne Boylan, Larry O'Malley, Deborah Kanter, Richard Boyer, Rebecca Horn, Judith Byfield, Darlene Clark Hine, Nell Painter, Michael Gomez, Saidiya Hartman, Tera Hunter, Sandy Darity, Carolyn Brown, Deborah Gray White, Nancy Hewitt, Steven Lawson, Allen Howard, John Gillis, John J. TePaske, Roberta Dunbar, Myron Dunston, Reginald Hildebrand, Genna Rae McNeil, and Harold Woodard. As a member of the black Atlantic project at Rutgers, I have been very fortunate to be surrounded by a stimulating and generous group of colleague-friends. Thanks should also be extended to the graduate seminar participants in the courses taught by Donald Kelley and Bonnie Smith.

Working with Indiana University Press, especially Robert J. Sloan, Jane Lyle, and Kendra Boileau Stokes, has been a professional and a yet convivial experience. Special thanks must, however, be reserved for my editor Kate Babbitt for taking an active interest in the project and whose enthusiasm helped rekindle my passion for the subject matter.

My friends and family are the center of my world. They are amazing, challenging, and always there. Thank you. Finally, I wish to thank Jennifer Lyle Morgan for a demanding and exciting life together as parents, partners, and colleagues.

Africans in Colonial Mexico

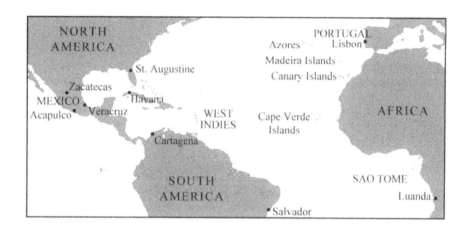

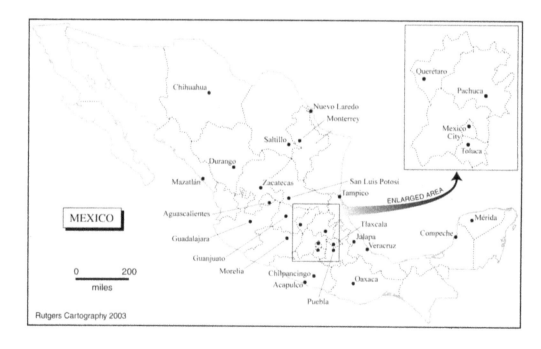

Rutgers Cartography 2003

Introduction
Africans, Absolutism, and Archives

Evidence is evidence only when some one contemplates it historically.[1]

In 1640, the year the Portuguese slave trade to Spanish America ended, the Kingdom of New Spain (colonial Mexico) contained the second-largest population of enslaved Africans and the greatest number of free blacks in the Americas.[2] In little more than a century following the successful expedition of Hernando Cortés against the Mexica (1519–1521), the Spaniards brought hundreds of African-descended servants and slaves into the colony. Over the course of a century, Portuguese slave-traders augmented this initial core with more than 110,000 enslaved Africans.[3] A 1646 census enumerated 35,089 Africans and 116,529 persons of African descent in New Spain.[4] With cessation of the slave trade, the enslaved population of New Spain steadily declined. The free black population, however, experienced continual growth and by 1810 numbered approximately 624,000, or 10 percent of the total population.[5] New Spain's seventeenth-century demographic distinctiveness—home to the second-largest slave and the largest free black populations—may come as a revelation to those unaccustomed to thinking of Mexico as a prominent site of the African presence. Even now, travelers familiar with the Afro-Mexican presence in the coastal states of Veracruz and Guerrero seem surprised to learn that a greater number of Africans and their descendants once resided in New Spain's interior.

In search of wealth, the Spaniards migrated from Tenochitlán, the capital of the Mexicas which acquired the name Mexico City, establishing a trail of towns and cities in their wake. In chartering villages, towns, and cities, the Spaniards underscored more than their physical presence and propensity for urban living.[6] The act of constituting an urban center heralded the arrival of royal authority, cloaked in laws and the ability to enforce them with violence if necessary. By establishing cities and towns—though the countryside contained the tribute, commodities, and land that they desired—the conquerors and first settlers unwittingly pitted their feudal ambitions against the centralizing Spanish monarchy intent on reining in its subjects. Cities thus became the locus of competing claims, and this contest, as we shall see, had important implications for the African presence.[7]

As servants and slaves, persons of African descent accompanied their masters into New Spain's nascent urban world. From the beginning, Africans and their descendants had deep roots in the urban landscape. By the end of the sixteenth century, they outnumbered Spaniards in many of New Spain's principal cities.[8] The growth of the urban African presence was linked to the restrictions that the Spanish Crown imposed on the use of native labor in Spanish households. As the available pool of indigenous labor declined, Spaniards employed ever-increasing numbers of Africans in their households and workshops. Urban slaves also plied the streets as carriers of people and goods, becoming indispensable to colonial city life. Spanish reliance on Africans in cities and towns throughout New Spain represents a peculiar and yet largely unexamined feature of New World slavery.[9]

As Africans labored in the urban milieu, they acquired the cultural insight necessary to navigate the colonial labyrinth. With a Christian-inflected cultural and legal consciousness, urban slaves and servants pressed for autonomy—time and mobility to interact with friends and familiars. Savvy in their quest for autonomy, urban Africans and their descendants acquired a legal consciousness composed of an awareness of rights and obligations, familiarity with the legal system, and the ability to initiate litigation that rallied the courts and its personnel in the pursuit of justice.[10]

With this legal consciousness, both enslaved and free persons established family and friendship networks predicated on an imagined identity. But in contracting Christian marriages—the centerpiece of family formation in New Spain—slaves and free persons, both of whom were defined as legal dependents, confronted opposition from patricians who interpreted certain marital alliances as a challenge to their authority.[11] In the ensuing struggles between paterfamilias and dependents, the latter, as we shall see, often prevailed with the assistance of royal or ecclesiastical authorities. This contest underscores how persons of African descent—both slave and free—appropriated strategies manifest among other dependents (wives, minors, and servants) in New Spain's urban milieu.[12] In doing so, Africans and their descendants shared and reproduced the legal consciousness that circulated between patricians and plebeians.

This legal consciousness was also instrumental in the decline of slavery and the growth of the free black population. Though scholars have long associated the slave population's precipitous decline with the cessation of the Portuguese slave trade and the negative growth rate among slaves, this formulation overshadows the contribution that the legal consciousness of urban slaves played in the ascendance of the free colored population.[13] Indeed, in Mexico City, a legal consciousness was part of the creolization process that Africans and their descendants experienced. In making this argument, I am staking out new claims for the cultural process identified as creolization.

Creolization's genesis in sixteenth-century urban New Spain resides in an immersion in the cultural practices of power. Becoming a creole literally involved navigating the judicial maze with the intent of exploiting the possibilities offered by legal obligations and rights. This definition reminds us that persons of African descent, the first people identified as creoles (*criollos*) before 1560, did not configure their culture through the physical environment, diet, language, beliefs, kinship practices, and community structures alone.[14] Creole culture included the customs, laws, and institutions that upheld the larger social structure and came to include an ability to navigate the various institutions of absolutism.[15]

Cognizant that their competing juridical identities created an exploitable tool, Africans and their descendants seized the opportunity. Though patricians posed a serious physical threat, individuals drew on their creole consciousness for specific tactics. In this process, their command of Spanish—which shaped the ability of Africans and their descendants to represent themselves before scribes, royal officials, and ecclesiastics as royal subjects and devout Christians —played an important role. Even recent arrivals from Africa, *bozales,* immersed themselves in a new linguistic environment soon after landing in New Spain, acquiring fluency in the Castilian lexicon and morphology of power.[16] Eventually, *bozales* learned to enlist the protection of crown and clergy, who, as representatives of the Spanish sovereign, often stood at odds with individual patricians.

This strategic awareness—the defining feature of creole consciousness— enabled the plebeian population, which included persons of African descent, to employ the law in their defense.[17] As litigants, persons of African descent modified their life circumstances, yet they rarely, if ever, threatened to undermine Spanish rule. But in enabling a semblance of cultural autonomy, the litigious nature of Africans and their descendants also insinuated both slave and free even further into workings of Spanish absolutism.

In Spanish America—where absolutism gained its fullest expression—the sovereign's authority reigned ascendant over all domains until the seventeenth-century culmination of the Baroque era. As an absolutist, the Castilian monarch assumed a prominent role in governing Spanish America, which stood in stark contrast to the English colonies, where the Crown assumed a more limited role and an individual's authority over private property reigned supreme.[18] In this respect, early modern Spanish expansion extended the traditions of the centralizing monarchies in medieval Christendom.[19] Castile's sovereigns subjected trade, discovery, and settlement to their authority in hopes of extending royal dominion. Even as merchant capitalism's extant pockets sustained the expansion of Christianity and colonization, it also required sanction from absolutist rulers in the form of charters. In return for real and symbolic obeisance, royal subjects requested and received approval to contract trade, discover new territories, and extend the Christian presence. In the absolutist era, such endeavors almost always necessitated royal authorization.

In paying scant attention to the imperial presence in the lives of Africans and their descendants, scholars have neglected the consequences of a slavery and freedom that flourished under absolutism. Spanish expansion fueled the emergence of New World slavery, while imperial absolutism constituted slaves as subjects; both profoundly shaped the African experience. Slaves, of course, represented both property and people.

But in early modern Spanish America, masters were not the only ones who defined the nature of slavery or even the most powerful authorities to manifest dominion over the enslaved. As Spain's absolutist rulers extended their dominion throughout the unfolding Atlantic world, they continually encroached on the domain of private property, which still occupied a tenuous place in the mercantile economy. Intent on consolidating imperial rule, Castile's sovereigns often transgressed the masters' domain even though Roman law accorded masters complete authority over slaves. The Catholic kings did not intrude on the sanctity of the master-slave relationship in an arbitrary manner, however. Instead, they relied on competing laws, especially canon law, which constituted converted Africans as Christian subjects despite their slave status. Jurisdictional conflicts surfaced with their attendant consequences for empire and slavery. In the process, the enslaved gained an acute awareness of competing obligations and rights, a form of ambiguity they willingly exploited by deploying regulatory devices in a manner that the Spanish monarchs never intended.

The competing and conflicting legal status of Africans in colonial Spanish America raises the questions of why, when, and how the enslaved emerged as beings other than as slaves. Under what circumstances did Africans acquire discrete subject positions? For instance, by applying canon law to a population that had entered the Americas largely as chattel, Spanish authorities assigned converted slaves Christian identities with defined obligations and rights formulated long before the European encounter with Guinea (the early modern Christian European referent for West Africa). On what grounds—theological or legal—did Spaniards rationalize this decision?

Similarly, why did the Spanish monarchy grant the tribunal of the Holy Office of the Inquisition authority over Africans and their descendants but exempt Amerindians? By demanding that converted Africans adhere to canon law and subjecting the sinners among them to the jurisdiction of the ecclesiastical court and the tribunal of the Holy Office, Spaniards perceived certain individuals of African descent as Old World persons. Yet studies of race and slavery in the Americas have posited Africans as the quintessential others.[20] If not the "other," what position did peoples of African descent occupy in the encounter between the Old and New Worlds?

By implicitly addressing these and similar questions, this book demonstrates that slave status—a legal category describing property in persons—merely represented one of several identities that enslaved Africans acquired in their forced migration from Guinea to the Indies (the Spanish name for the Americas). The circumstances under which these competing and conflicting identities emerged are central to the book's narrative structure. The genesis of the early modern African diaspora resides in imperial expansion, which included an unfolding political theory that informed the Christian European encounter with Guinea and its diverse inhabitants, and the process of transplanting some of those inhabitants to the Indies as slaves where they were also rendered vassals and Christians.

Simply put, the African diaspora—a lived experience—also constituted a field of identities made possible by the complexity of Spanish imperial ideology and Christian political thought, which assigned Africans discrete juridical identities as slaves, royal subjects, and persons with souls. For these reasons, the African diaspora as it emerges here represents both an experience and the product of regulation. African lives, as recorded by Spanish clerks, in Spanish records, for Spanish purposes, must be recovered from an archive that persons of African descent did little to construct in the first instance. Efforts to recover the "experiences" elicited by the diverse juridical identities that Africans acquired demands a careful delineation of the regulatory proceedings of absolutism.[21]

For students of the African diaspora, recovery of history remains a central preoccupation. But recovering histories of slaves and freedpersons also poses a formidable feat. "Africans"—an invention of the West—became "slaves" and "blacks" after they were rendered into commodities and removed from the land of their origins. They subsequently entered the absolutist archive as objects largely divorced from the material and ideological world of any past but that to which their owners ascribed.[22] Can the recovery of history avert the impact of colonial rule on the formation of an archive? Can historians produce an unmediated past capable of restoring subjects, agency, and narratives when absolutism constructed these very categories? I argue that it is impossible to recover an authentic and unmediated past since the fragments on which historians must rely emanated in regulation. The genealogy whereby "Africans" became "slaves" and "blacks" serves as a powerful reminder that the history of the enslaved and their descendants—free and enslaved—cannot be disengaged from the dominant historical process.[23] As Franz Fanon, the theorist of black existentialism, observed, "the black soul is a white man's artifact."[24] Though commenting on the late modern experience, Fanon understood that discerning a pure "experience" represented a quixotic quest akin to the act of authentic recovery—arguably social history's defining mission.[25]

At best, we can hope to contextualize the African past by delineating how, when, and why specific categories emerged. Given, as we shall see, the contingent nature of defining "black" (*negro*), "black creole" (*negro criollo*), and "mulatto" (*mulato*), among other terms, social labels never acquired fixed meanings.[26] The instability informing the classification process serves to question the existence of distinct African, slave, and black identities. Efforts to harness the surviving fragments in order to produce a history of the African diaspora requires careful attention to the overlapping ensemble of texts, traditions, and regulatory practices that constitute a discursive domain, that field of meaning through which specific terms, symbols, and behavior take on and impose significance.[27]

From the beginning of their initial encounters along the African littoral, Portugal's rulers and then the Spanish Crown monitored the experiences of Africans and their descendants. As the initial chattel raids gave way to mercantile relations, the Iberian monarchies imposed their preferred juridical terminology and through such language structured their relations with the Guinea's inhabitants.

We know that in Guinea of the fifteenth through sixteenth centuries, there was no such thing as an overarching African or black identity formulated in response to the European presence. Individuals largely identified themselves on the basis of lineages and occasionally on state structures, both of which were tenuous. The names of the port cities that were points of embarkation for groups of people from many disparate regions of Africa became the "ethnic" labels assigned to enslaved individuals. Thus, a person's "ethnicity" was assigned by Europeans through his or her encounter with slavery. The answer to the most basic of questions about identity—Who are you?—was defined by European categories of classifications from the moment of enslavement.

From the moment of enslavement the Portuguese and Spaniards categorized Africans as "ethnics," thereby ensuring both the legitimacy of the enslaving process and demonstrating their mastery over the enslaved. This distinction was important to the Europeans, since some Africans could not be legally enslaved. For example, the Portuguese until the middle of the seventeenth century recognized the vassal status of the subjects of the king of Kongo and prohibited their enslavement. There were, of course, exceptions, but in general the Portuguese respected the subject status of the Bakongo, which helps explain the dearth of "Congos" in the Americas prior to the middle of the seventeenth century. The identity of the African shaped who could legitimately be enslaved and, in turn, structured the slave trade. Consequently, the Portuguese and the Spanish focused on minutia of "identity," giving Africans labels that became the administrative categories in the New World and subsequently entered the colonial archives. When Africans in New Spain interacted with colonial authorities, they identified themselves as "from Angola" or "from Biafra land" or "from Terra Nova." These were not concepts that carried cachet with Africans in Africa; they represented European ways of categorizing.

It is evidence of the emerging legal consciousness of *bozales* that they adopted European nomenclature in their encounters with and uses of the European juridical systems. To accept that slavery is overarching is to lose opportunities to understand how individuals fashioned identities that were meaningful to them outside the system of slavery. Many *bozales* and persons of African descent whose stories entered the archives demonstrated great skill as they worked their way through the intricacies of European legal systems. As they did so, they used language that those in power could understand.

To ensure that crown favorites and their king's coffer benefited from the mercantile intercourse, officials carefully regulated the demand side through royal charters. During the second half of the fifteenth century, as Castilians challenged Portugal's purported hegemony over Guinea, the terms informing the charters and the language of the factors assumed even greater precision. By the sixteenth century, their trading monopoly with Guinea sanctioned by the pope, the Portuguese regulated the slave trade through European-derived concepts such as *asiento* (contract), *pieza de India* (a unit of measure representing an ideal male slave), and *bozal* (a slave directly from Africa). This regulatory language proliferated and subsequently mediated the trade in humans that extended to Iberia, the Atlantic Islands, and, finally, the Americas. But as this book illustrates, the terminology used to describe persons of African descent expanded over the course of the middle passage and beyond. By the time a slave ship landed in the Indies, the Africans on board already constituted slaves, royal subjects, and, in some cases, Christians. Through their prescribed juridical status, Africans and their descendants formulated New World identities that had valence during their encounters with absolutism. For this reason, identity was not a preordained essence for persons of African descent in the New World; it was carefully constructed.

Focusing on New Spain's slave trade and the formation of the African presence, Chapter 1 tracks the cultural shifts informing descriptions of the slave and free colored populations. Spaniards used a number of terms to refer to persons of African descent which reflected purported and actual differences among members of a constantly expanding population. In ascribing meaning to specific terms, royal officials, ecclesiastical authorities, and slave-owners underscored the regulatory intent of classification. Naming people and places signified mastery. Despite the power of dominant representations, the African-born and their descendants reconstituted their identities via diverse regulatory structures. But identities changed in accordance with the demographic, cultural, and social shifts among the population of African descent. Aside from describing these sociocultural shifts among persons of African descent, this chapter argues that New Spain, and in particular Mexico City, constituted a slave society—a society that Spain's sovereigns were intent on regulating.

Spain's rulers deployed various mechanisms to contain the threat of heresy presented by a population who was not Christian by birth. In an effort to discipline the African presence, the Spanish monarchy relied on the Catholic Church. An ally of, if not subservient to, royal absolutism, Catholic authorities complied, due largely to a fifteenth-century papal decree, with the Patronato Real, which granted Spain's rulers the authority to make all ecclesiastical appointments.

In regulating the African presence, ecclesiastical officials subjected converted black peoples to Christian norms. In the second half of the sixteenth century, the focus of Chapter 2, the ecclesiastical courts began policing the Christian commonwealth and disciplining the laity, who also represented the king's vassals. The ecclesiastical court insisted that the laity adhere to Christian orthodoxy and through conjugal laws determined the various cultural identities individuals could assume. The extant proceedings, recorded in the *bienes nacionales,* reveal how Mexico's ecclesiastical court regulated the behavior of Africans and their descendants in accordance with Christian mores. Spain's regulatory practices represented a novelty in the Americas because of their focus on the body, in particular sexual behavior, and the extent of their reach. This chapter demonstrates that the timing of absolutism's ascendancy prompted the Crown to extend greater authority over Africans as both property and vassals. Control over slavery, slaves, and the free colored population constituted an essential part of state-building. Christian courts and ecclesiastical sources aside; the formation of Spain's imperial state was demonstrated in its control of slavery, slaves, and free people of color.

Over the course of the sixteenth century, the limits of absolutism became readily apparent. Despite ecclesiastical vigilance, heresy proliferated in New Spain. While clerics saw verbal expressions that contravened the sacraments and canon law as heretical, following the Protestant Reformation, the term "heresy" expanded to include views and practices that challenged Catholic sovereignty. In 1569, Philip II was sufficiently alarmed to call upon the services of the Holy Office of the Inquisition—an institution regularly staffed by clerics but which in Spain and the Americas was under royal control. Indeed, it is critical to underscore that the Inquisition and the Catholic Church embodied two distinct institutions. Chapter 3 examines the effect of the Inquisition's powerful presence from its spectacular entry, bearing all the trappings of a *reconquista* (reconquest), to the spectacle of the initial auto-de-fé, a procession in which the guilty were paraded before the community in penitential clothing denoting their shame. Sometimes the guilty were publicly whipped, and on occasion individuals were executed. Despite its concerns with the Protestant heresy and the purported growth of the Jewish population, the Inquisition focused primarily on the Catholic laity, which was largely African. From the beginning, royal officials perceived Africans and their descendants as people of reason (*gente de razón*), according them a juridical status in the Spanish commonwealth (República de los Españoles) and thereby subjecting them to the jurisdiction of the Inquisition. In the eyes of the tribunal members, persons of African descent occupied a status distinct from that of the original natives of the Indies, who, as a result, were exempted from the jurisdiction of the Inquisition.

The intrusive nature of absolutism emerges fully in the inquisition proceedings mounted against persons of African descent. The tribunal never identified persons of African descent as a specific target, but nearly 50 percent of the inquisition proceedings involved Africans and their creole descendants. These proceedings, which figure prominently in this project, underscore both the extent of the African presence in New Spain and the Christian norms to which secular and ecclesiastical officials subjected Africans and their descendants. As the Inquisition sought to exorcise heresy from the realm and shore up the authority of the sovereign, Mexico's preponderance of Africans and their descendants witnessed the grim and gory spectacles of the auto-de-fé, orchestrated for a commonwealth and city composed principally of *castas*, a term referring to biologically mixed people.

After New Spain's initial auto-de-fé, Catholic reform assumed a less spectacular expression. Pedro Moya de Contreras's transformation from the initial inquisitor general to Mexico's archbishop symbolized the manner in which royal officials insinuated reform throughout the viceroyalty. Though the Inquisition remained an institutional fixture well into the nineteenth century, its modus operandi confined the tribunal's presence to those extraordinary moments when truly egregious acts surfaced among the laity.

The Episcopal Court, over which the ecclesiastical judge presided, held a more ubiquitous position with regard to the Christian flock. As archbishop, Pedro Moya occupied a role from which he could reform the Church and discipline the laity. A decade after his investiture, Pedro Moya had instilled royal authority throughout New Spain's clergy and Catholic reform stood ascendant. The Church's regulatory features presided over the cultural sphere that it had helped to create—baptism, confirmation, yearly confession, marriage, and the last rites.

An examination in Chapter 4 of over 4,000 marriage petitions from 1584 to 1640 highlights ethnic and cultural self-fashioning in an official context while illustrating the complexity of community formation, a process rarely discernible in histories of the African diaspora. Even though the clergy care-fully regulated cultural forms in accordance with Christian norms, in selecting their witnesses (*testigos*), New Spain's African-descended population simulta-neously manifested identities and expressed agency in a manner that Church officials never intended.

Chapter 5 examines how persons of African descent, free and enslaved, ac-tively navigated the cultural terrain of their rights and obligations as Christian subjects. Like the previous chapters, it delineates the regulatory sites in which persons of African descent emerged as subjects and the manner in which sub-ject status elicited specific depictions of their experience. This ethnography un-derscores how, in the prescriptive context which absolutism, Christianity, and Catholic reform imposed, the strategic performances of persons of African de-scent in New Spain—manifest in the use of language, cultural norms, and the law—reflected a cultural immersion rarely associated with Africans and their descendants. Christianity's regulatory impulse, in short, made possible a creoli-zation process among persons of African descent that included the acquisition of a legal consciousness alongside Spanish and indigenous cultural practices.

Chapter 6 offers an extended look at this creole consciousness among per-sons of African descent by examining some of the initial sixteenth-century inquisition proceedings involving the Hispanic population. The unequal dia-logue informing these trials again highlights the extent to which inquisition officials defined persons of African descent as Christian subjects with an obli-gation to adhere to Catholic mores. Catholic morality embraced more than a few discrete norms and practices. It constituted an elaborate belief and cultural system that defined gender conventions, sexual behavior, and kinship relations with great precision.

By embracing these mores—freely or out of fear—Africans and their creole descendants effected a profound transformation of their sense of self. The in-quisition proceedings, which delineate acceptable practices, enable us to see the speed of and the extent to which Christianity was insinuated into the lives of Africans and their descendants. In fashioning themselves and their narratives for the inquisitors, the innumerable witnesses both genuflected and performed, but in either case revealed a cultural sensibility that permitted them to navigate the judicial maze. By means of this awareness, persons of African descent also magnified the contours of the cultural arena that they inhabited. Although this arena thrived in a symbiotic relationship with Church and state, the trial pro-ceedings record the ways in which community boundaries differed from social status and the structures of social stratification.

Several studies have examined the experiences of the enslaved, offering im-portant assessments of slave life in New Spain. Mostly social historical works, these studies chartered new ground in the histories of the slave trade, the distribution of the enslaved, slave labor, the nature of slave treatment, social control, manumission, and race relations.[28] In analyzing the social experiences of slavery, the pioneering studies often left basic issues and common assumptions about the African presence in need of attention.[29] For instance, why was New Spain home at one time to the largest free black population in the Americas? In what ways was the growth of the free black population related to a natural rate of increase among the enslaved population? Unfortunately, Latin Americanists have largely moved on, believing that the early African experience remains irrelevant to the grand narrative of colonial Spanish America. Invariably, efforts aimed at recovering and redefining the African experience—including this one—start from a defensive posture designed to validate the study's significance and relationship to the history of power. In an effort to discern the workings of power, for instance, modern studies of slavery tend to focus on property and the authority that masters wielded over their chattel. This perspective rightly insists that the reality of power—most notably work—shaped the slave experience. Yet as a study of the urban experience of Africans and their descendants, this book does not privilege the laboring process. In devoting little attention to work, I do not deny that the laboring process shaped culture. It did, as Ira Berlin and Philip Morgan have reminded us.[30] Culture, in fact, emerged from the conflict between masters and slaves concerning the control of time. Still, I suggest that in the context of New Spain and particularly in Mexico City the laboring process was but one factor pressing on persons of African descent and their cultural formation. Labor simply did not have a monopoly over social relations.

My elision of labor is in part also a result of the sources I selected. Inquisition and church records offer invaluable depth into the lives and consciousness of New Spain's residents, providing a glimpse that cannot be reproduced for any other part of the early modern Atlantic world.[31] Yet work and master-slave relations have a limited presence in inquisition and ecclesiastical records. Although the archives contain records of how individuals identified their legal status, their masters, and the households in which they resided, they say very little about the culture of work. But at the same time, inquisition and ecclesiastical proceedings underscore New Spain's culture of power—absolutism's concern with the moral behavior of ordinary peoples. By attending to baptism, confirmation, marriage, death, and deviations from New Spain's sixteenth-century Christian norm, the ecclesiastical records and inquisition sources attend to critical episodes in peoples' lives and thereby in their Christian life cycle. I insist that in the period (1570–1640) and place (Mexico City) covered by this study, Christianity was just as—if not more—invasive than the patricians' authority over their African slaves and servants. Scholars have long known of these records, but only a few—Gonzalo Aguirre Beltrán, Colin Palmer, Solange Alberro, and Richard Boyer—have explored their potential for writing histories of Africans and their creole descendants.[32]

Despite their richness and countless testimonies, I treat inquisition and ecclesiastical sources with caution.[33] My central concern is who has the power in these stories and who does not. These sources were created because of the power of absolutism, and I do not feel that they can be viewed outside the context of the influence of that ideology. Concerns about power explain my insistence on determining the social logic behind the production of historical sources.[34] I initially wanted to know why Spaniards subjected persons of African descent to Christian norms and brought some of the purported sinners before the tribunal of the Holy Office of the Inquisition.

I view this book as a social history of absolutism that simultaneously constitutes a culturally inflected intellectual history. As such, this book does not purport to represent an exhaustive examination of urban Africans and their descendants in sixteenth-century Mexico—that history, if possible, needs to be written. I do, however, insist that the source material generated by Spanish absolutism at its epicenter—Mexico City—offers an unrivaled glimpse into the ways that Christianity and slavery produced specific gendered identities—or at least the strategic performance thereof—among Africans and their descendants. As the ecclesiastical authorities and the inquisitors subjected peoples of African descent to scrutiny, alien cultural practices did not represent the principal threat to the dominion of the sovereign of Spain in New Spain. For the clerics and members of the Holy Office, the gendered and sexual behavior of Africans was at issue. Absolutism, predicated on Christian patriarchal and conjugal norms, perceived an implicit threat in practices that did not conform to Christian orthodoxy. For this reason, Spain's absolutists expressed an interest in having the Catholic Church and the Inquisition regulate—by both recording and disciplining—the lives of Africans and their descendants. In examining this regulatory process, this project uncovers an exceedingly rich but neglected gendered, sexual, and conjugal history among Africans and their descendants.

Before us, then, is a history of the African presence under absolutism. Predicated on naming Africans and their descendants and identifying their lovers, kin, and enemies, this history—comprised of fictions, tales, and stories—reminds us that absolutism focused on controlling people. We should never forget that many of the persons whose experiences fill these pages were slaves—the property of others—or their immediate descendants. As a legal category, as a propriety relationship, as a labor-extracting mechanism, and as a form of domination, slavery shaped but did not determine African experience in urban New Spain. The emphasis on "lives," as opposed to "experience," seems appropriate for several reasons. For Church and state, the slave experience—as property, as a labor category, or as the subject of domination—and the African presence—alien and seditious by official definition—was not the issue. The concern resided with their gendered identities and sexuality, matters intimately associated with lives but not synonymous with the slave or African experience.

By exploiting the breach on the basis of their gendered identities, the African-born and their creole descendants used their lives to question the very meaning of the slave and colonial experience. Initially, slaves transformed Christian obligations into rights. As males and females, slaves were entitled to a Christian marriage, and as a couple they had a right to a conjugal existence. Conjugality resulted in visitation rights and restrictions on selling a slave husband or wife away from their spouse. By insisting on their rights as Christians, slaves circumscribed the masters' authority to treat them in any manner they saw fit. The ability to invoke these rights and mobilize the Church, state, and specific masters in their defense was the hallmark of a creole consciousness. In glimpsing this consciousness, however, we must remind ourselves that it emerged through regulatory proceedings, which invariably must temper our romance with the recovery of this knowledge. Still, the countless episodes underscore a cultural resourcefulness rarely if ever associated with African experience in the New World—a resourcefulness that the regulatory process highlights even if it only shows us strategic performances of Christian identities.

In recognizing the Church's involvement with converted Africans, I should emphasize that Christian discipline, not amelioration, informed this intervention. As the largest institutional owners of slaves in the Americas, the various Catholic corporations were not troubled by the enslavement of Africans. Yet the truly insidious part was the Church's commitment to transforming Africans into Christians, thereby distancing them from earlier selves. Can there be a question about the violence involved in remaking personhood? Even though persons of African descent used their rights as Christians to effect marriage—a process that brought their identities as individuals with souls into conflict with their status as chattel—the toll created by the negation of the past was enormous. Even if enslaved Africans willingly embraced Christianity and its social practices—baptism, gender norms, and matrimony—conversion to Christianity resulted in new ways of recognizing ontological distancing, a phenomenon that defined the African experience in the New World.[35]

1   Soiled Gods and the Formation of a Slave Society

> Continental Spanish slavery did not create a slave society—that is, a society domi-
> nated by slaveholders and marked principally by the pervasive influence of the
> master-slave relationship—but it did make possible enough concentrations of
> plantations and mines using black labor to create substantial pockets of masters
> and slaves within the wider society.[1]

New World slavery was ostensibly, but not exclusively, rooted in agricultural
production. Slaves spent their lives toiling on estates—haciendas, *engenhos*, and
plantations—cultivating cash crops.[2] In most regions of the Americas, slave labor also contributed substantial foodstuffs (cereal, grains, fruits, vegetables,
and livestock) to subsistence, household, regional, and domestic economies,
thereby reinforcing the perception that New World slavery constituted an agricultural institution.[3] The dominance of the plantation complex has obscured
the diverse African experiences that flourished within New World slavery.[4]
Though recent scholarship has done much to revise this perspective, studies on
the African experience largely remain focused on grand estates.[5] For this reason, scholars still identify slave societies with the plantation complex while associating cities as societies with slaves.[6] But in Spanish America, slave societies
and the African presence initially emerged in the urban crucibles of colonial
power—Lima and Mexico City—before extending into the rural periphery. To
define bondage in Spanish America, on the basis of its urban location, as mere
"pockets" of a slave society ignores Spanish colonial development. In contrast
to other European colonies, Spanish urban centers featured closer ties to the
countryside that have quite discernible implications for slavery and the early
African experience.[7]

Historical scholarship about slavery has also focused on labor instead of on
the multiple roles ascribed to slaves, which has drawn the attention of scholars away from comparing Peru and New Spain with Jamaica, Carolina, Saint
Domingue, Cuba, and Brazil. Similarly, scholars eschew positioning Mexico
City and Lima alongside Charleston, Havana, Rio, or Salvador.[8] One of the
most prescient scholars of slavery recently noted that "what distinguished societies with slaves was the fact that slaves were marginal to the central produc-
tive processes; slavery was just one form of labor among many."[9] Slavery on the
Spanish mainland, though far from insignificant, comprised one of several

ways in which the Spaniards organized labor, including that of Africans. In such societies, as Ira Berlin has noted, "no one presumed the master-slave relationship to be the social exemplar." For similar reasons, Eugene Genovese has determined that "continental Spanish slavery did not create a slave society."[10]

But as this and subsequent chapters illustrate, New Spain constituted a vibrant slave society in which the institution and its resulting mores informed patterns in the society at large. The ethos of slavery did, however, shape servant and dependent relations in general.[11] As a result, the African presence had a profound, though little-understood, impact on social formation in mainland Spanish America. Frank Tannenbaum concluded as much when he noted that "without the Negro the texture of American life would have been different— different in lore, family, *social organization,* and politics and, equally important, different in economy."[12] The impact of slavery was pervasive, constituting the "social exemplar" for race, gender, and dependent relations. But in Spanish America and throughout the New World, "slave" and "African" were eventually synonyms. Consequently, the slaves' impact was decidedly African in nature. To acknowledge this perspective offers the possibility of viewing New Spain as a slave society without demanding a complete reexamination of the historiographical tradition associated with Tannenbaum that argued for a benign interpretation of Latin American slavery when compared to bondage in Anglo-America.[13]

The emergence of New Spain's slave society coincided with the destruction of Tenochitlán and the founding of the viceregal capital, Mexico City. Even prior to the siege of Tenochitlán (1519–1521), the Nahua-speaking emissaries sent by Moctezuma to discern the intentions of the new arrivals from the east observed the obvious, that the strangers included persons of varying phenotype. As they assessed the strangers' presence, their strength, and the nature of their mission, the Nahuas saw all the new arrivals as deities, referring to the black strangers as "soiled gods."[14] Once they learned that the Spaniards did not represent gods, the Nahuas ascribed to blacks a less epic status as slaves. Though the Nahuas corrected their misperception, the initial observation underscores the presence of Africans in the earliest phase of the Spanish conquest, highlighting a reality that in the hands of Spanish chroniclers, as well as those of subsequent writers, still remains largely ignored. In victory and in history, the Spaniards posited the conquest as a binary encounter with Indians, thus flattening the triangulation that the ethnography of the Nahuas revealed. For Spanish chroniclers, Africans, even as members of the conquering party, merited no reference despite their numbers and the Nahuas' recognition of their presence.

Several years after the Spanish conquest (1521), enslaved Africans directly from Guinea, *bozales,* joined the initial African slaves and black servants who, because they had spent time among Spaniards, were identified as ladinos. These Africans sometimes allied themselves with Spaniards. Ladinos made informed decisions based on long-standing familiarity with individual Spaniards. The emotional intimacy that developed during years, if not a lifetime, of service in Iberian households enabled ladinos to acquire command of Portuguese or Spanish and thus navigate with ease in an Hispanic milieu.[15]

Like many ladinos, Juan Garrido was born on the African continent and was purchased by Portuguese slave-traders who carried him to Lisbon, where they sold him to an unknown merchant. The merchant shipped Juan to "Castile," where he became Pedro Garrido's possession.[16] Seven years later, when rumors circulated about the fantastic wealth in the Indies, thousands of Spaniards boarded ships bound for Hispañiola, Cuba, and Puerto Rico. Many of these fortune-seekers, including Pedro Garrido, arrived in the Americas with family members and servants in tow.[17] For many ladinos, their relationships to individual Spaniards were nonnegotiable even in the midst of the chaos that characterized the early encounters between Africans, indigenous peoples, and Iberians.

In the 1540s, Juan Garrido, by then an aging African conquistador, humbly informed Charles V of his exploits in the Indies:

> I became a Christian in Lisbon, of my own will, spent seven years in Castile, and landed in Santo Domingo . . . where I was for some time; From there I ventured to San Juan de Puerto Rico . . . where I spent considerable time . . . afterwards landing in New Spain; I was present at the taking of Mexico City and in other conquests, and later [went] with the Marquis to the island; I was the first to plant and harvest wheat in this land, from which has come all that there now is; and brought to New Spain many vegetable seeds; I am married . . . with three children . . . very poor and have nothing with which to sustain myself.[18]

Nearly twenty years after the defeat of the Triple Alliance, Juan Garrido still basked in his glorious feats on behalf of Christendom. Like many of his Iberian comrades, Juan Garrido never succeeded in parlaying his conquistador status into financial prosperity. Unable to enrich himself, this weary soldier laid claim to a greater mission—the conquest of Tenochitlán. As he recalled the circuitous route that led to his participation in that momentous event, Juan Garrido also revealed much about the formative experiences of Africans and their descendants—experiences characterized by movement (both of persons and cultures) social fluidity, and experimentation, which collectively produced the cultural hybridity that defined New Spain from its violent inception.[19]

Prior to joining the alliance between Spaniards and indigenous people that laid siege to Tenochitlán, Juan Garrido spent nearly a decade in the Caribbean. In 1510, he evidently landed in Hispañiola, where he spent seven years in Santo Domingo and subsequently settled in San Juan, Puerto Rico.[20] Soon thereafter, Juan enlisted with Hernan Cortés's *entrada* (expedition) that left Cuba for the mainland on February 18, 1519. Next to nothing is known about Juan's role in the expedition and subsequent conquest of Tenochitlán.[21] Vague and unsubstantiated assertions identify Juan as a survivor of la Noche Triste, when Cortés's army barely survived its retreat from the Mexica capital.[22] Juan Garrido allegedly built a chapel in Tenochitlán in memory of his fallen comrades after the reinvigorated multilateral alliance defeated the Mexica military.[23]

In 1523, Juan joined another conquistador, Antonio de Caravajal, on his exploration of the territory of the Tarascan people in the northwest. By August 1524, Juan had returned to the Mexicas' former capital, which the Spaniards had renamed Tenochtitlán–Mexico City, and settled on the outskirts of the *traza* (the Spanish urban center). Six months later, the Spaniards declared Juan a *vecino* (resident), allotting him a *solar* (urban plot) in the *traza*, on which he erected a house.[24] During the second phase of the internecine Spanish power struggle (1526–1527), Juan evidently lost his coveted position as *portero* (doorman) of Mexico's *cabildo* (town council).[25] He subsequently departed for the Zacatula province, which he had explored during the Caravajal *entrada*. By 1528, he possessed mining equipment and a gang of slaves who were panning for gold in the alluvial mines of the north west.[26] Years later, a fortune in gold remained an elusive quest and Juan returned to Mexico City. In the 1530s, Juan reunited with Cortés as the famed conqueror led an expedition into lower California. By 1536, with his thirst for adventure satiated, Juan returned to the viceregal capital, where he died in the late 1540s.[27]

Despite the extraordinary events that shaped Juan Garrido's life, a number of Africans shared similar experiences.[28] Although Iberians ascribed a subordinate status to peoples of African descent, the threat of annihilation tempered the social hierarchy considerably and motivated hundreds of Africans to actively participate in the New World conquests.[29] After major battles, Spaniards rewarded individual Africans who had served as retainers, soldiers, and auxiliaries with booty, freedom, and occasionally even an *encomienda*. In turn, the newly freed African beneficiaries often enlisted with the subsequent expedition in pursuit of fortune, if not fame. Juan Garrido's decision to join the Caravajal *entrada* and Cortés's mission in lower California typifies the shrewd behavior of many Africans during the conquest period. Yet this willingness to exploit existing opportunities came with a price.

The familiarity informing ladino-Spanish social interaction during the tumultuous formative years waned in the postconquest period (1528–). The rigid and feudal nature of Iberian social relations gradually replaced the fluid social mores of the conquest period. The arrival of thousands of Spaniards fueled commercial competition, including the African slave trade, and exacerbated the gulf between erstwhile allies. One symptom of the mounting tension between Africans and Spaniards manifested itself in 1537, when *bozales* planned a conspiracy that the Spanish authorities discovered and quickly quelled.[30]

In Juan's waning years, the ethos that equated slaves with Africans was ascendant in New Spain. Although this ideological construct was in place by the mid-sixteenth century, during the conquest period, the concepts underlying the marriage of "African" with "slave" remained fluid. As Juan Garrido recounted his exploits, he neglected to inform Charles V of his social legacy. The most notable yet elusive legacy Juan and others like him left behind involved the social ambiguity and cultural dexterity that characterized the experiences of Africans and their descendants throughout the colonial period. In the second half of the sixteenth century, the growing presence of *bozales* momentarily overshadowed Juan's legacy. But the constantly expanding population of freedpersons, most notably mulattos, contradicts our too-simplistic understanding of New Spain's African past. In a slave society, the presence and expansion of the free mulatto population was an essential index of the ambiguous nature of social relations and cultural forms. Juan Garrido and members of the conquest generation forged this legacy, which then defined the experiences of subsequent generations of Afro-, Euro-, and Indo-Mestizos.

By the mid-sixteenth century, people of African descent outnumbered Spaniards in New Spain and comprised the second-largest slave population in the Americas. The increase in the number of slaves from Africa occurred despite the existence of an abundant, though declining, supply of indigenous labor. Since Spanish colonial policy rested on ethnic segmentation, Africans filled a distinctive labor niche in New Spain's economy. Most Africans staffed Spanish households as domestics or toiled in an urban economy dedicated to the consumer behavior of Spaniards, an arena from which the Spanish Crown repeatedly sought to exclude indigenous peoples.

African slaves in the urban centers of New Spain fulfilled multiple roles for their owners. In Mexico City, they represented both labor and symbols of the status of their owners. In the colony's highly honorific culture, Spaniards used male domestic slaves to double as armed retainers, stewards, and pages, thereby demonstrating to their peers their economic status.[31] Thomas Gage, an Englishman and Dominican friar who in 1625 visited Mexico City, observed how

> the gallants of this city shew themselves, some on horseback, and most in
> coaches, daily about four of the clock in the afternoon in a pleasant shady
> field called la Alameda . . . where do meet as constantly as the merchants

upon our exchange about two thousand coaches, full of gallants, ladies, and citizens, to see and to be seen, to court and to be courted. The gentlemen have their train of blackamoor slaves, some a dozen, some half a dozen, waiting on them, in brave and gallant liveries, heavy wit gold and silver lace, with silk stockings on their black legs and roses on their feet, and swords by their sides. The ladies also carry their train by their coach's side of such jet-like damsels . . . who with their bravery and white mantels over them seem to be, as the Spaniards saith, "mosca en leche," a fly in milk.[32]

According to Gage, in this routine yet ritualized occurrence, Spaniards employed slaves as labor and, through conspicuous displays, as objects that conferred honor. Slaves offered real and embodied symbolic services to Spaniards intent on expressing their superiority.

Since urban slaveholding patterns geared toward domestic consumption and the symbolic importance of slaves in an honorific culture defy quantification, scholars have had difficulty assessing slavery's economic significance. For most scholars of colonial Latin America, silver mining constituted the centerpieces of the postconquest economies. From this perspective, the ensuing social relations between Spaniards and Indians over the access to labor represented the foundations of the colonial social structure. While mining and the control of indigenous mine laborers occupied an important place in the social fabric, this narrow focus on silver production and the process of labor extraction overshadows the African presence. The 29,000 Indians who toiled in the mines of Peru and New Spain during the late sixteenth and early seventeenth centuries were, of course, central to silver production.[33] But this total did not constitute the majority of the colonial labor force. The sizeable African-descended population—which in New Spain in 1646 alone totaled 151,618—questions the long-standing perception that the Indian miner was synonymous with the early colonial economy.[34]

The growth and size of the African and especially free black populations requires a reconsideration of the slave trade and the role of slavery in New Spain's economy. Persons of African descent filled an important economic niche that only increased with the growth of the free black population. In re-examining the role of Africans and their descendants, scholars need to move beyond the chattel principle (a perspective whereby analysis of persons of African descent is restricted to slavery and to slaves as laborers) and its effects on New Spain's economy. An urban free black labor force started to outnumber the slave population in the early seventeenth century. In 1646, the free colored population throughout New Spain numbered 116,529.[35] Free black labor surely surpassed slave and possibly Indian labor in terms of importance in the urban and certain regional economies. Much needs to be known about the New

World's first slave society, but we must also acknowledge that this society, from its inception, coexisted with the earliest and largest free black cultures in the Americas. From the beginning, New Spain's slave society was porous, as Juan Garrido's story and the following overview reveal. Though New Spain constituted a slave society, the experience of Africans, like all dependent relations within the colony, remained, within limitations, remarkably fluid.

The Structure of Slavery

Soon after the siege and destruction of Tenochitlán, Spaniards realized that the wealth they could extract from the Nahuas consisted of tributary payments, in kind and in labor. Initially, Spaniards appropriated tribute payments earmarked for the Nahua elite while distributing tributary labor, in the form of *encomiendas,* among themselves.[36] At the same time, the Spaniards initiated commercial ventures that tapped existing resources. A notable example is the Cuban sugar cane that Hernan Cortés planted in Santiago Tuxtla along the banks of the Tepengo River, where he also built New Spain's first sugar mill.[37] A year later, he initiated the construction of a shipyard in the Isthmus of Tehuantepec.[38] In 1532, Cortés erected another sugar mill, this time near the town of Cuernavaca. Afterward, he began assembling a water-powered sugar mill at Tlaltenango in the same vicinity.[39]

Cortés's compatriots engaged in similarly ambitious commercial schemes. Between 1524 and 1538, for instance, Antonío Serrano de Cardona, Bernardino del Castillo, Rodrigo de Albornoz, and Pedro de Estrada erected three water-powered mills and one animal-powered mill in Chiapas, Morelos, and Veracruz.[40] Many more *encomenderos* established estates on which they raised livestock, cultivated grain for urban settlements, or produced goods for local and distant markets. By the end of the 1530s, the Spaniards had largely channeled the resources derived from the indigenous population, including tributary labor, into the commercial economy that, in the postconquest countryside, provided the venue in which Africans, Amerindians, and Spaniards interacted with the greatest frequency.[41]

Despite their penchant for urban living, the Spanish elite gradually migrated into the countryside in order to tap provincial resources and indigenous labor. After establishing their rural enterprises, the most affluent *encomenderos* retreated to Mexico City or some provincial city, leaving distant relatives, illegitimate offspring, and impoverished Spaniards to preside over their interests.[42] From the beginning, free and enslaved Africans joined this motley crew of Spaniards who together formed the nascent core of Spanish colonialism.[43]

Persons of African descent, both slave and free, initially resided in urban centers, where they worked as domestics, personal servants, artisans, and day laborers. This brought them into daily contact with Spaniards and, to a lesser extent, the indigenous peoples. Throughout the Americas, the descendants of Africans also cultivated the Spanish-owned gardens, orchards, and vineyards adjacent to urban settlements.[44] At dusk, they abandoned the fruit and vegetable plantations for nearby villages, towns, or cities; the initial persons of African descent in New Spain cannot be categorized as rural residents. As the *encomenderos* devised new ways to profit from their tributaries, they relied on acculturated Africans and the miniscule but growing mulatto nucleus to serve as intermediaries and supervisors over indigenous laborers. Hispanicized after spending years either on the Iberian Peninsula, Spain's Atlantic possessions, or the Caribbean islands, acculturated Africans had few qualms about representing the *encomenderos'* interest.[45] Throughout the 1530s, a constant stream of *bozales*—recent arrivals from Africa unfamiliar with Portuguese or Spanish and ignorant about Iberian customs—joined acculturated Africans (ladinos) and mulattos already present in the countryside. One scholar has estimated that during the first half of the sixteenth century, nearly 500 Africans annually entered New Spain.[46]

In the 1540s and 1550s, Spanish commercial activities rapidly expanded throughout New Spain. The availability of land, which Spaniards rented or purchased from the indigenous peoples, acquired as land grants, or simply appropriated through force and guile, facilitated mid-century commercial expansion. As the Spaniards accrued more land, they maintained a tenuous grasp over their tributaries. Yet they never exclusively depended on indigenous tributaries for labor. From the colony's inception, the Spaniards employed various labor strategies, including draft labor (whereby a native community was obligated to provide uncompensated labor for a designated period of time), work for wages, and slavery, often relying on all three simultaneously. By 1549, for instance, the resident labor force on Cortés's sugar mill in Tlaltenango included 186 indigenous workers and 80 enslaved Africans.[47] During the 1550s, the Spaniards steadily increased their dependence on wage and slave laborers of various hues.

By midcentury, commercial agriculture, livestock estates, and the mining industry essentially relied on a multiracial workforce composed of draft labor, enslaved Africans, and salaried workers. This variegated labor force profoundly shaped the composition of the community, the experiences of its members, and the formation of culture in New Spain. At midcentury, Africans were so numerous in New Spain that it alarmed the viceroy, Luís de Velasco. In 1553, he wrote Prince Philip requesting "an order limiting the license for bringing blacks since in New Spain there are more than twenty thousand who are increasing and will eventually spread confusion in the land."[48]

Despite Velasco's warning, Spaniards annually imported over 500 Africans into New Spain. By 1570, the colony had received an estimated 36,500 Africans, of which 20,000 had survived.[49] Among the approximately 36,500 Africans who entered New Spain by 1570, 80 percent came from the "Guinea of Cape Verde" and especially the "rivers of Guinea." A census taker in 1570 reported finding 8,000 black slaves and 1,000 mulattos in Mexico City alongside only 8,000 Spanish males.[50] The nearly 60,000 Nahuas residing in Mexico City's Indian neighborhoods, however, easily outnumbered both groups.[51] Though a disproportionate number of Africans and their descendants lived in Mexico City, by the end of the sixteenth century, they collectively rivaled, if not outnumbered, Spaniards throughout New Spain. In Puebla, for instance, the population of African descent constituted 40 percent of the nonindigenous population. In Veracruz, persons of African descent constituted 63 percent of the nonindigenous population. In Guanajuato, the 800 African slaves represented 66 percent of the Hispanic population. Even in remote Antequera, the descendants of Africans accounted for 31 percent of the nonindigenous population. These figures illustrate the preponderance of Africans in sixteenth-century New Spain and also highlight their presence in urban centers.[52]

Africans also flourished in the countryside.[53] In 1570, the archdiocese of Mexico included approximately 150 livestock estates on which 200 Spaniards, 300 slaves, and 50 mulattos resided. In Michoácan's diocese, which had 300 livestock estates and two water-powered mills, there was a population of 400 Spaniards, 200 mulattos, and "more than seven hundred slaves." The Tlaxcala diocese, in contrast, had 200 estates, 300 Spaniards, and 400 slaves of African descent. Oaxaca's diocese had 100 estates, on which 150 Spaniards and 200 slaves resided. Although imprecise, this census underscores the growth of the African and creole labor force in the mills of Morelos, Veracruz, and Michoácan; the livestock estates in the Isthmus of Tehuantepec, Oaxaca, Guerrero and Michoácan; and the large cocoa plantations along the Pacific coast.[54]

After 1570, the presence of Africans and their descendants continued to expand throughout New Spain. The commercial economy fueled much of this expansion and transformed the social landscape.[55] By the closing decades of the sixteenth century, events in Africa, Europe, and the Americas affected the cultural composition of the transatlantic slave trade's cargo. Because of political events and economic changes along the Atlantic periphery, the seventeenth-century slave trade, which began in 1595, brought Africans to Spanish America who identified and were identified as Angolans. Although Portuguese slavers primarily transported Angolans to the Americas, they continued to ship Biafaras, Brans, Gelofos, Mandingas, and Terra Novas to Castile's various Atlantic provinces.[56] The lingering West African presence among the *bozales* underscores Portugal's trading legacy in the "Guinea of Cape Verde."[57]

By 1640, the Spaniards had imported over 110,000 ethnic Africans.[58] For the period 1521–1639, this amounted to a little more than 900 per year. This longitudinal perspective, however, obscures the vicissitudes of the slave trade. Spaniards received more enslaved Africans during the first four decades of the seventeenth century than they had throughout the entire sixteenth century. Ebbs and flows also characterized the seventeenth-century slave trade (1595–1639), which roughly corresponded to the union of the Portuguese and Spanish Crowns. In 1609 and again in 1619, the Spaniards imported over 6,000 slaves, but between 1611 and 1615 they legally managed to acquire a total of only 476 Africans.[59] Despite these fluctuations, the seventeenth-century slave trade in New Spain averaged 1,871 persons annually; it reinforced the African presence while simultaneously augmenting the creole population.[60] By 1646, an estimated 151,618 persons of African descent inhabited New Spain, of which 62,814 resided in the Archdiocese of Mexico. In the dioceses of Michoácan and Tlaxcala, Africans and their descendants of various legal categories respectively numbered 23,480 and 22,915. The remaining 42,409 were dispersed throughout the dioceses of Oaxaca, Nueva Galicia, Yucatan, and Chiapas.

Creoles clearly experienced phenomenal growth during the second half of the sixteenth century and the initial decades of the seventeenth century. In a 76-year period (1570–1646), the creole population grew fifty fold, from 2,437 to 116,529. Mostly free mulattos, they constituted the largest freed and free population in the Western Hemisphere—a position that creoles maintained well into the nineteenth century. The 35,089 residents of New Spain who were born in Africa represented only 30 percent of the "black" population; the 116,529 creoles accounted for the remainder.[61]

Creoles, as Africans born in New Spain were known, emerged as a significant presence soon after the conquest. Throughout the sixteenth century, the growth of the creole population proceeded slowly but unabated. By the mid-sixteenth century, the creole population had proliferated to such an extent that the colonial authorities finally took notice. Despite the impressive growth of this population, initially it could not compensate for the high mortality rates among the descendants of Africans. Yet toward the end of the sixteenth century, steady growth among surviving persons of African descent augmented the expanding nucleus of creoles. By 1650, this nucleus had produced a nearly balanced sex ratio in many regions throughout New Spain, which in turn sustained the reproduction of the creole population.

Ironically, as creoles began to outnumber the African-born population, the institution of slavery became more tenuous. In fact, seventeenth-century estate inventories underscore the existence of two population trajectories among persons of African descent. While the Spaniards imported significant numbers of Africans during the first half of the seventeenth century, the demographic balance gradually shifted in favor of creoles and free mulattos. By 1589, the heirs of Cortés on the Marquesado del Valle's livestock estates in the Tehuantepec region had had over fifty years of experience with African, indigenous, and Spanish laborers.[62] In 1589, the full- and part-time resident work force included forty-one slaves, fifteen free mulattos, and nineteen indigenous wage laborers.[63] Among the enslaved, there were twenty-one *bozales* and twenty creoles. Ten years later, only twenty-five slaves remained; the population of free mulattos and indigenous peoples had also diminished.[64] By 1616, the presence of thirty-two slaves and nine free mulattos signaled the revitalization of Tehuantepec's African and creole labor force.[65] Six years later, however, enslaved mulattos ascended into the majority among the slave population while free mulattos rivaled and gradually eclipsed enslaved Africans as laborers.

Despite new African arrivals, natural reproduction ensured that mulattos retained their primacy among Tehuantepec's slave labor force. Between 1588 and 1629, for instance, mulattos constituted 58.3 percent of the slave children born on the Tehuantepec estates.[66] Despite these indices of growth, the decline of the slave population was irreversible. By the third decade of the seventeenth century, a permanent free mulatto majority had emerged on the Tehuantepec estates that, together with the indigenous laborers, comprised the bulk of the workforce.

The sugar industry in Morelos, which by 1570 had one of the largest slave populations in the Americas, experienced a similar pattern whereby creoles gradually replaced African-born individuals as laborers.[67] During the first half of the seventeenth century, the Spaniards steadily acquired more land, on which they extended the cultivation of sugar cane and constructed additional water-powered mills. The expansion of the sugar industry created a demand for more labor, and Spaniards promptly imported a mass of enslaved Africans. Consequently, the African and creole population of Morelos soared to new heights. While older estates continually clamored for labor, the greatest demand came from owners of newly established sugar estates well positioned at the beginning of the seventeenth century to compete in New Spain's labor market.[68] Juan Fernández de la Concha, for instance, rapidly accumulated slave labor for his growing estate. In 1616, Juan Fernandez purchased the Guajoyuca estate, which had no laborers at the time. Fourteen years later, his labor force included eighty enslaved Africans, making him one of the largest slave-owners in Spanish America.[69] Andrés Mendes's Atlihuayan estate, founded in 1627, grew even faster.[70] A mere five years after its construction, his estate also included a labor force of eighty enslaved persons.

Although persons defined as Angolans predominated among the African-born in seventeenth-century ethnic New Spain, the slave labor force in Morelos was not exclusively African. Black and mulatto slaves had a significant presence on the estates of Morelos, and during the first half of the seventeenth century, they began to outnumber Africans.[71] Estate inventories reveal that the *marque-*

sado's mill, Tlaltenango, represented the only seventeenth-century sugar plantation on which Africans constituted at least 30 percent of the slave population.[72] Even on the newest estates, such as Atlihuayan and Guajoyuca, creole and mulatto slaves easily outnumbered enslaved Africans. In 1680, sixty-four years after its construction, the Guajoyuca estate had only two African-born slaves, thirty-two blacks, and thirty mulattos.[73]

Around the same time, the Atlihuayan estate included ten *bozales*, sixty-two blacks, and forty-four mulattos in its slave labor force.[74] Surviving estate inventories from Morelos reveal that on average blacks and mulattos accounted for 81 percent of the slave population during the seventeenth century. The growth of the black and mulatto population did more than offset the waning African presence; it also contributed to the expansion of free mulattos who, along with indigenous peoples, constituted the core of eighteenth-century labor force at Morelos.[75]

The African and creole population of Michoácan experienced the same demographic pattern manifest throughout seventeenth-century New Spain. By the seventeenth century, African slavery was flourishing at Michoácan. In 1624, the provincial capital, Valladolid, included 1,116 servants and 229 enslaved persons distributed among 220 households.[76] The majority of enslaved Africans and creoles, however, lived on estates that grew livestock, cotton, tobacco, and, of course, sugar.[77] During the first half of the seventeenth century, the sugar planters—the largest owners of slaves—enslaved 525 Africans and creoles distributed among fourteen estates.[78] The largest concentration of slaves resided on an unnamed estate in Tacámbaro, the Parandían plantation near Pintzándaro, and the Jorulla hacienda located in the Alima valley, which all claimed eighty persons. Since Michoácan's sugar planters produced exclusively for a regional market, most slave-owners owned fewer than eighty slaves.[79]

Existing sources make it difficult to be precise about the ethnic composition of Michoácan's slave population. As active participants in New Spain's domestic slave trade, Michoácan's planters probably acquired a number of enslaved Africans during the first half of the seventeenth century. In 1635, for instance, when José de Figueroa y Camporío authorized his brothers-in-law to purchase twenty slaves on his behalf, they were likely to find persons defined as Angolans and Congos overrepresented among the available pool of slaves.[80] Doña Isabel Guillen's seventeenth-century estate inventory reveals the proliferation of Africans among the enslaved labor force at Michoácan. This same inventory also underscores a significant black and mulatto presence among the labor force.[81] Based on Doña Isabel's inventory, it seems that blacks and mulattos rapidly proliferated in seventeenth-century Michoácan.

Baptismal records from Michoácan support the contention that the black and mulatto populations steadily expanded during the first half of the seventeenth century.[82] The creole population's fecundity precipitated a phenomenal growth rate during the second half of the seventeenth century among persons defined by themselves and others as blacks and mulattos. In due course, free creoles, especially free mulattos, eclipsed the African and enslaved population.[83]

With the exception of the Cordóba region, the evolution of the African and Afromestizo population preceded along similar lines in seventeenth-century Veracruz. At the beginning of the seventeenth century, a substantial African labor force resided in Jalapa. During the period between 1597 and 1610, planters at Jalapa acquired 330 Africans, or 70 percent of the total African population they would purchase overall. This expansion of African-born slaves was unprecedented in Jalapa; prior to 1597 and after 1610, the number of Africans that entered that region rarely exceeded two or three per year.[84] Most of the 478 Africans sold to Jalapa's nascent plantocracy toiled on the sugar estates. After 1610, Jalapa's planters were not aggressive buyers of enslaved Africans. Jalapa's withdrawal from the international slave trade effected a social and demographic transformation among its resident labor force. By midcentury, Africans had lost their numerical ascendancy among the enslaved and resident laborers, and free persons outnumbered slaves.[85]

The demographic patterns on the Santisíma Trinidad sugar plantation vividly illustrate the precipitous decline of African slavery in New Spain. In 1608, the slave labor force on the estate numbered 200; thirty years later, only fifty-four remained.[86] By 1670, the number of slaves had increased but now represented a smaller percentage of the estate labor force. Meanwhile, the number of free mulattos and persons of African-Indian heritage (*pardos*) had increased to such an extent that they, along with the indigenous peoples, filled the ranks of the wage labor force. Although the size of Santisíma Trinidad's labor force was exceptional, the ethnic patterns and social changes apparent in its labor force manifested themselves throughout Jalapa. At the end of the seventeenth century, the importance of African slaves as a source of labor had waned in Jalapa. Ironically, as slavery contracted in Jalapa, the institution expanded in Cordóba, thus making the region an exception in eighteenth-century New Spain.[87]

As in other areas of New Spain, the waning number of African immigrants precipitated the decline of the slave population. The decline of slavery in New Spain, however, was not synonymous with a decrease in the population of creoles there. From 1575 to 1675, the percentage of Afro-Veracruzanos, or creoles, in the slave labor force fluctuated from 33 percent in 1575 to 14 percent in 1615 to 51 percent in 1675.[88] Despite the marked decrease in relative terms between 1575 and 1615, the creole population continued to grow in absolute terms. The diminishing gap between males and females of African descent sustained this growth. By the end of the seventeenth century, the ratio of male to female slaves had nearly reached parity. This represented a dramatic shift from the beginning of the seventeenth century, when the balance favored males over females three to one.[89] Among the free descendants of Africans, who by the end of the seventeenth century largely constituted female creoles, such patterns seemed even more pronounced.

Demography as Culture

The estate inventories from New Spain reveal two demographic trends among people of African descent beginning in the second half of the sixteenth century—the rapid increase of individuals born in Africa and the spectacular growth of the creole population. By 1646, the creole population, largely free and comprised of mulattos, numbered 116,529, whereas the predominantly African slave population totaled 35,089. The dramatic growth in the number of creoles underscores a dazzling rate of natural increase among that population and signals that not all persons of African descent were slaves. By the second half of the sixteenth century, most enslaved persons were Africans and their children were invariably defined as "black creoles." But the census materials and estate patterns also highlight that at the same time most persons of African descent were free or had been freed. With the abatement of the international slave trade in 1640, people of African descent entered communities in New Spain in three ways: they were born there, they voluntarily moved there from other regions, or they were brought there as laborers. While the periodic influx of Africans via smugglers and the occasional sanctioned trader affected the growth and cultural patterns of creoles, local factors had a greater impact on the growth of the creole population.

Local slaveholding patterns and indigenous communities shaped the idiosyncratic nature of the transformation process in fundamental ways. In those areas with a small African population liberally dispersed, the descendants of Africans tended to blend physically and culturally, eventually acquiring identities as Indians or Spaniards but most likely as mestizos, the offspring of Spaniards and Indians. Manifest throughout New Spain, this pattern of absorption or "disappearance" occurred in both urban and rural areas. In contrast, in those areas with a significant enslaved population congregated on large estates —Veracruz, Guerrero, Guanajuato, Oaxaca, Morelos, and Michoacan—the African population retained its distinctive physical presence for a longer period. Yet even in these areas, Africans and especially their descendants gradually blended into the local population. The pace of this process varied according to locality.

In describing this process as *mestizaje,* most scholars have characterized it as the "whitening" of the African population, the assumption being that Africans and their descendants largely interacted with Spaniards. Such views, though reflective of an imperial policy that repeatedly encouraged Spaniards to restrict the black and mulatto presence from indigenous towns and peoples, were far from ever being realized. During the earliest contact between members of both commonwealths—the crown-sanctioned *república* that separated Spaniards from Indians—persons of African descent, as Spanish agents in the countryside, interacted with indigenous peoples. It stands to reason that individuals of African descent facilitated the Hispanicization process among Amerindians.

In fact, the initial cultural exposure that many indigenous peoples experienced during the sixteenth century rarely emanated directly from those individuals defined as Spaniards. With the exception of the itinerant pig farmer and the occasional priest, most contact—physical and cultural—took place between Spanish-speaking Africans and Amerindians. Moreover, this interaction between Africans and Amerindians increased after midcentury when recent arrivals from Africa arrived on the rural estates, where they worked alongside indigenous persons. Though the crown restricted the labor demands of the *encomenderos* on the indigenous population, this did not result in diminished contact between Africans and Amerindians. Throughout the colonial period, indigenous persons toiled on Spanish estates as salaried employees, often alongside the free black and mulatto employees. Furthermore, Spanish estates were often adjacent to Amerindian communities. This proximity meant that enslaved Africans and free mulattos interacted continuously with the surviving Amerindians, and from this process Afromestizos emerged.

While scholars have acknowledged the growth of Afromestizos in the sixteenth century, their focus has been confined to urban centers. Yet rural areas, including the indigenous corporate communities, represented important centers where Africans and blacks interacted with Indians. The estates situated among or in proximity to indigenous communities represented the dominant spheres of interaction in which persons of African descent encountered native peoples. Even during the greatest decline of the indigenous population, Indians still constituted a significant minority, if not the majority, of laborers on or adjacent to local haciendas, plantations, and ranchos. As their numbers increased in the second half of the seventeenth century, a large number of men and women migrated to local estates in search of a livelihood. Thus, Africans and Amerindians eventually produced the third-largest population group in seventeenth-century New Spain, a position Afromestizos retained throughout the colonial period. Taking all this into account explains the phenomenal growth that all mestizo categories experienced in the seventeenth century.

While the Afromestizo population's seventeenth-century growth was linked to the demographic recovery of the indigenous population and sexual interaction between those of African descent and Amerindians, the term "mestizo," like all racial and cultural terms, owed less to biological pedigree than it did to social appearance and behavioral patterns. The term should not obscure the interaction between individuals of European and African descent that was responsible for the emergence of mulattos, who also represented an important feature of rural society. Colonial records rarely contain evidence of rural *mestizaje*, since the clergy recorded interracial marriages only sporadically before the eighteenth century and in many instances defined those indigenous persons who tried to marry individuals of African descent as mestizos. However, it must be noted that most sexual contact did not lead to marriage. The limited documentary evidence, especially marriage records, strongly supports the scholarly contention that indigenous peoples were restrictive in terms of spouse selection. Even at the end of the colonial period, endogamy represented the norm among most indigenous persons in the central south and northwest. Such regions, in fact, recorded endogamy rates of 90 percent or more. Yet the ease with which indigenous persons could pass as mestizos and the proclivities of the clergy make marriage records a problematic though impressionistic source with regard to definitional precision. Most persons of indigenous descent who formed liaisons or petitioned for a marriage license with non-Indians defined themselves for pecuniary, if not other, reasons as mestizos or were characterized as such. Also, one cannot ignore the static views that governed Spanish perceptions of who constituted an Indian. Despite the fluidity between the categories of Indian and mestizo, Spaniards continued to imbue these terms with rigid, idyllic, anachronistic, and mutually exclusive meanings. Patterns of interaction were clearly not uniform throughout New Spain. Variations did occur, and in some regions of the central south and the northwest, where indigenous communities retained their corporate identities along with their corresponding social taboos, *mestizaje* with persons of African descent happened with less frequency. In this respect, endogamy among the indigenous population coincided, unintentionally, with Spain's imperial design to keep the purported races separated.[90]

This demographic overview underscores several neglected dimensions of New Spain's African presence. From New Spain's inception, Africans had a discernible presence. As this population increased in the postconquest period, New Spain became the largest slave society in the Americas. But in the second half of the seventeenth century, two related population trends emerged among the slave population that affected the trajectory of slavery and the formation of culture in New Spain. Among the enslaved, creoles emerged as the most populous. As the creole population increased, the free black population also reached new heights, becoming the largest such community in the Americas. Though mulattos constituted an important component of this community, in the countryside, Afromestizos comprised the majority of freedmen and freedwomen. Afromestizo ascendancy suggests that the African presence ultimately shifted toward the countryside. Yet until the middle of the seventeenth century, and the sizeable rural estates notwithstanding, slavery and the African presence was decidedly urban.

Slavery in the Capital

Scholarly portrayals of slavery in New Spain have thus far emphasized the institution's rural nature. From the sixteenth century, Africans labored on the rural estates of Morelos, Michoácan, Oaxaca, and Veracruz. Their variously defined descendants—both slave and free—would inherit these roles, but with the decline of slavery, they increasingly contributed to the growth of the rural peasantry. In New Spain, however, the African presence was not strictly rural. Africans, both slaves and servants, occupied an important niche in urban centers.[91] While African labor was essential for the workings of the Spanish domestic economies, blacks also doubled as symbolic capital for a Spanish community perpetually anxious about status. In urban New Spain, Spaniards valued persons of African descent both as laborers and for the cultural capital that they conferred. This duality is essential to an understanding of urban slavery during this time period. Analysis of urban slavery cannot be restricted to chattel slavery with its emphasis on labor. Slaves worked, of course, but they and their descendants also bestowed honor on their owners. Those Spaniards with the greatest pretense to honor owned several slaves, while even modest members of the Spanish community strove to possess at least one slave.[92] In essence, the perceived need to own a slave underscores slavery's centrality in Spanish America's urban cultural arena. Consequently, in defining a slave society, greater weight should be ascribed to a culturally determined need that led to the pervasive ownership of slaves. This perceived need explains why Mexico City constituted a slave society alongside Morelos, Michoacan, Oaxaca, and Veracruz.

As the Spanish capital, Mexico City represented New Spain's most important cultural center. Within this urban crucible, a new cultural synthesis emerged which was both peculiar to Mexico and representative of New Spain's ever-shifting cultural moorings. In Mexico, the community of colonizers manifested their vision of enduring dominance over the land and its once-sovereign occupants. Nowhere else in New Spain were the competing expressions of colonial power—imperial absolutism, Christian colonialism, and Spanish patrician authority—as deeply rooted or as explicitly manifest.[93] To invoke New Spain was to speak of Mexico City.

While Mexico's architects reconfigured the social landscape into two distinct *repúblicas*, one for the Indian majority and the other for the Spanish minority, they neglected to allot distinctive social space to Africans who lived there. But this omission was not simply an oversight. The African presence— mediated by the experiences of slavery and servitude—represented an extension of Spanish expansion; as such, it did not warrant a distinctive *república*. Mastery over Africans and their descendants, in other words, accompanied the Spanish conquest. In the confrontation between Old and New Worlds, the African presence embodied Spanish cultural continuity.[94]

By establishing their cultural dominance, the conquerors imposed long-standing Spanish cultural norms and practices, including a recently acquired mastery over African slaves and servants, as their legacy. From this perspective, Africans and their descendants stood for more than labor; they constituted symbolic capital doubling as a cultural legacy. Like writing, walled cities, wheat, olives, and wine, Spaniards relied on the servile African population to signify their cultural identity as the civilized. By the time of the conquest, mastery over Africans was tantamount to being a Spaniard.[95] Spanish mastery, however, resided not in the Africans' race but in the authority and honor conferred in displays of conspicuous consumption.[96]

Travelers routinely commented on the symbolic importance of New Spain's African presence. These comments often followed standard refrains about Spanish sloth, ostentation, and arrogance. For several observers, including Thomas Gage, these qualities, along with the African presence, contributed to the rampant vice, sin, and moral degeneracy that they saw enveloping Mexico City.[97]

In 1625, Thomas Gage spent five months in Mexico. Like many other observers, Gage was awed by the "noblest city in all India." The city's grandeur, the size of its streets and promenades, and its structures impressed him, as they did other contemporary visitors. More than once, Gage remarked that "buildings are with stone and brick very strong. . . . The streets are very broad; in the narrowest of them three coaches may go." On the basis of the structural splendor, Gage identified Mexico as "one of the greatest cities in the world."[98] Wealth accompanied grandeur. Dazzled by the display of wealth, Gage described in detail the liveries. He remarked upon "the beauty of some of the coaches of the gentry, which do exceed in coast the best of the Court of Madrid and other parts of Christendom, for they spare no silver, nor gold, nor precious stones, nor cloth of gold, nor the best silks from China to enrich them."[99] After this assessment, Gage pointed out that "men and women are excessive in their apparel, using more silks than stuffs and cloth." The excess of the Spaniards was evidently quite contagious, since "nay, a blackamoor or tawny young maid and slave will make hard shift, but she will be in fashion with her neck-chain and bracelets of pearls, and her ear-bobs of some considerable jewels. The attire of this baser sort of blackamoors and mulattoes . . . is so light, and their carriage so enticing, that many Spaniards even of the better sort (who are too too [*sic*] prone to venery) disdain their wives for them."[100] In Mexico, a culture of excess had emerged, in which even slaves and their descendants participated. This explains Gage's insistence that he found little but "sin and wickedness."[101]

Sensitive to the ways that Africans figured in the ostentatious displays of honor and status, Gage nonetheless did not refer to Mexico City as a slave society.[102] Through his observations, however, Mexico's slave society comes into relief—a society in which "the master-slave relationship provided the model for all social relations."[103] Present in significant numbers, both African slaves and Afro-Mexican servants occupied prominent roles in an economy structured by circulation, production, and consumption. But rather than describe Mexico City as a slave society on the basis of the slaves' role as labor in the economy, Gage captured something much more elusive. He glimpsed the Africans' prominence in spectacles of ostentation that, in turn, mirrored social relations at large.[104]

In lieu of sources capable of delineating with any precision sixteenth- and seventeenth-century urban slaveholding patterns, we must rely on other sources related to the slave experience in order to understand urban slavery. Such records, as we shall see, suggest that most urban slaves labored as domestics, artisans, and vendors, occupations that placed them in daily contact with persons similarly defined and with a host of plebeians of various hues. They, of course, interacted with a diverse range of Spaniards. In doing so, the enslaved learned to navigate in and between the households and various institutions comprising Spanish society. Though life in cities offered the enslaved a specific challenge— constant supervision—it also afforded them opportunities to circumvent their masters' authority. As urban masters imposed their authority over the enslaved, they confronted royal and ecclesiastical officials who respectively defined slaves as vassals and persons with souls. Africans and their descendants learned that conflicting obligations and rights accompanied the disparate identities ascribed to baptized slaves. Many, as the subsequent chapters reveal, became adept at manipulating their conflicting status as chattel, as vassals, and as Christians.

2 "The Grand Remedy"

Africans and Christian Conjugality

What is a Negro slave? A man of the black race. The one explanation is a good as the other. A Negro is a Negro. He only becomes a slave in certain relations.[1]

Slaves posed numerous problems for masters intent on defining them solely as chattel. In their epic struggle, masters and slaves repeatedly clashed while attempting to impose their respective visions of slavery. As persons, slaves limited the extent to which masters could classify them as property. Slaves had to be made and constantly refashioned. Yet in the Spanish New World, masters and slaves did not represent the only parties concerned with defining the slave experience. The Crown and the Catholic Church displayed a keen interest in shaping the social landscape—a landscape in which African slavery played a prominent role. As royal and ecclesiastical officials struggled to implement their vision of society, they steadily encroached on the masters' domain. Through secular legislation and ecclesiastical law—by classifying slaves as the king's vassals and baptizing Africans as Christians—royal and church officials overrode the masters' authority to define chattel solely as property. A jurisdictional contest emerged involving the Spanish monarchy, the Catholic Church, and New World masters over whose definition—vassal, Christian, or chattel—would prevail. Obligations as vassals and Christians predominated over status as a slave, especially in urban areas where institutional power concentrated. In their effort to control—not ameliorate—the slave experience, crown and clergy overrode masters' authority. In this and the following chapter, we shall see how the Spanish monarchy regulated and thereby defined the slave experience from its inception. Even before establishing control over the unfolding New World, the Spanish monarchy subjected slaves to its authority. In doing so, the Spanish Crown consistently intervened on the masters' purported domain.

A master's rights over property, including chattel, constituted a hallmark of Western Europe's evolving legal systems. In law, the master embodied absolute authority in all matters pertaining to his property. So complete was this dominion that the master constituted the final arbiter in deciding if his *res* (property) warranted death. In the course of institutional consolidation, church and state rarely challenged authority over property. The rediscovery and implementation of Roman law in the eleventh and twelfth centuries bolstered dominion. With the codification of canon law in Western Europe, the Church, however, gradually encroached on the master's domain by delimiting Christian obligations. In an effort to secure their authority, rulers of territorial states in the high Middle Ages increasingly arrogated jurisdiction in capital crimes, in the process of which they trespassed on the masters' authority. In formulating its earliest definitions of treason, most notably regicide, monarchs launched their greatest assault against a master's dominion. A slave who revealed a plot against the monarch that implicated his master, for instance, received unconditional freedom. This and other examples wherein a master could forfeit his property rights underscores that by the late Middle Ages, secular and ecclesiastical legal statutes superseded the master's authority, though the fiction of his dominion prevailed.

Students of early modern and colonial slavery have been instrumental in preserving the legal fiction of the master's absolute authority. In their efforts to discern the workings of slavery, scholars of the Americas initially displayed a marked interest in the extant slave laws. As scholars subjected slave laws, most notably the Siete Partidas and the Code Noir, to scrutiny, they observed the ambiguous status accorded masters vis-à-vis slaves.[2] They concluded that, in theory, at least, the master's authority was far from absolute precisely because the laws limited the owners' authority over property.

Practice represented another matter. As a field, scholars understood that laws could not reveal the meaning of the slave experience. Inquiries about the law, therefore, quickly fell from grace as scholars shifted toward producing histories of specific slave societies. For Spanish America, this trend in scholarship—which features a conflation of civil law with all laws—has been especially problematic, since canon law played a very important role in shaping slavery. The pioneering studies of colonial Spanish American slavery acknowledged the Siete Partidas and its importance as a mediating factor in the master-slave relationship, but these studies isolated that legal code from canon law. Roman law, of course, defined the master-slave relationship. But in adjudicating over human affairs, even when individuals were defined as masters and slaves, crown and clergy assumed primacy. In the course of their evolution, ecclesiastical and royal laws competed for jurisdiction in most affairs and steadfastly encroached on the master's domain. Jurisdictional conflict ensued. Initially, the Church prevailed by subjecting all individuals to the dictates of canon law. In due course, the centralizing monarchies appropriated similar authority in the contest for primacy with the Church. As the most powerful Iberian monarchies ventured into the Atlantic with the Church in tow, ecclesiastical and secular authority reigned ascendant over the master's power.[3]

Extra Ecclesiam

Scholars of slavery have long recognized that church and state wielded influence in the Spanish-American slave codes and, therefore, in the master-slave relationship. One of the most prescient observers, Frank Tannenbaum, declared that the Church bestowed a "moral personality" on the slave. In an effort to protect this personality, the Church intervened in the master-slave relationship in an attempt to ameliorate slavery's excesses. But the focus on amelioration and treatment overshadowed a critical aspect of ecclesiastical law. Even before the traders introduced the modern incarnations of slaves—Africans—in Europe, the Atlantic Islands, and then the Indies, the Church had accorded the individuals regarded as slaves status as "persons." On the basis that they represented non-Christians, the Church also identified Africans as the *extra ecclesiam* (an ecclesiastical term applicable to all persons who did not profess Christianity) and thus gave them rights that competed with their slave status. In constituting the *extra ecclesiam,* the Church relied on the rediscovered teachings of the ancients, the Bible, natural law, customary law, commentaries, canon-law precedents, theological treaties, and papal bulls. Collectively, these texts and institutional practices outlined the obligations and the rights of non-Christians both within and beyond an imagined Europe. Such rights and accompanying obligations prevailed until the individual *extra ecclesiam* embraced the Christian faith. If enslaved Africans elected to become Christians, the Church amended these rights and obligations. In its encounter with Africans, the Church focused less on amelioration than on regulation of slaves. According to crown and clergy, Christian slaves had to conform to Christian orthodoxy.

As Christian explorers and conquerors encountered diverse peoples, their interactions with these peoples were shaped by a canonical tradition dating from Innocent IV's thirteenth-century commentary. Prior to his election as Pope Innocent IV in 1243, Sinibaldo Fieschi was an influential canonist. As pope (1243–1254), he took an active interest in Christian-Moslem relations because the Christian Crusades, the reconquest, and Christian territorial expansion lacked a firm legal basis in canon law. In his influential commentary, Innocent IV raised the question: "Is it licit to invade the lands that infidels possess, and if it is licit, why is it licit?"[4] According to one scholar, "Innocent was not . . . interested in justifying the crusades; the general theory of the just war did that. What interested him was the problem of whether or not Christians could legitimately seize land, other than the Holy Land, that the Moslems occupied. Did . . . Christians have a general right to dispossess infidels everywhere?"[5]

Innocent acknowledged that the law of nations had supplanted natural law in regulating human interaction such as trade, conflict, and social hierarchies. Similarly, the prince replaced the father as the "lawful authority in society" through God's provenance, manifesting his dominion in the monopoly over justice and sanctioned violence. As did the ancient Israelites in selecting Saul as king, all "rational creatures" were entitled to elect their rulers—a right which in the Old Testament was not predicated on living in a state of grace. Viewing infidels as "rational creatures," Innocent deemed that they also could decide on their rulers. The pope, however, bore responsibility for the infidels' souls.[6]

In outlining his opinion, Innocent delineated a temporal domain that was simultaneously independent of yet subordinate to the Church. Laws of nations pertained to secular matters, a domain in which a significant proportion of Church members, known as the "dualists," showed increasingly less interest. But in spiritual matters, the pope's authority prevailed, since all humans were of Christ even if they were not members of the Church. "As a result," the medievalist James Muldoon notes, "the pope's pastoral responsibilities consisted of jurisdiction over two distinct flocks, one consisting of Christians and one comprising everyone else."[7] Since the pope's jurisdiction extended by law over infidels, he alone could call for a invasion of an infidel's domain by Christians. Innocent maintained that even then, however, only a violation of natural law could precipitate such an attack. By adhering to the beliefs of their gods, infidels and pagans did not violate natural law. Thus, such beliefs did not provide justification for Christians to invade non-Christian polities, dispossess the inhabitants of their territory and freedom, and force them to convert. The importance of Innocent IV's contribution resided in the fact that he accorded pagans and infidels sovereignty and therefore the right to live beyond the state of grace.

Some canon lawyers questioned the assertion that infidels and pagans possessed rights—including Henry of Segusio, a former student of Sinibaldo Fieschi known widely as Hostiensis—but "by the end of the fourteenth century Innocent IV's commentary . . . had become the *communis opinio* of the canonists."[8] Half a century later, the imperial activities of Christian rulers again raised the issue of the infidels' dominion. While Innocent IV's commentary prevailed and continued to mediate European imperial expansion and Christian interaction with non-Christians, the strength of the Christian princes and their growing autonomy vis-à-vis the papacy along with their desire for legitimacy brought renewed interest in Hostiensis's commentary. Despite the shifting alliance that characterized church-state relations in the late Middle Ages, temporal authorities in Christian Europe legitimized their rule and defined their actions on scriptural and spiritual grounds. Christianity represented their ontological myth, the source of their traditions, and the banner under which they marched against infidels.

The Christian princes were reluctant to distance themselves from this founding ideology, since to discard Christianity would mean that their dominion rested merely on the might of one particular lineage over another. Moreover, by abandoning the pretense of just war against the infidels, Christian sovereigns risked revealing that profit motivated their desire for expansion. In the context of the late Middle Ages and the beginning of the early modern period, commercial considerations stood in opposition to the purported interest of the Christian sovereigns in honor and justice.

In the early modern period, Christianity still served multiple secular purposes: it legitimized the ascendancy of a particular noble house while sanctioning dominion of the elite over the nonelite. In the face of a powerful noble lineage, the position of the nascent absolutist rulers remained tenuous at best, and the prince was reluctant to dispense with the protective veneer that even diminished papal authority provided. Still, the ambitious Iberian monarchs were willing to interpret canon law in a manner that furthered their claims over infidels and Christians. As a result, secular authorities relied increasingly on commentaries of Hostiensis and those theologians who displayed less conformity than canon lawyers on the rights of the *extra ecclesiam*.[9]

Developments in Christendom also brought the dominion of the *extra ecclesiam* under renewed scrutiny. Since the Church defined all nonbelievers, including Saracens (a widely used term for infidels or those who willfully rejected the Christian faith) and pagans (individuals who existed in ignorance of the Christian faith), as the *extra ecclesiam*, it utilized the same laws and traditions in their treatment. In effect, the Church did not distinguish between the non-Christian minority in Europe and the *extra ecclesiam* residing beyond its de facto jurisdiction. Therefore, laws and practices that shaped the relations of church and state with nonbelievers in Europe set the precedent for Christian interaction with non-Christians in the wider early modern Atlantic world. Beginning in the thirteenth century, and in the context of the reconquest, Christians on the Iberian Peninsula began to undermine the corporate bodies of Jews and Saracens by ordering those populations to adhere to Christian legal precepts and Iberian customary laws.

While indicative of the Christians' victory over the Moors, such practices represented a departure from reconquest ethics. Throughout much of the reconquest, victorious Christians and Moors often allowed adversaries who remained under their territorial jurisdiction to adhere to their own beliefs and traditions. By the thirteenth century, when the tide favored Christians, the victorious rulers displayed less willingness to respect Moorish and Jewish corporate institutions and practices. This intransigence flourished at the very moment that Castilian scholars rediscovered and codified Roman civil law in the Siete Partidas. Following this legal transformation, the Christian monarchs continued to restrict the judicial autonomy of their Jewish and Moorish populations. In 1412, this culminated in the most draconian legislation to date, which "forbade Jews and Moslems alike to have their own judges. Thenceforth their cases, civil and criminal, were to be tried before ordinary judges of the districts where they lived. Criminal cases were to be decided according to Christian custom."[10] Though the temporal authorities relaxed the 1412 legislation with a decree in 1479, the systematic assault against customary courts of non-Christians continued unabated.

Though inimical to Innocent IV's commentary granting the *extra ecclesiam* sovereignty, the practice of curtailing Jewish and Moorish traditions reflected the ascendant hegemony of Iberia's Christian rulers. These sovereigns, though zealous Christians, saw all corporate privileges as a threat to their centralizing aspirations. In their opinion, all inhabitants of their territory were subject to the sovereign's laws. Jews and Moors were not an exception. By their actions, Iberia's Christian rulers contrived new forms of personhood. In a world defined by corporations with their accompanying rights and obligations, Jews and Moors subject to the victorious Christian rulers embodied corporateless beings that despite their own legal traditions and customs were expected to adhere to Christian laws and customary norms.

By undermining Jewish and Moorish courts, the Christian rulers redefined more than their relations to Jews and Moors. As they dismantled the courts through which Jews and Moors reproduced their distinctive juridical status, the Catholic monarchs actually reconstituted what it meant to be a Jew or a Moor. Standing before Christian courts and secular officials whose rulings owed much to Christianity, Jews, Moors, and enslaved Africans on the Iberian Peninsula lacked the protective shield of a culturally sanctioned judicial status. As such, they embodied one of the distinguishing features of the early modern period—individualism.[11]

In the fifteenth and sixteenth centuries, the Church still maintained a hold over the Christian princes' expansionism and their interactions with the *extra ecclesiam* both in and beyond Christendom. In regulating this interaction, the Church drew on a rich corpus of texts but relied primarily on canon law, especially the ecclesiastical consensus that formed around Innocent IV's commentary on *Quod super his,* a decretal of his predecessor, Innocent III. On the basis of canonical precedent, the Church increasingly intervened in the domain of laws of nations as it adjudicated over the affairs of Christians, infidels, and pagans. Even as the secular domain gradually acquired dominance, temporal authorities still needed to contend with Christian dogma's lengthy history, even though some postulated that their activities were subject to the law of nations. Well into the early modern period, the Christian Church presided over the imperial activities of secular authorities and even after the Protestant Reformation still meddled in the nascent but not entirely secularized domain of "Catholic sovereigns": the affairs of state.

While such affairs increasingly defined treaties and trade between nations as "secular" matters and property relations as the sole provenance of individuals, on the grounds of spiritual considerations and concerns about orthodoxy the Church continued to assert its dominion over the temporal realm. As for the infidels and pagans who fell into Christian hands as chattel, the Church and, to a lesser extent, the Crown, manifested a keen interest in their spiritual well-being. Well into the sixteenth century, canonists and theologians agreed that the *extra ecclesiam* could legitimately live beyond a state of grace, but in areas where Spanish absolutism was dominant, a growing number of ecclesiastical authorities equated such views with heresy. As a new orthodoxy swept Spain in the wake of the final phase of the reconquest, royal authorities brought an end to *conviviencia* (coexistence) and imposed new Christian norms on all persons in the domain of their sovereign.[12]

Intent on coercing the most prominent *extra ecclesiam* into abiding by Christian practices, Spanish Christians during the late medieval period began systematically undermining Jewish and Islamic judicial bodies. As Spain's sovereigns attacked the Jewish and Islamic institutions in order to eradicate the most prominent expressions of heresy, they gradually defined Jews and Muslims residing in Christendom as individuals—persons without judicial institutions to regulate their distinct social practices. During the earliest phases of the reconquest, Christians grudgingly respected the judicial institutions of Jews and especially Muslims, often recognizing the distinct administrative jurisdictions manifest among the various "peoples of the book."

Despite a history of antagonism and occasional pogroms, strategic imperatives favored *conviviencia* during the high Middle Ages. As Christian fortunes changed vis-à-vis the Cordoba-based caliphate's shifting ethnic composition, the Christian princes—with the approval and at times at the behest of the Church—steadily restricted the judicial privileges of the infidel population. Over the centuries, as Christianity began to dominate the peninsula, restrictive measures became increasingly draconian, culminating in 1412 with a Catholic decree banning Jewish and Islamic courts altogether. Indeed, within fifteenth-century Christendom, secular and ecclesiastical authorities subjected the *extra ecclesiam* to Christian law irrespective of their faith. In the absence of judicial institutions that historically shaped the ways Muslims and Jews experienced themselves as the faithful, for instance, Spain's minorities became individuals subject to the full extent of Christian laws and practices. The rulers of Spain's fragile hegemony forbade tolerance for the unorthodox, interpreting leniency toward heretics as a threat both to their rule and to Christendom. As Miguel Angel Ladero Quesada has noted, "In the political situation of the 'modern state' inaugurated by the Catholic Monarchs, the unity of religious faith was an indispensable condition of the social order and a premise for the exercise of power." Thus, in order to uphold the nascent, expanding, but still fragile Christian social body, Spain's Catholic sovereigns opted to regulate the *extra ecclesiam* in their midst. According to Deborah Root, "The construction of royal and religious sovereignty in Spain was precisely the production and interpretation of cultural and ethnic differences as something to be delineated and controlled, as well as the institution of communal recognition of those differences." [13]

Despite this internal transformation in western Christendom, European expansion still had to contend with the canon-law tradition that granted the *extra ecclesiam* sovereignty, including the right to exist beyond a state of grace. Christians, especially canonists, grudgingly recognized that non-Christian princes represented sovereigns. But what about the uprooted *extra ecclesiam* who lived under the dominion of a Christian sovereign? Though canon law prevailed in western Christendom, the ascendancy of medieval territorial states alongside the rising secular rulers gradually restricted its jurisdiction. As secular rulers promulgated vernacular legal codes, they steadily curtailed the *fueros* (special juridical privileges) of their subjects, including the rights of the *extra ecclesiam* sanctioned by canon law.

As tolerance waned in Christendom, secular rulers insisted that their subjects —new and old—adhere to recently decreed orthodoxy. The personnel staffing the new instruments of secular authority wielded increasing control over the subject population's diverse customs and social practices. This period of political consolidation and colonial expansion witnessed the introduction of new legitimating acts that authorities performed on the bodies of all subjects. Through displays of power—including the changing of names, branding, severing of kinship ties, and forced Christian conversion—secular and ecclesiastical authorities symbolically incorporated their victims. Such symbolic practices characterized the enslavement of Africans, marking the genesis of New World slavery.

In this sense, the process signified both an end and a beginning. For enslaved persons from "the land of blacks" (a fifteenth-century referent for West Africa), such practices highlighted their introduction to a Christian colonialism firmly intent on regulating body and soul. As gestures of humiliation and subjugation, these acts also marked the dominion of the secular sovereign over the enslaved person's body. But as "reasonable beings," the enslaved also fell under the secular Church's jurisdiction, where authorities held them accountable, as they did old and other new Christians alike.[14] The ecclesiastical authorities manifested their dominion over the African body on the basis that it contained a rebellious soul. The Crown aided the Church in this effort. Aside from chronic efforts to control the unsupervised, restrict fugitive flight, and prevent an armed black presence, the Crown limited its regulation of enslaved Africans and their descendants to what it called "good customs," by which it meant Christian conversion and a conjugal life. Understandably, the majority of sources that touch on African customs and those of their descendants had an ecclesiastical provenance. The manner in which Christian colonialism produced and then constituted itself around black bodies—bodies that represented the metaphorical territory that housed their souls—is highlighted by the archive. For the well-being of the commonwealth, all bodies had to be regulated and made to confirm to Christian norms. Whereas the Spanish conquest inaugurated the regulatory process, the less-dramatic Christian conquests that followed inscribed the process on the social landscape.[15]

Laws and the African Presence in the Indies

On August 18, 1518, Charles I—who, after his election as emperor in 1519, became Charles V—granted Laurent de Gouvenot permission to ship 4,000 enslaved Africans, "both male and female, provided they be Christians," to the Indies.[16] Charles's concession entitled this member of the royal council "or persons who may have his authority" to transport human chattel to lands "already discovered or to be discovered." By means of his order, Spain's sovereign sanctioned the importation of *bozales*, enslaved Africans directly from Guinea (West Africa) who did not speak Spanish or Portuguese and had not been exposed to Christianity beyond the problematic baptism as they boarded the slave ships. Ostensibly a charter permitting the direct importation of Africans into Spanish America, Charles's order underscored how quickly Spanish demand for a familiar commodity outstripped the available supply of ladinos (persons conversant in Portuguese or Castilian who often displayed knowledge of Christianity and Iberian customs). But the order also indicates the extent to which the Catholic sovereign attempted to regulate the slave trade and especially its victims, who, on arriving in Spanish America, became his vassals. As early as Columbus's initial landfall, Charles's maternal grandparents—Ferdinand and Isabel—attempted to control the flow of people, including slaves, to Spanish America.

By insisting that their subjects obtain a license to migrate to Spanish America, Spain's rulers sought to secure royal dominion. Even before realizing his dominion's extent in the New World, Spain's recently crowned sovereign insisted that order prevail throughout his real and imaginary patrimony. While theologians, canonists, lawyers, and chroniclers grappled with the novelty of America, Charles acted decisively to secure his authority over the newly discovered lands. For these reasons, he subjected the African presence, both slave and free, to intense scrutiny. From the inception of the slave trade, royal scrutiny was intent on regulating the forced migration of Africans and the ever-expanding population of African descent. Royal concerns mounted as the number of *bozales* and ladinos and their variously defined offspring increased. Though eager to regiment persons of African descent, the king did little more than decree additional legislation. At no time did Charles or his successors conceive of installing institutions specifically designed to regulate slaves and freedpersons after their arrival in the Americas. The Spanish king simply deployed the same instruments with which he regulated his other subjects. *Bozales,* above all else, had to adhere to Christian orthodoxy. By insisting that orthodoxy prevail, King Charles precluded masters from wielding supreme authority over slaves.[17]

By stipulating that Africans should "become Christians on reaching each island," Charles identified the customs to which crown officials subjected the recently enslaved.[18] For *bozales,* it meant conversion, baptism, and conformity to an elaborate set of beliefs, norms, and rituals predicated on distinct notions of body and soul, one's worldly existence, and the soul's eternal location in the hereafter. For those outside the Catholic fold, Christian conversion represented nothing less than a transformation of cosmic proportions. Ironically, most scholars of African conversion in the New World have separated "culture" from kinship patterns and familial mores. While the middle passage transformed Africans into slaves, scholars have rendered Christian conversion into a cultural abstraction in which static worldviews—both African and European —overshadow the actual mechanisms whereby Christianity insinuated itself into the lives of the enslaved.[19] Through customs and taboos and especially through a legal system that included natural, divine, canon, and Roman law, Spaniards defined Christianity in concrete terms.

Whereas faith retained its elusive nature, Christianity as a kinship and marriage system was subject to greater control. Feigning compliance always remained an option for heretics, but an individual could only manifest her/his beliefs by risking severe ecclesiastical sanctions. Thus, behavior, and thereby the body, became more susceptible to ecclesiastical discipline than did the soul. Laws intent on regulating the soul actually achieved greater control over the enslaved person's body. Christian compliance literally represented command performances in which the body, but not necessarily the soul, adhered to the colonial script.

Christian colonialism rested on the mistaken assumption that the body and soul acted in concert. Subscribing to the view that ascribed identities reflected the lived reality of the Christian conscience, officials believed that they could orchestrate the human drama in Spain's newly acquired provinces. As the Spanish king sought to impose Christianity on his subjects, royal and ecclesiastical authorities sought to mold those Africans rendered by the enslavement process into slaves—in their image. Spain's monarch engendered the imagined Africans by steadfastly attaching the adjectives "male and female" to the nouns "slaves" and "negroes," all the while insisting that the human chattel be Christian or "become Christians on reaching each island." Charles thereby underscored that enslaved Africans constituted humans and much more. He revealed that their overlapping identities as enslaved, Christian, and gendered beings would compete with, if not overshadow, their status as commodities.

On May 11, 1526, nearly eight years after Castile's sovereign permitted the importation of *bozales,* Charles V sought to restrict ladino migration to the Indies. Ladinos became desirable to the Crown and individual masters, who early on staffed their New World households with them. As commodities, ladinos initially commanded a higher exchange value than indigenous labor or unacculturated Africans. William Fowler, an English merchant who frequented Spanish America in the 1560s, observed that

> a Negro of good stature and yonge of yeres is worthe and is commonlie bought and soulde there at Mexico and the maine lande of the West Indias for 400, 500, and 600 pesos. For if a negro be a Bossale that is to say ignorant of the spanishe or Portugale tonge then he or she is commonly soulde for 400 and 450 pesos. But if the Negro can speake anye of the foresaide languages any thinge indifferentlye (which is called Ladinos) then the same negro is commonlye soulde for 500 and 600 pesos as the negro is of choise and yonge of yeres And this Deponent seythe that the best trade in those places is of Negros.[20]

While Fowler's assessment may obscure the skills a ladino might have acquired during a brief residence on the Iberian Peninsula, it still reflects how in the Indies Spaniards placed importance on language as a marker of civility and value.

As domestics and as symbols of wealth, ladinos initially acquired a reputation for their pliable nature and aversion to heresy. During the first two decades of the sixteenth century, King Ferdinand periodically sent black slaves, usually ladinos of various degrees of acculturation, to Hispañiola in order to work in the royal gold mines and the estates of his favorites. But twenty-four years after Columbus's momentous discovery, ladinos had fallen out of favor because of intractable behavior that purportedly threatened the orthodoxy of the commonwealth. From the Crown's perspective, the pliability of ladinos now represented a liability and a source of concern that royal authorities quickly projected onto mulattos, among other hybrids. The ladinos who initially arrived with Columbus's second voyage (1493–1496) absconded from their owners and periodically raided Hispañola's Castilian colony for supplies. Despite such insurrectionary behavior, the Crown seemed to harbored greater anxiety about ladinos because they were cultural insiders who defied orthodoxy. Such anxiety was manifest in the frequent orders to officials to regulate ladino behavior and social mobility.

In a precariously balanced social order, interlopers constituted a perennial threat because their very presence defied the conventions on which Castilian dominance rested. The capacity of ladinos to flaunt the various incarnations of the Castilian dichotomy (Christian versus barbarian, New Christians versus Old Christians, Spaniard versus Indian, and, among others, enslaved blacks versus free whites) alarmed officials intent on maintaining a rigidly defined order. Their inability to do so eventually prompted officials to embrace an insurmountable division predicated on blood and genealogy. Though this language was typical of the age of exploration, Castilians initially employed a division based on faith and customs rather than on race.

For these reasons, when ladinos proved intractable, Castilians turned to *bozales*. Seeking to curtail rebellious behavior, Charles decreed that "from here forward in time no one can or will carry the said negros ladinos from these our kingdoms nor from other parts if they are not bozales, because such bozales are those that serve, are peaceful and obedient." By imposing an import restriction on "negros who have been herein in our Kingdoms or in the Kingdom of Portugal for a year," Charles contradicted the notion that Christian conversion produced pliable subjects.[21] But despite the regulatory limitations of Christianity, secular and ecclesiastical authorities saw it as the only way to govern the growing population of those of African descent. On June 28, 1527, the emperor expressed his anxieties about Hispañola's growing African presence and its threat to orthodoxy. He noted how "each day many negros come to the Island of Española," and then maintained that "having few Christian Spaniards, it will be a source of some restlessness or uprising among the said negros."[22]

But instead of subjecting persons of African descent to greater military vigilance, Charles attempted to rectify the situation through marriage. In the Spanish monarch's eyes, "the grand remedy" would be to command "the negros that come here from now on and those that are here now" to contract marriage.[23] Matrimony, according to the king, represented an effective way to curb the seditious behavior threatening the commonwealth.[24] As a Christian sacrament, matrimony was the instrument through which Castilian officials tried to impose orthodoxy on its new subject population.

In his attempts to temper the insurrectionary spirit of the enslaved through marriage, the king stipulated how persons of African descent should experience their gendered identities. Charles, in fact, mandated that slavers "be obligated to come with half . . . males and the other half females." This demographic balance, Charles surmised, would facilitate coupling and enable the enslaved to marry "on their own."[25] Then the king granted Hispañiola's slaveowners fifteen months to comply with the new ruling but warned them not to coerce their dependents "because matrimony has to be free and not burdensome."[26] But the authorities did not favor any union. They wanted person of African descent to restrict spouse selection to individuals similarly defined. The growing frequency of African-Indian unions in the Caribbean and subsequently on the mainland worried colonial officials, who perceived an imaginary alliance that could challenge Spain's fragile hegemony. Though alarmed by interracial sex and especially by racial exogamy, neither the Crown nor the Church banned such behavior. In keeping with Christian law, the Crown did not decree endogamy. Such a practice would have violated free will, both a Christian belief and a widely held Iberian norm.

Instead, efforts to both restrict African-Indian unions and control the insurrectionary impulse among persons of African descent underscore a concern with the body and intentions to regulate it through Christian gender and sexual norms. The specter of sedition brought the gender and sexual identities among the variously defined persons of African descent (*bozal,* ladino, *negro,* mulatto, *lobo, coyote,* and *pardo*) into relief but only as something that needed to be contained and controlled. In regulating this population, the Spanish authorities did not treat them as a race apart. Both Crown and clergy dealt with Africans and their descendants as Christian subjects whom they judged and disciplined on the basis of canon law, the rules (canons) whereby the Christianity community established and judged its social and cultural practices. As the principal source of New Spain's moral code, canon law addressed illicit behavior from the perspective of heresy and explicit gender norms. In an attempt to suffuse Spanish America with orthodoxy, royalists actively curtailed the authority of potential competitors. The desire for order relegated property rights to a secondary concern. Royal and even ecclesiastical interests wielded precedence over the master's civil authority. In Spanish America, a person's subject status as the king's vassal prevailed over his or her identity as property largely because the fledgling polis necessitated the Crown's jurisdiction over all subjects, even the master's chattel. As paterfamilias of the realm, the king's interest reigned ascendant over others claiming authority as head of household. Jurisdictional conflicts magnified the slave's multiple identities—identities accompanied by discrete but competing obligations and rights.[27]

Concerned that the enslaved might see marriage as a route to freedom, Charles ordered masters to correct this assumption. "They should not think of themselves as free persons but slaves as if the said marriage never occurred."[28] A year earlier, in fact, Charles had declared that neither conversion nor marriage would affect the slave's legal status. Slavery and Christianity were not antithetical. In an order granting Alvaro de Castro, dean of the Church of Conception on the island of Hispañiola, license to important 200 slaves "half men and the other women," Charles stressed Christianity's compatibility with slavery. The king observed how "it will be of service to Our Lord and benefit the land to make the said slaves marry according to the law and benediction in order to teach them and make them live like Christians." Though he feared that marriage would encourage "the said slaves and their children" to press for their liberty, Charles insisted that "the laws of our Kingdoms" made the clamor of the Christianized slaves for freedom a baseless demand. To avoid groundless petitions, Charles instructed his officials to inform prospective neophytes that conversion to Christianity would not bring about a change in their status. By encouraging serial monogamy, the emperor intended to regulate, not ameliorate, the slave's behavior. Christian matrimony based on specific gender and sexual conventions constituted the preferred instrument with which the emperor and his authorities attempted to regulate persons of African descent.

Enslaved Africans, however, evidently continued to perceive Christian marriage as an avenue that would lead to freedom well after the king commanded officials to inform neophytes of the contrary. In 1538, Bartolomé de Zárate, a royal official, sent a report to Spain lamenting the cynicism with which the enslaved entered the state of matrimony. Zárate stated that after their arrival, enslaved African men "cohabit with Indian and black women in and beyond their masters' houses" until their owners demand that they marry. According to Zárate, the enslaved men, once married, "say they are free and have obtained liberty."[29] Such sentiments, the magistrate claimed, undermined the sacrament and threatened the commonwealth's precarious balance. The specter of liberty did not pose a challenge to the social order. But the consciousness of slaves that they could use Catholic sacraments as a strategy to obtain freedom was a threat.

Zárate's concerns reveal that the enslaved utilized the sacrament of matrimony—imposed as an obligation—in order to appropriate rights for themselves. Even the recently enslaved understood that in this jurisdictional contest between their status as slaves and their status as Christians, the latter status prevailed, at least in theory. By means of marriage, the enslaved acquired rights as Christian subjects in the commonwealth that tempered the scripted role that colonialism and slavery imposed. Anxious to avert the spread of similar claims among the enslaved, Spain's monarch again instructed his representatives to correct this misunderstanding. Marriage, according to canon law, did not free the enslaved. Some of the enslaved nonetheless utilized their conjugal rights and obligations to their advantage. This consciousness that one could use Christian rights as a personal strategy will be the focus of subsequent chapters.[30]

As the Castilians tried to impose conjugality on *bozales* and their descendants, gender assumed critical importance. Even among the lowest-ranked members of society, gender, and its link to reproduction, garnered royal attention. By allowing the royal favorite, Gouvenot, to import "both male and female . . . in whatever proportion he may choose," Charles acknowledged the slave population's reproductive capability. Charles's insistence that this population be or become Christians underscores his desire to regulate the enslaved and their offspring in accordance with Christian mores. Such norms had a transforming effect on the slaves' lives since they defined the ways in which males and females could experience themselves as Christian men and women. Among the *bozales* who landed in the Indies, sexual differences represented a fundamental division. Iberian slavers worked with Africa's diverse sovereigns in order to conform to the gender ratios of the royal decrees. But in the Indies, Spaniards subjected perceived sexual differences according to Christian-inflected gender norms.

Spaniards stipulated how Africans could experience themselves as females and males in the Indies. In fact, the sacrament of matrimony rested on a historically constituted system based on gender, kinship, and morality through which Spanish Christians defined how men and women experienced their maleness and femaleness, reckoned descent, and legitimately expressed desire. Consequently, when Charles decreed that slave traders transport a balanced ratio of females and males to the Indies, he offered a glimpse of the gender and moral system prevailing in early modern Spain and the Habsburg Empire. Through this elaborate system and its gendered scripts, persons of African descent had to process and perform their identities as men and women in accordance with Christian norms, even though adherence to these norms occasionally brought the roles assigned to slaves as vassals and Christians into conflict with their identity as property.

On Becoming Christians

The absence of a distinct conversion policy for Africans poses important questions about their Christian identity and the methods that the clergy employed to instruct *bozales* in the faith. As a requirement for baptism and a Christian life, Christian instruction represented more than an aside. Without Christian instruction, a person could not abide by the commandments, observe the sacraments, or participate in the rites of the Church. These practices represented the bare essentials for a Christian life, placing the individual in the community of the faithful and granting them access to the rituals that accompanied the Christian life cycle. In stating that he "became a Christian in Lisbon, of my own will" Juan Garrido, the ladino who participated in Cortés's conquest of the Nahuas, revealed his complicity in the conversion process. Unfortunately, he left few traces of the process whereby the clergy inaugurated him into the Christian faith. Similar glimpses exist for the second half of the sixteenth century and beyond. But for the earlier period, the encounter of the *bozales* with Christianity remains largely undocumented. The historical record abounds with insinuations that priests baptized hundreds of the enslaved as slave-traders herded them on board. Diverse anecdotes also attest that priests waited at the ports to administer the sacraments to the enslaved soon after they landed in the Indies. Yet how, when, and under what circumstances did the clergy introduce *bozales* to Christianity? Posed differently, how did Charles envision that "the said negroes male and female, become Christians on reaching each island?" Canon law complicates this question since it forbade forced conversion.[31]

In 1524, three years after the Nahuas surrendered to Cortés, the mainland conquest entered a new phase. The arrival of the twelve Franciscans signaled the beginning of the Christian conquest and the "methodical evangelization" of the native inhabitants. Initially the mendicant orders (or the regular clergy, as the Franciscans, Dominicans, and Augustinians were known) acquired jurisdiction over the indigenous population. In order to administer the sacraments to the Native Americans—the normal function of the secular clergy—the regulars received papal dispensations. Alongside the multifaceted Christian conquest, the arrival of the twelve Franciscans also inaugurated the primitive phase of the Episcopal Church. From its roots in Rome, the episcopacy expanded from urban centers into the adjacent countryside. In New Spain, the Church strove to replicate this pattern. Centered on a cathedral and its bishop, a diocese contained several parishes whose staff included a pastor and priests, vicars, and an ecclesiastical judge. Known as the secular clergy, they and the cathedral staff presided over the full extent of the laity's spiritual life. While regulars and seculars shared a common goal—the Christianization of New Spain and its inhabitants—they focused their energies on distinct populations. Dividing New Spain's population into two camps—Indians and everybody else—the regulars converged on the native peoples, largely leaving the Hispanic laity to the secular clergy.

Beginning in Hispañiola with the assistance of the regulars, the Crown tried to separate the Hispanic laity from the indigenous population. Through a policy of residential separation known as *congregación,* the Crown decreed that native peoples should reside in makeshift parishes under the supervision of regulars until they had sufficient exposure to Christianity. In the aftermath of the mainland conquests, the Spanish authorities implemented the congregation policy in New Spain, separating the indigenous population from the Hispanic invaders by restricting the latter from making their homes in rural areas. Over the course of the sixteenth century, the clergy debated the efficacy of this and other evangelizing methods, devising various schemes for converting indigenous peoples to Christianity. In successive ecclesiastical synods, the clergy subjected their methods to examination, which highlights the multiplicity of opinions about how best to convert the indigenous population. In a 40-year period (1524–1565), New Spain's clergy met in five Juntas Eclesiásticas (1524, 1532, 1539, 1544, and 1546) and two Concilios Provinciales (1555 and 1565) in order to expound upon and refine their tactics.

Though ostensibly focused on the conversion of the indigenous population, the church councils also addressed themselves to the beliefs and practices that prevailed in the República de los Españoles. In the period of Catholic renewal, orthodoxy emerged as a pressing concern, prompting the convocation of New Spain's First and Second Provincial Councils. Even as the Tridentine Reforms brought the laity and its customs into relief, the clergy initially manifested little interest in discerning distinctions among the faithful and the nonindigenous *extra ecclesiam*. In relation to the Indians, the clergy simply defined *bozales*, Spaniards, and new Christians among other corporate groups as old Christians. As late as 1585, Fray Pedro de Feria, bishop of Chiapas, reflected such sentiments when he observed how "there are two differences among Christians. Some are old Christians, which are Spaniards along with others from our diverse kingdoms and provinces in Europe. And the others are new Christians: the natives of this new world the Indies."[32] While Pedro de Feria's sentiments underscore the juridical status separating old and new Christians, they also imply the absence of a distinct conversion process for *bozales*. Perceiving Africans and their descendants as an Old World and thus a familiar population, the clergy subjected both ladinos and *bozales* to the same methods they used with Spaniards. In matters of faith and the administration of sacraments, the Episcopal Church never accorded *bozales* the same neophyte status they bestowed on Indians—which offered the indigenous population limited protection from Christianity's most onerous demands and discipline.[33]

In the postconquest period that roughly corresponded with the period of Catholic renewal, episcopal officials finally manifested greater vigilance over the heterogeneous mass of persons defined as "people of reason," though some behavior defined as heretical did not properly belong in the Church's domain. As the secular clergy displayed more interest in the lives of its flock, they insisted on an order in which the sacrament of matrimony had a prominent role. By demanding conformity to Christianity's hallowed institution, the clergy stressed more than dogma. Through marriage, the clergy defined how members of the República de los Españoles should experience life and their gendered selves. For many born in Africa and even some of their creole descendants, Christian conjugality represented a phenomenon of epic proportions.

Intent on imposing Christian norms on the commonwealth's Hispanicized inhabitants—including persons of African descent—the clergy mobilized the ecclesiastical courts.

Then Philip II installed the tribunal of the Holy Office of the Inquisition in his Spanish possessions. By linking orthodoxy, good customs, and order, officials defined cultural practices as political manifestations. Heterodoxy, in all its manifestations, emerged as a synonym for political instability. From the perspective of royal and ecclesiastical officials, the commonwealth's fornicators, adulterers, and bigamists represented a comparable threat to the Protestant menace personified by John Hawkins and his band of interlopers. In both instances, the inquisitors acted decisively to curb the threat. In the era of Catholic renewal, royal and ecclesiastical authorities magnified New Spain's Christian norms and defined the ways in which persons of African descent could experience themselves as black females and males. Such norms challenged the master's domain since they imposed gendered identities on the enslaved—identities accompanied by specific obligations and rights. But the long-standing scholarly tradition of ascribing Roman law (as enshrined in the Siete Partidas) primacy in discussions of slavery has restricted this rich history from view and confines the African and slave experience to bondage. This perspective ignores the ways in which the Spanish monarchy and the Catholic Church shaped the slave and black experience by bestowing multiple juridical identities on persons of African descent.

3 Policing Christians

Persons of African Descent before
the Inquisition and Ecclesiastical Courts

> The Spanish monarchy administered its realm largely through its judiciary. At
> the apex of what might well be termed the "judicial state" of the antiguo regi-
> men stood the monarch, whose prime function, according to the medieval Siete
> Partidas, was to "govern" and maintain the empire in justice.[1]
>
> Representing power was essential to reproducing domination.[2]

In keeping with the Council of Trent (1545–1563) and at the behest of Charles
V and Philip II, New Spain's secular clergy manifested greater vigilance over
the laity during the second half of the sixteenth century.[3] As the Old World
population in the Indies expanded due to voluntary and involuntary migration, royal and ecclesiastical officials called for greater discipline. Though the
idolatry of the indigenous population remained a concern, the secular clergy
directed their attention at the expanding República de los Españoles. Despite
mounting ecclesiastical vigilance, influential royal officials such as Juan de
Ovando, Rodrigo de Castro, Melchor Cano, and Bernardo de Fresneda believed that New Spain's clergy could not enforce the orthodoxy on which their
Catholic sovereign's dominion rested. England's imperial ambitions—to foster
a growing Protestant presence in the Atlantic world—and the imagined converso (descendants of baptized Jews) menace heightened royal concerns.[4]

In 1569, alarmed by the threat of Protestant and converso interlopers, Philip
II extended the jurisdiction of the Holy Office of the Inquisition to his New
World dominions. As an instrument of Catholic renewal, the Inquisition focused on exorcising the heresies that threatened the Catholic realm and its
faithful. As Catholic stalwarts, the Habsburg emperors and rulers of Castile—
especially Charles V and Philip II—linked their authority as sovereigns with
the cause of the Roman Church and spearheaded the Catholic offensive in
Europe against the growing Protestant minority. Protestant interlopers presented more than a threat against orthodoxy. As they ignored the fifteenth-
century papal accords, the Protestants challenged the Castilian sovereign's dominion and the ideology—Catholicism—on which it rested. As a threat to
Catholicism and papal authority, they undermined the very source of Spanish and Portuguese imperial expansion. In the context of the Protestant Reformation and Catholic renewal, royal and ecclesiastical authorities labeled the

schism as heretical and a rebellion against their sovereign's authority.[5] According to Richard Greenleaf, "The line between heresy and treason became very vague, and since heretics robbed the community of its faith, sacraments, and spiritual life, it was deemed just to execute them as traitors and fomenters of social revolution."[6] In Spain and its New World dependencies, the Inquisition tried to stave off any threat to the sovereign's authority.

Aimed in the first instance against foreign enemies of the faith, the ominous tribunal also sought to imbue New Spain's Catholic laity with awe for Crown and clergy. Though Protestants and then conversos represented the stated foe, the composition of the Christian commonwealth underscores another menace. As the majority among New Spain's República de los Españoles, persons of African descent constituted an implicit threat to Spanish rule. In Mexico City in 1571, the site and year of the Inquisition's installation, the variously defined persons of African descent numbered 11,645 while Spaniards totaled 9,495.[7] Martín Enríquez, New Spain's viceroy from 1568 to 1580, viewed these figures with alarm. According to the cultural historian Irving A. Leonard, Viceroy Enríquez believed that "the social effects of the rapidly growing Negro element constituted the gravest problem of the realm."[8] Miles Philips, an Englishman who resided in New Spain during this period, candidly observed that "the Negros also doe daily lie in wait to practise their deliverance out of that thraldome and bondage, that the Spaniardes doe keep them in."[9] Twenty years after Viceroy Luís de Velasco's dire warning about the slave trade, persons of African descent had, in the eyes of officials and some observers, finally "put the land in confusion."

If the Inquisition intended to instill order in the realm, it had to inspire awe and quiescence in the Christian commonwealth's African majority. The specter of insurrection magnified the anxiety of Spanish elites and officials about the growth of the African population. In addressing this perceived threat, officials typically passed ordinances that prevented Africans and their descendants from associating in large numbers or at night. Officials denied black males the right to carry weapons, an emasculating gesture in an era when most men sported knives or swords.[10] Philip II even instructed Viceroy Enríquez that all persons of African descent, especially free persons, had to reside under Spanish supervision.[11] Despite this legislation, the Crown believed that Christianity represented the most effective means of social control. Christianity, according to Charles V, especially the sacrament of marriage, represented the "grand remedy." The Inquisition, in effect, sought to invigorate the Christian faith of the viceroyalty's inhabitants. The inquisitors intended to instruct and unite the laity. Through its spectacular displays, designed to punish the most egregious behavior, the tribunal also issued an ominous warning—conform or risk the wrath of the inquisitors.

Notwithstanding the Inquisition's century-long presence in New Spain, the tribunal never attempted to replace the routine interaction between priest, parish, and parishioner. As an instrument of absolutist authority, the Inquisition deliberately remained episodic and selective. But by intervening in the lives of the enslaved, the tribunal underscored the Spanish sovereign's willingness to subject slaves to his authority even at the expense of their masters' dominion. Accustomed to exuding mastery, members of the tribunal understood that their sovereign's fragile Catholic hegemony necessitated drama in order to keep the mass of slaves and freedpersons in check. This was the goal of the spectacles of the Inquisition. From the perspective of the authorities, the Inquisition's *entrada*—the ritualized entrance announcing the presence of a new viceroy or archbishop—represented an effort to reconquer New Spain from an internal enemy defined as old Christians whose faith had lapsed. The auto-de-fé, in turn, symbolized both exorcism and reconciliation. For the majority of the tribunal's victims, however, the Inquisition's *entrada* signaled a heightening of Christian moral discipline. For enslaved Africans and the free black population, the tribunal's presence represented another instrument intended to define the essence of personhood, since this, the latest regulatory institution to arrive in the Indies, sought to regiment behavior in accordance with Christian gender, kinship, and marital norms. Consequently, many of the proceedings focused on the laity's sexual behavior.

In the historiography of the Inquisition, the experiences of Africans and their descendants remain largely unexplored. Even though they outnumbered Spaniards, the Africans in New Spain rarely have invited comment. For the most part, scholars have confined the cultural significance of the African presence—the majority among the República de los Españoles and the largest sector of Mexico City's population after Amerindians—to slave insurrections and *mestizaje,* thereby obscuring the Inquisition's regulatory activities among *bozales,* ladinos, and *negros criollos.* But nearly 50 percent of the 1,553 volumes of surviving inquisition tomes involve persons of African descent as the accused.[12] From its installation, the tribunal subjected persons of African descent to its jurisdiction. By adjudicating over Africans and their descendants and not the indigenous population, the tribunal magnified the ways in which the dichotomy between New and Old World informed the divergent experiences of the colonized.[13]

Inquisition scholar Solange Alberro has observed that "they [Spaniards] could not justify this difference." Both groups represented newly converted Christians, and "nothing indicates . . . why African neophytes ought to receive more severe treatment than the natives." Thus, Alberro speculated, "It is very likely that considerations of a political type contributed to Spaniards showing less rigor with the indigenous population and exempting them from the inquisitorial jurisdiction though they represented the majority of the vice-royalty's population."[14] For Alberro, the crux resided in the Africans' assumed familiarity with Christianity, which in Spanish eyes defined them as an Old World population. As Old World inhabitants, Africans were subject to the Christian orthodoxy that stipulated existing obligations, and violations thereof exposed the offender to ecclesiastical censure.

By adjudicating over Africans and demanding that recently converted Africans adhere to Christian mores, the tribunal disregarded the rights of the *extra ecclesiam* to reside beyond grace. In the voyage from Guinea to the Indies, the rights of the *extra ecclesiam* eventually gave way to the demands of the Castilian sovereign. Absolutism, in other words, emerged ascendant from its jurisdictional conflict with canon law.

In the Indies, the Patronato Real—a 1508 accord in which the Pope granted the Spanish monarchs the rights associated with being head of the Church—enabled the Castilian king to act in defense of his interests, including subjecting Africans to Christian morality—especially those individuals who willing embraced Christianity. While the ecclesiastical courts presided over most moral offenses involving members of the República de los Españoles, in the event of bigamy, blasphemy, and witchcraft, the Inquisition's tribunal assumed jurisdiction. In its desire to reform the laity's behavior, the tribunal did not exempt persons of African descent. To do so would have represented a major omission. Yet in subjecting the behavior of enslaved Africans to scrutiny, the tribunal—as an instrument of absolutism—intervened in matters most scholars of slavery have mistakenly confined to the master's domain. For the tribunal, matters related to bigamy, blasphemy, and witchcraft were too essential to leave in the hands of paterfamilias and masters. Similarly, the officials presiding over the ecclesiastical courts defined certain behavior manifest among the laity as belonging to their jurisdiction, thus circumscribing the paterfamilias dominion over children, wives, and servants.

Christian Strangers

At midcentury, nearly twenty years before the Inquisition's installation, Catholic officials began scrutinizing the presence of Protestants in New Spain, revealing that the Church's vigilance preceded the Counter-Reformation's offensive. From New Spain's inception, the clergy attempted to monitor and correct the laity's behavior. New Spain's Catholic Church professed jurisdiction over all Old World peoples. Long-standing customs offered little, if any protection, from the Church. In many cases they merely invited closer scrutiny. Irrespective of its claims of universal jurisdiction and, therefore, of implied impartiality, New Spain's Church was a decidedly Castilian institution, which ecclesiastical officials manifested institutionally through the Patronato Real. Anxious to maintain its temporal hegemony over the Indies, royalists identified foreigners as a threat. Through the xenophobic prism of absolutism, even Christian foreigners evoked Castilian suspicion. Royal and ecclesiastical officials acted quickly to stop the behavior of any stranger who emerged as an active threat. As New Spain's authorities regulated and purged their sovereign's domain, they tried to elicit a sense of community, in opposition to the presence of strangers, among the king's heterogeneous subjects. In New Spain's stratified social milieu, Protestants and conversos, as opposed to Africans, represented the most identifiable strangers.

As the following example demonstrates, in the context of Protestant Reformation, the English offered a threat that Spanish officials took very seriously. Robert Tomson, one of the initial Englishmen who was tried and convicted by Catholic officials, stated that a considerable number of his countrymen resided in New Spain. Identifying New Spain's vibrant English presence with Protestant expansion, Tomson suggested that the Hispanic population displayed great interest in England's heretical beliefs.[15] In turn, Catholic officials saw Tomson and his heresies as a threat that needed to be exorcised. In 1555, after spending a year in Seville, where he went "to learn the Castillian tongue and the customes of the people," Robert Tomson departed for the Indies in the company of the English merchant John Fields and his family.[16] Tomson readily acknowledged his financial motives; he had "seene the fleetes of shippes come out of the Indies to that citie [Seville] with such great quantity of gold & silver, pearles, precious stones, sugar, hides, ginger, and divers other rich commodities."[17] During a brief sojourn in the Canary Islands where they awaited the fleet, Tomson's party found hospitality among "certaine Englishmen merchants."[18] Eventually, the entourage sailed for New Spain via the island of Hispañiola. Off the coast of Veracruz, a storm dispersed and then destroyed the fleet, but Tomson and a few others managed to make it ashore.[19] After a harrowing journey from the coast to the highland, Tomson's entourage finally arrived in Mexico, although three days later, Tomson's employer and patron, John Fields, perished. Tomson sadly recalled that "of eight persons that were of us of the saide company, there remained but foure alive." By befriending Thomas Blake, "a Scottishman borne, who had dwelt and had married in the said Citie above twentie yeares before I came to the said Citie," Tomson secured employment with "one of the first conquerours," Gonzalo Cerezo, with whom he resided for eighteen months.[20]

During this time, Tomson expressed sentiments that led church officials to try and convict him. Tomson recounted that one evening while at dinner in the company of Spaniards, "They began to inquire of me being an Englishman, whether it were true, that in England they had overthrown all their Churches and houses of Religion, and that all the images of the Saints of heaven that were in them were throwen downe, broken, and burned . . . as they had been certified out of Spaine by their friends."[21] "It was so," Tomson replied, noting that the images and the adoration of them "was cleane contrary to the expresse commandement of Almighty God, Thou shalt not make to thy selfe any graven image."[22] The Spaniards were astonished by the audacity of the English, and a theological conversation ensued in which some, according to Tomson, lauded the actions of the English while others defended Catholic practices. Finally, Tomson called on the Catholic defenders to "looke into the Scripture your selfe, and you shall find it." Troubled by such sacrilegious sentiments, "a villanous Portugal" retorted "It is enough to be English in order to know all this and more." The next day, the offended party "went to the Bishop of Mexico, and his Provisor, and said, that in a place where he had bene the day before, was an Englishman, who said, that there was no need of Saints in the Church, nor of any invocation of Saints."[23]

The Church officials acted with haste against the heretic, seizing him "for the same words here rehearsed, and none other thing."[24] In 1557, he was imprisoned for seven months. The ecclesiastical judges presiding over the Apostolic Inquisition (1533–1571) then subjected Tomson and the Genoese Augustin Boacio, who also had been convicted "for matters of Religion," to processional penance and public ridicule—the auto-de-fé. Dressed in a *sanbenito*—the penitent's yellow frock inscribed with two red crosses—church officials escorted the foreigners through Mexico's principal streets toward the "high Church of Mexico" where "at least five or sixe thousand" people looked on in somber amazement. Tomson recalled that many had trekked great distances "to see the saide Auto (as they call it) for that there were never none before, that had done the like in the said Countrey, nor could not tell what Lutheranes were, nor what it meant: for they never heard of any such thing before."[25] Aside from punishing the heretics, the clerics utilized the spectacle to instruct their flock in righteous behavior. Through the foreigners, they reminded those present of the Church's omnipotence and the consequences of heresy. Tomson recounted how the clerics told those in attendance that he and Boacio "were heretiques, infidels, and people that did despise God, and his workes, and that wee had bene more like devils then men, and thought wee had had favor of some monsters, or heathen people." According to Tomson, however, the spectators questioned the Church officials,

> saying, that they never sawe goodlier men in all their lives, and that it was
> not possible that there could be in us so much evill as was reported of us,
> and that we were more like Angels among men, then such persons of such

evill Religion as by the Priests and friers wee were reported to be, and that it was great pitie that wee sholⅾ ⱱee so used for so small an offence.[26]

Despite such protestations, the proceedings continued. In the cathedral, the clerics displayed the two penitents on a newly constructed scaffold "which was made before the high Altar." Following mass, the presiding officials issued lengthy indictments against the "heretiques," sentencing Tomson to three years in prison while condemning Boacio to a life term. The clerics eventually sent both men to Spain.[27]

Such inquisitorial proceedings by New Spain's clergy did little to impress influential royalists and tridentine prelates in Castile. The most ardent royalists argued that New Spain's clergy was incapable of upholding Catholicism and the interests of the monarch. Representing a powerful constituency at court, Castile's orthodox and royalist prelates continually implored Philip to take the religious offensive in the Indies. England's imperial aspirations, which fostered a growing Protestant presence in the Atlantic world, finally persuaded Philip to act decisively by establishing the Holy Office of the Inquisition in his New World dominions in 1569.

On Friday evening, November 2, 1571, two years after the Inquisition began in the Indies, a town crier repeatedly made his way "through the major streets and plazas of Mexico."[28] Each time, he exhorted Mexico's inhabitants to attend Sunday's mass at the cathedral and witness the installation ceremony of the Holy Office of the Inquisition. As the town crier delivered his message, several of the newly appointed inquisitors accompanied him through the *traza*'s neighborhoods and the various public squares.[29] "Attracted by the novelty" and the fanfare, a large "multitude of persons of varies social classes" joined the gathering of dignitaries.[30]

Despite the gaiety exhibited by the procession's hangers-on, the town crier issued serious tidings. Every so often, as his voice rose above the cacophony, he announced that "all and what person, men as well as women, irrespective of status and stature that they be, from twelve years up, must come the following Sunday . . . to the principal church of this city to hear mass, a sermon and vows of the faith . . . under the pain of excommunication."[31] Mexico's inhabitants knew that the authorities would carry out this ominous threat. Two days later, hundreds assembled in the cathedral while latecomers gathered outside, anxious for mass to begin. As the assembled waited and others scurried through the streets in the direction of the city's epicenter, many more sought to avoid mass altogether. Perhaps some, watching the Inquisition's solemn procession move toward the cathedral, changed their minds. Accustomed to the spectacle of the *entrada*, Mexico's inhabitants saw this somber procession, with its crimson banner inscribed with a silver cross, as a novelty.[32] Individuals familiar with the banner realized that the tribunal of the Holy Office of the Inquisition had arrived in New Spain.

For some, the town crier's earlier threat took on added significance.[33] As the massive procession plied through the viceregal capital on November 4th, participants and observers alike witnessed the performance of power and the hierarchy of the colonial order. The procession—with its ostentatious display of pomp, precision, and strict observance of hierarchy—symbolically positioned the Inquisition in the sovereign's realm.[34] Thus, Dr. Moya, the newly appointed inquisitor general, stood at the physical rear but spiritual head of the procession with the viceroy, Martín Enríquez, at his right and the *audiencia*'s president and deacon, Judge Villalobos, to his left. The tribunal's *fiscal,* Licenciado Alonso Hernández de Bonilla, preceded the heads of the corporate bodies, carrying the crimson standard. In turn, the *audiencia*'s judges, Puga and Villanueva, walked slightly ahead of Bonilla but behind the Inquisition's *alguacil mayor,* Verdugo de Bazan; the treasurer, Arriarán; and the notary, Pedro de los Ríos. Mexico City's *regidores* flanked the Inquisition officials while the university's illustrious doctors proceeded apace just behind their students who, of course, marched in accordance with their status.[35] As this ostensibly secular procession approached the cathedral, it merged with the awaiting secular clergy and monastic orders. Together, secular and ecclesiastical officials entered the cathedral —according to rank within their respective corporate bodies—while Inquisitor Dr. Moya, Viceroy Enríquez, and Judge Villalobos, at the apex of power, came last.[36] Following Fray Bartolomé de Ledesma's sermon, the newly appointed notary—Pedro de los Ríos—ascended to the altar and read the sovereign's instructions to the assembled mass. The king, de los Ríos announced, implored the faithful "neither to permit nor to consent to heretics being among them but to denounce them to the Holy Office."[37] As a demonstration of their faith, he called on all "men, women and children [to] raise the right hand" and in unison shout "I swear." After this pledge, de los Ríos descended the altar and with silver cross in hand approached the viceroy, who was to swear the following oath:

> I swear to God the all powerful and Holy Mary his mother and the sign of the cross and the holy apostles, as a good and faithful Christian from now and always to assist and defend our Holy Catholic faith and the Holy Inquisition, her officials and ministers . . . to protect and defend their exceptions and immunities and not to hide their heretics and enemies and to prosecute and denounce to the Inquisitors who are here and those that follow and to accept and to comply and to do all that is contained in the said edict of judgment.[38]

And so he did, as head of the secular government, as did all the officials present that day.[39]

After the administration of the oaths, Dr. Moya—in his ecclesiastical splendor—climbed the altar and reminded the assembled of their Christian obligations. He instructed those in attendance in matters of the faith, noting "with great detail the things that they [members of the tribunal] considered punishable."[40] He then prohibited "the confessors from absolving" any penitent "who knew some of these things, without appearing to manifest them."[41] Finally, Dr. Moya exhorted confessors, the faithful, and penitents to report suspicious behavior within six days "under the threat of excommunication."[42] With the Edict of Faith, the decree and oath which placed the burden of regulation in public hands, Dr. Moya sought to secure the Inquisition's dominion over New Spain's moral domain. Taking their Catholic sovereign's concerns seriously, Dr. Moya and the other inquisitors implored New Spain's Christian inhabitants to resist Protestantism, among other heresies. According to Dr. Moya, Mexico's residents took his message to heart. In a letter to Philip II, Dr. Moya proclaimed that New Spain's inhabitants "with great honor and much frequency" were to divulge "things about bigamists and foreigners of which there are plenty in these parts and of all nations."[43]

Despite the preponderance of "bigamists," the inquisitors initially focused their attention on "foreigners," including the survivors of John Hawkins's disastrous third voyage, who, defeated at the hands of the Spanish fleet, briefly eluded capture by escaping overland.[44] Soon after their arrival in 1571, the inquisitors interrogated the surviving Protestants but eventually released them to secular authorities. The authorities, in turn, parceled them out as servants to wealthy Spaniards.[45] As a result of subsequent heresy allegations, however, most of the sailors soon landed in the hands of the inquisitors again. The ensuing investigations, in which the inquisitors employed judicial torture, led to the conviction of most of the sailors. Although their sentences varied, the inquisitors subjected the convicted Protestants along with various Hispanicized heretics and bigamists to New Spain's tribunal first auto-de-fé—its ultimate display of power.

In the early hours of February 28, 1574, less than a year and a half after the Inquisition's installation, more than the usual commotion took place in the plaza of Santo Domingo. Amidst the cock's crowing, the incessant barking of dogs agitated by men on horseback, and the ambulatory vendors who hawked their wares, hundreds of people assembled in front of the Inquisition's office. A few gave specific orders, many more yelled, the occasional person grumbled or pleaded, but most simply complied. As a processional line took shape, sumptuary distinctions became noticeable. The individuals on the inner line wore the *sanbenito*, nooses around their necks, and each carried a large unlit green candle. As the onlookers gazed at the nearly 100 assembled men and women dressed in their "fooles coats," some recalled the notices issued during mass, the town crier's endless prattle, and the spate of construction near the cathedral. Those individuals in "fooles coats" represented "Gods enemies," and February 28, 1574, was the day of their atonement.[46] As the Inquisition's *alguacil mayor* and his various lieutenants cajoled and prodded the ominous gathering, two deputies positioned themselves alongside each penitent. Soon thereafter, this somber procession made its way through Mexico's principal thoroughfares, which were lined with thousands of onlookers. On reaching the *plaza mayor*, the inquisition officials escorted the colorful procession of penitents up the second highest of several recently constructed scaffolds. At the top, the officials directed each person to a designated seat, where they awaited the arrival of another procession. Miles Philips, an English survivor of John Hawkins's third voyage and victim of the auto-de-fé, vividly recounted the ordeal in his memoirs:

> And so about eight of the clocke in the morning, we set foorth of the prison, every man alone in his yellow coat, and a rope around his necke, and a great greene Waxe candle in his hand unlighted, having a Spaniard appointed to goe upon either side of every one of us: and so marching in this order and manner toward the scaffold in the market place. . . . We found a great assembly of people all the way, and such a throng, that certain of the Inquisition officers on horseback were constrained to make way, and so coming to the scaffold, we went up by a paire of stayres, and found seates readie made and prepared for us to sit downe on, every man in order as he should receive his judgment.[47]

As the last penitent sat down, members of the Inquisition's procession entered the massive *plaza mayor*. The theatrics of order again reminded participants and observers of the corporate hierarchy. As the formation made its way through the crowded plaza, the ecclesiastical and secular *cabildos* led the way, respectively occupying the right and left. The chancery's *alguacil mayor* and his lieutenants followed on their heels while minor inquisition officials trailed behind. Licenciado Bonilla, the tribunal's *fiscal*, came next but walked alone with the crimson banner in hand. The *audiencia*'s judges, organized according to rank and seniority, followed the *fiscal* but preceded the bishop of Tlaxcala, who had been asked to deliver the principal sermon. The viceroy, along with Dr. Moya and another inquisition official, brought up the powerful rear.[48] As the Inquisition's procession ascended the highest of several scaffolds and its members located their seats, hundreds of Dominican, Franciscan, and Augustinian friars paraded onto their respective platforms. Miles Philips noted that after all had been seated and prayers were said "then presently beganne their severe and cruell judgment."[49] After the authorities publicly proclaimed the sins and "judgment" of the penitents, the inquisitors called on the remaining two "enemies of God," whom secular officials summarily dragged from the scaffold, garroted, and burned before the assembled mass.[50] For the survivors, the ordeal did not end that day. Miles Philips recalled that

> the next day in the morning being good Friday . . . we were all brought into a court of the inquisitors pallace, where we found a horse in a readiness for every one of our men which were condemned to have stripes, and to be committed to the gallies . . . inforced to mount up on horsebacke naked from the middle upward, were carried to be shewed as a spectacle for all the people to behold throughout the chiefe and principall streetes of the cities, and had the number of stripes to every one of them appointed, most cruelly laid upon their naked bodes with long whips.[51]

As this blood-ridden procession proceeded through the city, Mexico's residents realized that the spectacle involved more than atonement. Through the massive display of power and with English bodies, the inquisitors reminded the 21,140 members of the República de los Españoles—of which 11,645 were of African descent—that Catholicism and the Castilian sovereign reigned supreme. In a letter to Philip II, Dr. Moya noted that the juxtaposition of the Spanish and the English may have confused his heterogeneous flock, who were allegedly not accustomed to differentiating between Christians—read whites.[52] Although Dr. Moya clearly underestimated the ability of the Hispanicized mass to distinguish between Europeans, his allusion underscores the ways in which the auto-de-fé gave the heterogeneous mass of Catholics a fleeting but ultimately illusory cohesiveness.[53] As the auto-de-fé purged the newly ascendant colonial society, it momentarily simplified the drama of community. The large presence of English penitents enabled the elite and the subalterns of various hues, colonial officials and the public, and masters and slaves to identify themselves as Catholics and subjects of the Castilian sovereign. Above all, however, the auto-de-fé depicted power and whiteness for a crowd that largely included Africans and Indians. The presence of Englishmen in the auto-de-fé may have obscured this symbolism during the first auto-de-fé, but the various *entradas,* the ceaseless interrogations, and the subsequent spectacles of power would remind the crowd about the stakes involved.

Africans in the Midst

While the drama of the *entrada* and the tribunal's initial auto-de-fé highlight the Catholic offensive against the foreign heretical menace, it also signified renewed efforts to instill Christian orthodoxy in the República de los

Españoles. Protestants represented the initial victims of the tribunal's auto-de-fé. Conversos and the rest of the *república* followed the Protestant population. Among the penitents were forty inhabitants of the *república,* including persons of African descent, who were charged with heretical propositions, blasphemy, and bigamy. Their presence in the proceedings alerted the crowd that the tribunal had also located heresy among members of the *república.* In the period before and after the tribunal's arrival, officials voiced growing concerns about the intractable nature of the *bozales* and their harmful presence in the *república.* Mulattos exacerbated these anxieties, since the elite and officials perceived hybrids, including mestizos, as the greatest internal threat to the social fabric.

In 1568, the king expressed these anxieties, once again noting that he had been informed that "in that land there are a large quantity of negros that marry and consort with negras and indias bearing many mulatos, who are badly inclined." In requesting a report on their activities, Philip II wanted to know whether mulattos and blacks adhered to the sumptuary legislation that forbade them to ride horses and carry weapons.[54] A decade later, the king repeated his concerns about the growing presence of Africans, mulattos, and mestizos. He observed how, "being universally ill inclined," mulattos, blacks, and mestizos were disseminating their vile habits among the indigenous population. In order to curtail this practice, the king asked his officials to interrupt all forms of intercourse among Indians and blacks.[55] Given that the king periodically repeated this legislation throughout the Indies, including New Spain, this policy evidently failed.[56] The anxieties about persons of African descent, nonetheless, determined the tribunal's agenda in New Spain. The tribunal invariably harnessed its activities around local concerns, an implicit feature of the Edict of Faith.[57]

Even before the tribunal's arrival, the laity knew that if their behavior transgressed Christian orthodoxy, the increasingly vigilant clergy would discipline them. In the second half of the sixteenth century, the clergy of Mexico's archdiocese extended their authority over the laity by hauling an increasing number of moral offenders before the ecclesiastical judge. Before the second half of the sixteenth century and the arrival of the tribunal, the Monastic Inquisition (1522–1533) and Apostolic Inquisition (1533–1571) assisted the bishop in monitoring old and new Christians. Judging the increasingly heterogeneous República de los Españoles in accordance with canon law, the secular clergy constantly reminded the faithful that only Christian moral conventions would be tolerated. Although they were briefly overshadowed by the Inquisition's tribunal, the ecclesiastical courts bore the responsibility for instilling morality among the laity. A large part of morality in early modern Christianity focused on sexuality. Consequently, the clergy assigned to the ecclesiastical court intervened in the most intimate matters—matters that placed the clergy in conflict with the intent of the paterfamilias to regulate legally defined minors (his wife, children, unmarried women, servants, and slaves) in their household. For the clergy, sexual matters were of paramount concern since order (*policía*) in the *república* depended on orthodox practices. The laity's gender and sexual conventions, including those practiced by *bozales, negros criollos,* and mulattos, constituted matters of grave concern.

The mutual interest of the Crown and the clergy in the illicit highlights a domain in which slaves and servants, as Christians, were subject to royal and ecclesiastical jurisdictions irrespective of their status as property and dependents. Similarly, a husband's authority over his wife did not prevail when orthodoxy came into question. Even in New Spain's patriarchal moral economy, as the following vignette underscores, the interest of the *república* as defined by canon law prevailed over male desire. The Galician Juan de Llanes learned, before the installation of the Inquisition, that an individual could not act with impunity in moral matters. Reinvigorated by the tridentine reforms, New Spain's secular clergy displayed greater vigilance after midcentury by initiating judicial proceedings against moral offenders.

On April 26, 1564, nearly seven years before the arrival of the Inquisition, a frail and feeble Galician appeared before the archdiocesan *provisor*. Four days in an ecclesiastical cell had visibly shaken Juan de Llanes. Thus, he approached God's representative with deference and a modicum of fear. Steadfastly determined and convinced of the injustice of his incarceration, Juan humbly reiterated that "under no circumstance would he make a life with Juana Díaz, his wife," described as a mulatto. Adherence to this statement had initially landed Juan in ecclesiastical custody. Aware that his resolve sealed his fate, Juan informed the presiding officials that "the reason I said this was because after she married me . . . and to this day she has committed and commits adultery with many persons." This revelation no longer burdened Juan. As he stood before an audience of Spanish men, Juan paid little attention to his male honor. "Out of fear that she does not kill me or have me killed," Juan simply begged the ecclesiastical judge "Do not make me live with her."[58]

Apparently, Juan did not convince the judge that his case had merit. On April 28th, he reappeared before the ecclesiastical judge still pleading for permission to "not have a life with her." At that moment and under the threat of excommunication, Juan officially accused his wife, Juana Díaz, of adultery. Two additional days in the dank ecclesiastical dungeon finally convinced Juan to risk the wrath of his wife and her lovers, who allegedly included "many honorable people of this city."[59] He then gave the *provisor* a detailed description of Juana's indiscretions and the physical attacks she had directed against him. Juan revealed that his wife had "committed adultery numerous times casting herself carnally with many different persons."[60] Juana evidently acted on her desires with little concern about her marital status or an irate and vengeful husband. Juan noted that due to his age and infirmity, he could neither control his arms nor Juana. Work in the Pachuca mines had exacted a heavy toll on Juan's body and left him largely dependent on Juana for financial and physical support. Juana, in turn, resented having a doddering, infirm, and impoverished spouse who constantly exhorted her to toil on his behalf. Juana manifested her resentfulness in violent outbursts. Juan recounted one of these assaults, which occurred after he ordered his wife to "help in discharging her matrimonial duty." For that purpose, he purchased a cart for Juana so that she could traverse the city selling bread. On this occasion, Juan's actions elicited a violent response from Juana, who, angered by this imposition, approached him with a group of "indios and indias." Juan recalled how, with their help, Juana "seized me grabbing my beard and knocked me on the floor where they left me severely wounded after administering many punches."[61] Juan insisted that Juana and her hired thugs often repeated such thrashings. He divulged how "many other and diverse times she has put her hands on me wanting me dead." For instance, after having been scolded by her husband for her "bad life," Juana retaliated with the assistance of two young Flemish men, one of which had sired her daughter. The trio easily overwhelmed the feeble old man, who recalled how the men "grabbed my arms" while Juana, armed with a stick, "hit me many times." Afterward, Juana and her escorts left a severely battered Juan for dead. The tenacious old man recovered from the brutal attack but remained paralyzed in both arms. For Juan, the matter came down to a life alone or death with Juana. He informed the ecclesiastical judge that his wife merely "pretends to want a life with me . . . in order to kill me or to have a shield for her bad deeds."

Fearful of an untimely demise, Juan again implored the *provisor* to grant them permission to go their separate ways, "because my life will not be safe being with her." Evidently, the *provisor* did not share Juan's concerns and never authorized a divorce, since a decade later the inquisitors tried the mulatto Juana for bigamy. Nor did the testimony of Pedro de Villalón or Francisca González persuade the *provisor*. Only extenuating circumstances warranted a divorce; marital infidelity did not abrogate the bonds of marriage. Though confronted with these allegations, the ecclesiastical court did not simply side with a Spaniard against his mulatto wife. In the interest of order, on which royal authority rested, the ecclesiastical court placed greater weight on the sanctity of marriage than on charges of adultery.

The testimony of the witnesses, although they corroborated Juan's allegations, underscores the magnitude of Juana's sexual indiscretions. Pedro de Villalón, a 50-year-old Spaniard and resident of Mexico City, recalled that more than seven years previously, Juana had had "carnal access" in his house with his friend Morillas.[62] The relationship between Juana and Morillas was a protracted affair. Pedro testified having seen "both eating together at one table and sleeping together in one bed as if they were husband and wife and she washed Morillas' clothes and respected all that he ordered and said."[63] Despite the apparent stability of the affair, Pedro highlighted the fleeting nature of the relationship. He testified that Juana "gave her body to whomever asked and paid for it."[64] With this statement, Pedro touched on more than Juana's character and her sexual proclivities; he implied that she made her living as a prostitute.

Another witness, the mulatto Francisca González, gave additional details. Francisca, a former resident of Pachuca's mining community, related how when Juan went to work "Juana locked herself up in a room of her house with men and spent much time enclosed with them and she put a daughter of hers at the door as a spy who stood there until Juana opened the door of the house and when Juana was enclosed she was confined with only one man although many came to her." Francisca's emphasis that Juana had been "confined with one man although many came to her" clearly suggests that Juana was sexually active with her visitors. Although any woman who invited a man into her house raised the specter of sex, being secretly "confined" confirmed people's suspicions. Francisca noted that Juana behaved in an adulterous manner, but confining herself "with only one man although many came" implied something more. Beyond the insinuations that Juana worked as a prostitute, Francisca's testimony also indicates the multitudinous affairs that the mulatto had despite her marriage to Juan.[65]

According to Francisca, Juana also had a lengthy affair with Gaspar Díaz in Mexico City and Pachuca. Evidently Juan knew of his wife's behavior and repeatedly ordered her to stop seeing Gaspar. Francisca recalled how Juan had scolded Juana "to act and live like a good woman." Thus, as we have noted, he purchased his wife a cart with which she could peddle bread as a means to sustain herself and her family. From Francisca's perspective, Juan bought the cart so that Juana could "support herself with honor." Juana, however, did not comply and, according to Francisca, had even showed herself unwilling to do so during her courtship with Juan. Juana clearly pursued her extramarital affairs with abandon and callousness. More than once, Juan found his wife in bed with another man. On one occasion, rather than being contrite, Juana flung herself against Juan and began beating him. Eventually neighbors rescued the feeble Spaniard and placed Juana in *depósito* (female custody) in Francisca's boarding house. Francisca recalled how Juana had bested her husband; he bled profusely from bite wounds to his chest and hands. This was not, however, an isolated display of violence. Francisca testified that four months previously

Juan had been "stabbed . . . in front" by a former consort of Juana during an attempt on his life.[66] Such evidence convinced Francisca that "Juan's life is not secure."

Despite Francisca's concerns and the incriminating testimony, the *provisor* did not rescind his order that called on Juan to respect the sanctity of marriage by returning to Juana. Whether Juan actually returned to the matrimonial fold and for what length of time remains unclear. Ten years after petitioning for divorce proceedings, Juan was still alive. Perhaps Juana's decision to move away and subsequently marry Gaspar Pereira explains why the alleged assassination never took place. On the other hand, Juan may have simply concocted rumors of a murderous plot in an effort to bolster his case for a divorce.[67] Interestingly enough, the *provisor* manifested almost no concern about Juan's allegations. As the Church's representative, his imperative resided with protecting the conjugal union, even though Juan and Juana were clearly incompatible.[68] Still, the *provisor* displayed remarkable indifference to the issue of compatibility. In fact, a husband's authority and will could not prevail in matters related to orthodoxy. As a Christian sacrament, the clergy had to protect matrimony even in the face of a Spanish husband's opposition to his mulatto wife's behavior. Countless other cases highlight the *provisor*'s vigilance while simultaneously revealing his tolerance for "minor" moral transgressions. The laity, in turn, seemed well versed in the hierarchy of sins, while the accused readily confessed to minor transgressions but denied culpability for major moral infractions.

Confession and contrition constituted an important aspect of all proceedings. The *provisor* and his staff relied on the hearsay of the laity, accusations, corroborating testimony, and, to a lesser extent, on confessions. Without the participation of the laity, the clergy would have been less than effective in regulating its flock. As the following vignettes demonstrate, informants came from the communities of the accused. By bringing illicit behavior to the fore, informants gave the clergy, and subsequently the Inquisition, access to the sheltered lives of ordinary people. Thus, in a routine manner, the lives of Africans and their descendants came to the fore because they were so widely represented among the laity. But the ecclesiastical raids also demonstrate the clergy's intent to reform the laity. Such efforts were directed at the sexual behavior of the *república*'s inhabitants—behavior that allegedly introduced disarray in the commonwealth. As a result, the clergy steadily pursued fornicators and those who cohabited unlawfully, practices which plebeians widely engaged in. While the ecclesiastical proceedings underscore the Church's moral expectations, the cases also uncover a richly textured world in which persons of African descent figured prominently.

In 1570, one year before the Inquisition's installation ceremony, Gabriel de Buenaventura, a resident and native of the viceregal capital, stood humbly before the officials of New Spain's archdiocese. Identifying himself "in the Mexican language" as a 28-year-old Indian, Gabriel informed the *fiscal* that mulatto hatmaker Cristóbal and María, whom he defined as an Indian, had "cohabited publicly" for a year. According to Gabriel, the couple's behavior fostered "scandal and murmurs in the neighborhood where they live." Even worse, he saw Cristóbal and María "sleeping together in one bed . . . dining at one table and treating each other as husband and wife." Finally, Gabriel noted that their behavior represented a "bad example to the Christian republic." Catalina Pérez de Zamora, a 25-year-old mestiza, resident of Mexico, and wife of Luís Sanchez, concurred. Employing the same formulaic yet vivid language that Gabriel used and that we saw in the cases already highlighted, Catalina recalled seeing Cristóbal and María "sleeping together in one bed, eating and dining at one table and treating each other as legitimate husband and wife." For the *provisor*, Catalina and Gabriel's testimony constituted sufficient proof to warrant an investigation, and he ordered the *alguacil* to arrest the errant sinners.[69]

María Salome trembled as she stood before the ecclesiastical officials. Each time the *fiscal*, Don Gutiérrez, directed a question at María she listened intently before turning toward the court's interpreter. The 20-year-old Indian acknowledged "in the Mexican language" having had a four-month relationship with Cristóbal. María, in fact, confessed to knowing the mulatto hatmaker "carnally many times." Despite clear evidence of her moral turpitude, María convinced the *provisor* that this represented her only lapse. As a result, he simply admonished María, warned her to stay clear of Cristóbal, and fined her a gold peso.

After concluding the proceedings against María, the clerics directed their attention to Cristóbal Hernández. On learning that Cristóbal was still a minor, the *provisor* ordered that a defender (*procurador*) be named for the 17-year-old mulatto. Assured that his orders had been followed, the *provisor* reconvened the judicial proceedings. Contrary to María's testimony, Cristóbal confessed to having known the young Indian for two years, during which they had cohabited for a year. But, according to Cristóbal, their relationship had ended over a year ago and since then "he [Cristóbal] has not seen nor has had further interaction with her." Indeed, Cristóbal informed the *fiscal* that he did not know of María's whereabouts. Evidently, Cristóbal did not convince the *provisor* of his innocence, because the ecclesiastical judge fined the mulatto two gold pesos and warned him to steer clear of María.[70]

Once a case had been brought before the *provisor*, contrition instead of excuses represented the best defense. But in a case involving a mulatto and an Indian, contrition may not have been the only issue. In their attempts to protect Amerindians from persons of African descent and their purported habits, secular and ecclesiastical officials vilified the latter and punished them with greater vigor.[71] As ecclesiastical vigilance mounted in the second half of the sixteenth century, denunciations from members of the laity become more common.

Once informed of their Christian obligations, some individuals were reluctant to withhold allegations of impropriety from the clergy. In 1570, for instance, Don Gutiérrez initiated a suit against the mulattos Francisco de Acevedo and Juana de Rozas for cohabitation. Agustín Ponce, a 24-year-old mulatto, and Francisca de Alvarado, a 26-year-old *india ladina,* served as corroborating witnesses. According to Francisca, countless people in the barrio of San Juan knew of Francisco and Juana's illicit affair. Both Francisca and Agustín recalled seeing Francisco and Juana live together; their decision to do so had caused great consternation among their neighbors. When questioned about the allegations, Juana denied being familiar with Francisco de Azevedo. The young mulatto revealed that "I know many men who are called Azevedo but I do not know anyone who is called Francisco de Azevedo." Despite this response, Don Gutiérrez pressed Juana on her alleged relationship with Francisco de Azevedo. Again, she denied any involvement with the "said Francisco" but confessed to "knowing Duarte Pérez de Azevedo carnally." Yet this relationship, Juana noted, never involved cohabitation. At the conclusion of her cross-examination, the *provisor* fined Juana two gold pesos and threatened her with a year of exile and a 20-peso fine if she were seen with Francisco de Azevedo in any "suspicious place."[72]

Although the above cases involved plaintiffs with racial identities different than those of the defendants, race did not seem to prompt the denunciations. In some instances, the accusers and the accused actually shared the same social classification, but this was of little significance. On April 6, 1574, the *provisor* and vicar general, Dr. Estéban de Portillo, sat in judgment as the free black Luís Marín denounced Alonso and María, a mulatto couple. After taking an oath "to God, Holy María and the sign of the cross" and promising "to tell the truth," Luís Marín informed his audience that Alonso, the servant of Barajona, and María, who worked in the house of Benavides, had lived together for the past four months. For the couple's neighbors in the Santo Domingo barrio, this affair was common knowledge and a source of scandal. According to Luís, the couple made no effort to conceal their relationship, since they were seen "touching each other and kissing one another" while confining themselves to a single room at night. Four days after Luís's testimony, the ecclesiastical court heard further evidence from an enslaved black woman named Beatriz. On informing the cleric officials that she was a "Christian and baptized," the *fiscal* subjected 26-year-old Beatriz to the customary religious oaths. Afterward, Beatriz revealed that Alonso entered the house of María's employer with some frequency, leading her, Beatriz, to believe that they were married. In fact, Beatriz recalled that the couple spoke publicly about being "married." Possibly,

Beatriz's testimony led the *provisor* to question the *fiscal*'s case against Alonso and María, since the proceedings ended abruptly and inconclusively.[73]

In some instances, ecclesiastical officials (as opposed to scandalized neighbors) took a more active role in pursuing moral offenders. On November 3, 1571, the *fiscal* filed suit against 26-year-old Spanish silversmith Juan García and 25-year-old Juana de Aviles for cohabitation and presented Diego de Molina and Juan Rodriquez as witnesses. Diego, a Spaniard and the *alguacil* of markets, testified that Juan and Juana "had been and are publicly cohabitating." Diego had firsthand knowledge of this moral infraction since he and the *fiscal* "entered Juana de Aviles' house where the so said [were] together in a bed . . . as if they were husband and wife." Diego's mestizo servant, Juan Rodriquez, supported this accusation. He too had been present "between ten and eleven at night" when the *fiscal* and *alguacil* surprised the couple in bed. Juan Rodriquez left little to the imagination once he disclosed seeing Juan and Juana "naked in a bed together." Juan and Juana, however, denied any wrongdoing. Juan, a 26-year-old Spaniard and silversmith, noted emphatically that "what happened the night before last . . . was the first night [I] knew Juana de Aviles carnally." Juana, a 25-year-old mulatto, expressed similar sentiments. She testified that the *fiscal* had apprehended her "the very day" that they met.[74] In this instance, the *provisor* did not give Juan and Juana the benefit of the doubt. Perhaps the same rumors that prompted the *fiscal*'s raid persuaded the *provisor* to convict and fine these errant members of his flock.

With Dr. Moya's ascension as archbishop in 1573, the episcopate fully entered its era of Catholic renewal and invigoration.[75] Raids increased, convictions mounted, and regulation—manifest in the *relación*—became the norm. Even before Philip II decreed the establishment of the Inquisition in New Spain, the ecclesiastical courts became more activist about pursuing moral offenders. This flurry of ecclesiastical activity can, in fact, be traced to the initial Christian conquest, the Monastic Inquisition, the post-Tridentine provincial councils, and the Apostolic Inquisition. The tribunal of the Holy Office's pending arrival, however, instilled the clergy with added urgency, which they expressed in their aggressive posture toward the laity. By means of this increased vigilance, the routine behavior of the laity, including that of Africans and their descendants, entered the administrative record. Such proceedings offer an unprecedented glimpse of the experience of blacks in New Spain.

In 1571, the *provisor* sat in judgment on another case unearthed by an ecclesiastical raid. One day after a sweep through the San Juan barrio, *fiscal* Don Diego Anaya de Chavés pressed charges against Marcos Pérez and Isabel López. Don Diego relied on the *alguacil mayor*'s deputies, Jerónimo de Benavides and Alonso de Ballesteros, as corroborating witnesses. Jerónimo informed the *provisor* that during the *fiscal*'s raid they "entered a house" in the Santa Ana neighborhood "where they found the said Marco Pérez in a shirt" while in the company of Isabel López. Alonso de Ballesteros supported Jeronimo's testimony, adding that Marcos Pérez had recently been advised to distance himself from Isabel. According to Alonso, "last night . . . between eleven and twelve," they entered a house in Santa Ana in which Marcos Pérez and Isabel López were found scantily clad. Pablo, an *indio ladino* and the *fiscal*'s servant, was even more explicit. He recalled entering the house with "his master" along with other members of the raiding party and seeing Marcos and Isabel "naked . . . in a bed together."[76] In her defense, 30-year-old mulatto Isabel López acknowledged that she knew "the said Marcos Pérez carnally." She denied, however, the more serious allegations, stating that Marcos had left her eight months before to rejoin his wife in Zacatecas.

Marcos Pérez, a 32-year-old Spaniard, reiterated Isabel's claims. He confessed that he had known Isabel for "seven or eight years," during which time "he had carnal access with her several times." But Marcos vehemently denied the charges that he had cohabited with Isabel. As a married man and a Spaniard, Marcos risked being charged with cohabitation and adultery, which represented a more serious charge. Marcos's willingness to lie underscores both his familiarity with Christian morality and a consciousness of the strategies he might use to avoid the clergy's wrath. In his defense, Marcos noted that for the past year "more or less" he had been in the San Martín mining center from which he just returned. Though the authorities found them in bed, Marcos insisted on his innocence, stating "he did not have carnal access with Isabel López."[77] Despite the testimony of Isabel and Marcos, the *provisor* had sufficient proof to prosecute the culprits. He fined Isabel "two pesos" and ordered her to avoid being "in any suspicious place day or night" with Marcos Pérez. The *provisor* informed Isabel that if she failed to comply, a 20-peso fine and "a year of exile" awaited her.[78]

The clergy's propensity to regulate the behavior of their flock during the second half of the sixteenth century did little to assuage Philip II's concerns that the inhabitants in the Indies needed even greater vigilance. Although it was overshadowed by the Inquisition, the ecclesiastical court and its staff remained active throughout the colonial period. Responsible for keeping the laity's morality in check, the ecclesiastical court often overlapped with the jurisdiction of the Inquisition.[79] In seeking to shape and regulate the morality of the laity, both institutions relied on the cultural intelligence that plebeians usually hid from the elite and officials. As we have seen, the *provisor* and his staff depended on an informal network of informants in order to gain knowledge of the laity's practices.

From its installation, the Inquisition's tribunal tapped a similar network. The Edict of Faith called on good Catholics to clear their conscience by divulging all heretical and illicit behaviors to the tribunal, its staff, and its *familiares* (trustees). Though Dr. Moya emphasized the need for the laity to act as informants, the primacy of individual agents as disseminators of Christian morality has been overshadowed by the scholarly attention on Church and state. Yet individuals actively insinuated Christianity into people's lives. Even before the installation of the tribunal, the laity served as the eyes and ears of absolutism, which relied on hearsay, rumors, and personal interaction to extract evidence of illicit and sinful behavior. For many reasons, thousands of individuals revealed incriminating evidence to inquisition officials.[80] Informants for the Inquisition were not part of a network of strangers who spied on others by frequenting the public spaces or subterranean haunts in search of moral offenders. Instead, they were family members, neighbors, employers, coworkers, and passing acquaintances who drew facts from the innocuous gossip, idle chatter, and innumerable rumors circulating in New Spain. These informants brought the most egregious cases to the attention of the inquisitors.

On February 26, 1574, Spaniard Juan Bautista Gallegos appeared before Mexico's *provisor* while some inhabitants of the viceregal capital finalized the preparations for the Inquisition's first auto-de-fé. As was customary, Juan Bautista employed the ritualized language of wanting to "discharge his conscience" and drew attention to the fact that he had "read . . . the general letter." After his formulaic introduction, he accused mulatto Ana Caballero of heresy. While passing Ana's house in the company of his wife, Doña Luísa Villalobos, and their page, Juan testified that they heard Ana telling others "it is much better to be happy cohabiting than poorly married." "We were scandalized," Juan proclaimed. They walked on so as not to "see what happened afterwards." Now Juan stood before the *provisor* in order to report Ana's sacrilegious remarks.[81] Juan's accusation illustrates how rapidly the Inquisition established a network of informants who were familiar with those they denounced. As was invariably the case, Juan overheard Ana in public—the neighborhood store that also served as her abode.[82] Informants rarely had to seek out immorality. More frequently they inadvertently stumbled upon or heard about questionable behavior in their communities. Juan did not need to scurry unobtrusively through neighborhoods, taverns, or the innumerable street gatherings. Sheltered from the obtrusive gaze of officials and the elite, immorality flourished publicly. Consequently, every neighbor, family member, and friend represented a potential informant. The inquisitors structured their interrogations in such a manner that the accused and witnesses could easily relate hearsay, gossip, and rumors, thus serving unwittingly as informants themselves.[83] Inquisition officials sought to reproduce the omnipotent domain of the Church through this discursive ritual. In turn, the ecclesiastics expected the pious and the mass of the unfaithful to genuflect rhetorically and to reveal all that they knew, symbolizing their Christian sensibility. Even though the judges ruled against her, Ana nearly performed this role to perfection. She skillfully employed the ritualized dialogue of the contrite—a spectacle in its own right—which underscored her awareness of what constituted transgressive behavior.

A few days after Juan Bautista and Doña Luísa scurried passed Ana's store in the company of their page, the young mulatto paid Doña Luísa a social call. Evidently, Ana was unaware that she had offended the moral sensibility of her neighbors. But when she entered the young couple's household, Juan informed Ana of the investigation pending against her.[84] And soon afterward, the tribunal issued a warrant for Ana's arrest. From the very beginning of the proceedings, Ana knew that the inquisitors would scrutinize her every word.[85] She quickly implored the *provisor* for formal charges "so that she could use her rights and request justice."[86] Ana realized that her defense depended on knowing the charges brought against her and being able to portray herself in a favorable manner—a manner which focused on her Christian background and religiosity, her Hispanic upbringing, and her female virtue. As such, Ana's confession represented a performance in which she recited the dialogue that the inquisitors had scripted.[87] Though produced in the context of a cross-examination, Ana's narrative underscores her keen understanding of Christian morality.

As was customary, Ana's confession began with a brief biographical sketch. She defined herself as a 30-year-old Castilian of African descent from San Lúcar de Barrameda, a port city in southern Spain. Ana identified her father, Fernando de Grajales, as a Spaniard and labeled her mother, Brianda Rodriguez, a black woman. The Spanish-born mulatto gave no indication of how or when she had come to New Spain.[88] Unlike most women in Mexico City, Ana had sufficient capital to operate a small store, from which she sold bread and wine. Following this brief autobiographical sketch, the inquisitor queried Ana about the reason for her incarceration. By means of this procedure, the inquisitor hoped to elicit incriminating evidence about Ana or her acquaintances. As a result of her *instancia,* Ana knew the cause for her arrest and stated as much to the inquisitor. Then the inquisitor called on Ana to "express and discharge her conscience if she at any time . . . [had] made some bad sounding pronouncements against Our Lord and Our Holy Catholic faith." The inquisitor ended his exhortation with an ambiguous threat. He promised Ana "justice" if she told the "truth" but cautioned that failure to do so would result in serious punishment.[89] Undaunted by this threat, Ana did not plead guilty. She maintained her innocence, stating that "I did not recall having expressed bad sounding sentiments against Our Señor God at any time because I am a good Christian fearful of God and my conscience." Ana insisted that this conscience had prompted her to surrender. On three separate occasions, Ana had conferred with the *provisor*, reiterating how she had left his offices on her own recognizance.

Despite Ana's lengthy testimony and insistence on her innocence, the *fiscal* pursued the same line of inquiry. He repeatedly pressed Ana about having told visitors "in the store of her house" that it was "better to cohabit than be poorly married." Ana noted emphatically that "she had never expressed such sentiments," again reiterating that she had turned herself in. "As the Christian that I am," Ana remarked, such comments would have prompted a denunciation by her and a request for forgiveness. Ana's response did not appease the inquisitor, who simply turned it into another question. If "you have never said the said words . . . why did you come before the said provisor to denounce yourself? What moved you to do it?" Ana replied that "the said man" informed her of the allegations and her conscience moved her to act. Stymied by Ana's replies, the inquisitor asked her "if any person had counseled her to deny the truth." "I am a woman of reason," Ana responded. She quickly dismissed the allegations, declaring that "I value my spirit more than all things there are in the world." Yet Ana did not persuade the inquisitors of her innocence. Two days after her confession, the judges appointed Arias de Valdés as the prosecuting attorney and received authorization from Ana permitting Juan Mendez to serve as her defender.[90]

While the inquisitors ostensibly tried Ana for blasphemy, perhaps her unwillingness to recant was also at issue. The inquisitors saw vocal, independent thinkers as a threat, but females who spoke their minds on church doctrine represented something even more ominous. As a free woman of color who was financially independent and culturally conversant, Ana symbolized an insidious and potentially dangerous interloper. If Spaniards wished to retain their ascendancy over the brown and black majorities, they could neither ignore nor neglect to punish Ana Caballero and those like her.[91] As such, Ana's guilt as a blasphemer may not have been the sole issue for which the inquisitors tried her. During the subsequent proceedings, Ana again denied that she "said such words in her life." Even after being coerced to attend mass and pray, Ana stuck to her initial testimony. In her defense, she drew attention to her Christian conscience. Ana said "I have never said such in my life" and "to hear it makes my body tremble."[92] On May 14th, the inquisitors subjected Ana to yet another interrogation and possibly judicial torture, but she still did not retract her initial confession. Eight days later, the inquisitors presented Ana with the depositions of Juan Bautista and Doña Luísa. She simply denied their allegations. In an effort to undermine the testimony of Juan Bautista and Doña Luísa, Ana's lawyer asked why the page "did not hear the words that the said Doña Luísa and her husband say that were said."[93] It remains unclear if the inquisitors examined the page, but on August 11th they finally ruled against Ana Cabellero. Despite her testimony, the inquisitors found the "woman of reason" guilty. In this credibility contest, the rules of evidence favored the words of a white male over those of a black woman. A few days after her conviction, Ana stood topless and barefoot in the Inquisition's chapel with a candle in hand. Standing before her neighbors, and presumably her accusers, Juan Bautista and Doña Luísa, Ana's humiliation was complete.

Public humiliation had a powerful effect on New Spain's inhabitants. Perhaps more than the lashes and eternal damnation, the fear of ritualized punishment led to behavior modification. While some individuals modified their beliefs and sexual practices, others simply became more guarded about their thoughts and intimate affairs when the tribunal arrived. The public nature of the Inquisition's activities also led some to question whether their behavior was in conformance with canon law. Plagued by doubts, some individuals such as Luísa de Abrego approached their priests with hopes of absolution but nonetheless came before the Inquisition. Far from being limited to Spaniards, self-scrutiny brought more than a few persons of African descent to the Inquisition's attention.

After nearly a year of confinement, Luísa de Abrego emerged slowly from the Inquisition's dank and dreary dungeon with tentative steps. Gradually her senses adjusted to Mexico's familiar aromas, its dry and dust-filled air, and the cacophony that poured forth from all directions. As she left the Inquisition's offices on February 17, 1576, and walked in the direction of Santa María, Luísa finally realized that her ordeal was over. Luísa's incarceration, however, was merely the second or the judicial phase of her ordeal, which had begun when "without being called" she appeared before the Holy Office in order to "discharge her conscience."[94] As Luísa put distance between herself and the Inquisition, the burden she had carried for three years gradually lifted. Earlier in Zacatecas, Luísa had witnessed the arrest of an accused bigamist, which had raised doubts about her own innocence.[95] Frightened, this believer revealed her concerns to a confessor and eventually to the inquisitors in Mexico City.[96] After her self-indictment on February 28, 1575, the Inquisition's constable led the frightened woman into the fetid cellars to await her fate. It would take almost a year before God's earthly agents absolved this 30-year-old Spaniard of African descent and self-described *vecina* (resident) of Mexico City.[97] By absolving Luísa, the judges lifted the burden that had motivated the confession—a spiritual burden that provides a glimpse of Luísa's consciousness.

Luísa's ordeal began in 1561 in Jérez de la Frontera, sixty miles south of Seville. That year, Jordan de Herrera, a free black, approached Luísa's employers requesting permission to marry their 15-year-old servant. Juan Luís and his wife promised their blessings if Luísa consented. But Jordan did not act with haste. Luísa recalled that "one day while cleaning and with my mistress absent," Jordan "[re-]entered the house." He asked if "I had reflected on my masters' promise" to which "I said yes." Then Jordan "took my hands" and asked "me to be his woman and wife as ordained by the Holy Mother Roman Church." Luísa acquiesced and Jordan stated that "he [received] me as woman and wife and [consented] to be my husband." Following this brief ritual, the newlyweds continued to hold hands and embraced and kissed, but, according to Luísa, did nothing else since they "did not have the place for more."[98] In the eyes of both the clergy and practitioners of the faith in sixteenth-century New Spain, this ritual had the binding force of marriage. After this ceremony, Luísa and Jordan saw each other "two or three more times," yet always in the presence of Juan Luís. Luísa recalled that Jordan "did not speak to me." Instead, Jordan interacted with Juan Luís, since he wanted "to take" Luísa with him to Doña Esteban's house. Juan Luís was skeptical of this arrangement, which he demonstrated by questioning Jordan about his legal status and his ability as a "man . . . to maintain and sustain" Luísa. Evidently, the two men haggled without resolution, leading Luísa to remark that "I never saw Jordan again."[99]

Despite the failed negotiations, Luísa and Jordan's relationship actually floundered for different reasons. After the matrimonial pledge—tantamount to an engagement—Luísa left Juan Luís for another but unknown employer, in whose house she fell gravely ill. During Luísa's absence from Jérez, her acquaintances, including Jordan, believed that she had actually departed for Seville, her birthplace. After two months, she recovered and returned to Jérez de la Frontera, where she lived with mulatto Juana de Granado. Soon Luísa learned that Jordan had abandoned her for another woman. As a group of female servants passed the house, Luísa recalled asking "them where they were going and they informed me that they were heading to Jordan de Herrera's wedding."[100] Luísa's initial reaction was "to go and disrupt the wedding," informing those present that "I was his wife," but she could not "prove it" in the absence of witnesses. Instead, Luísa returned to Seville, her birthplace, and during her 5-year tenure there met Miguel Rodriguez, a Segovian sheep-shearer and soldier with whom she eventually sailed for Florida.[101] In the San Augustine *presidio,* the couple exchanged wedding vows in the presence of garrison officials and Miguel's comrades.[102] Nine months later, the newlyweds were on the move again; they eventually settled in Zacatecas.

There, Luísa witnessed the arrest of an alleged bigamist, which prompted feelings of fear and guilt. "I was scandalized in my heart," Luísa noted, "about what had happened with Jordan." Luísa informed Miguel about her concerns, and he responded by soliciting the advice of friends.[103] They concluded that Miguel was the legitimate spouse, an observation that did little to assuage Luísa's conscience. Thus, she sought her confessor's advice, and he decided in favor of Jordan. Alarmed by Luísa's confession, Father Curiel informed Miguel that a "plot of the devil" had been uncovered.[104] He exhorted Miguel to keep Luísa at bay, cautioning that continued "carnal access" would constitute "mortal sin." While Miguel claimed to have heeded Father Curiel's warning, Luísa offered opposing testimony.[105] By February 1575, the combination of guilt and fear finally compelled Luísa to throw herself at the mercy of the inquisitors.

Luísa's behavior was not atypical, but the timing of her self-indictment, which followed her denunciation by one Juan de Pinillos, calls the motives prompting the confession into question. On March 26, 1574, nearly a year before Luísa turned herself in, Juan, a 34-year-old Segovian smelter and resident of Mexico, appeared at the Inquisition "without being called." He informed the *fiscal* that his compatriots, Juan de Vega and Blas de Avila, "had told him" that another Segovian, Miguel Rodriguez, had recently separated from the "negra whom he had married in Florida" since she was already married."[106] The following day, Juan de Vega provided corroborating evidence. The 40-year-old former soldier and smelter stated that he, "Blas de Avila and other soldiers" saw Miguel marry a "negra who was named Luísa de Abrego."[107] He noted that they had separated on the advice of their confessors but "until now they have had a married life together." That same day, the inquisitors also heard from 52-year-old clothier, ex-soldier, and resident of Mexico Blas de Avila. Blas simply revealed that Miguel Rodriguez was married "by the hand of a cleric . . . with a negra named Luísa."[108] Luísa was not oblivious to the indictments that the three Segovian friends leveled against her.[109] In fact, Luísa probably saw Blas de Avila just before he delivered his deposition, since the latter noted having seen her "in the portals of this Holy Office."[110] Conceivably, the sighting convinced Luísa to come forward on her own. Purported sinners often believed that an unsolicited confession would ameliorate their punishment. The Church encouraged such views, thereby insinuating its ideological presence into the consciousness of the laity.[111] Although the chronology of the accusations of the Segovians cast doubts on Luísa's motives, the fact that she was Spanish and Christian undermines the theory that she approached the inquisitors for purely strategic reasons.

Indeed, the glimpses gleaned of Luísa's material world and belief system reveal the depth of her immersion in the Iberian cultural milieu. Creolization shaped Luísa's mores, which included her understanding of guilt and sin, and facilitated her cultural navigation of the Hispanic domain. Luísa, who was alternately described as a "negra" and "de color negra," toiled as a domestic in the household of Juan Luís. In a household filled with retainers and servants, Luísa was probably the lone person of African descent.[112] Her employers clearly manifested a paternalistic interest in their 15-year-old domestic, which suggests that Luísa had been in their employ for some time. While Jordan Herrera's interaction with Juan Luís underscores this paternalism, it also accentuates his own cultural awareness. Rather than approach Luísa directly with his romantic intentions, Jordan requested Juan Luís's permission to marry Luísa. Even after the marriage—the exchange of words and promises—Jordan continued to solicit Juan Luís's approval as he sought "to take" his new wife to his employer's, and by implication his, domain. Juan Luís, in turn, displayed his paternalistic concerns by interrogating Jordan about his ability as a "man . . . to maintain and sustain" Luísa. Such behavior, though motivated by self-interest and the desire of a patriarch to control, reveals Juan Luís's affection for Luísa—a typical expression indicative of the personal and cultural proximity between master and subject.

While Juan Luís's paternalism underscore, among other things, Luísa's Hispanicization, her behavior and sense of guilt highlight the magnitude of her Christian conscience. After listening to her confession, the *fiscal* queried Luísa about her religious beliefs. He asked if she thought of Jordan as "her legitimate husband" after their exchange of vows.[113] "Yes," Luísa replied, but when "I saw that he married another woman I did not think of him as such nor did I understand that the marriage was validated."[114] Then the *fiscal* asked if Luísa had "copulated" with Jordan "as if with her husband and how many times." Luísa retorted that she had not had intercourse "nor any other interaction" but the holding of hands, embracing, and kissing "because there was no place for more."[115] At this point, the interrogation ended but resumed at eight o'clock the following morning. After some brief introductory remarks, the *fiscal* again questioned Luísa about having carnal interaction with Jordan "as if between husband and wife." Luísa insisted that "since I was cleaning near the door," there was no place to have intercourse. "For this reason," she claimed, they abstained.

Evidently convinced by her sincerity, the inquisitors acquitted Luísa de Abrego. With the acquittal, Luísa fades from sight, leaving the reader to ponder subsequent developments in her life. Did she return to Spain once her relationship with Miguel had been declared illicit? If not, what forces confined her to New Spain or other regions in the Indies? In what ways, moreover, did Luísa's marital status affect her subsequent relationships? Since the inquisitors and the clergy quickly focused on other alleged sinners, answers to these and other questions remain elusive. Though the inquisitors subjected Luísa to their scrutinizing gaze, she literally disappeared from the tribunal's memory when she no longer represented a sinner.[116] Of course, Luísa continued to make and live within history, but routine behavior was not of interest to the Inquisition and only rarely to crown and clergy. Luísa's narrative, like those cited above, emerged from and then entered into the historical record, as does much of the African past, only through regulatory sources.

The emergence of an African majority and a steadily increasing mulatto population diverged radically from the ideals of Church and state. The anxieties of elites and officials were manifest in the tribunal's proceedings. It is significant that Ana and Luísa represented two of the first persons that the Inquisition subjected to its proceedings. Clearly their gender and cultural hybridity played an important part in the proceedings. Their previous residence in Spain had exposed them, in theory, to Christianity and its moral code. Surely this fact was not lost on members of the tribunal. As Spanish creoles, Ana and Luísa personified the culturally ambiguous individuals that Castile's authorities perceived as a threat to their sovereign's dominion. Crown and clergy believed that cultural interlopers—mulattos, ladinos, *negros criollos*, conversos, and *moriscos* (Christians of Moorish descent)—had to be controlled if orthodoxy was to prevail in the *república*. The tribunal's initial proceedings, which included ladinos and mulattos, underscore the perceived threat that the culturally ambiguous posed. What better way to discipline peoples of African descent than to subject a few of the most culturally conversant to the wrath of the Inquisition? Though the inquisitors punished errant sinners for their purported behavior, the public nature of the trial proceedings and the auto-de-fé also operated as a cultural deterrent. For the inquisitors, the selection of a victim bore a relationship to the crowd's composition and acted as a deterrent against the threat of heresy. The decision to include mulattos reflected localized concerns that persons of African descent represented a numerical majority among New Spain's República de los Españoles. Since the king displayed an unwillingness to suspend the slave trade, royal officials and the elite made an effort to control *bozales, negros criollos,* and mulattos. Fearing that the clergy would not be able to control persons of African descent by routine methods, the Spanish elite welcomed the reconquest that the Inquisition inaugurated, even though the tribunal, like the ecclesiastical courts, curtailed their authority over their servants and slaves.

4   Christian Matrimony and the Boundaries of African Self-Fashioning

> Order and classification are the beginning of mastery, whereas the truly dreadful enemy is the unknown.[1]

In 1584, an exceptionally dark black man entered the Sagrario, a parish church adjacent to Mexico City's cathedral, and, in the presence of his small entourage, petitioned the ecclesiastical scribe for a marriage license. In voicing his request, the self-identified black man, Francisco, simultaneously proclaimed his nationality and Christian sensibility. "I am from the land of Biafara," declared Francisco and then stated that he was single and wished to marry Catalina. At the conclusion of this testimonial, Catalina, a member of the entourage, re-enacted the spectacle. As she announced her desire and single status, Catalina also revealed that she too was "from the land of Biafara." The scribe recorded the testimony of the couple, but before presenting the ecclesiastical judge with the marriage license, he noted that Francisco and Catalina belonged to the same master.[2] As the judge examined the petition, the master's absence caused him no concern. He simply asked Francisco and Catalina if they acted in good faith and of their own volition. Assured of the propriety of the case, the *provisor* ordered Francisco and Catalina to offer proof of their single status and lack of impediments. At that moment, Andrés and Victoria stepped forward. Andrés, a 25-year-old, acknowledged having known Francisco ever since he had arrived from "his bozal country" eight years before. Andrés did not mention Catalina. But the presiding official assumed that if the Spanish-speaking black man, enslaved by the same master, had an awareness of existing impediments, he would have revealed them then. If he did not, he would face the Inquisition's wrath for willful deception—a fate dozens had suffered in the decade since the Inquisition's installation.[3] Victoria, Francisco and Catalina's second witness, simply noted that she too came from the "land of Biafara." In lieu of specific information about the nature and length of her familiarity with the couple, Victoria's purported ethnicity legitimized her testimony about Francisco and Catalina's eligibility for marriage. Consequently, the judge attached the customary proviso—a public reading of the banns in conjunction with mass in the prospective couple's parish church—a ritual designed explicitly to elicit information about potential impediments from the couple's friends, family members, or neighbors within twenty-one days.[4]

In spite of the ritualized nature of the proceedings, the ecclesiastical authorities acted rather perfunctorily. Matrimony constituted a Christian sacrament to which all "qualified persons" could aspire—one that medieval canonists stipulated could be extended to pagans and contrite infidels, the *extra ecclesiam,* irrespective of their legal status.[5] The *provisor* scrutinized Francisco and Catalina's petition like that of other Christians despite their status as slaves. On the basis of their names and actions, one can assume that Francisco and Catalina were Christians with more than a rudimentary understanding of the faith's mystery and its ritualized proceedings. After all, by identifying themselves as "Francisco" and "Catalina," they underscored their exposure to the baptismal font. As Christians, though enslaved, the couple had a right to a married life and could even enter a marriage contract without their master's consent. In conformance with Christian norms—dating from the Fourth Lateran Council (1215) which the Council of Trent (1545–1563) had reaffirmed as a counterreformation measure—a parish priest simply needed the couple's verbal consent that they wished to marry. After this declaration, the couple had to prove that they were both single and that no blood or spiritual kinship ties existed. An existing marriage or kinship ties constituted marital impediments. Spiritual kinship ties, forged through Christian rituals—sponsorship of baptism, confirmation, or marriage—however, were the most common impediments. In those cases, unless a couple received an ecclesiastical dispensation for existing impediments, a zealous priest would withhold the sacrament. With its customary rigor and by means of the marriage petition, the clergy questioned all couples about potential impediments.

Couples carefully selected persons who could speak with intimate familiarity on their behalf. Invariably, they asked individuals with whom they had a long-standing relationship, if not actual or spiritual kinship ties, to serve as their matrimonial sponsors. Sponsors needed an awareness of the bride or groom's genealogy to substantiate claims about the lack of impediments and of mutual consent. Before delivering their testimony, the witnesses identified themselves by name, purported nationality or race, legal status, the name of their master, residence (if not birthplace), marital status, and age. The scribe would occasionally mention their command of Spanish, their phenotype, and even the way a person dressed. After these details were registered, the witnesses would state how long they had known the bride, groom, or both, and the circumstances surrounding their relationships. In extreme cases, a couple marshaled only one person, but usually the prospective bride and groom would produce two or more witnesses.

From 1584 to the culmination of the colonial period in 1810, thousands of *bozales,* ladinos, and creoles petitioned for marriage licenses. The Church's penchant for order led the clergy to extract biographical details from members of the flock in order to more effectively regulate the *república*. The initial marriage petitions date back to Dr. Moya's tenure as archbishop, which began in 1572. Because of Dr. Moya's reform efforts, the reformed clergy demonstrated its growing control of the laity by means of the marriage petition, which the Church used to record and store biographical details about the *república*'s inhabitants.[6] For the period 1584 to 1650, the extant marriage petitions that involve at least one person (but usually two persons) of African descent contain the testimony of approximately 4,400 marriage witnesses. As a product of Christian regulation, this testimony remains largely formulaic. Yet its sheer volume and ethnographical minutiae make the petitions an invaluable source. The act of questioning the wedding party about themselves and their relationship to the prospective couple constituted a discursive site through which the witnesses, the groom, and the bride, in tacit complicity with the ecclesiastics, acquired a juridical status sanctioned by canon law. By means of this procedure, the Church enabled Africans and their descendants to manifest their recently constructed New World identities in the Christian *república*.

As they stood before an audience of peers and clergymen, *bozales*, ladinos, and creoles actually defined themselves. In this ritualized context, they articulated identities sanctioned by Church officials that had standing in the República de los Españoles. But the marriage petitions also accorded its recipients the right to a marriage contract that was recognized through custom and supported by the force of law, even in the case of enslaved Africans. Such marriages, in the eyes of the Church, constituted legitimizing and legitimate acts which even the most malicious had to respect in theory if not in practice. The marriage contract also accorded the couple heterosexual rights to a married life by preventing either party from being sold beyond a certain geographical distance.

As husbands, in theory at least, men acquired conjugal rights over their wives. After all, Christianity structured conjugality along patriarchal lines. The marriage contract also bestowed on men the status of paterfamilias and granted them dominion over potential offspring. But by requiring *bozales*, ladinos, and creoles to define themselves in accordance with Christian categories, ecclesiastics also established the official boundaries of self-fashioning. Decidedly Western European in origin, these fabricated identities reflected the European explorer's penchant for naming and the colonizer's need to define and invent territorially based social categories for the recently subjugated. As a product of regulation, the petitions privilege formal and intimate relationships over haphazard and routine social interaction. *Bozales*, ladinos, and creoles fashioned themselves, their ethnicity, and the ethnicity of others through Christian metaphors. The subjective sense of self, as it emerges from the petitions, reflects Christian temporal, spatial, and social precepts. Yet even as strategic performances of cultural identification, the testimony of the witnesses provide a glimpse of Mexico's extensive and diverse social networks. These networks—based on real and imagined kinship ties, long-standing interaction, and shared experiences—underscore some of the symbolic markers that shaped the formation of community in the first half of the seventeenth century. Indeed, the petitions highlight some of the essential markers of community boundaries. As individuals identified themselves during the ritualized proceedings, they defined and often refined these boundaries—boundaries whose symbols tempered the salience of race and slavery in the process of community formation.

Indeed, community boundaries acquired importance through physical proximity and interaction. Individual Africans forged relationships based both on face-to-face interactions in New Spain and their New World identities, largely imaginary in scope, which underscore the important roles that process and experience played in identity formation. Much current scholarly literature assumes that race and slavery as the materiality of oppression constituted the guiding principle for a black slave identity which served individuals as they organized their lives. I argue that specific experiences, memories, and events that took place in the context of slavery but nevertheless transcended that reality brought individuals together and, more important, sustained their relationships. Africans and persons of African descent created communities that expanded the boundaries of the households in which they served as slaves and bridged cultural divisions. Yet even as "Angolans" formed communities with individuals from "Lamba land," for example, they retained their newly imposed ethnic identities. What was once simply a European-imposed label acquired meaning for individual Africans in New Spain as specific cultural experiences in the Americas—experiences that they chose and sought out—shaped their memories and the course of their lives. The choice of a marriage partner represents a perfect example of such experiences.

Although individuals played a critical role in stating how they defined themselves, the colonial sources privilege formalistic identities. For instance, during the first half of the seventeenth century, enslaved Africans established elaborate social networks along ethnic lines in Mexico City. But the colonial records do not reflect the instability characteristic of early modern ethnicity. As enslaved persons whose servile status was contingent on early modern racialist notions, Francisco, Catalina, Andrés, and Victoria constituted a symbolic community. But what were the symbols that defined their community? In the experiences of Francisco, Catalina, Andrés, and Victoria, race and legal status constantly competed with ethnicity, spatial proximity, and Christianity for primacy. As this chapter underscores, throughout the sixteenth and seventeenth century, peoples of African descent embraced, modified, and occasionally even discarded the symbolic categories around which they and the authorities as-sembled ever-shifting community boundaries.

The Geography of Households

In Mexico City's socially reconstituted urban landscape, elite house-holds constituted an important site in and through which the salient symbols for community formation circulated. In New Spain's viceregal capital and in urban centers throughout Spanish America, wealthy and powerful Spaniards resided in the *traza,* the spatial epicenter of Mexico City. From the time when ladinos and *bozales* were introduced, a majority of Mexico's enslaved popula-tion staffed elite households. As slaves and servants, Africans and their creole descendants lived in a decidedly urban milieu and acquired a prominent pres-ence at the viceregal epicenter. Indeed, it is within this epicenter that they built their elaborate social networks. Couples who lived together invariably used cultural strategies when they selected witnesses from different households. Since the elite routinely staffed their households with Indians, mestizos, *casti-zos* (offspring of a Spaniard and a mestizo), Spaniards, mulattos, and blacks of various kinds, the couple's decision to draw their marriage witnesses from different households often transcended demographic considerations. By ask-ing acquaintances dispersed throughout the *traza* to serve as marriage wit-nesses, individuals brought into focus symbolic categories—embodied in spe-cific relationships—that informed their choices. Many ladinos, *bozales,* and creoles established strong relationships with individuals who were owned by the same master, who worked in the same household, and who lived and toiled nearby.

Such relationships, as the witnesses reveal, reflected more than spatial con-venience. In 1628, Luís Picaro, an enslaved mulatto, and Francisco, an enslaved person "from Angola," testified on Manuel and Catalina's behalf. The 50-year-old Francisco informed the *provisor* of his 30-year relationship with Manuel, who also claimed to be from Angola. According to Francisco, he had known Catalina ever since she arrived "from Lamba land" twenty years ago. In con-trast, the 80-year-old Luís dated his interaction with the prospective groom and bride at twenty-nine and twenty years respectively. As fellow members of Luís Gutierrez's household, Luís Picaro and Catalina "from Lamba land" had sustained a long-standing relationship with Manuel.[7]

In that same year, Beatriz de los Reyes, a 24-year-old free mulatto, informed the *provisor* that Juan de la Cadena and Luísa de la Cruz, both of whom were also free mulattos, were single and unencumbered by impediments. Beatriz cited her 8-year relationship with Juan and her lifelong familiarity with Luísa, which began at birth, "for she [was] her sister . . . and they always had lived together." Don Juan de Savedra Guzman had evidently employed Juan de la Cadena as a household servant eight years previously, and there the young mulatto met Beatriz de los Reyes and her younger sister, Luísa. Though Juan entered Don Guzman's employ in 1620, he was not new to Mexico or a recent acquaintance of members of the household. The other witness, Juan de Santiago, a 34-year-old enslaved mulatto, testified that they had known Juan de la Cadena four years longer than Beatriz had and acknowledged that he had known Luísa for twelve years. Juan de Santiago's testimony indicates that Juan de la Cadena's familiarity with members of the Guzman household predated his employment there. The household structures and residential patterns of elites enabled individuals in their employ to structure their lives around other members of their community over the long term. While the *traza*'s cartography provided all residents with a shared spatial consciousness, individuals invariably made finer distinctions when they defined their community. For Juan de la Cadena, Luísa de la Cruz, Beatriz de los Reyes, and Juan de Santiago, the Guzman household constituted the tangible site in and through which they manifested their mulatto identities.[8]

Similarly, in 1629, free mulattos Bernabe de la Cruz and María de Solís, a couple, relied on Jusephe de Salamanca, an enslaved creole, and Antonío de Solís, an enslaved mulatto, as marriage witnesses. Antonío, a 40-year-old, had known both Bernabe and María ever "since he could reason and recall," for they all had been raised in Don Fernando de Figueroa's house. Jusephe, a 25-year-old, could not match Antonío's lifelong interaction with the couple. But his 8-year relationship with Bernabe and María represented a significant accomplishment.[9]

The marriage petition of Diego Gutiérrez and Catalina de la Concepción also brings into relief the importance of the household as both the basis for and a site of community formation. In 1628, 25-year-old free mulatto Catalina de la Concepción consented to marry Diego, a Spaniard and native of Guatemala City. In seventeenth-century New Spain, interracial marriages were a novelty; prior to that time, interracial couples largely engaged in nonmarital sexual activity. Francisco Aretega, a 30-year-old Spaniard, had known Diego since the age of 16. Mestizo Diego Gracía also dated his relationship with the prospective groom from the time he was a teen. Despite their long-standing acquaintance, the nature of Francisco Aretega and Diego García's relationship remains unknown.

Catalina's witnesses, however, acknowledged the importance of shared space in the formation of community, whether the members were neighbors or members of the same household. Francisco Miranda, a 24-year-old Spanish sacristan, testified that he had known Catalina for sixteen years "because we are neighbors." Jacinto de los Reyes, who was also a 24-year-old Spaniard, stated that he had interacted with Catalina for six years, since "they had lived together in the same house." Catalina, Francisco, and Jacinto's familiarity—forged through spatial proximity—crossed the racial divide that customarily separated the descendants of Africans from others. As a product of a multiracial household, Catalina moved with ease in the *traza*'s racial milieu but rooted herself among Spaniards. Catalina's cultural orientation, coupled with her ambiguous genealogy, made her a familiar of Spaniards and ultimately an acceptable spouse.[10]

Deciding on a marriage witness constituted a highly subjective process. It comes as no surprise that *bozales* and creoles displayed reluctance to select Spaniards as their matrimonial sponsors. As Spaniards, masters and employers might seem like ideal sponsors, but the descendants of Africans thought otherwise. In the ritually charged petitioning process, *bozales,* ladinos, and even creoles rarely called on them as witnesses. This reluctance reveals the manner in which the descendants of Africans perceived Spaniards, even Spanish plebeians. By keeping Spaniards at bay, *bozales,* ladinos, and creoles highlight the strategies they used to select sponsors and the intimacy that united members of the wedding party.

In some instances, however, strategy and intimacy did involve Spaniards. In 1629, a prospective couple relied on individuals with whom they shared a residence. This time, two enslaved mulattos, Andrés and Juan; Gregorio Serrano, a Spaniard; and Francisco, an enslaved person "from Angola," offered evidence on behalf of María and Juan Francisco, the prospective bride and groom. Juan, a 35-year-old, had known the couple for eleven years, while the 28-year-old Andrés testified that he had had an 11-year friendship with Juan Francisco, an enslaved mulatto. Master Gregorio Serrano (an exception among witnesses since very few individuals called on their masters to offer testimony on their behalf) acknowledged having known María "from Terra Nova" on the grounds that until the previous month she had been his property. According to 30-year-old Francisco, María had resided in Gregorio Serrano's household for at least ten years prior to her departure. Even after María became the symbolic property of André and the actual property of Pedro Sierra, the decade-old ties still flourished between Francisco, Gregorio, and their erstwhile housemate María. For María, the change of households did not transform her social network; she maintained ties with Pedro Sierra's slaves and servants.[11]

On August 26, 1645, four members of García de Losada's household entered the cathedral. Nicolás Galban, a black creole, and Madalena de la Cruz, "from Angola," had come to request a marriage license. After the couple provided the requisite biographical details, the scribe's attention shifted to Juan de Torres and Antón Duque. Juan, a 50-year-old Spaniard and the steward of Tomas García de Losada's mill, had known the couple for seven years. Juan had evidently arrived years after Nicolás and Madalena entered the García de Losada household. Antón Duque, a 50-year-old bondsman "from the Congo" who had spent decades in the García de Losada household, had interacted with the couple for twenty years. Over the course of those two decades Antón, Madalena, and Nicolás had watched their owner, Tomas García de Losada, employ a number of stewards before he engaged the services of Juan de Torres. As longtime members of the same household, Antón, Juan, Madalena, and Nicolás formed an identifiable core community that extended beyond a single racial, social, or residential status.[12]

The ties uniting Juan, Ysabel de Santiago, Nicolás de Ayala, and Spaniard Juan de Robredo reflect enduring bonds forged over the years in and around the Ayala household. On October 2nd of the same year, Juan, Ysabel de Santiago, Nicolás de Ayala, and Juan de Robredo initiated marriage proceedings by approaching an ecclesiastical scribe in Mexico's cathedral. Juan, a Mandinga and widower of three years, requested a marriage license in the absence of his prospective bride Ysabel. A sense of urgency informed Juan's request, since Ysabel, a creole enslaved to Ana María, had recently fallen ill. Now, after two years, the couple wanted to legitimize their illicit affair. Juan requested an ecclesiastical dispensation, marshaling Nicolás de Ayala and Juan de Robredo, with whom he lived in Father Benito Ayala's household. Nicolás, a 26-year-old enslaved mulatto, and Juan, a 24-year-old Spanish servant, had known Ysabel longer than they had known their housemate, Juan. Juan probably entered the Ayala household two years after Nicolás and Juan de Robredo had established a relationship with Ysabel. Ysabel's illness helps explain Juan's decision to select Spaniard Juan de Robredo as a marriage witness. But Juan de Robredo's proximity to Ysabel and Juan in all likelihood nurtured an abiding relationship that encouraged the enslaved couple to circumvent the social divisions in colonial Mexico.[13]

Pascual and María's marriage also evinced little change in their social networks over time. Though both Pascual, enslaved and "from Congo," and María, enslaved and "from Angola," resided with their respective masters Don Esteban Castellano and Mateo Barroso on the Street of the Holy Spirit, the meanings they ascribed to their West Central African identities shaped their relationships with members of both households. Francisco and Antón, for instance, both identified themselves as being "from Angola." Francisco, described by the scribe as a 40-year-old, had known María for five and Pascual for eight years. Antón, a 28-year-old, testified only on Pascual's behalf, noting that they had been acquainted for eight years. Their relationship comes as no surprise, since Don Estéban Castellano owned both of them. But Antón's unfamiliarity with María seems perplexing, given their shared ethnicity and their respective interactions with Pascual and Francisco. Pascual, María, Francisco, and Antón magnify the ways in which ethnicity spanned the Street of the Holy Spirit to link some of the West Central Africans in the Castellano and Barroso households.[14]

The Angolan wedding party that entered the parish church Santa Veracruz on May 7, 1635, also manifested a pattern whereby ethnicity spanned barrios and specific streets that linked disparate households. As Ambrosio and Gertrudes petitioned for a marriage license, the couple manifested no concern about a married life without actual cohabitation. As the respective property of Agustín Rincon and Tomás del Castillo, Ambrosio and Gertrudes had sustained their relationship for a number of years despite residing in different barrios. While Ambrosio selected his perspective spouse from a distant neighborhood, he selected Francisco, his neighbor, as his matrimonial sponsor. Francisco, a 38-year-old Angolan who, like Ambrosio, resided on Aguila Street, had known the prospective groom for six years. Even as a resident of a different household and neighborhood, Francisco had also maintained a 6-year relationship with Gertrudes. The same was true for Antonío, a 50-year-old enslaved Angolan who belonged to master carriagemaker Juan Nabaro. Despite laboring and residing on Tacuba Street, Antonío had known his ethnic compatriots for six years.[15]

A similar pattern prevailed among some of the enslaved in the Alamaras, Barriento, and Sánchez households. In 1640, after a lengthy illicit affair, two enslaved persons "from Angola" owned respectively by Don Diego de Barriento and Don Antonío de Almaras requested a marriage license. The lovers, María and Pedro Sánchez, both asked Juan de la Cruz and Ana María, who were also lovers, to serve as witnesses. Juan, a 30-year-old, had known Pedro for fourteen years "since he . . . is the companion of this witness and slave of the said his master." Juan added that Pedro had been a widower for five years. Juan testified that in the aftermath of the death of Pedro's wife, his compatriot and María had been "in a bad state much of the time." Ana María, a 50-year-old, acknowledged having known Pedro for more than twenty-five and María for twelve years. Ana María's relationship with Pedro probably began in her master's household, the same person from whom Pedro acquired the Sánchez surname. Years after Pedro left the Sánchez household, he still retained the Sánchez surname and his New World ethnicity as a person "from Angola." Self-consciously defining himself as an Angolan, Pedro sustained his purported ethnicity through his friendship with Juan de la Cruz and his affair with María, both of whom also claimed to be from Angola.[16]

Ethnicity also manifested itself when Domingo, Esperanza, Lorenzo de la Cruz, and Pedro entered the cathedral on December 26, 1644. Lorenzo and Pedro, two enslaved Angolans, informed the *provisor* that the couple, their compatriots Domingo and Esperanza, with whom they shared an 8-year rela-

tionship, were single and free from impediments. An 8-year relationship represented a significant feat, especially since Domingo and Lorenzo lived in different barrios than Esperanza and Pedro, who both resided in San Agustín yet in
different households. If race or ethnicity alone had shaped the consciousness
of Domingo, Lorenzo, Esperanza, and Pedro in the 1640s, they could have easily
found ethnic compatriots in their respective barrios of San Pablo, Santo Domingo, and San Agustín. Instead, they ascribed specific meanings to their Angolan ethnicity—meanings produced in the context of particular friendships,
experiences, and memories.[17]

On August 26, 1645, four individuals "from Angola" entered Santa Veracruz's
parish church to request a marriage license. Diego, a widower enslaved to Pedro
Gómes de Pineda, and Margarita, a widow enslaved to Juan García Calabe, both
repeated a performance with which they were intimately familiar through their
previous marriages to Cristiana and Juan. Six years after his wife's death, Diego
wanted to marry his compatriot, who had been a widow for two years. In 1639,
around the time that Diego's wife Cristiana died, Margarita had entered his
life in the barrio of Santa Veracruz. Antón, an enslaved 50-year-old, dated his
relationship with the prospective groom to 1625. Although Diego no longer
resided with their master Pedro Gómes de Pineda, Antón implied that they
still interacted with great frequency. Antón connected his 6-year familiarity
with Margarita to the death of Diego's wife. Pablo, the other witness, was also
initially Diego's friend. A 30-year-old "from Angola," enslaved to blacksmith
Sebastian de Nieba, who lived on Cuba Street, Pablo had known Diego twelve
years. He testified that Diego had been single since 1639, which was also when
he first met Margarita and her husband. For Pablo, Diego, Margarita, and Antón, the parish boundaries delimited the geographical contours of their community. Throughout the seventeenth century, thousands of *bozales,* ladinos,
and creoles toiled in Spanish households and traversed through the streets of
Santa Veracruz on behalf of their Spanish masters and employers. Yet in the
traza's microcosm, individuals such as Pablo, Diego, Margarita, and Antón
constantly moved between the overlapping communities to which they belonged.[18] In this, as in numerous other cases, the urban landscape enabled
individuals to embrace a New World ethnicity that they expressed through
chronological referents dating back decades.

Most prospective brides and grooms were not fortunate enough to live with
or near each other and their respective marriage witnesses. In 1620, Juan de la
Cruz and Isabel de la Cruz, two enslaved persons "from Angola" who belonged
to Pedro Martín de Loa, petitioned for a marriage license. Instead of asking
their master or his respective servants to stand in as witnesses, the prospective
couple relied on two other enslaved persons "from Angola." Both 45-year-old
Luís and 34-year-old Pascual had known the couple for eight years.[19] Despite

the difficulties that living in separate households imposed, Juan, Isabel, Luís, and Pascual maintained contact and sustained their New World ethnicity.

On July 1, 1644, another coterie of Angolans highlighted the confluence of elite residential patterns and African ethnicity when they assembled in Mexico's cathedral. As Antón and Catalina presented their marriage petitions, the enslaved Angolans belonging respectively to Don Alonso de Gonzalez de Villalba and Juan Rendon presented Domingo and an unnamed enslaved person from Angola as their matrimonial sponsors. The unnamed 26-year-old Angolan belonging to Doña Magdalena de Orduña had known the couple for eight years, as did the 35-year-old Domingo, an Angolan enslaved to Isabel de la Cruz. Since both Domingo and Catalina lived in the barrio of Santo Domingo, they had ample opportunities to see and possibly interact with one another. The same was true for Antón and the unnamed Angolan. Because of the elite status of their owners, they also saw and conversed with Domingo and Catalina in the numerous alleys, thoroughfares, and plazas of the *traza*.[20]

Mexico City's numerous artisans resided in distinct barrios or streets with others who practiced their craft. Some neighborhoods, as a result, doubled as workshops for the various smiths, cobblers, tanners, and other artisans. As slave-owners and employers, artisans—who were located in specific geographical areas—enabled their charges to forge ethnic and cultural ties with neighbors whose employers and owners shared the same occupation.

On July 12, 1631, Manuel and Francisca petitioned officials in the cathedral for a marriage license. Manuel, an enslaved Angolan who lived on San Francisco Street, had a long-standing relationship with an enslaved Angolan woman. Although both of them resided on San Francisco Street, the occupation of Francisca's owner aided her interactions with Manuel and their matrimonial sponsors. Mateo de Bega, Francisca's owner, was a peanut vendor and probably employed her as a street hawker. Francisca thus had the mobility to forge ties with Manuel and also with Pedro and Matheo. Matheo, "from the Congo," had known the couple for seven years. As the property of another peanut vendor, Matheo probably enjoyed the same mobility as Francisca. This mobility and their relationship, the product of occupational ties and much more, enabled this disparate aggregate of individuals to sustain their interaction. Manuel and Matheo defined themselves as Congos while Francisca and the 50-year-old Pedro claimed an Angolan ethnicity. Over the course of eight years, Pedro and Francisca had imbued their Angolan identity with specific meaning—a meaning they forged through their personal interactions yet one that did not exclude intimacy with Manuel and Matheo, who, as Congos, had engaged in a similar process.[21]

The relationship between Francisco, Catalina, Antón, and Cristóbal illustrates the confluence of occupational specialization, residential patterns, and ethnicity. On August 23, 1645, four Angolans entered Mexico's cathedral and initiated marriage proceedings. The couple, Francisco and Catalina, presented Antón and Cristóbal as their witnesses. Antón, a 30-year-old, had known the couple for six years. Like Francisco, Antón belonged to Francisco Mexia, a tanner who resided in the barrio of San Pablo. Cristóbal, a 24-year-old, also had known the couple for six years. Enslaved to Bartolomé García, another tanner who resided in the San Pablo neighborhood, Cristóbal labored and lived in close proximity to Francisco, Antón, and a host of his ethnic compatriots.[22]

Likewise, the marriage petition of Antón de la Cruz and Gracía de la Cruz highlights the intersection of occupational ties, elite residential patterns, and the centrality of the household as a site of community formation. On September 2, 1645, Antón and Gracía, who were both from Angola, entered the cathedral in order to legitimize their relationship. Although Antón and Gracía knew that marriage did not ensure that their residential status would change, they still wanted the blessing of the Church. Antón, who had been a widower for eight years, understood the difficulties that marriage to a member of a different household imposed, especially since the demands of his owner would invariably precede his familial obligations. Even if the respective owners of Antón and Gracía, Pedro de Gustamante and Doña María de Ocampo, permitted them unrestricted access or even cohabitation, slavery made marital life inherently difficult. Nonetheless, Antón and Gracía embraced the challenge and asked Simón de la Cruz and Agustín de Salazar to serve as their marital sponsors.

Both Simón and Agustín had had a 20-year relationship with Antón de la Cruz. Despite their status as enslaved persons belonging to the miller Bartolomé de Cardoso, Simón and Agustín found time to initiate and maintain relationships in and outside of their household. Both witnesses had also interacted with Gracía for a period of five years. As Antón and Gracía's entourage stood before the ecclesiastical party, they underscored the ways in which the spatial landscape of household and occupational ties and elite residential patterns enabled *bozales* and creoles to temper, if not circumvent, the physical burdens that slavery imposed. On September 2, 1645, the *provisor* and scribe perhaps unwittingly registered how household, extrahousehold, occupational, and residential ties intersected with legal status, ethnicity, race, and a Christian consciousness. The existing social networks, forged in diverse spatial contexts, extended from their initial locus and ultimately linked specific individuals who were dispersed throughout the urban labyrinth.[23]

In 1633, Juan Bautista de la Cruz, a black creole, and Lucrecia, an Angolan-born enslaved person who belonged to a different owner, testified on behalf of Antón and María de la Cruz. Lucrecia, a 40-year-old, had had a 6-year relationship with Antón and María de la Cruz. Juan, a 37-year-old, revealed that his interactions with the couple had thus far lasted eight years.[24] In 1640, Francisco and Gracía, both "from Angola" and enslaved to Juan Goméz, also manifested their ethnicity when asking Juan Antonío and María to be their marriage witnesses. Enslaved by a different master, the 30-year-old Juan Antonío "from Angola" had forged a 20-year relationship with Gracía and had known Francisco for a period of three years, "which is when he [Francisco] came as a bozal from Guinea." María, likewise "from Angola," dated her interaction with Francisco from 1637, soon after he arrived from Guinea. María's relationship with Gracía, however, spanned more than a decade; she testified that she had known Gracía for sixteen years.[25] Such long-standing relationships should not surprise us. In Mexico and throughout New Spain, a number of residents who were born in Africa, as we shall see, dated their familiarity in decades.

Time, Space, and African Ethnicity

In 1628, Francisco and Dominga, two enslaved persons claiming to be "from Calabar," selected as marriage witnesses residents of separate households who defined themselves in similar terms. Instead of relying on their master or his other servants, Francisco and Dominga called on Cristóbal and Francisco, with whom they had maintained a 5-year relationship.[26] Through their actions, the prospective couple highlighted their ethnicity as persons "from Calabar." But during the 1620s, and throughout the seventeenth century for that matter, individuals such as Francisco and Dominga confronted serious odds in their quest for culturally compatible witnesses. By the seventeenth century, the population in New Spain from West Africa had seriously declined and found it difficult to establish relationships with persons similarly defined.

This stood in contrast to the experiences of people from West Central Africa. In the 1620s, late West African arrivals such as Francisco, Domingo, Cristóbal, and Francisco faced greater obstacles in maintaining their "Calabar" networks than did Juan, Isabel, Luís, and Pascual; many among Mexico's *bozal* population defined themselves as persons "from Angola." Still, these two cases, among numerous others, highlight the tenacity with which individuals adhered to ascribed cultural labels and ethnicities. By defining themselves as being "from Calabar" or "from Angola," Africans simultaneously revealed their subjective sense of self, both new and old, and the discursive limits of self-fashioning. Spanish authorities stipulated the forms that these identities assumed, but such limits did not preclude immigrant Africans from manifesting distinct identities beyond definitions created by their encounter with ecclesiastical authorities or from investing these newly constructed categories with different meanings. Yet despite the ongoing contest over definitions and their meanings, the ritually charged nature of the marriage petitions had some effect on the ways that Africans identified themselves in less formalized contexts.

Even in relationships in which ethnicity played a more limited role, collective and individual identities informed the selection of marriage witnesses. Diego and Ana, for instance, manifested a particular cultural predilection in selecting two "Angolans," Francisco and Domingo de la Cruz, as their matrimonial sponsors. Although Ana identified herself as a black creole and Diego claimed to be "from Angola," the couple did not indiscriminately select persons of African descent as their witnesses. When they recruited Francisco and Domingo to testify on their behalf, Ana and Diego deliberately avoided members of their master's household. While ethnicity clearly guided Diego's decision, Ana's motives remain obscure. In any case, Ana had had a long-standing relationship with 40-year-old Francisco and 36-year-old Domingo. Both Francisco and Domingo had known Ana and Diego for eight years.[27]

Esteban, a creole, and his prospective spouse from Angola, Isabel, also relied on witnesses who lived in separate households. Rather than depend on Don Diego Zarate's beneficence or that of his kin, servants, or slaves, Esteban and Isabel asked Martín, an enslaved person of undefined ethnicity, and Antón, "from the land of Bran," to vouch for them. Antón, at the time 60 years old, had interacted with the couple for ten years. The 30-year-old Martín had had a 5-year relationship with Esteban and Isabel. Despite Martín's obscure ethnicity, this and other wedding parties underscore that the communities of participants in the ritual were culturally heterogeneous. Even though Isabel and Esteban identified themselves respectively as being "from Angola" and a creole, they did not randomly embrace similarly defined individuals to serve as their witnesses. Instead, the couple called on acquaintances. In their case, a long-standing friendship—forged through work and recreational experiences—stood in for ethnicity.[28]

Selectivity also informed the behavior of Manuel and Ana. In 1629, Manuel, "from Congo," and Ana, "from Angola," decided to forgo asking members of Don Fulgencio de Vera's household to serve as their marriage witnesses. They relied on Manuel, a 30-year-old "from the land of Biafara" and Francisco, a 46-year-old "from Angola." Although the members of the wedding party resided in three distinct households and defined themselves differently, both Manuel and Francisco acknowledged having had extensive relationships with Manuel and Ana. The relationships between the bride, the groom, and the marriage witnesses underscored a discernible, though not rigid, pattern. In lieu of an obvious cultural pattern, *bozales* and criollos depended on friendships established long before in the course of their recreational activities and labor routines to stand in for cultural affinity.

Even as early as 1584, the nature of African ethnicity was anything but simple when Miguel and Inés petitioned the *provisor* for a marriage license. The couple presented Juan, Domingo, and an unknown person as witnesses. Procedurally speaking, this represented a typical case. After convincing the ecclesiastical judge of their desires, Miguel and Inés presented three witnesses willing to testify that they were single and unrelated. This case, however, reveals more than customary Christian practice. Miguel, Inés, Juan, Domingo, and the unknown person all claimed to be from "Guinea."[29] But neither their shared births in Guinea nor their legal status as slaves displaced the nuances with which they described themselves. Miguel, Inés, and Juan also identified themselves as being "from Angola." While Domingo (or the scribe) failed to register his ethnicity, the nameless person noted that he was "from Terra Nova."

This case, like all examples that underscore the Church's penchant for specificity, highlights the interactions of *bozales* and creoles. Such interactions belie assumptions that social networks were narrowly defined on the basis of birthplace, race, or legal status. If these categories alone defined their identities, Miguel and Inés could have indiscriminately selected a spouse and marriage witnesses from the thousands of persons of African descent who resided in the viceregal capital. Yet they selected particular *bozales* and possibly individuals that shared their ethnicity. But why did they elect Juan, Domingo, and the nameless man? In the case of Miguel and Inés, the timing of their arrival "from Angola" and the 3-year relationship between the couple and some of the witnesses suggests that these constituted the ties the bride and groom had forged during and immediately after the harrowing middle passage. Domingo and the nameless person both acknowledged that they had known Miguel and Inés for three years. Perhaps soon after their arrival in Mexico City, Miguel and Inés met their witnesses through members of their respective households—an introduction that the urban landscape facilitated. In this case, we cannot know what precisely their ethnicity meant to Miguel and Inés or how that ethnicity was formed or the significance it played for them. Yet in this and numerous other marriage cases, a discernible pattern emerges. Though they were from Guinea and were enslaved on the basis of race, *bozales,* negroes, and mulattos utilized specific cognomens that revealed the primacy of certain representations over others.

In 1605, Matias and Catalina, two enslaved black persons "from [the] land of Angola," requested a marriage license and asked Pascual and Antón to serve as their matrimonial sponsors. Identifying himself as a 30-year-old enslaved black man "from Biafara," Pascual informed the authorities that he had known both Matias and Antón for three years. Antón, a 53-year-old who was also from Biafara, provided a similar testimony. Like Pascual, Antón had known Catalina for three years, but he had known Matias "ever since he came from Angola" four years previously.[30] This case, in all likelihood, involved multiple expressions of identity. Catalina and Matias defined themselves and sought to contract a marriage on the basis of being from Angola. But they relied on two individuals who identified themselves as being "from the land of Biafara" to serve as their marriage witnesses—revealing how Africanity informed the behavior, if not the consciousness, of Catalina, Matias, Pascual, and Antón.

This scenario repeated itself on September 19, 1633 when Biafarans Domingo and Anton testified on behalf of Angolans Felipe de la Cruz and Juliana de la Cruz. In their testimonials, both Biafaran sexagenarians acknowledged having had 20-year ties with the Angolans. Despite residing in four separate households, Felipe, Juliana, Domingo, and Antón had sustained relations dating back to 1613, a period when West Africans had a viable presence in Mexico City. The ties uniting the Biafarans and the Angolans demonstrate how enduring personal ties produced an imagined Africanity. In this instance, members of the West African charter group and the subsequent migrants from West Central Africa bridged existing cultural divisions, including those based on the time of arrival from Guinea.

Although the petitions demonstrate personal ties based on Africanity, the sources simultaneously obscure the history of such ties. The diverse peoples of African descent assigned symbolic meanings to their arrival in New Spain that shaped subsequent patterns of interaction and the process of community formation. New arrivals often assigned elder status to members of the charter generation of African immigrants and saw them as repositories of cultural and ancestral heritage.[31]

As the elders Domingo and Antón offered their testimony on Felipe and Juliana's behalf, the *provisor* may have inadvertently witnessed the valence that subsequent arrivals from Guinea accorded members of the charter generation. The Catholic Church encouraged individuals to privilege certain criterion when they selected marital sponsors, including status as an elder and a long-standing Christian identity. But as this case demonstrates, couples also crossed ethnic boundaries when they chose their sponsors. Perhaps in this particular case, the timing and the circumstances of their encounter played a significant role in sustaining cross-cultural relationships. For subsequent arrivals from Angola, a similar interaction may have been unthinkable, since the arrival of large numbers of Angolans in Mexico affected the *bozal* population's cultural options.[32]

During the first half of the seventeenth century, peoples of African descent transcended the African-creole dichotomy. While Africanity manifested itself in New Spain, especially through the very use of the term *bozal*, ethnicity represented a more widely employed referent. Individuals born in Africa defined themselves and were identified as Angolans, Biafrans, and Congos. Of course, these cognomens acquired specific meanings in New Spain—meanings that disappeared in the second half of the seventeenth century when the number of residents of New Spain who had born in Africa began to decrease. But during the course of the slave trade, ethnicity retained its salience as a cultural artifice, a geographical referent, and a symbolic trope that tempered the development of an imagined African, slave, or even black community. Prior to 1650, ethnicity—not Africanity—played the dominant role in the lives of *bozales*. Individuals invariably manifested forms of panethnicity, but distinct patterns often typified boundary-crossing at the most intimate levels of their lives. In crossing ethnic boundaries, for instance, West Central Africans in New Spain almost always did so with persons from the contiguous cultural areas in Africa. As can be seen in the following examples, Angolans generally limited their panethnicity to Congos.

In 1628, three Angolans and a free mulatto offered testimony on behalf of a Congo couple seeking a marriage license. Pedro, a 40-year-old enslaved Angolan, and Manuel, a 36-year-old enslaved Angolan, had known the bride and groom, Cristina and Mateo, for five years. A different Manuel, another enslaved Angolan who was 30 years old, dated his relationship with Manuel to 1620, when they had resided in the city of Puebla. Two years previously, however, Mateo's master had departed for Mexico with his Congo slave. In 1626, Manuel's master followed suit, thus enabling the Angolan to reestablish contact with his Congo mate. Francisco, a 34-year-old free mulatto, offered a similar testimony but acknowledged that he had interacted with Mateo for fifteen years. As former Poblanos (residents of Puebla) in the viceregal capital, Francisco, Manuel, and Mateo maintained their culturally expansive ties despite the existence of extensive mulatto, Angolan, and Congo nuclei. Yet in selecting a spouse, Mateo sought a companion who shared the specifics of his ethnicity.[33]

The scribe recorded a similar case in the following year. In 1629, as they stood before the ecclesiastical authorities, Domingo and Isabel, two enslaved Congos belonging to different masters, presented their compatriot, Bartolomé, as a witness. The enslaved 40-year-old Congo testified that he had had an 8-year relationship with the prospective married couple. Diego Luís, a 50-year-old enslaved Angolan, had known Domingo and Isabel ten years. A 10-year relationship represented a considerable feat for *bozales,* especially for members of two ethnic groups that had the requisite numbers to sustain endogamous social networks. After a decade of interaction, ethnicity played a limited, if not a nonexistent, role in the relationships between Diego Luís, Domingo, and Isabel. Although Domingo and Isabel thought of themselves as Congos, through their relationship with Diego Luís they also defined themselves as West Central Africans. Perhaps this change began, as it did for Pedro de Fonesca and María, soon after their arrival in Mexico City.[34]

Also in 1629, two enslaved Angolans who belonged to different masters entered the ecclesiastical domain for a marriage license. Both Manuel and María presented Sebastian and Pedro de Fonesca as their witnesses. Sebastian, a 30-

year-old enslaved Portuguese, acknowledged that he had known the couple for five years, as did Pedro, who added that he had known María "since she arrived as a bozal." As a survivor of the middle passage, María searched instinctively for familiar sites in her new surroundings. In this context, she initially met Manuel, Pedro, and Sebastian, each of whom had contributed to the way she defined herself. Through their relationships with each other, María, Manuel, Pedro, and Sebastian, became Angolans, West Africans, and enslaved migrants.[35]

Another case from 1629 involving Congos Juan and Luísa and Angolans Domingo and Juan simultaneously reified ethnicity and a West Central African consciousness. Although the Congo couple, Juan and Luísa, lived in separate households, they wanted a Christian wedding. At a time when a significant Congo presence flourished in Mexico, Juan and Luísa selected Angolans Domingo and Juan as their matrimonial sponsors. At the time the Angolans offered their testimony, they had had a 5-year relationship with Juan and Luísa despite residing in separate households. Antón and Esperanza replicated this pattern in 1633, when the Congo couple relied on two Angolans, Francisco de la Cruz and Juan de la Cruz, as their conjugal witnesses. Evidently being residents of four different households did not pose a problem for Antón, Esperanza, Francisco, and Juan. While Francisco dated his relationship with the couple back to 1623, Juan had known them for eight years.[36] Over the years, the friends maintained their respective ethnicity even as they constructed an Africanity with a distinctive Congo-Angolan texture.

As a marriage witness in two separate proceedings, Pedro, a 50-year-old enslaved Angolan, illustrates the seemingly perfunctory manner in which individuals mediated between their ethnicity and their Africanity. On July 12, 1631, Pedro, a 50-year-old enslaved Angolan, and Matheo, an enslaved Congo, offered testimony on behalf of Manuel and Francisco. Despite his Angolan ethnicity, Pedro had had an 8-year relationship with the Congo Manuel. Pedro also acknowledged interacting with his compatriot and with Manuel's prospective bride, Francisco, for a period of eight years. In the course of those years, some combination of ethnicity and Africanity had bridged the cultural and spatial divide that separated the members of the wedding party. Five days after Pedro offered his testimony, he once again stood before the *provisor* as a matrimonial sponsor. This time, however, Pedro's presence lacked ethnic ambiguity since he testified for and alongside persons who defined themselves as Angolans. As Pedro presented evidence of his compatriots' single status, the scribe recorded the very same testimony that five days earlier had revealed the existence of a restricted Africanity. Pedro's testimony now stood in as an index of Angolan ethnicity.[37]

In the seventeenth century, as the petitions make clear, individuals usually manifested their ethnic ambiguity only in the selection of a matrimonial sponsor; rarely do we find an individual who selected a spouse from another ethnic group. Even when a more heterogeneous population made endogamous marriage a possibility, most individuals in New Spain chose spouses from within their own ethnic group. As such, the marriage between the Angolan Ambriosio and Ana, "from the Congo," represented an anomaly. Ambriosio had had a long-standing interaction with Congos, most notably Bartolomé and Juan, who testified on his and Ana's behalf. Even as a resident of distinct household and irrespective of the large Angolan presence, Ambriosio sustained intimate ties with Congos dating back more than a decade, a cultural process that ultimately informed who he chose for a spouse.[38] In the seventeenth century, those who transcended ethnic boundaries to choose a mate usually resided in close proximity to one another and often, as in Manuel and Ana's case, belonged to the same master.[39] In some instances, forced proximity, a cultural process in its own right, tempered the salience of ethnicity.

Throughout the first half of the seventeenth century, slaveholding patterns in Mexico enabled and sustained a discrete ethnicity which invariably tempered broader ethnic alliances. In 1621, Ana de la Cruz and Pedro, a New World widow and widower "from Congo," asked two other persons "from Congo" to be their marriage witnesses. Simón Matias, a 30-year-old doorman, had known Pedro eighteen years and Ana de la Cruz ten. Similarly, the 36-year-old Rodrigo acknowledged having known the bride for ten years and the groom for twelve. During the course of their interaction, the couple had shared personal information and experience with both witnesses, which they, in turn, manifested in their testimony. Simón Matias and Rodrigo both knew that Pedro's wife, Francisca, had died in 1620. Yet only Simón mentioned Ana's loss in 1618. Even in the disease-ridden world of seventeenth-century Mexico, Simón Matias's eighteen-year-old relationship with Pedro was not an unusual occurrence. Simón's declaration before the *provisor* brings into relief the spatial and temporal referents whereby witnesses legitimized their testimony on behalf of a prospective couple.[40]

This Congo network may have but did not necessarily include Juan, Antonía, Manuel, and Anton, who appeared before the *provisor* in 1622. Although Juan and Antonía, both "from Congo," belonged to two different masters, they met in New Spain and subsequently married. Yet rather than relying on their respective masters or members of their households as witnesses, Juan and Antonía called on Manuel and Antón, long-standing intimates and compatriots. Manuel, a 22-year-old, testified that he had known the couple five years, and the 50-year-old freedman, Antón, had known them just as long.[41] The existence of this network is not surprising. A significant number of individuals from Congo arrived in Mexico as part of the New Spain's seventeenth-century slave trade that largely drew its victims from West Central Africa. Consequently, "blacks from Congo" constituted one of several ethnic tropes that proliferated in seventeenth-century Mexico and through which some *bozales* identified themselves to ecclesiastical scribes.

In the first half of the seventeenth century, "Terra Nova" (defined in other parts of the Indies as Lucumis and Yoruba) was another ethnic signifier that was present in New Spain. In 1621, Dominga and Catalina, enslaved persons "from Terra Nova" who belonged to two different masters, relied on two witnesses who were similarly defined to certify that they were free to marry. The 70-year-old Francisco recalled having known the couple for three years, but the 36-year-old Antón had known them even longer. According to Antón, he had known Domingo "ever since he came from Guinea and . . . the bride for five years."[42]

The following year, in 1622, another couple "from Terra Nova" called on their compatriots to serve as marriage witnesses. Despite residing in four separate households, the members of the wedding party had known each other on average for five years. Pedro, a 44-year-old belonging to Doña Agustín de Valdez, stated that he had known Catalina, Manuel, and Manuel's deceased wife, also called Catalina, for five years. Luís de Albornoz had known the bride Catalina six years and Manuel five. Since Manuel's wife had died only five months before, Luís had thus been familiar with Catalina prior to her romance with Manuel. Catalina's ethnicity probably shaped her relationships with Luís, Pedro, and Manuel. But in Manuel's case, the death of his wife Catalina transformed him from a mere compatriot to an acceptable spouse.[43]

In 1628, Juan and Isabel, two enslaved persons from Terra Nova owned by different masters, asked two of their compatriots to serve as marriage witnesses. Francisco, a 54-year-old free person, had known Juan ten years and revealed that he had been a widower for two years. An enslaved person, also named Francisco, acknowledged knowing both Isabel and Juan. Indeed, Francisco's 6-year relationship with Isabel predated the death of his wife two years previously.[44] Juan and Isabel's affinity evidently facilitated the transformation of their relationship to an amorous one. In the seventeenth century, some ethnicities had a balanced gender ratio that enabled one to have spouses and sexual companions of the same ethnicity as oneself.

The persistence of the pattern in which the couple and the witnesses shared the same ethnic identity highlights the importance of that variable. In 1629, for instance, Pedro and Catalina sought to contract marriage although they belonged to two different masters. Identifying themselves as enslaved persons from Terra Nova, they asked María and Pedro, both of whom were also from Terra Nova, to serve as their marriage witnesses. In their testimony, María and Pedro testified having had an 8-year relationship with Pedro and Catalina.[45] Though the precise meaning that Pedro and Catalina ascribed to their "Terra

Nova" ethnicity remains elusive, it acquired a privileged position in their lives, since some of their most intimate and more established associations were with persons similarly defined. Individuals in a position to interact with their compatriots often manifested endogamous behavior at critical junctures in their Christian lives—moments during which Spanish authorities inscribed their identities and called on the participants to define themselves for the sake of legitimacy, orderly procedure, and the existence of a good *república.*

In 1584, four years after the union of the Portuguese and Spanish Crowns which granted Spain "legitimate" access to the coast of Guinea, Miguel and Inés petitioned the ecclesiastical authorities for a marriage license. At the time, Angolans still constituted a distinct minority among African-born residents of New Spain. As part of the vanguard of a forced migration of Angolans, Miguel and Inés confronted greater obstacles than did later arrivals from Angola in their efforts to establish endogamous social networks. During the initial years of the seventeenth-century slave trade, individuals identifying themselves as Angolans lacked the demographic base that could sustain endogamous social interaction.

The wedding party of Miguel and Inés underscores their ethnic isolation. Among their three witnesses, only Juan, an enslaved 30-year-old, identified himself as an Angolan. According to the scribe, Miguel's witness Domingo was an enslaved 25-year-old creole who had known the prospective groom three years. Inés's nameless 33-year-old informant from Terra Nova had known the bride-to-be for three years.[46] Prior to the massive introduction of Angolans in the 1620s, persons who identified and were identified as such faced serious challenges if they wanted to organize their lives with persons similarly defined. In the case of Miguel and Inés, the two Angolans clearly placed value on their ethnic identification, but why they selected Domingo and the nameless person from Terra Nova as their matrimonial sponsors remains a mystery. While the petitions highlight the possible importance of race, legal status, and shared experiences—produced during the middle passage, the seasoning process, and various spatial contexts—they do not reveal the underlying meanings that Miguel and Inés and other Angolans may have attributed to spouse and sponsor selection. Without other clues, we can only speculate about the criterion Miguel and Inés used when they selected the members of their wedding party.

At most, the *informaciones* underscore the presence of existing symbols—race, legal status, and possibly shared experience—marshaled during the petitioning process. They do not, however, reveal the range of contingent meanings present during and beyond the ritualized transactions. Even with symbols for which some precision can be established, the contingent nature of experience imbued meanings with a chronic fluidity. Sixteenth-century Angolan endogamy represented something distinct from the pattern of the 1630s and 1640s. In the sixteenth century, Angolans were less likely to establish endogamous social networks, since a requisite core did not inhabit Mexico City. During this time, Angolans, along with other West Central Africans, manifested a more expansive ethnic consciousness, as reflected in the composition of their wedding parties.

In 1595, fifteen years after Spaniards gained direct access to the Guinea coast, two enslaved persons, Pedro and Isabel, requested a marriage license. Although Isabel had just completed the seasoning process, she wanted to marry Pedro, an Angolan from a different household who had been in Mexico for at least five years. As a *bozal* "from São Tomé" who had arrived in Mexico in 1592, Isabel had established contact with other West Central Africans. She petitioned to marry an Angolan and brought forth two witnesses whom she had known in São Tomé and with whom she may have shared her ethnicity. One witness, a nameless 30-year-old female *bozal*, had known Isabel for eight years.

In 1587, the nameless woman simultaneously became an ethnic African, a slave, and a registered 22-year-old Christian. These categories, along with the shared experiences on São Tomé, during the middle passage, and in New Spain tempered the existing ethnic differences. Luísa, Isabel's second witness, indicated as much in her testimony. Identifying herself as an Angolan, the 25-year-old Luísa noted that her relationship with Isabel had flourished for "many years because they grew up together in São Tomé where they interacted and communicated very closely until three years ago more or less they came to New Spain together on one boat." Although in Mexico Isabel and Luísa entered separate households, the friends, fellow shipmates, and co-residents of Mexico still maintained contact with one another. Pedro's witnesses did not reveal the existence of any transatlantic ties. Both the 30-year-old nameless Angolan and the 20-year-old nameless Congo had interacted with Pedro for five years. In the absence of a core population of Angolans, Pedro manifested an Angolan identity and his consciousness as a West Central African through the selection of his marriage witnesses and prospective spouse.[47]

By 1605, New Spain's colonists had imported over 13,000 enslaved Africans. In that year, when Matias and Catalina identified themselves as Angolans, they brought a multiplicity of symbols that shaped their ethnicity to bear on the marriage petition. The steady introduction of Angolans enabled both Matias and Catalina to find a spouse who was also Angolan. But both of their matrimonial sponsors identified themselves as Biafarans who dated their familiarity with the couple to the time when they arrived from Angola.[48] During the seasoning process, Matias and Catalina probably met and interacted with dozens of Angolan survivors who labored throughout the *traza*. Still, they selected the Biafarans Pascual and Anton as their sponsors. Of course, their decision reflected the complex interplay between Africanity, legal status, residential proximity, and shared experiences. What exactly united Matias, Catalina, Pascual, and Anton remains a mystery. Such ties serve as a powerful reminder of cultural dexterity in a context in which endogamy was on the rise. At a moment at which Angolans had the necessary demographic base for endogamous social practices, Matias and Catalina found community with individuals who, in ethnic terms, defined themselves differently. The Angolans who selected non-Angolans as their spouses and their matrimonial sponsors represented a distinct minority who highlighted the porous nature of ethnic boundaries and the plethora of symbols around which individuals organized their lives.

Although speculation about the origins of this community invokes ties to "Guinea," the peoples "from the land of Angola" largely forged these networks in the Americas. In this sense, African ethnicity, like creole cultures, largely represented New World creations. The preponderance of persons claiming the "land of Angola" as their birthplace ensured that Angolan networks prevailed among the *bozal* population in the first half of the seventeenth century. The figures from New Spain's seventeenth-century slave trade underscore the fact that persons claiming affinity with "the land of Angola" had the material basis from which to sustain relatively exclusive social networks. As the following vignettes illustrate, a significant number of individuals chose this option.

Ethnic endogamy prevailed during the course of the entire seventeenth-century slave trade (1595–1622). Corresponding with the massive influx of Angolans, individuals manifested their endogamous sentiments immediately after being seasoned. During the seasoning process, survivors of the middle passage gradually acclimatized to Mexico City's disease environment and immersed themselves in the Hispanic cultural milieu. Since a number of persons from the "land of Angola" acknowledged knowing their compatriots anywhere from six to nine years, it seems safe to assume that most Angolans passing through the marriage market did so before the 1640s. For many individuals, marriage also represented a cultural transition—a culmination and a beginning —indicating perhaps that Mexico City's seasoning process was shorter than that in rural areas and plantation regions throughout the Americas. Evidently, after three years, individuals acquired the cultural, if not linguistic, dexterity that enabled them to realize the advantages that would accrue from formal marriage ties. Acting on this awareness allowed individuals to formalize their relationships and, by implication, their New World ethnicity. Above all else, the formalizing of relationships reflected the demographic foundation on which ethnicity sustained itself. Even though more individuals staked their identities around Angola, it is important to remember that the slave trade, as a particular political practice and a discursive site, subordinated the more discrete meanings attributed to "Angolan" ethnicity. And individuals did not always manifest rigid adherence to ethnicity. As we have seen, a variety of factors, including the slaveholding pattern, shaped existing social networks.

While the composition of the seventeenth-century slave trade and slaveholding patterns enabled an Angolan ethnicity to flourish, the atomization process, the numerical ascendancy of the creole population, and the presence of other ethnic groups underscore how spouse and sponsor selection represented a strategic decision. Such was the case in 1628 when the two Angolans, Manuel and Gracía, selected two enslaved Angolans named Catalina as their marriage sponsors. Manuel's and Gracía's choice of spouse and sponsors reflected the importance they accorded their ethnicity. As the chattel of two different masters, their relationship would, unless they acquired their freedom, be subjected to their masters' whims and would invariably be ranked behind the demands placed on their labor. Undaunted by slavery's spatial and temporal rigors, Manuel and Gracía insisted on a Christian marriage. Perhaps the couple's long-standing relationship with their compatriots, the two Catalinas, convinced Manuel and Gracía that they could sustain their marriage irrespective of their separation. Having maintained one set of ethnic relationships for six years, Manuel and Gracía opted for what may have represented the ultimate ethnic act—marriage to one another.[49]

The prevailing pattern that emerges from the petitions indicates that a significant number of Angolans forged their New World ethnicity on a continuum that began with an individual's arrival in New Spain, continued with initial contact with other Angolans, and culminated with a marriage to a person similarly self-identified. Of course, the structures that slavery imposed channeled the cultural process, but some agency resided with Angolans as they struggled to reshape their subjective sense of self. The testimony of Juan and Agustín on behalf of Susana and Juan delineates the contours in which individuals forged and sustained their Angolan ethnicity. After identifying themselves (and their compatriots) through Western European and Christian metaphors, Juan and Agustín they proclaimed their familiarity with the prospective Angolan couple, noting that they had known them five years, "which is the time the so said arrived as bozales." Five years after their initial encounter in Mexico's *traza*, Juan and Agustín still interacted with the former *bozales* who, like them, eventually inhabited ladino and Angolan identities. In the cultural process of becoming ladinos and Angolans, the presence of Juan and Agustín in the lives of Susana and Juan remained, like slavery, a constant.[50]

In 1629, Juan and his prospective bride, Lucía, both "from the land of Angola," entered the Sagrario to petition for a marriage license. There had been a recent flood and chaos still gripped the viceregal capital, but the couple insisted on being married. As recent survivors of the middle passage and as chattel belonging to Spaniard Pedro de la Madrid and the free black Juan Fulano, they were accustomed to adversity. Indeed, by entering the Sagrario, Juan and Lucía demonstrated their ability to navigate the Hispanic cultural arena—slavery, elite households, and Spanish-imposed institutions. With and through their request, Juan and Lucía also demonstrated awareness of their ethnicity. As persons "from the land of Angola" they asked two individuals residing in disparate household but who shared their legal status and alleged ethnicity to be their marriage witnesses. Antonío de la Cruz, a 22-year-old, and the 30-year-old Agustín had known the couple for four years, indicating that Juan and Lucía's seasoning had ended four years after their 1625 arrival in Mexico City.[51] It is a paradox that Juan and Lucía utilized Christianity to mark their rite of passage and affirm their identities as Angolans.

While numerous Angolans manifested their ethnicity through Christian conjugality, individuals such as Francisco acted as cultural brokers. In 1629, 46-year-old Angolan Francisco and Francisco Hernández, a 36-year-old enslaved Congo, both testified on behalf of the Angolan couple Simón and María. Although they lived in separate households, both Franciscos certified that they knew Simón, who was previously known as Mateo. Francisco also revealed that he had served as Simón's baptismal sponsor and godfather when they lived together in Bartolomé de Olite's household. Francisco acknowledged that soon after Simón arrived in New Spain, he had exposed his compatriot to Christianity. In 1629, three years later, the neophyte engaged his new faith more firmly by petitioning for a marriage license, reaffirming his adherence to Christianity. Francisco's testimony outlines the cultural trajectory whereby previous arrivals from Guinea introduced subsequent migrants to the Christian faith. But through ritual assistance he also shored up Simón's New World ethnicity as an Angolan—an identity that owned much to Christian and Western tropes.[52]

In that same year, 1629, Mateo and Gracía, "from the land of Angola," enslaved but belonging to separate masters, asked Francisco and Manuel, who shared their ethnicity, to testify on their behalf. Despite having different masters, the 50-year-old Francisco and the 34-year-old Manuel had known the couple for eight and seven years, respectively.[53] Also in 1629, a couple "from the land of Angola," Diego and Catalina, who lived in separate households, asked María and Matheo, who also defined themselves as Angolan, to sponsor them as marriage witnesses. María, a 45-year-old who was the property of Juan Martínez, had known the couple for six years. Matheo, a 30-year-old, acknowledged that he had known the couple for the same amount of time.[54]

Pedro and Juliana joined the spate of couples "from the land of Angola" that requested marriage petitions in 1629. As they stood before the *provisor,* Pedro and Juliana, owned by Doña López de Estrada and Doña Altamirano, respectively, presented two of their compatriots as marriage witnesses. Manuel, a 46-year-old who was González Sánchez's chattel, had known the couple for eight years, whereas Francisco de Cuyoacan, a 64-year-old freedman, had known them for nine years.[55] Domingo and Inés seemed fortunate when they petitioned for a marriage license in 1629. Both the bride and groom lived on San Francisco Street, ensuring them perhaps continual access to one another. Despite their proximity, Domingo and Inés established ties with persons "from Angola" who lived in distant households. This included 45-year-old Antón and 25-year-old Pedro de la Cruz. Both men had known the couple for six years.[56]

Beyond Race, Culture, and Slavery

In 1629, seven years after New Spain received its last ship of slaves under the Spanish-Portuguese accord unifying both countries (1580–1640), Simón de la Cruz and Magdalena de San Bernadino expressed their conjugal desires to the ecclesiastical authorities. After the prospective groom, an enslaved Angolan, and his 22-year-old creole bride completed the required proclamations, they presented a battery of witnesses whose respective subjectivities underscore Simón and Magdalena's cultural expansiveness. In the 1620s, as a self-identified Angolan, Simón doubtless saw, if not interacted with, persons similarly defined. Yet in selecting a spouse and his sponsors, Simón chose a free creole, a free *chino* (a former inhabitant of the Spanish Philippines), and an enslaved Congo. Simon's decision to marry Magdalena and to ask another Simón and Sebastian de la Palma to be his matrimonial sponsors reflected the contingent nature of community formation in which long-standing relationships acquired sufficient symbolic weight to compete with ethnic and cultural divisions. The 38-year-old free *chino* Simón and the 40-year-old Congo Sebastian de la Palma highlight the ways that long-standing relationships bridged cultural divisions. Simón acknowledged having had a 9-year relationship with Simón, half the time that Sebastian had known him but still a relationship of considerable duration.

In the turbulent world of seventeenth-century Mexico, individuals accorded relationships of this duration the same valence as Magdalena's cultural ties with her witnesses. Gaspar de la Cruz, an 18-year-old enslaved creole, and Nicolás Bravo, an 18-year-old enslaved mulatto, both had had an 8-year relationship with the prospective bride. As members of the same household and as creoles, they shared an ethnic identity with Magdalena. In contrast, her husband-to-be, Simón, seemed to value length of acquaintance over shared ethnic identity when he chose his sponsors. Despite this manifestation of Magdalena's creole sensibility, she found solace with Simón, an Angolan but one whose long-standing presence in New Spain made him a ladino and possibly an acceptable mate.[57]

In the case of Juana and Sebastian, the groom's ladino identity also made him an acceptable partner. In the Pérez household, Sebastian's process of becoming a ladino acquired its cultural specificity and enabled the enslaved Angolan and Juana, an enslaved black creole, to define each other as desirable mates. In fact, the couple requested their marriage license well into Sebastian's transformation. As Sebastian petitioned for a license in 1631, he requested a dispensation because of his 2-year common-law marriage with his housemate Juana, who was "about to die." Alonso de Reyes corroborated Sebastian's confession, noting that he had known the couple for five years, during which they were "in a bad state interacting carnally." Juan, a 22-year-old free ladino tailor, was just as candid. Having had a 9-year relationship with Sebastian and having known Juana "since birth," Juan testified that the Angolan-creole couple had lived in a "bad state" for two years.[58] According to this testimony, in 1631, Sebastian had been a ladino for at least nine years. Over the course of these years, the Angolan Sebastian gravitated toward individuals with whom he had shared cultural affinity. For Sebastian, Alonso, and Juan, years of familiarity transformed initial affinities—symbolic and experiential—into something enduring and meaningful beyond the inaugural encounter. As far as Juana was concerned, Sebastian had become her actual lover years before while the two of them labored and lived together in the Pérez household. Through the confluence of space and time, *bozales* and *criollos* mediated important cultural divisions—chasms which race and slavery, as abstractions, seemed unable to bridge.

When the enslaved Angolans Antón de la Cruz and Catalina entered the cathedral on August 18, 1631, their respective masters and the ecclesiastical authorities surely defined them as enslaved *bozales* from Angola. Through this process of classification, with its emphasis on legal status, cultural orientation, and national origins, the Spaniards ascribed meanings and behavior to Antón and Catalina. Even though they used the classification system of the Spaniards, the enslaved Angolans invested the inherited lexicon with meanings that enabled them to have both an endogamous marriage and a wedding party that included a 50-year-old free creole, someone they had known for ten years.[59]

Over the course of the seventeenth century, this scenario constantly repeated itself, revealing the importance of specific relationships, especially longstanding ones, as vehicles of community formation and the means whereby individuals, not collectivities, transcended social divisions. For instance on September 20, 1645, a 6-person entourage entered the cathedral in the quest for a marriage license. As the wedding party stood before the presiding officials, the four witnesses acknowledged having known the couple for an average of thirteen years. This assortment of Angolans, enslaved black creoles, and one free black creole had interacted with the prospective bride and groom María de la Cruz and Lorenso de la Cruz for a combined fifty years. Lucía, a 40-year-old enslaved Angolan, had had a 16-year relationship with her compatriot, Lorenzo. Juan Francisco, a 40-year-old enslaved creole, dated his interaction with Lorenzo back fourteen years. Both Jacinto de Torres and Dominga de la Cruz had known the prospective bride, the *india* María, for ten years. For this multicultural wedding party, years of sustained contact, mediated by their residence in Mexico's elite households, produced a community of familiars that the architects of the *república* had neither envisioned nor yet legislated against. It was possible for an indigenous free woman to take an enslaved Angolan as her spouse, but, more important, the couple maintained binding ties with individuals across one of the many imaginary divides.

Before sanctioning her purported transgressive behavior, the *provisor*, as a final reminder, asked María if she, a free woman, really wanted to marry a slave and thus agree to accompany him wherever he might be sent or sold. Even though the ecclesiastical judge brought legal status, and by implication race, into sharp relief, María insisted on marrying Lorenzo de la Cruz, her Angolan lover. Years of interaction with the enslaved and therefore allegedly distinct persons of African descent enabled María to transcend imposed differences. Juan Francisco, Dominga de la Cruz, Jacinto de Torres, Lucía, and Lorenzo de la Cruz also engaged each other and their familiars throughout the *traza* in a similar manner.[60] Three days after María de la Cruz and Lorenzo de la Cruz petitioned for their marriage license, another wedding party entered the cathedral. María and Lorenzo's Angolan entourage also manifested decade-old ties. Juan and María de la Cruz, the Angolan couple who served as Gracía and Francisco de la Cruz's witnesses, had maintained a 12-year relationship with their compatriots. Because of their ethnicity as Angolans, Francisco de la Cruz, Gracía, Juan, and María de la Cruz forged their ties through years of interaction in the *traza* during frequent daytime and nocturnal gatherings.[61]

Ethnicity, like cross-cultural ties, constituted a social expression. In the context of existing constraints, individuals made efforts to sustain specific relationships. Such relationships—initiated on the basis of symbolic similarities, linguistic affinities, spatial proximity, the experiential, and by chance—carried multiple meanings that scribes rarely captured. Despite the tendency of scholars to assign symbolic meanings to identifiable ethnic, racial, and cross-cultural patterns, the networks that emerge from the petitions reflect above all a process. Individuals established and sustained relationships with others who enabled them to define and acquire a specific cultural identity.

Process, as opposed to some immutable cultural essence, explains the ethnic composition of the wedding party of Gracía and Francisco de la Cruz, and the same dynamic explains why six days later Juan and Esperanza selected as witnesses the individuals that they did. Juan, an enslaved Angolan, and Esperanza, a black creole enslaved to Doña María Herrera, asked Juan Manuel and Pedro de Bustamante to serve as their matrimonial sponsors. Juan Manuel, a 40-year-old enslaved Angolan who belonged to Doña Ysabel de Estrada, had nurtured a relationship with his compatriot Juan for fourteen years and acknowledged having had more than a decade of interaction with Esperanza. Pedro, a 70-year-old enslaved Congo, testified that he had known Esperanza for a decade and Juan for eight years.[62]

Gregorio de la Cruz and Pasqual, two self-identified Angolans, informed the *provisor* that they had a relationship with their compatriots that dated back at least a decade. On July 9, 1631, 54-year-old Gregorio de la Cruz testified that his interaction with the couple Juan and Luísa began in 1619. Pasqual stated that he had known the couple for a period of ten years. Although Juan, Luísa, Gregorio, and Pasqual resided with their respective masters—Sebastian Gómez, Fabian Jimeno, Doña Luísa de Yslaba, and Licenciado Pedro de Galves —they frequented the streets beyond hearth and home in order to interact with persons similarly defined.[63]

Eight days after Gregorio and Pasqual requested their marriage petition, Alexandre and Margarita, like numerous other Angolans, petitioned the ecclesiastics for a marriage license. Although they were human chattel, they nonetheless longed for the sanctity of a Christian marriage even if this solemn ritual would not obligate their respective masters, Francisco Moran and Diego Juárez, to grant them actual cohabitation rights. Despite the possibility of a married life marked by physical separation, Alexandre and Margarita wanted the Church's approval. They had been atomized for years, and separation represented a normative condition around which Alexandre and Margarita organized their lives. This would explain why and how the marriage witnesses Pedro and Francisco maintained an 8-year relationship in spite of living in four different households. Pedro, an enslaved 40-year-old, lived near the barrio of Santa Clara while 30-year-old Francisco called Santo Domingo home. Alexandre and Margarita, in turn, resided respectively near the Hospital of the Holy Spirit and on the Street of the Doncellas.[64]

In that same year, Juan and Isabel, both "from Angola," also petitioned for a marriage license. Even though they resided in different barrios, Juan and Isabel had sustained their relationship and forged associations with others similarly defined. Both Manuel, whom the scribe described as a 30-year-old, and the self-identified 20-year-old Marcos had known the couple for six years.[65] In a different case two years later involving a marriage petition, four enslaved persons again brought into relief the long-standing and geographically extensive ties that united individuals from Angola. The 60-year-old Juan Francisco acknowledged having known Pedro and Cristina for an undetermined number of years, while Juan de la Cruz, a 30-year-old, had known the couple for eleven years. Although Juan Francisco and Cristina resided in the same neighborhood,

Santo Domingo, they belonged to different households. Ethnicity clearly bridged the physical chasm separating these two households and the distance between Cristina's barrio of Santo Domingo and Pedro's Santa María la Redonda neighborhood.[66] Despite ethnicity's bridging qualities, slavery—as a legal process, a form of labor, and, most important, an extension of each master's will—could metaphorically and actually lengthen distances between households and neighborhoods.

In contrast to most couples from Angola, Domingo and María seemed rather fortunate. Being owned by the same master enabled the couple to live together as husband and wife. Although their relationship flourished as a result of spatial proximity, Domingo and María consciously contracted ties with persons in different households who shared their ethnicity. Two of these individuals, García and Felipe de la Cruz, had known them both for eight years—a significant feat, given that their status as slaves placed onerous demands on their time and recreational mobility.[67] In Pablo and Lucretia's case, Pablo's occupational mobility as a fruitseller's slave enabled the couple to overcome their residential separation. In any case, they had sufficient mobility—occupational and recreational—to maintain an 8-year relationship with Miguel and Domingo, both "from Angola" yet owned by Diego Ramos.[68]

Mateo de la Cruz and Paula de la Cruz, enslaved and "from Angola," overcame their atomization. When their marriage witnesses, 36-year-old Diego de Torres and 30-year-old Domingo de la Cruz, came forth to testify on their behalf, both acknowledged having known Mateo and Paula for nine years.[69] In the same year, Pablo and Esperanza, who lived in separate households, also petitioned for a marriage license. Like countless other persons "from the land of Angola," this couple also asked their compatriots to sponsor them. Both 40-year-old Antonío de la Cruz and 20-year-old Marcos had known the prospective bride and groom for six years.[70]

Four years later, in 1637, Sebastian and Gracía also manifested their ethnicity. For them, roots in Angola played a crucial role in their selection of spouse and sponsors. After all, Gracía's owner Francisca de Reino, a free mulatto, underscored the limits of racial consciousness. Perhaps Gracía's *bozal* status initially prevented Francisca from manifesting a racial awareness that included her slave, but in 1637, at the time of the marriage petition, Gracía had been in New Spain for at least nine years. Pedro de Serrano, "from the land of Angola" who served as the couple's marriage witnesses, had known both Gracía and Sebastian for eight years. Sebastian, the second witness and Gracía and Sebastian's compatriot, had a 9-year acquaintance with the couple.[71] In 1640, 40-year-old Pablo and 36-year-old Gaspar de la Cruz, both enslaved and "from the land of Angola" informed the *provisor* that they knew and had interacted with the similarly defined Mateo de la Cruz and Gracía for twelve years.[72]

Table 4.1. Length of Time Witnesses of Angolan Couples
Were Acquainted with the Bride and/or Groom, 1595–1650

Amount of Time	Number of Individuals	Percentage
One year or less	3	—[1]
2–3 years	22	2
4–5 years	128	11
6–7 years	444	37
8–9 years	349	29
10–11 years	138	11
12–13 years	67	6
14–15 years	14	1
16–17 years	7	—[1]
18–19 years	2	—[1]
20–21 years	17	1
"Many years"	5	—[1]
Total	1,196	100[2]

1. Less than one percent.
2. The percentage total equals 100 percent once the relationships that accounted for less than one percent are factored in.
Source: AGN, Matrimonios.

By the 1640s, familiarity of this length was not unusual. On December 23,
1644, at the time that Antón, a 48-year-old, testified on behalf of the couple
Gaspar and Victoria, he had sustained a 6-year relationship with his compatriots. Pedro de la Cruz, in contrast, had known Gaspar for an undetermined
number of years but had interacted with Victoria for ten years. Antón, Pedro
de la Cruz, Victoria, and Gaspar had maintained their ties despite the fact that
they lived in diverse households throughout the viceregal capital.[73] Similarly, in
1645, at the time that he was 30, Juan had had a 12-year relationship with Francisco de la Cruz and Gracía, his compatriots from Angola. Juan had known his
wife, María de la Cruz, who was Francisco and Gracía's second witness, for at
least twelve years. María, a 40-year-old free creole "from Angola" also acknowledged knowing the prospective couple for twelve years though she lived in a
separate barrio.[74] As Francisco, Gracía, Juan, and María stood before the cathedral's presiding ecclesiastical officials on September 23, 1645, they literally embodied the thousands of Angolan social networks that flourished between the
1620s and the 1640s. Even as recently created communities, the Angolan networks had acquired a temporal depth that underscored individual tenacity and
the salience of ethnicity.

In fact, as Table 4.1 shows, 77 percent or 931 of the marriage witnesses in cases
involving persons "from Angola" testified having known the bride and groom
from six to eleven years. Although the largest number of witnesses, 37 percent,

had known the couple between six and seven years, 29 percent claimed a familiarity with the prospective bride or groom that had lasted between eight and nine years. Eighteen percent of the witnesses registered a relationship with one or both of the *novios* of between ten and thirteen years. Ten to thirteen years represented a substantial amount of time considering that most individuals were survivors of the middle passage, were enslaved, were unrelated, and resided in different households. The existence of such ties highlights the temporal, if not emotional, depth that the Angolan networks acquired prior to 1650. In the immediate aftermath of their arrival, the seemingly atomized individuals "from the land of Angola" had established a formidable, enduring, and mutually satisfying close-knit community.

Creoles

Creoles, who were largely but not exclusively defined as mulattos, also established extensive ties within the *traza*'s labyrinth, where some labored as slaves but most lived as freedpersons. Just as their parents defined themselves in relationship to symbolic geographical referents—the Indies, Guinea, and Castile—seventeenth-century creoles ascribed cultural meaning to New Spain as their birthplace. But New Spain's diverse and growing creole population displayed a marked affinity for other blacks and mulattos in the selection of matrimonial sponsors. Although this pattern reflected the currency of hypergamia —the phenomenon wherein one parent's heritage carried greater weight in defining the offspring—it also magnifies the metamorphosis of race into culture. In constructing and reproducing their networks, blacks and mulattos formalized what has been construed as racial endogamy. In actuality, these networks constituted a cultural dynamic in which the birthplace was racialized and lent a tenuous cohesiveness to the amorphous black and mulatto population.

In 1628, Ventura Díaz and his prospective bride, Ana, entered the Sagrario and requested a marriage license. Ventura, an enslaved mulatto, and Ana, an enslaved black woman and native of Mexico, belonged to Pedro Sierra, a textile-mill owner. The creole couple asked Andrés, Francisco, Mona, and Jusephe, all of whom were enslaved except Jusephe, to be their marriage witnesses. Andrés, a 40-year-old enslaved mulatto who labored in Pedro Sierra's textile mill, testified that he and Ventura had interacted for four years. Jusephe, the only free person among the witnesses, had known Ventura for an equal amount of time. Although the nature of Jusephe and Ventura's relationship remains a mystery, the former probably had been Pedro Sierra's employee. Francisco, a 26-year-old black man, stated that he had known Ana for a decade. Similarly, Mona, a 40-year-old mulatto, acknowledged having had an 8-year relationship with Ana.[75]

In contrast to Ana, a longtime resident of Pedro Sierra's textile mill, Ventura joined the sweatshop's labor force in 1624. Four years, however, constituted sufficient time for Ventura to establish enduring ties with his workmates. Ventura and Ana's decision to enlist Mona, Andrés, and Francisco as sponsors reflected more than their spatial proximity and creole heritage. A range of ethnic and cultural choices existed among Pedro Sierra's servant and slave population. Andrés, Juan de la Cruz, Manuel de la Cruz, Pedro Losano, and Nicolás de la Cruz were all creoles who toiled in Pedro Sierra's textile mill. What then explains Ana and Ventura's decision to choose Jusephe, Andrés, Francisco, and Mona to sponsor them?[76] Of course, a number of *bozales*, ladinos, mestizos, and Indians also toiled in the textile mill. Since creoles generally favored other creoles as confidants and companions, Ana and Ventura probably did as well.

As we shall see, most creole-*bozal* interaction centered on real and imagined kinship ties. Such ties and affinity born of a long-standing acquaintance narrowed the supposed cultural chasm distinguishing mulattos and black creoles from *bozales*. Indeed, from New Spain's inception, kinship and the memory of kin constituted key ingredients in community formation.

In 1628, Juan de la Cadena and Luísa de la Cruz, two free mulattos, asked Beatriz de los Reyes and Juan de Santiago to be their marriage witnesses. Juan de Santiago, an enslaved 34-year-old mulatto, had known the couple for twelve years. Beatriz, a 24-year-old free mulatto, had known Juan eight years and Luísa "since she was born because she is my sister . . . and we have always lived together." In choosing Beatriz, Luísa employed, from the Church's perspective, the ultimate legitimizing manifestation of sponsor authority—kinship. In mobilizing kinship, she also underscored the intimacy that existed between a prospective couple and their marriage witnesses.

Also in 1628, Francisco de Albarado, an enslaved mulatto widower, requested his second marriage license. Four years after his free mulatto wife, Juana Baptista, died, Francisco sought to marry a free mulatto, also called Juana. The prospective couple presented four witnesses who spoke with conviction about Francisco and Juana's single status. Juan, a 40-year-old enslaved Spanish-speaking African man "being from Mandigo country" testified that he had known the groom for a long time. Juan recalled that Francisco's first wife, Juana Baptista, had died four years earlier. Isabel de la Cruz, a 50-year-old black creole and native of Mexico, claimed a lifelong association with Francisco "since he is my cousin." Juana Baptista, the prospective bride, materialized ties of similar depth. Pedro Ramirez, a 50-year-old free mulatto, had known Juana "since [she was] a little girl." Ana María, a 50-year-old enslaved black creole, had known Juana "since she was born."[77]

Similarly, in 1629, an unnamed 50-year-old enslaved woman "from the land of Biafara" noted that Juan de Lomas, the prospective groom, was "her cousin."

The woman also had known María de Caseres, the prospective bride, for six years. Melchor Hernández, a 22-year-old free black creole and tailor, invoked his 8-year relationship with Juan and María to lend his testimony credence. The interaction between Juan de Lomas, María de Caseres, and Melchor Hernández probably began in their early teens, and nearly a decade later these ties still flourished.[78]

In 1629, Juan Esteban de San Diego and Pascual, two black creoles, relied on individuals similarly defined as creoles to be their marriage witnesses. The couple, however, also selected African-born sponsors who claimed kinship ties to the prospective bride. Juana de Ayala, a 46-year-old enslaved black creole, employed the language of kinship to describe her lifelong familiarity with Pascual. Juana proclaimed, "She is like [my] daughter." Simone Pérez, a 70-year-old person "from Mozambique," also employed kinship to buttress her testimony. But unlike Juana de Ayala, Simone invoked consanguinity ties. Simone informed the ecclesiastical judge that she had known Pascual since birth "due to being [my] daughter." Although both mothers, the real and the symbolic, resided in different households, they sustained their familial network—a network initially forged in Doña María de Castillo's household, where Juan de Ayala, Simone Pérez and possibly even Pascual once lived. Juan Esteban did not, however, mobilize kin. Instead, he called on two witnesses with whom he had a long-standing relationship. For Juan Esteban, such ties probably resembled those that Pascual shared with her two mothers.[79] Juan, a 50-year-old black creole, had known Juan Esteban—whom he referred to as Esteban—for twelve years. Francisco Hernández, a 34-year-old enslaved person "from the land of Congo," also testified the he and Esteban had interacted for twelve years. For the *provisor*, 12-year ties represented intimate familiarity and in all likelihood he granted Juan Esteban and Pascual their marriage license.

Also in 1629, Juan Pérez and María de Jesus presented Pasqual, Juan Fernández, Domingo, and Miguel Hernández as their marriage witnesses. Juan Fernández, a 22-year-old free mulatto, had known Juan for three years and recalled that his wife had died three years earlier. Pasqual, a 36-year-old free mulatto, did not raise the issue of Juan Pérez's first wife. Pasqual simply noted that he had known Juan "since he has the use of reason for he is my brother." Domingo, a 46-year-old "from the land of Bran," could not invoke such binding ties with María de Jesus. Still, Domingo informed the *provisor* that he had interacted with the prospective bride "many years" and that her mulatto husband, Bartolomé de Durante, had died eight years previously. Miguel Hernández, a 30-year-old enslaved black creole, simply testified that he had known María for nine years. In lieu of a legitimizing kinship relationship, Miguel relied on his long-standing familiarity with María.[80]

An identical case involved Francisco Rodriguez and Juana de Bustamante, mulattos who were enslaved to different masters. Miguel Sánchez, a 30-year-old mestizo, and Juan de Alcala, a 36-year-old free mulatto, testified that they had known Francisco for eight years and recalled that his wife had died two months previously. In contrast, María de Bustamante, a 38-year-old free mulatto, had known the bride "since she was born because she is her sister." Ana de Bustamante, a 60-year-old free black and wife of Miguel, a Spaniard, spoke with even more authority, claiming that "she [was] the legitimate mother of Juana de Bustamante," to whom she had given birth twenty years before.

In 1633, Catalina, an enslaved 56-year-old "from Terra Nova" also evoked the ultimate signifier when she acknowledging knowing Diego Pascual, an enslaved black creole, whom she claimed was single and free to marry. "He is my son," exclaimed Catalina when asked why and how long she had known Diego. Domingo Nicolás's testimony on his friend's behalf paled in comparison. The 26-year-old mestizo had known Diego for only five years. Juan Diego and María Magdalena, two Nahuas, informed the *provisor* through a translator that they had known the 25-year-old Nahua, Juana Francisca, Diego's prospective bride, for twelve and ten years respectively.[81]

A final case from 1633 involved Pedro, an enslaved mulatto, and Ana María, his 18-year-old mestiza girlfriend. Andrés Reyes, a 25-year-old enslaved mulatto, had known the groom for twenty years "because he is his brother." Andrés also had known the prospective bride, Ana María, but only for five years. Antón de la Cruz, a 48-year-old free negro and poultry vendor, informed the *provisor* that "since he was a little boy" he had known the widower Pedro. Like Andrés, Pedro's brother, Antón had known Ana María for only five years. Relatives and friends often dated their acquaintance with a prospective bride or groom with the onset of courtship rather than reveal the actual length of their familiarity. Andrés and Antón were probably familiar with Ana María longer than indicated in their testimony but only noted the length of time that she and their Pedro had been a couple.[82]

Individuals often reckoned familiarity in several different ways, two of which—the initial encounter and the onset of courtship—were probably inscribed into the historical record as testimony. But as the following case illustrates, this was not always true. In 1635, Diego de Solís, a 32-year-old enslaved mulatto, and Juana de Ortega, a free mulatto, approached an ecclesiastical scribe to request a marriage license. The scribe recorded their testimony and that of the marriage witnesses, Jusephe de Ortega and Miguel de Angus. Miguel, a 30-year-old mestizo servant, acknowledged having known Diego "a long time" and the bride for three years. According to Jusephe, a 42-year-old enslaved mulatto, both Diego and Juana were free to marry. Jusephe justified his claims because he had known Juana "since . . . she was born and . . . [in] respect of being his daughter."[83] Jusephe clearly had known Diego for some time, but that relationship was sure to change with Diego's impending marriage to his daughter. Surely this marriage would transform their friendship, or mere acquaintance, into something more elaborate and binding.

The same held true for Juan Antonío and Pedro de Torrijo, two free mulattos. In 1640, Pedro and his girlfriend Gregoria Hernández, a free mulatto, petitioned for a marriage license and presented Francisco de Caraballo and Juan Antonío as their witnesses. Francisco, a 40-year-old free mulatto, had known Pedro five years and Gregoria "since she was born." Juan, a 40-year-old, had known the prospective groom for twenty years and Gregoria since birth, for, as he noted, "she is my daughter." Since Pedro had begun courting Gregoria, his daughter, the relationship between the two men had probably changed. But after a 20-year relationship, their ties may not have been significantly affected by the marriage.[84] Kinship represented formidable ties, but so did a 20-year relationship. Ties of such longevity often approximated biological ties in depth and meaning.

In 1640, Ignacio de Figueroa, an enslaved black creole, and his prospective free mulatto bride, Ana María, called on Gerónimo Gómez and Juan Antonío as marriage witnesses. Juan Antonío, a free black, had known the couple "since they were children." Similarly, Gerónimo Gómez, a 54-year-old free black, testified that he lived in Don Figueroa's house and had interacted with Ignacio and Ana María "since they were infants." As long-standing intimates, Gerónimo and Juan Antonío probably constituted the core of Ignacio and Ana María's social network.[85]

A final example illustrates how creoles conflated long-standing familiarity and kinship ties. In 1646, Nicolás de Buena Ventura, an enslaved black creole, and Juana de la Cruz, a free mulatto, presented Nicolás and Jusephe de Eschevaria as their marriage witnesses. Nicolás, of whom nothing is known except his age, had known the couple for twelve years, or since the age of six. Jusephe, a free mulatto, had known Juana ten years and Nicolás for many years more, "for he was his brother."[86] Such ties, as we have seen, were far from unusual. Although creole and ethnic African networks were New World creations, creoles marshaled many more relatives as marriage witnesses, who, in turn, used the language of kinship as the legitimizing source in their testimony.

In 1628, Nicolás Sánchez de Contreras, an enslaved mulatto, and Catalina, an enslaved woman "from Terra Nova," asked Diego de la Cruz and Antonío to sponsor them as marriage witnesses. Antonío, a 25-year-old enslaved mulatto, had known both Nicolás and Catalina eight years, although the nature of their relationship remains a mystery. Diego, a 26-year-old black creole, had known the prospective groom for five years and the bride for ten. Nicolás and Catalina's marriage petition underscores the cultural diversity of some creole communities. Nicolás, an enslaved mulatto whose mother was "from the land of Congo," wanted to marry a West African woman. Bride and groom relied on two enslaved creoles, both of whom they had known for a long time, as their marriage witnesses. Clearly, a multiethnic African-creole network united Nicolás, Catalina, Diego, and Antonío.[87] This and similar such networks reflected the cultural diversity manifest even among these seventeenth-century descendants of Africans. But cultural diversity does not explain how multiethnic and multicultural social networks emerged. Most African-born individuals and, especially, creoles resided among a plethora of servants and slaves. Still, many had the desire and the means to establish ties with persons of their choosing, most notably individuals similarly defined. Persons who maintained culturally diverse networks irrespective of ethnic and cultural boundaries did so willfully.

In 1629, Cristóbal and María, two enslaved persons from Angola belonging to two different masters, petitioned the ecclesiastical judge for a marriage license. The couple presented Pascual, an enslaved mulatto, and Diego Hernández, Antonío Hernández, and Pablo de la Cruz, three enslaved Spanish-speaking Africans, as their marriage witnesses. Pablo and Diego only revealed that María's first husband had died that previous year, thus implying that she was free to marry Cristóbal. Antonío and Pablo informed the *provisor* "in the Castillian language" that they had known Cristóbal ten years. Although the genesis of their relationship remains unknown, after ten years, firm, if not binding, ties probably united the trio of Antonío, Pablo, and Cristóbal. Even Pascual, Diego Hernández, and María shared a long-standing relationship. Both witnesses knew precisely when Pablo, her former husband, had died. During the marriage proceedings, revelation about the death of a spouse superseded familiarity. After all, the Church's interest resided with impediments, actual and potential, and not with the length of time a witness had known the bride or groom. Nonetheless, in this case, cultural differences manifested themselves. Although María, "from Angola," had previously married a man "from the land of Bran," now she wished to marry her compatriot. Despite their affinity as persons "from Angola," the couple relied on various individuals whose command of Castilian obscured their ethnic and cultural identities. Spatially separated members of the wedding party still maintained contact despite the influence of ethnicity.[88]

In the same year that Cristóbal and María petitioned for their marriage license, Gregorio de Esperalta and Pascual de Alohera also requested permission to marry. The mulatto couple lived in different households and did not share the same legal status. They presented a diverse assortment of marriage witnesses, including Lucas and Ana, enslaved black creoles, and Miguel, an enslaved person "from the Congo," all of whom resided with their respective employers. Though atomized, the prospective bride and groom and their witnesses had interacted for years. Lucas, a 25-year-old, had known Pascual fifteen years and Gregorio eight. Ana, a 40-year-old, had known Gregorio "since . . . he was an infant and afterwards saw him grow." Miguel, a 50-year-old "from the Congo," had known Pascual for ten years, but the circumstances of their interaction remains unknown.[89] In any case, the familiarity maintained over many years represented something meaningful to this diverse assortment of friends and familiars. In fact, their ties stood in for kinship. Ana signified as much when she stated that she had known Gregorio "since . . . he was an infant and afterwards she saw him grow."

Similarly, Diego de Medina, a free mulatto who was a shoemaker, informed the *provisor* in 1629 that he had known Matheo Rodriguez, the free mulatto who wished to contract marriage with Maríana Carces, also a free mulatto, "since he [had] the use of reason [for] they grew up together in the city of Oaxaca." Pedro, a 23-year-old enslaved mulatto, expressed similar sentiments when testifying that he had known Matheo "since he knew how to remember." For Pedro and Diego, their lifelong relationship with Matheo, which began in Oaxaca, constituted familial ties. Indeed, on the basis of their ages, the three mulattos may have been childhood playmates who as adult friends saw and spoke of one another as brothers. Maríana, in contrast, did not select matrimonial sponsors who had known her as a child in a distant province. She called on Juana Bautista, a free mulatto who had known her for merely five years, and Juana Lopez, a Nahua woman who had known her for fifteen years.[90] Such ties paled when contrasted with Matheo's but they were meaningful to Maríana and, above all, sufficient for the *provisor*.

In 1633, Juan de la Cruz and Agustína de Nava, both free mulattos, presented two other free mulattos as their marriage witnesses. Juan de la Cadena, a 35-year-old, had known Juan and Agustína nine years. Luísa, the second witness and Juan de la Cadena's 24-year-old wife, also had known Juan for nine years but acknowledged having known Agustína "since the so said was an infant." Evidently among creoles a continuum existed in which childhood friends became lovers and confidants. And it is from this same pool that creoles selected their matrimonial sponsors, underscoring the importance individuals accorded the role.

Middle Passages

The African-born and creoles skillfully circumvented the existing structural and spatial constraints that isolated them from their ethnic compatriots, cultural affines, relatives, and long-standing friends. While most of these constraints reflected elite residential and slaveholding patterns, their mobility—across the Atlantic and throughout the Indies—represented another obstacle.

Although elite migratory patterns and the mobilization of labor truncated affinity and consanguinity ties among *bozales* and creoles, a number of individuals still maintained contact with friends and relatives after traversing the Atlantic. The extant testimony of marriage witnesses underscores the tenacity with which *bozales*, ladinos, and creoles sustained ties forged in Africa. Even as the most dispersed and atomized individuals of a culture in movement, they made conscious choices about the composition of their social networks.

In 1584—soon after marriage petitions became a regular feature in New Spain—Duarte and Polonia requested a marriage petition.[91] Duarte, a slave "from Bio-Bio land" declared that he had arrived in New Spain "more or less" three years before. He then presented Antón as his witness. Antón vouched for Duarte's single status, basing it on their familiarity not only in Guinea but especially in Biafara, from where they had left together for New Spain. Polonia, Duarte's future wife, claimed to originate from "the land of the Brun." She also drew on ties that extended across the Atlantic. Her first witness, María, identified "the land of the Mandinga" as home. María attested that she had known Polonia "in Guinea." Next, María observed that they, together "with other black men and women, *bozales*, were brought on a ship to Santo Domingo and from there to this land [New Spain] and afterwards arrived in Mexico City."[92] Francisca was one of those *bozales* brought over with Polonia and María. She served as Polonia's second witness. The 25-year-old slave recalled having known Polonia for five years "because we came together on a boat from the land of Brun."[93] After considering the testimony of persons who had known the couple prior to becoming "Duarte" and "Polonia," the *provisor* issued the required license.[94]

The *provisor* also granted Gaspar and María a marriage license after hearing the declarations of their witnesses.[95] Gaspar, simply identified as a black slave, presented four witnesses—Juan, Andrés, Juan, and Juan. Juan, who claimed to be "from the land of Congo" had known Gaspar ten years, declaring that "he knew him in Jérez de la Frontera in the kingdoms of Castile." After going their respective ways four years previously, they had reestablished contact in Mexico.[96] On the basis of this intimacy and continued contact in Mexico— though they had different masters—Juan testified that Gaspar was single. Andrés, a mestizo of 31 years, also dated his familiarity with Juan back to Castile. In his statement, Andrés acknowledged having known Gaspar "since he was a boy of four in Jérez de la Frontera." In Mexico, the two men reconnected after a gap of several years and now interacted with regularity.[97] The second Juan, a black slave, also dated his interaction with Gaspar back to Castile. Aside from this detail, he had no more to say. The third Juan, a Spaniard, provided the ecclesiastical judge with more specific information. As a native of Jérez de la Frontera, he recalled that "since I could remember" Gaspar had always been in his life. From Castile, the childhood acquaintances had traveled to New Spain on the same ship. The extent of their interaction assured the *provisor* that the third Juan could vouch for Gaspar's single status.[98] María did not offer witnesses who had known her in Jérez de la Frontera. In fact, the free mulatto had never been to Castile. Instead she presented a Spanish-speaking Indian who was her sister. As sisters with the same mother "but not father," the woman testified that on the basis that she had known her "since she could remember," María was single. In addition to her sister, María also offered her employers, Doña Petronila and Francisco de Casteñeda, as witnesses. Both dated their acquaintance with María to four years before, when "she began to serve in our house."[99] With this evidence, the *provisor* granted the prospective husband and wife their required license.

In 1591, Antón and María, two enslaved persons who respectively came "from the land of Bran" and "from Terra Nova," requested a marriage license. As María and Antón manifested their desires in accented Spanish, the couple presented four African-born marriage witnesses. Even as forced migrants and chattel of different masters, the wedding party had maintained their ties to each other—ties forged prior to their arrival in the Indies. Indeed, these ties highlight the symbolic weight accorded to the middle passage—a forced migration that began on the African continent and only ended when the victims had entered elite households in Europe or the Indies—as a defining experience. Francisco, a 30-year-old enslaved person "from the land of Bran" informed the ecclesiastical authorities of his 6-year relationship with María. Francisco probably introduced María to his compatriot and her future husband, Antón, soon after the latter's arrival in Mexico in 1586. Antón, a 40-year-old enslaved person "from the Congo," had known María for a year longer than had Francisco. A second Francisco, who was also enslaved and "from Bran land" testified that he had known Antón for five years. Francisco revealed how he initially interacted with Antón on Cape Verde Island "in the land of Guinea, where they embarked on a boat for this New Spain and they came together on the said boat to the port of San Juan de Ulua." Antón, another enslaved person who experienced the middle passage with Francisco and Antón, also noted that his interaction with the latter had begun on Cape Verde five years ago. After shipping them to Veracruz, the captors of both Antóns and Francisco transported their human cargo to Mexico City, eventually selling them to separate owners. Despite their separation, the former shipmates continued to interact. An imagined ethnicity as "Brans"—in which Cape Verde and subsequently Mexico City constituted mediating sites—shaped the relationships among Francisco, Antón, and the Francisco with whom María had a long-standing association. The ties that were formed during the trauma of the middle passage, which individuals experienced with persons of other ethnicities, precluded the emergence of an exclusive "Bran" social network. Francisco and Antón defined themselves as being "from the land of Bran," but the terror they experienced with the other Antón created a bond with him that tempered any desire for ethnic exclusivity. At the time of Francisco's and Antón's arrival, "Brans" found it very difficult to sustain their most intimate interaction with persons similarly defined; the proliferation of West Central Africans and creoles overshadowed the former ascendancy of the West Africans.[100]

A marriage petition from 1631 underscores Cape Verde's importance as both transitory port and cultural site. Whereas Francisco and Antón invoked Cape Verde as a mediating referent, Pablo de la Cruz actually relied on the island for his ethnicity. In petitioning for a marriage license, Pablo de la Cruz identified himself as a "negro from Cape Verde." His witness, Antonío Mendoza, also claimed Cape Verde as his territorial referent, noting that "since he has the use of reason he has known Pablo de la Cruz . . . for he is like his brother and he knows that he never has married." Evidently, Antonío and Pablo had arrived in Mexico in 1625, since the former testified that he had known the prospective bride for six years, whereas Felipe, enslaved and "from Angola," had known the prospective groom for the same amount of time. In turn, Miguel de la Cruz, enslaved and "from the land of Angola" dated his interaction with his compatriot and Pablo's prospective bride, Luísa, back to 1624.[101] As these and numerous other examples illustrate, individuals accorded the passage across the Atlantic great significance that, in turn, mitigated the differences that had distinguished them in Guinea and in the Indies. In short, the shared experience of the middle passage could and often did obviate the symbolic boundaries around and through which difference flourished.

For a brief moment in the seventeenth century, as we have seen, persons claiming "Angola" as their symbolic referent confronted circumstances that enabled those who so desired to establish ethnically cohesive social networks. Although the intimacy uniting "Angolans" largely represented an American creation, some individuals maintained relationships initially forged on or adjacent to the African continent. In 1595, a 25-year-old enslaved woman "from Angola," Luísa, testified that Isabel was single and thus able to contract matrimony with Pedro, also "from Angola." Luísa, a resident of Mexico City since 1592, testified that her relationship with Isabel had begun on São Tomé, where as children "they had interacted and communicated very closely." In 1591, their lives on the Atlantic island ended abruptly when the Portuguese shipped both to New Spain. The childhood friends and compatriots still maintained contact in Mexico and even interacted with other persons "from the land of Angola" who were owned by different masters. In 1595, three years after her arrival,

Isabel petitioned to marry Pedro, another recent arrival "from the land of Angola." Isabel asked her shipmate, compatriot, and friend, Luísa, to testify on her behalf.[102]

The maintenance of preexisting relationships was far from unusual. Despite the preponderance of cultural affines, *bozales* often interacted with individuals with whom they had shared transoceanic voyages. The frequency of this pattern reveals that individuals who were isolated from their affines used the middle passage as a marker of community. For many individuals, ties forged in the fetid confines of coastal factories and in the stench-filled holds of the slave ships constituted the ontological moment from which they dated their new identities. Invariably and irrespective of existing identities, some individuals defined those who had shared the coffle with them on the middle passage as kin and relied on them as marriage witnesses.[103]

In 1610, Anton and Petrona requested a marriage license. They were enslaved by different masters, and ethnicity had become a salient feature of their New World existence. Petrona identified herself as a "black woman from Biafara land" and presented Francisco and Ana as her witnesses. Francisco, a 50-year-old compatriot from the "land of Biafara," had known Petrona for ten years, while Ana, a 40-year-old "from the land of Bran," had interacted with the prospective bride for eight years. Anton, in turn, asked Juan and Francisco de la Cruz to be his witnesses. Juan, a 25-year-old enslaved *chino*, testified that he had known Anton for seven years, four in Manila. Francisco, a 30-year-old enslaved *chino*, had known Anton for four years and recalled that "he knew [him] and interacted in the city of Manila where they interacted a year and at the end of the said year they traveled together . . . on a boat."[104]

Juan del Castillo and María de Esquivel's marriage petition represented a similar scenario. Juan, an enslaved mulatto and native of Spain, asked Francisco and Antonío, long-standing acquaintances, to serve as his marriage witnesses. Francisco, 34, enslaved and "from Terra Nova," had known Juan "nine years in Seville where both were slaves of distinct masters and came to Mexico on the same fleet five years ago." Antonío, a 23-year-old native of Ayamonte in Castile identifying himself as an enslaved black man, declared that he had interacted with Juan for eight years in Seville and they had come to Mexico together on the same fleet. María, an enslaved *china* "from the Portuguese Indies," also relied on ties forged prior to her arrival in New Spain. She called on Lorenzo de Molino, a 30-year-old enslaved *chino* who had known her twelve years. According to Lorenzo, they initially met in Manila but had interacted in Mexico for ten years "because they came on the same ship." In Mexico, María established contact with other *chinos*, including Nicolás de Govera, an enslaved 30-year-old, with whom she had an 8-year relationship at the time that she petitioned for a marriage license.[105] The increasing presence of *chinos* in the archival records indicates that Mexico's *chino* population experienced growth in the first half of the seventeenth century.

In 1629, Jacinto de Torres, an enslaved *chino*, and Gertrudis de San Nicolas, his enslaved mulatto lover, petitioned for a marriage license. Although they lived in separate households, the couple had interacted for years and even relied on the same marriage witnesses. Pedro de la Cruz, a 30-year-old enslaved *chino*, acknowledged having known Gertrudis for five years and Jacinto "since he knew how to remember for they grew up together as little boys in the city of Manila." Five years after their arrival in Mexico, even though they lived in different households, they sustained a relationship initially forged in the Philippines. Simon Lopez, a 38-year-old free *chino*, had probably introduced Jacinto to Gertrudis, since he had had an 8-year relationship with the latter and met the former soon after his arrival in Mexico.[106]

Despite the growing presence of *chinos* in the archival record and their proclivity for partners of African descent, most preexisting relationships among the enslaved involved individuals from the Atlantic world or the Spanish Indies. In 1612, Juan, an enslaved creole from Peru, and María, a free mulatto, entered the Sagrario and petitioned for a marriage license. Juan de Astudillo, an enslaved mulatto, and María, a Spanish-speaking Indian, testified on María's behalf. Juan, an 18-year-old, had known María eleven years, which suggests that the two of them had been childhood playmates who maintained contact as adults. María's acquaintance with the prospective bride was relatively new. The two women had known each other for only four years. Similarly, Pedro, a 30-year-old enslaved person "from the Congo," had known the groom for three years. But Juan, an 18-year-old enslaved mulatto, had a long-standing relationship with Juan, the prospective groom, which began in Peru.[107]

Similarly, Juan de Angula, a free black creole and a 39-year-old widower, asked Alexandro and Juan Alonso, acquaintances from Peru, to serve as his marriage witnesses. Alexandro, a black creole, had known Juan ten years and noted that his wife had died three years previously. Both he and Juan, according to Alexandro, left "the city of the Kings in Peru" and arrived "in this kingdom together . . . two years ago." Juan Alonso, an indigenous servant, native of "the city of the Kings, Peru" and a "ladino in the Castilian language," stated that he had known Juan for eight years. Juan Alonso, Alexandro, and Juan, in fact, had arrived in New Spain together and there utilized their identities as Peruvians as markers of community. In contrast, Juan de Angula's prospective bride, Clemensia, a black creole who was a lifelong resident of Mexico, only marshaled Anton, enslaved and "from Angola," whom she had known for eight years.[108]

In 1633, a different creole couple demonstrated the geographic range that relationships could span. In that year, Diego de la Cruz and Joanna de Jesus, enslaved black creoles who belonged to different masters, petitioned for a marriage license. What is interesting about this case is that the witnesses knew both the bride and the groom. It is thus likely that Diego and Joanna had been acquainted for some time, since creoles, in contrast to *bozales* and ladinos, rarely shared marriage witnesses. In any case, their witnesses Francisco and Lucas had both known Diego for six years. The enslaved creoles and former Cartagena natives expressed greater familiarity with Joanna, for they had known her since childhood. Francisco, in fact, testified that "they came together to this city where they now are." For Lucas, Francisco, and Joanna, the ties forged in Cartagena represented formidable links with the past and still resonated in their present lives.[109] As the extant marriage petitions illustrate, creoles, like those born in Africa, often sustained relationship that spanned vast distances, including the Atlantic Ocean.

In 1620, Juan, an enslaved black creole "from the city of Toledo in the kingdom of Castile" informed the *provisor* that he had known Francisco, a Spanish-speaking African and native from the Palm Islands, for eight years. Juan, a 20-year-old, noted that their acquaintance had begun in Seville and continued in "this kingdom." A different Juan, who was also 20 years old, enslaved, and a creole but a native of Seville, testified that he had known Juan, the prospective groom, for six years "in the city of Seville and in this kingdom." Magdalena, Juan's prospective bride, identified herself as an enslaved native of Mexico. Nonetheless, she relied on two enslaved men, one "from Angola" and the other a black creole from Cartagena, as her witnesses. Miguel, a 40-year-old "from Angola," and another Miguel, a 20-year-old black creole, had known Magdalena for six years. The reason they knew each other remains rather elusive.[110]

In Diego de Sevilla and Agustína's case, however, the relationship between the marriage witnesses and the prospective couple is quite explicit. In 1628, Agustína, a free mulatta, petitioned to marry Diego, a free black man. Though Diego migrated from Seville, he, in contrast to Agustína, maintained formidable ties with kin and affines, who subsequently served as his marriage witnesses. Juana Machado, a 40-year-old free mulatto, informed the *provisor* that she had known Diego "since he was born for he was her nephew." Juana also testified on behalf of Agustína, whom she had known for eight years. Petronilla, a 26-year-old Spanish-speaking black woman, could not claim consanguinity ties but noted that she had known Diego "since he was born." In the *provisor*'s eyes, Petronilla's appropriation of symbolic kinship metaphors validated her testimony. Like Juana, Petronilla stated that she had known Agustína for eight years, indicating perhaps that Agustína had been a long-standing associate of theirs prior to becoming Diego's companion.[111]

In 1629, Francisco, "a black man from the city of Lisbon, Portugal" requested a marriage license to marry Juana, "a *negra* from Seville." According to Juan de

Rojas, a Spaniard like Juana, Francisco had been a widower for one of the seven years that he had known him. Francisco, a 30-year-old enslaved black creole, had known Francisco, the prospective groom, and his former wife for five years. Juana drew on more geographically expansive ties in selecting her marriage witnesses. She asked Juan Francisco, a 40-year-old free black who had known Juana in Seville for nine years; Juan recalled that she had come to Mexico City five years previously. Francisco, a 32-year-old enslaved Wolofo, had known Juana twelve years—five in Mexico and seven in Seville, "being both the slaves of the Capitán." Felipa, a 30-year-old enslaved woman "from the Congo" had known Juana fifteen years. She recalled the ten years they had spent together in Seville and that they had arrived in the Indies "on the same ship and fleet." After the "Capitán" sold them in Mexico, Felipa, Francisco, and Juana maintained contact. For them and for Francisco, Europe symbolized the site of their cultural formation—a phenomenon that Francisco and Juana manifested in their marriage to each other and the selection of their marriage witnesses.[112]

Simón de la Cruz demonstrated a similar tendency. In the same year that Francisco and Juana petitioned to contract their marriage, Simón and Francisca de la Concepción, an enslaved woman "from Angola," also requested a marriage license. Simón, who defined himself as an enslaved black man and native of Lisbon, had resided in Mexico City for eight years prior to his marriage petition. Eight years after they left together on the same fleet, Simón still maintained contact with Antonío Juárez, an enslaved person "from the land of Bran" whom he had known "since the so said had been an infant in the city of Lisbon." Despite Antonío's ethnicity and Simón's cultural status as a Portuguese of African descent, they both held steadfastly to ties forged in Europe. As a result of Antonío's nationality, however, Simón met and subsequently interacted with Domingo, a 30-year-old who was also "from the land of Bran," who testified that he had known the prospective groom for eight years. Although Francisca, the prospective bride, contracted marriage with a Portuguese, she drew on her nationality in the selection of a marriage sponsor. Antonío Lopez de la Cruz, an enslaved 40-year-old "from the land of Angola," acknowledged having known the bride for seven years, while Lucretia, a 44-year-old who defined herself similarly, testified that she had known Francisca for six years.[113]

In that same year, 1629, Juan, an enslaved mulatto and native of Seville, and Juana, an enslaved mulatto, requested a marriage license even though they belonged to different masters. Even though she was a native of New Spain, Juana lacked long-standing ties with individuals on whom she could rely as marriage witnesses. Juan, a 28-year-old enslaved creole, had known Juliana for a mere four years, and Pedro, a 20-year-old mestizo, claimed a 5-year relationship. In contrast, the testimony of Juan's witnesses reveals an emotional depth that united him with Gerónimo and Antonío de Roma. Gerónimo, a 36-year-old free mulatto, had known Juan for fourteen years and noted that six years earlier they had come to New Spain on the same ship. Antonío, a 36-year-old "from the land of Mozambique," recalled how he and Juan had been enslaved in Sevilla but had come to New Spain six years previously. Even with different masters in Seville and in New Spain, Antonío and Juan sustained their relationship. Again, we see how ties forged on the Iberian peninsula survived the Atlantic passage and enabled individuals in disparate households, though divided by nationality, culture, and legal status, to draw on these formative relationships at critical moments.[114]

In some instances, individuals brought actual kin across the Atlantic. Both Antón Sardina, an enslaved mulatto from Castile, and Ana de la Concepción, a free mulatto, called on their respective kin as marriage witnesses. For Antón, this was somewhat more difficult, since he identified himself as a native of Castile. Pedro de Moratella, a 50-year-old Spaniard, had known Antón for some sixteen years and dated their relationship back to Castile. Gaspar Ramírez, another Spaniard, had known Antón thirty years, noting that "they had grown up together." Gaspar, a 40-year-old, informed the *provisor* that nearly thirty years after his departure from Castile they had reestablished contact. Isabel, a 60-year-old enslaved woman "from Angola," referred to her relationship with Antón in kinship terms. Recalling that she had known Antón since his birth, Isabel stated that Antón "is like her son and they came to New Spain together" nearly three years before. Domingo Xuárez, a 38-year-old enslaved mulatto, had known Ana for fourteen years. According to Domingo, Ana had been a widow for some time and was free to remarry since Marcos, Ana's first husband, had drowned several years after he escaped from a textile mill. Lazaro de Navaez, a 43-year-old black man, also recalled that Ana was a widow. For the *provisor*, evidence of a former marriage and the legitimate means whereby it ended seemed far more important than the exact number of years that Lazaro and Ana actually had known each other. Isabel, a 44-year-old free woman, invoked the ultimate expression of familiarity when she told the *provisor* about her sibling tie to Ana. But as Ana's sister, Isabel did not divulge more than Domingo or Lazaro about her sister's former marriage. She merely noted that Marcos, her former brother-in-law, had fled from a textile mill eleven years previously but had later died in a river near the port of Acapulco. With regard to her sister's marriage, Isabel did not know or perhaps was unwilling to reveal any more than Domingo and Lazaro. For the *provisor*, however, Isabel's information sufficed, and he granted Ana and Anton their marriage license.[115]

Sustaining ties across the scope of the Spanish world was an impressive feat for merchants and officials. For enslaved persons, however, this constituted a truly remarkable accomplishment. As persons whose mobility was restricted in accordance with their masters' whims, ties of this magnitude speak to the value that individuals placed on them. It would always have been easier to select a passing acquaintance as a matrimonial sponsor. But the creoles and *bozales* who petitioned for a marriage petition forsook that option. This decision highlights the symbolic weight *bozales* and creoles accorded to sponsor selection.

By 1650, Mexico City's resident *bozales*, ladinos, black creoles, and mulattos were sustaining elaborate social networks that crisscrossed the viceregal capital, New Spain, and the monarch's diverse kingdoms. As slaves and servants, the African-born utilized elite residential, slaveholding, and migratory patterns for unintended purposes. Together with the growing number of black creoles and mulattos, they formed their social networks within the structural confines of the masters' world. As the diverse persons of African descent constructed their communities, they disregarded the compartmentalized perspective of the master-slave divide and the social design of imperial policymakers. For Africans and their creole descendants, the imposed patterns of social stratification and their own community boundaries were very different phenomena.

The marriage petitions, which capture the minutiae of community formation, highlight the social channels that touched virtually every elite household and in the process defined the *traza*'s human cartography. The marriage petitions, like other regulating sources, reify forms of identification precisely because they capture a specific moment in the Christian life cycle during which the Church and members of the flock called on individuals to substantiate truth claims and as sponsors to usher others along the Christian path. At crucial moments in the life cycle—baptism, confirmation, marriage, and extreme unction—when individuals interacted with the regulatory features of the Church, they called on persons with whom they had the most established relationships, notably family, friends, and clients, and, occasionally, patrons. Like the moments themselves, the individuals called upon varied according to the situation and circumstances. Yet in all cases, the ecclesiastical proceedings required individuals to identify themselves by existing classificatory schemes. Although they are not a reflection of the more haphazard and routine social interaction that typified the experiences of people in Mexico City and New Spain, these invaluable sources reflect a regulatory moment that accentuated and reinscribed formal relationships.

5 Between Property and Person
Jurisdictional Conflicts over Marriage

> The effort to reconstruct the history of the dominated is not discontinuous with
> dominant accounts or official history but, rather, is a struggle within and against
> the constraints and silences imposed by the nature of the archive—the system
> that governs the appearance of statements and generates social meaning.[1]

On April 2, 1579, the ecclesiastical judge and vicar general of New Spain's archdiocese, Dr. Don Sancho Sánchez de Muñon, received a petition from Antón,
an enslaved black man who resided in Mexico City with his owner, Alonso de
Estrada. In his petition, Antón noted that several years previously he had married Inés, an enslaved black woman in "the Holy Mother Church." After the
death of the couple's mistress, Antonío de Reinoso, a resident of Puebla, purchased the couple. Reinoso, in turn, sold Antón to Alonso de Estrada, a resident
of Mexico, but retained Inés. Antón lamented that "my master wanted to buy
. . . my wife" but Reinoso, his erstwhile owner, simply refused. Undaunted by
Antonío de Reinoso's callousness and insisting on having a married life with
Inés "as my legitimate wife," Antón implored the ecclesiastical judge to act on
his behalf.[2]

Two days after receiving Antón's petition, the *provisor* instructed Antón to
substantiate his marital claims. On April 6th, Antón presented Lucas, an enslaved black man who lived in Mexico with his master, Don Luís de Sosa.
The 55-year-old Lucas testified in the presence of a notary that he had a long-
standing relationship with both Antón and Inés. Lucas, who was present at
their wedding in the cathedral, proclaimed that the couple "were betrothed and
married in accordance with the Holy Mother Church." He also recalled seeing
Antón and Inés in Juan Alonso de Sosa's household behaving as "husband and
wife." Lucas concluded his testimony, noting that "he heard it said" that Inés
lived with another master in the city of Angeles, a vernacular reference to
Puebla.[3]

The next day, Antón stood before a different notary with Juan Alonso de
Sosa in tow. Acquainted with both Antón and Inés since the time they served
his wife, Ana de Estrada, Juan Alonso recalled that the couple had lived in his
household "as husband and wife." He also noted that after his wife's death, Antón and Inés moved in rapid succession from one master to another. Juan
Alonso owned the couple until his wife's death and then António de Reinoso

acquired possession of Antón and Inés. Like Lucas before him, Juan Alonso acknowledged that António de Reinoso kept Inés after selling Antón.[4] With this testimony, and merely four days after he received Antón's petition, Sánchez de Muñon ordered António de Reinoso to send Inés to Mexico, "where she is freely able to have a married life with the said Antón her husband." He also decreed that António de Reinoso should not remove Inés from Mexico "nor impede the marriage between the so said." By threatening this Spanish master with both excommunication and a stiff fine unless he complied within six days, the *provisor* acted decisively to unite Antón and Inés.

Though the ecclesiastical judge positioned himself, and thus the Catholic Church, between master and slave, his ruling did not represent an extraordinary feat. In Spain and throughout the Indies, ecclesiastics regularly intervened between masters and slaves. "The church," according to one of the most judicious students of slavery and the law, "could and did thunder its opposition to the sins committed against the family—against all Christian families, regardless of color and regardless of status."[5] The master's private affairs deferred to ecclesiastical matters, most notably to Christian mores and the regulation thereof. In the patristic tradition, order in the Christian commonwealth revolved largely, but not exclusively, around moral considerations. In the quest for orthodoxy, the Christian Church subordinated even the master's will and dominion over chattel.[6]

Ecclesiastics adjudicated over behavior that threatened the moral order and, by implication, the *república*. By aligning himself with Antón and Inés, Sánchez de Muñon acted in defense of the conjugal couple and, in doing so, protected the *república*'s moral order. Even as chattel, the rights of Antón and Inés as a married couple superseded the will and personal authority of their master. As husband and wife joined by the Catholic Church, Antón and Inés represented subjects of the Christian *república* with defined privileges that the clergy steadfastly observed. As Christians, the enslaved could enter matrimony independent of the opposition of their masters. The Church, in tacit complicity with the Crown, granted couples a married life, ensuring the enslaved regular conjugal visits, if not actual cohabitation, and protection from physical separation that would threaten the marriage. Persons owned by different masters could request that they be sold or their spouse be purchased in order to effect a reunion.

Once married, individuals like Antón and Inés could petition ecclesiastical authorities for a conjugal existence that meant living in the same household but generally resulted in being sold to an owner in the city where the supplicant resided. Of course, in the contest of wills, Antón and Inés, as slaves, confronted formidable odds. As a slave-owner, free person, and a Spaniard, António de Reinoso had cultural and institutional recourses that could impede the reunion of the enslaved couple. Once he employed the services of one of New Spain's numerous and infamous lawyers, Reinoso could stymie the threat of excommunication and inaugurate a protracted legal battle between himself and Antón. Even with the *provisor*'s aid, the conflict could linger indefinitely, perhaps outlasting the supplicant.

But as Antón's petition and ability to marshal witnesses underscore, the enslaved were not easily deterred. As a slave, he understood his rights and had the presence of mind to utilize the ecclesiastical authorities to effect a reunion with his wife. In this, Antón exhibited acumen shared widely among New Spain's enslaved population. In the 1570s, Guinea's former inhabitants and their free and enslaved New World descendants routinely relied on existing ecclesiastical channels to voice grievances and modify their life circumstances. Though they depended on scribes and, to a lesser extent, on their masters to formally channel their grievances, both the enslaved and freedpersons understood that certain rights derived from their status as Christians. While even the most recent arrivals from Guinea quickly learned how to navigate the economy of rights and obligations, ladinos and creoles truly mastered it.[7]

By the second half of the sixteenth century, the enslaved—like the indigenous population—navigated juridical and institutional channels with ease and a frequency that generated mixed feelings among royal officials and especially masters.[8] A number of sixteenth-century viceroys saw the legal dexterity of their sovereign's vassals as a threat to Castilian dominion, a concept whose meaning constantly vacillated but always implied Christian conquest and royal authority. In contrast, the judges who sat in judgment at the various royal courts seemed not to share such concerns. Ecclesiastical authorities, many of whom were also ardent royalists, similarly expressed little worry about the ability of subalterns to use judicial avenues to express their grievances and seek justice. By deeming conjugality the principal means through which the laity, including baptized slaves, could lead orthodox lives, church officials actually encouraged a certain degree of litigiousness. In the eyes of the Church, Antón's behavior might undermine the master's personal authority, but the advantages of a Christian marriage outweighed the benefit of uncontested dominion.

As Antón's petition underscores, conjugality constituted an effective and pervasive metaphor through which the diverse population of individuals born in Africa and their New World descendants represented themselves—or were represented—before the ecclesiastical authorities in order to effect a semblance of cultural autonomy.[9] Though mediated by a scribe, Antón's very phrasing—"my wife" or "my legitimate wife"—reveals a familiarity with Christian tropes that aided his legal strategy.[10] All married Christians possessed conjugal rights. Appeals to matrimony or the maintenance of a Christian marriage energized the clergy to act swiftly on behalf of the supplicants. In cases involving opposition from patricians, kinfolk, and the larger community, ecclesiastical officials invariably sided with the couple, whether free or enslaved, African or Spaniard.[11] As believers in the divine nature of individual or free will—which assumed precedence over temporal concerns—church officials championed a couple's desire to marry. Though this behavior routinely pitted the Church against the Spaniards most likely to own slaves, "free will" constituted a powerful Christian and Castilian ideal, which ecclesiastics guarded tenaciously regardless of the status of the petitioners. As one of the cornerstones of the *república,* conjugality—symbolizing the Christian family, community, and polity—occupied a prominent place in the Christian imagination.

It is impossible to know whether Antón's petition and sense of entitlement were grounded in the elaborate ecclesiastical discourse about conjugal rites. Still, Antón's actions underscore a familiarity both with his and Inés's conjugal rights and with the channels whereby he could effect a desired result. The petition, however, reveals next to nothing about his actual beliefs or a deeper understanding of the tenets of Christianity. The depth of Antón's Christian consciousness was not, however, at stake. Ecclesiastics rooted their behavior in the canonical discourse irrespective of Antón's awareness. As defenders of the faith, church officials acted in accordance with a litany of dogma, theology, and canon law. By means of this discourse, compiled and inscribed over centuries, church officials accorded Christians rights and obligations with which they also regulated them.[12] In this respect, Sánchez de Muñon acted in accordance with long-standing views that granted Christians, including the enslaved, conjugal rights on the basis that they had willingly entered the state of matrimony. Antón's petition reveals a sense of entitlement that implicitly underscores Christianity's defense of individual will. It also highlights the extent to which a couple simultaneously existed as property, as Christians, and as husband and wife. Though the petition embraced all of these identities, the status of Antón and Inés as Christians prevailed in the Christian commonwealth.[13] In the hierarchy of status, Christian status reigned ascendant. Thus, the master's domain, though seemingly omnipotent, paled in contrast to that of the Church. After all, the Castilian monarch, a powerful sixteenth-century sovereign and lord of countless subjects, still deferred, ritually at least, to the pope and the Christian God.[14]

Whereas Antón's petition explicitly manifests his rights, as husband, to have a married life, it also implicitly embodied obligations. From the very moment they baptized individuals, Church officials demanded that the faithful adhere to Christianity's basic tenets. In this sense, Antón's rights as a husband also obligated him to a monogamous, exogamous, and indivisible union. As a faithful husband, Antón had to observe his marital debt to Inés and provide for her and for the subsistence of any potential offspring. Through his petition, Antón claimed both his rights and obligations that, in turn, flowed from his status as a Christian subject.

The petition also magnifies the multiple and even competing juridical identities that he inhabited—identities that entitled and compelled. In this respect, the petition represented much more than Antón's desire to have a married life with Inés. As a cultural artifact, it underscores the manner in which the Catholic Church defined the enslaved as Christian subjects.[15] In outlining their Christian obligations, ecclesiastical officials introduced the slaves to church laws, the rudimentary mysteries of the faith, and the norms governing behavior. But in teaching the commandments and the sacraments, the clergy also conferred an understanding of the rights to which all Christians were entitled. In effect, by regulating the enslaved laity, the clergy also extended privileges to slaves. Thus, the Church steadfastly encroached on the master's domain in its efforts to minister to all Christian subjects.

The enslaved, as we shall see, utilized this jurisdictional breech to their advantage. As Christians, they acquired an understanding of the obligations and rights they invoked to effect changes in their lives. As perceptive observers of the political landscape, they learned to mobilize the Church on their behalf. Invariably this strategy involved relying on the Church to effect a married life. Marriage represented the cornerstone of the Christian commonwealth and the hallmark of "good customs." Extended to all Christians, irrespective of status, matrimony constituted a sacrament, which the Church counseled all Christian adults to embrace. As Christianity's founding social institution, matrimony allegedly tempered base human instincts. Believing in the institution's ameliorating features, the Church equated marriage with order (*policía*). Matrimony was so critical to the orderly functioning of the *república* that the clergy sided with couples even when parents mounted vociferous opposition to their children's spousal selection.

In the case of slaves, the same imperative informed the clergy's actions. In the face of free will, even masters had to defer. In defense of a potential couple, the clergy mobilized the might of ecclesiastical law and one of its most powerful weapons, excommunication. Over the course of the colonial period, the enslaved developed an acute understanding of their right to a married life and drew on the clergy for assistance when a parent or master proved obstreperous in honoring their will. Individual will or "free will" occupied a central role in matrimony.[16] The Church exhorted couples to follow their desires, which they classified as "will" and which reflected the workings of the divine. As couples petitioned for a marriage license, the clergy questioned the prospective bride and groom individually about their desire. In protecting the sanctity of marriage, the clergy made every effort to avoid coerced unions.[17] Priests routinely asked legally recognized minors—women, children, servants, and slaves—to declare that the pending marriage reflected their will.[18] In affording individuals this opportunity, the clergy transcended ritualized formalities. As a sacrament, matrimony needed to be entered by individual accord. As the following case illustrates, the clergy pursued the slightest hint of impropriety—even among the enslaved—with customary rigor.

On July 21, 1572, Juan de Yepe informed the *provisor* of Mexico's archdiocese that the Sagrario's priests had previously declined to extend nuptials to his slaves Antón and Isabel. He petitioned the judge, Dr. Estéban de Portillo, to examine the matter on their behalf. The following day, the *provisor* questioned his assistants about their decision. They, in turn, told the judge how "the said negro declared that he was marrying the said negra under duress and against his will." On that basis, they declined to proceed. If this did in fact reflect Antón's views, the priest acted appropriately. But the *provisor* wished to verify the situation. He commanded the couple to appear before him and proceeded to question Antón and Isabel.[19] As Antón stood before Dr. Portillo, the slave proclaimed that he wanted Isabel as his wife. In manifesting his will, Antón declared that "neither his master or any other person threatened, nor forced him" into this decision. Isabel was just as adamant. Standing before the *provisor*, the enslaved woman insisted that in marrying Antón she obeyed her will. Persuaded by the couple's declaration, the *provisor* commanded his subordinates to join Isabel and Antón in holy matrimony. Perhaps Antón had previously voiced contrary sentiments, but in expressing his desire to Dr. Portillo he was unequivocal, and Dr. Portillo formulated his order on Antón's personal assurance that the pending marriage reflected his will. The concerns raised by the intervention of the priest and Dr. Portillo underscore the zeal with which the clergy approached matrimony. With regard to matrimony, the clergy respected the humblest will. For the clergy, coercion could play no role in marriage.[20]

In their vigilance, the clergy carefully examined the will of the couple. Fraud constituted a grave concern. How could the priests be certain that the persons receiving a petition also represented the same individuals asking to be joined in holy matrimony? In regulating the marriage petition and thereby the laity, the clergy displayed its customary rigor. The clergy even subjected slaves to the most careful scrutiny. By recording the Christian names, ages, place of birth, and residence of slaves and the names of their owners, the clergy institutionalized their social identities. In the tumultuous world of slavery, this regulatory act reflected a monumental challenge. In scope, the clergy's efforts underscored the importance they attributed to the knowledge gathered from couples and matrimonial sponsors. As they received petitions, the clergy constantly reminded *bozales* and creoles of the reverence with which all Christians must view marriage. As the previous chapter illustrated, Africans and their descendants responded by carefully selecting their witnesses. Even the slightest discrepancy nullified a marriage license. Errors encouraged greater scrutiny and called for correction before the priest would perform the wedding ceremony. In Mexico City at least, the clergy's penchant for detail suggests that the Church acted decisively in limiting social ambiguity.

On September 26, 1633, another Antón reappeared before the *provisor*. Earlier, he and Esperanza had petitioned for and received a marriage license. But when the couple attempted to legitimize their union, the priest noted a discrepancy in the name of Esperanza's owner. During the petitioning process, the scribe wrote that Esperanza belonged to Sebastian Jiménez instead of Sebastian de Arizmendi. On grounds of this discrepancy, the priest refused to unite the couple. In order to effect their marriage, Antón and Esperanza had to resolve this matter. Again the couple offered Pedro, a "negro from Bran land," and Manuel de Silva, a "negro from Banguela land," as witnesses. They corrected the identity of Esperanza's owner. Afterward, the *provisor* dispatched a second license enabling the marriage to take effect.[21]

A similar scenario repeated itself a year later. On October 5, 1634, Juan related how the scribe had falsely recorded his name as Francisco on the marriage license. Unaware of this error, the couple and their wedding party entered the Sagrario only to be turned away by the priest. Now Juan implored the *provisor* for another license. After presenting their witnesses, the couple reapproached the priest, who ascertained the legality of the petition and then issued the required banns. Finally, after twenty-one days, he performed the wedding ceremony.[22] Orthodoxy demanded vigilance, which the reformed clergy displayed with zeal.

In regulating the laity, the clergy rarely permitted laxity. After receiving a couple's marriage petition, the priest issued the required banns and would only then preside over the ceremony. On a few occasions the clergy did permit exceptions. Marriage constituted an indissoluble contract that only the highest authorities could rescind. But the clergy acknowledged that human frailty demanded procedural modification. A pending death after a life of sin represented a typical case in which the Church amended the regulatory procedure.[23] In such cases, as the following example illustrates, the clergy acted with urgency. In their haste, the clergy abbreviated the process. Couples, however, still had to present witnesses and demonstrate their lack of impediments. On October 10, 1633, Catalina Gutiérrez proclaimed her single status and desire to marry Juan de la Cruz. The mestiza and native of Tasco petitioned for the license in Juan's absence since the free mulatto lay ill in the hospital. Catalina requested that the *provisor* "in the service of God Our Lord" dispense with the customary banns.[24] As witnesses, Catalina presented Jacinto de Alfaro, Diego de Esquível, and Juan González. All three acknowledged their familiarity with the couple and attested to the single status of Catalina and Juan.[25] Jacinto and Diego also revealed how the couple had lived "in a bad state knowing one another carnally." As lovers and therefore sinners, Juan's pending death brought the afterlife into relief. Jacinto and Diego noted the gravity of the matter, stating that Juan was at death's door. Though vigilant, the clergy also derived pride from being merciful. With sufficient proof of the couple's single status, the *provisor* granted Catalina and Juan a marriage license that dispensed with the requisite banns.

The clergy's vigilance underscores the importance it attributed to the institution of marriage. Clerical activism on behalf of a couple could be mounted only if the couple adhered to the procedural obligations. If they were to challenge the authority of masters and parents, the clergy needed assurances that they would be acting from a firm legal basis. Though the Church was willing to transgress the authority of paterfamilias, they respected dominion and its legal standing. To minimize jurisdictional contests, couples had to carefully observe propriety. Armed with knowledge that proper procedures had been met, the clergy tenaciously defended lovers. In the process of according couples rights as Christians, the clergy circumvented the wishes of masters and parents.

Not even the powerful had a right to deny Christians, even slaves, a married life. On February 8, 1612, a young Spaniard, Pedro González, stood before the *provisor* of Mexico's archdiocese and petitioned for a marriage license. Pedro identified himself as the son of Pedro González and Barbola Gómez and said that he had been born in Salamanca "in the kingdoms of Castile." After offering this biographical detail, Pedro petitioned for the formalities that would allow him to marry the mulatto María de Brito. In María's absence, Pedro characterized his bride as a native of Extremadura and the slave of García de Santillan. He noted that while "in an illicit state," he had pledged marriage to the Spanish mulatto. Pedro then asked the *provisor* to place María in *depósito* since her master intended to send her away "because he does not want her to marry me."[26]

On completing his petition, Pedro presented four Spaniards as witnesses. Spaniards Martín Velas Asensio and Alonso Navarro spoke on behalf of Pedro and María. Both acknowledged that the couple had been cohabiting. In selecting Spaniards Diego de Cobos and Cristóbal as witnesses, Pedro underscored his legal acumen and the importance the clergy placed on long-standing acquaintances. Diego had known Pedro in Salamanca prior to arriving in New Spain. Cristóbal also shared ties forged in Salamanca and Seville, noting that they had sailed for New Spain together. In the clergy's eyes, the testimony, even though it was a routine declaration, demonstrated substantial familiarity. Pedro did not, therefore, represent a disreputable character. With this proof, the *pro-*

visor granted the couple a marriage license, ordering García de Santillan to offer up his charge. He also admonished García not to sell María or impede the marriage.[27]

Undaunted by this order, García stalled. The *provisor* then threatened García with excommunication. Even after receiving the *provisor's* threat, García refused to comply. In fact, he actively sought to undermine the order by selling María and by attempting to hide her in successive households until the new owner arrived. Wise to García's strategy, Pedro presented witnesses who appraised the *provisor* of the situation. Francisco de Silva, a 15-year-old Spaniard, observed seeing García de Santillan "transport María de Brito from his house on a mule . . . to San Pablo where he hid her." Two days later García hid María in Doña Juana de Escobar's house. "Yesterday morning," Francisco revealed, García had moved María again. Though uncertain of María's location, Francisco recalled how "he heard it said that her master carried her to Morquecho's house." The mestizo Juan Pérez offered similar testimony, observing that he had seen a shackled María being led throughout the streets. García, in other words, had no intention of complying with the *provisor's* orders.[28]

In a slave society, a shackled slave did not represent an anomaly. As García escorted María through Mexico, the spectacle probably invited little scrutiny. But under the cover of night, García was not transacting routine business. He was attempting to circumvent the law and knew that associates of Pedro and María kept abreast of his movements. Francisco asserted as much when stating that "he heard it said that her master carried her to Licenciado Morquecho's house." Pedro and María's will, which had the blessing of the Church, made García a fugitive. Several masters came to García's defense by offering their homes as refuge. Through their actions, they became co-conspirators who sanctioned García's strategy and approved of his tactical obstruction. In their eyes, García simply championed the authority of masters. In the moral universal of the slave master, the Church, though respecting the rights of Christian subjects, transgressed the rule over property.

In the jurisdictional conflict, however, the rights of Christian subjects prevailed over the master's authority and the Church acted decisively to uphold due process. Cognizant of the law and the couple's superior claims, García recognized the limits of obstruction. His defense did not invoke the authority of masters. Instead, he attempted to persuade the *provisor* that Diego Martín and Juan Patiño had proof that Pedro González had previously contracted a marriage in Castile.[29] Initially García's strategy worked. The *provisor* rescinded the marriage license until García's witnesses could offer their testimony in person. By the middle of August, the *provisor* became impatient when his officials could not locate Diego Martín or Juan Patiño. On August 17th, when it became clear that no one knew of the accusers, the *provisor* delayed the proceedings for two more days, noting that their failure to appear in person would lead to a dismissal of the allegations.[30] As a last-ditch effort, García tried to convince the *provisor* that Diego and Juan were underway "with goods," which prevented their appearance.[31] Unconvinced, the *provisor* reinstated the marriage license, allowing Pedro and María to enjoy their nuptials. After several difficult months, Pedro and María finally prevailed.

García, however, harbored lingering resentments. In a fit of rage, García demonstrated his anger on María's face. He knifed her badly and through this act reminded Pedro that his wife, María, still represented "my slave." The Church's response to this gruesome behavior remains unknown. The record ended inclusively with Pedro incarcerated for an unrelated offense. In any case, as María's master, García acted within his rights. Beyond ensuring a conjugal existence, the Church manifested little concern in defending the enslaved from the excesses of their owners' savagery. As García de Santillan's legal and extra-legal maneuverings reveal, in opposing conjugality, masters, not slaves, stood on the defensive. Conjugality circumscribed the rights of masters to act with impunity in matters concerning human chattel. Slaves knew this and with this acumen explicitly thwarted the masters' authority.

In a remarkable example of audacity manifested by a slave, Juan de Matos invoked his rights as husband to have his wife María de Leonor, a convicted bigamist and an enslaved Angico, returned to him.[32] Aware that Francisco Ansaldo, Leonor's master, planned to sail for Castile on the next fleet, Juan feared permanently losing his wife. On April 23, 1618, Juan de Matos, who identified himself as a slave in the port city of New Veracruz, sent inquisition officials in Mexico a letter in which he requested the tribunal to act on his behalf. Having recently learned that the inquisitors had convicted Leonor of bigamy, Juan de Matos implored the tribunal to enforce the order that "her master sell her in the region and place where her first husband resided." Though suffering her abandonment and the assault on his masculinity, Juan welcomed Leonor's return. In an effort to appeal to the sentiments of the inquisitors, Juan declared that "in the service of god, I should receive particular mercy because I want to spend my captivity in her company which shall absolve many offenses against God."[33] Astutely aware of Leonor's status as property, Juan skillfully added, "I have many persons who in order to accommodate my plight would want her." By instructing Francisco Ansaldo to sell Leonor to a resident of New Veracruz, the inquisitors would reconcile husband and wife.

Juan's letter represents a striking testament of legal acumen, resourcefulness, and guile. Here was a slave of the *encomendero* Francisco Rodriguez, who resided several days distant from the viceregal capital. Yet he knew of Leonor's conviction, the tribunal's sentence, and Francisco Ansaldo's pending departure. Juan also understood that he could force a master's hand; in fact, he had interested buyers. As husband, Juan had preeminence, even in the case of a convicted bigamist. The tribunal, an instrument of the Crown, recognized as much. The inquisitors actually ordered Leonor's reunion with Juan. Even in the face of adultery and bigamy, matrimony represented an indissoluble union.

It remains unclear how the inquisitors resolved this matter. The records end abruptly and inconclusively. Though Juan alerted the tribunal to the urgency in the matter, we do not know if the inquisitors acted with haste. If Francisco Ansaldo had succeeded in departing New Spain with Leonor in tow, crown and clergy could still have pursued the matter. Though the tribunal's jurisdiction was limited to the Indies, judgments in New Spain applied in Castile, and crown and clergy would insist that Francisco Ansaldo respect Juan's rights as husband. Even in its incompleteness, the case highlights Juan's entitlement irrespective of his slave status. Of course, any of the potential buyers, including his master, could have prompted Juan's actions.[34] Yet for this purported plot to work, Juan had to demonstrate agency. Only by mobilizing his status as husband could the judicial machinery be stimulated into action.

As paterfamilias, fathers wielded mastery over their charges—wives, children, servants, and slaves. In Castile and New Spain, the father's authority prevailed in the household and in the public world. In their capacity as legal minors, wives, children, and slaves deferred to fathers, who represented family members in contractual agreements and courts.[35] At the age of 25, boys legally became men, but mothers, daughters, and female dependents always represented minors in the presence of paterfamilias. For slaves and servants, reaching the age of majority had no effect on their status. In civil and public matters, the master's authority reigned. Yet, in relation to marriage and a couple's will, even parental authority was less than absolute. The Church, as the following narrative illustrates, sided with lovers even in the face of parental opposition. The groom's slave status did not temper the clergy's zeal. Individual will intent on marriage trumped differences in legal status.

On August 2, 1633, the enslaved black creole Nicolás de la Cruz informed the ecclesiastical judge of his single status and desire to marry the free mulatto Gertrudis de San Nicolás. The native of Mexico and slave of Juan de Tavares asked the *provisor* to send notice to Francisco de la Torre, Gertrudis's father, who opposed the union by placing his daughter in a convent.[36] After voicing his request, Nicolás offered two black creoles, Catalina de la Cruz and Juana de Todos los Santos, as matrimonial sponsors. Both women testified that bride and groom lacked marital impediments, and they also noted that Francisco de la Torre objected to his daughter's marriage to Nicolás.[37] As the black creoles concluded their respective declarations, they offered no reason for Francisco's objections. In fact, the trial proceedings—comprised largely of the testimony of the witnesses—never revealed his motive.

Francisco de la Torre had a motive, which initially prompted him to place Gertrudis in the convent of Regina Celi. His motive, however, seems to have had no basis in law since he took his daughter from the convent and attempted to hide her with relatives. Several witnesses recalled how Francisco and an aunt, in lieu of verbal persuasion, began hitting Gertrudis in an effort to change her mind. Gertrudis refused. Eventually she eluded her tormentors and appeared before the *provisor*. Gertrudis professed her desire to contract marriage even after the *provisor* warned her that in "marrying him she had an obligation out of matrimonial respect to go with him where his master sent or sold him." Gertrudis agreed. Afterward, the ecclesiastical judge issued the couple a marriage license. To avoid further obstruction, the *provisor* dispensed with the banns, threatening any person that impeded the couple's union with excommunication and a 10-peso fine.[38] With his decree, the *provisor* acted decisively. He manifested no interest in a declaration from Francisco de la Torre. For the clergy, all that mattered was an expression of individual will. Parental authority, like that of masters, played no role when couples wanted to contract marriage. Francisco de la Torre knew as much when he sequestered his daughter among relatives. In the confines of a relative's home, he administered a thrashing with the intent of bending Gertrudis's will. Gertrudis, not her father, had the power to stop the pending marriage.

In trying to determine his daughter's selection of a spouse, Francisco had no legitimate recourse. Even Nicolás's slave status did not constitute an impediment. Gertrudis simply had to declare her willingness to follow her husband, who was another person's slave. But what were Francisco's motives? In the absence of his declaration, such an inquiry reflects at best informed guesswork. In principal, Francisco did not register a blanket opposition to his daughter being married. One witness testified that Francisco intended for Gertrudis to marry "a mestizo from Zacatecas."[39] Yet Gertrudis resisted her father's desire. Francisco insisted that his daughter defer to his authority. As a black creole in a slave society, Francisco's authority did not represent an abstraction. The ability to claim his daughter as symbolic possession represented a notable feat in a society where freedom and elaborate kinship ties were usually not associated with a person of African descent. As a father and a free person of African descent who could claim lateral kinship ties—recall the aunt—Francisco drew his authority from his status as paterfamilias. His daughter's marriage to a slave would contract, not extend, his authority. Nicolas's time belonged to his master, and the wife of a slave had to accommodate herself to that owner's whims. As the wife of a slave, Gertrudis would have to provide for her own sustenance, since the slave husband had no right to divert resources from the master to his wife. From Francisco's perspective, Gertrudis's pending marriage symbolized a potential drain for him, his daughter, and their larger family. In an effort to defend his limited resources and preserve his authority, Francisco manifested tenacity and considerable malice.[40] In the face of canon law, however, neither masters nor masterly fathers could prevail.

Even officials sworn to uphold the law found it difficult not to act as masterly fathers. As individuals, some officials acted in contradistinction to the very law that sanctioned their authority. Ironically, they utilized their position to cloak their surreptitious deeds. For couples, the confrontation with such men required an acute sense of entitlement, determination, and resourcefulness. Even then the playing field was far from even. Only through the Church's intervention could dependents hope to successfully challenge the authority of an individual who simultaneously occupied an official position. The Church, as the following case demonstrates, took on all masters and fathers, even when such men held the highest office in the land.

On November 8, 1612, the free mulatto Rodrigo Gallegos initiated ecclesiastical proceedings against one of New Spain's most powerful men. In his request for a license to marry the mestiza Francisca, Rodrigo noted that the bride languished in the Colegio de las Niñas, where the master had placed her in order to impede the marriage.[41] The young mulatto asked the *provisor* to order Francisca's release and intervene on his behalf against Don Antonío Rodriguez, judge of the royal court. Don Antonío represented a formidable opponent for the young mulatto Rodrigo. Besides the viceroy and the handful of other judges, Don Antonío was the highest crown official in New Spain. In challenging Don Antonío's authority over Francisca, Rodrigo confronted a man who stood at the pinnacle of power.[42]

In his quest to marry Francisca, the intrepid mulatto did not enlist the assistance of a particularly impressive array of witnesses. He simply presented a priest and two indigenous women conversant in Castilian. The priest, Miguel López, acknowledged having known Rodrigo for six years and attested to his single status. He recalled that two months before, Rodrigo had come to him very upset, declaring that he wanted to marry a woman who had been a virgin, but that her master, Don Antonío, opposed the marriage.[43] Rodrigo wanted to ask the *provisor* for the license, yet he feared that Don Antonío would have him incarcerated before he reached the ecclesiastical judge. In his testimony, Miguel underscored Don Antonío's heavy hand. He stated that the royal judge had issued a warrant for Rodrigo's arrest while remanding Francisca to the Colegio de las Niñas.[44] Spanish-speaking Indians Francisca de San Miguel and Inés Ana María offered a similar story. From their perspective, Don Antonío was stewing because Francisca had not approached him before publicly declaring her will to marry Rodrigo. The royal judge, according to the two women, denied that words carried the force of law.[45] For Francisca de San Miguel and Inés Ana María, Don Antonío's strategy was obvious. By denying Rodrigo and Francisca access to the *provisor,* the royal judge intended to annul the effects of the verbal pledge.[46]

With this testimony, the *provisor* had enough to act. He ordered Francisca's release and demanded that she inform him of her will. The next day, Francisca complied. From her declaration, we learn that as an orphan from birth, Francisca had spent her life in Don Antonío's household. So complete was Francisca's identification with the judge that all she could register about her background was that "since a little girl I was reared in the house of Señor Licenciado Antonío Rodriguez." She simply had no knowledge of her age, her birthplace, or the names of her parents. In response to questions about the circumstances of her relationship with Rodrigo Gallegos, Francisca observed that she had met the young mulatto while accompanying Don Antonío and his wife and daughter. "Having given Rodrigo a verbal promise of marriage," Francisca confessed to "knowing him carnally." Now she wanted to fulfill her earlier pledge and marry Rodrigo. After this declaration, and assured by Francisca that she and Rodrigo had no impediments, the ecclesiastical judge granted the couple a marriage license. Of course, the priests still had to issue the banns and wait for three successive Sundays before the nuptials could be performed, but Don Antonío had been served notice that the couple had the Church's protection.[47]

In taking on Don Antonío, the *provisor* acted rather perfunctorily. The ecclesiastical judge knew that canon law sanctioned his actions. No Christian subject stood above the law. With this understanding, the *provisor* acted decisively in favor of Francisca and Rodrigo. In the face of canon law, even a powerful royal judge had to bow. Of course, Don Antonío could have mounted a defense that would have occupied the couple and the ecclesiastical court for months, if not years. Extralegal means also were an option. Don Antonío had already issued one warrant for Rodrigo's arrest and placed Francisca in custody. As a man of influence and affluence, the royal judge had unlimited ways to stymie the pending wedding. If Don Antonío had employed these options, he would have found that the Church, as the couple's protector, constituted a formidable adversary.

As a man of means, Don Antonío tried to retain his patriarchal authority over Francisca. Yet he was no fool. He knew his limits and avoided a battle. Of course, he abused his position. In the end, however, the young mestiza did not warrant a heedless contest. Don Antonío acted like countless other masters. Though Francisca was free, by residing in Don Antonío's household she constituted a legal minor. By definition, Don Antonío was Francisca's master. As master, he had significant say in her life, but that did not include her choice of spouse. Beyond residing in Don Antonío's household since birth, the record does not reveal the nature of their relationship. Perhaps he was her father or relative. Though Rodrigo insisted on having enjoyed Francisca's virginity, Don

Antonío may have been an earlier lover or even violator. In any case, Don Antonío felt spurned by the manner in which Francisca informed him of her marital choice. In presenting the matter as a fait accompli, Francisca probably offended Don Antonío's sense of propriety and patriarchal authority. After his initial response, the young mestizo would have to live with the consequences of her actions. In marrying Rodrigo, Francisco replaced one master with another, a father for a husband. The choice was hers and, according to the Church, a reflection of Francisca's will.

Patriarchs and masters did not simply acquiesce to the assault on their authority. Even upstanding Christian masters defended their moral and civil authority against ecclesiastical encroachment. Some masters acknowledged the higher authority of canon law but obstructed justice through extralegal means. Masters hoped that by threatening, sequestering, and beating slaves their will would prevail. Such efforts, as we have seen, could have the opposite effect. In the end, masters employing such surreptitious tactics conceded the legal ground to the Church and the couple.

It is not known how many masters engaged in such illicit tactics. Still, they defended their rights as patriarchs to determine the fate of legally recognized minors and property. For some, the court embodied an arena in which lawyers, the legal petition, and time constituted the weapons of choice. In complex and prolonged cases, the couple often emerged as the losers. Such cases also took their toll on ecclesiastical authority. Since the Church's authority hinged on an unquestioned morality anchored in canon law, cases raising the question of legal merit and jurisdiction steadily undermined ecclesiastical hegemony. Judicial contests had other consequences as well. In their contentiousness, supplicants and defendants used the language of rights in their mobilization of witnesses and their involvement of familiars. The very procedure of litigation, by drawing a community that included servants and slaves into the courtroom, socialized others in the knowledge of rights and a married life.

Some masters simply did not care. An obstructionist master was often too worried about his authority and winning the pending case to care whether the slave enlisted on his behalf would later turn that legal knowledge against him. The arrogance of power precluded some masters from initiating preventive measures aimed at restricting the emergence of a legal consciousness among slaves. Keenly aware of the deleterious effects of slaves in courtrooms, masters in other European colonies often closed ranks as whites.[48] But in a society with competing legal traditions, this proved difficult.[49] In the Spanish Indies, Castilian law, as positive law, occupied a secondary position to canon law, which was derived from divine and natural law. As the following case makes clear, clergymen tenaciously defended the Church and its laws even when their actions positioned them as the allies of slaves. As a collection of powerful white men and slave-owners, the clergy broke ranks with secular masters by defending the rights of all Christians to enjoy conjugality.[50]

On August 12, 1615, Antonío Martín, a resident of Mexico who was anxious to relocated his household to Oaxaca, stood before the *provisor*. He had made several unsuccessful attempts to purchase the slave Lorenzo from Pedro Coquete, and he felt the *provisor* represented his best recourse. Antonío noted that he owned the black women Gracía, who years ago as a person of single status and "not subject to matrimony" had decided to marry Lorenzo. Until a year ago all had been well. But then Lorenzo's mistress, Catalina Ortíz, died, and her heirs sold the slave to Pedro Coquete. Away from Mexico at the time, Antonío Martín missed the opportunity to buy Lorenzo. Now he endeavored to move to Oaxaca "with my entire household" and out of respect for Gracía's marriage tried to persuade Pedro Coquete to sell Lorenzo. In addressing the *provisor*, Antonío bemoaned Pedro Coquete's refusal. "Since the black woman does not want to be separated from her husband," Antonío asked the *provisor* to intervene on his behalf, stating that "I am the senior owner." Even in asking for ecclesiastical intervention, Antonío acknowledged Pedro Coquete's rights as master and offered to compensate him after certifying "the amount he [Lorenzo] cost."[51]

The *provisor* was quick to act. Antonío Martín's plea had legal merits, and Gracía was entitled to a conjugal existence. The *provisor* issued an order demanding that Pedro Coquete sell Lorenzo to Antonío Martín for "the price he was justly valued and cost." Aware that this case touched on a civil matter— ownership and property value—the *provisor* also requested that both parties present their bill of sale. To assure a prompt response "within six days" and because he was anxious to avoid needless obstruction, the ecclesiastical judge threatened both men with excommunication for failure to comply.[52] Though excommunication routinely accompanied the *provisor*'s orders, the threat and the merits of Antonío Martín's case persuaded Pedro Coquete to engage a solicitor. Though the law and, seemingly, the *provisor* stood on his side, Antonío Martín knew that civil matters complicated the case. As a result, he too secured an attorney.[53]

In compliance with the *provisor*'s order, Antonío Martín presented his bill of sale. By means of this bill we learn that Gracía, who in the proceedings had been listed only as a black woman (which implied that she was a creole), was actually a *bozal*. Soon after landing in Cartagena, Gracía, the "negra from Biafra land," was purchased by Juan Gómez Pinto, who took her to Mexico. In 1599, "more or less" when she was 17, Antonío Martín had bought Gracía for the sum of 470 pesos. Pedro Coquete responded in kind by offering a counter-petition. His attorney, Pedro Gómez, observed that Pedro Coquete would not concede ownership, protesting that "it is not lawful to make him comply with the sale." Pedro Gómez noted that at the time when Lorenzo married Gracía "she was a resident and inhabitant of Mexico." Again through his attorney, Pedro Coquete denied the existence of any "legitimate reason for me to sell the said slave residing in this city if the other party wanted to move, in conformance with the rules of law the wife should follow the husband not the husband the wife." Having raised the issue of gender propriety, the solicitor then stated that Lorenzo was so industrious that "his [Pedro Coquete's] whole bakery depended" on his labor. The lawyer explained that in selling Lorenzo, Pedro Coquete would lose an invaluable slave and thereby jeopardize his financial well-being. Attuned to the matter of conjugality, the attorney observed his client's willingness to purchase Gracía and stated that since he owned the male, "he has more basis in the law."

In defending his client, Pedro Coquete's solicitor acknowledged the primacy of canon law. Yet he insisted that canon law's gender conventions privileged the male or the owner of the male. In that civil law accorded Antonío Martín rights as owner, Pedro agreed to purchase Gracía so the couple could enjoy a married life. The attorney skillfully avoided questioning canon law; he simply underscored that gender complicated matters.[54] But the attorney argued that civil law precluded his client from selling Lorenzo if the transaction would cause him financial harm. In this intricate defense, the attorney exposed the jurisdictional conflict and manipulated it in his client's favor.

Antonío Martín's attorney responded that his client represented the more senior owner. As such, the recent owner "who has not had him for more than one year . . . should [permit the slave to] go where his wife in her master's service goes in order to have a married life." Martín's attorney also added that the couple had always resided with him. He then disputed claims about Lorenzo's priceless service. Martín's attorney maintained that this assertion was "an invention . . . since the profession in which he is occupied is so easy and accomplished by any other slave even a bozal in a very short time . . . could be able to help him [Pedro Coquete]."[55] Gracía, in contrast, was an invaluable servant. After all, she "is the governess of his house with whom he confides his business." In his counterargument, Antonío Martín's attorney insisted that canon and civil law privileged his client. Instead of clarifying matters, however, he merely reaffirmed the jurisdictional conflict.

Four days after this legal sparring, Lorenzo entered the fray to try to direct the case back to his rights as husband. Defining himself as a creole "from Terranova," Lorenzo observed that Antonío Martín had absconded with his wife. Surmising that they had left for Oaxaca, he implored the *provisor* to "dispatch someone with a letter of justice against Antonío Martín . . . so that my wife be returned to this city."[56] In support of his allegations, Lorenzo presented two slaves, including Antón García, who belonged to Pedro Coquete. Both men testified that Antonío had left for Oaxaca with Gracía in tow.[57] In light of the recent legal sparring, Antonío Martín's departure represented an affront to the *provisor*. He immediately dispatched an order to his counterpart in Oaxaca demanding Gracía's return.

In response to the order, Antonío Martín justified his actions.[58] Martín, however, assured the *provisor* that in the event of a negative judgment he would release Gracía. He simply had pressing business in Oaxaca that could not wait while the court weighed its options. His actions revealed that Pedro Coquete's strategy had taken a toll on his patience. As the instigator of the case, Antonío Martín initially felt that canon law favored him. But jurisdictional conflict complicated matters. Anxious to begin his life in Oaxaca, he grew tired of a conflict that revolved around the married life of slaves. In departing from Mexico, Antonío Martín simply retreated from the legal stalemate. The *provisor* saw matters differently. By taking Gracía to Oaxaca, Antonío Martín acted like so many masters who resorted to extralegal means when they confronted a potentially unfavorable ruling. Antonío Martín had become what he accused Pedro Coquete of being—an obstructionist. In this case for which there is no resolution in the archival records, Antonío Martín's behavior became the *provisor*'s most pressing concern. Gracía, Lorenzo's wife, had to be returned to Mexico.

Despite Antonío Martín's transition from supplicant to defendant, Lorenzo and Gracía represented the real victims. Their lives as a conjugal couple had been placed on hold as the attorneys of their masters debated precedent and jurisdiction. Though it is plausible that Pedro Coquete encouraged Lorenzo to inform the *provisor* of Antonío Martín's flight from Mexico, the hapless slave may have been genuinely motivated by his desire to be reunited with Gracía. Perhaps both dynamics operated simultaneously. Lorenzo may have utilized Pedro Coquete's prodding as an opportunity to remind the *provisor* that underneath the legal tangle and verbal sparring, the stakes involved his life with Gracía. Of course, the *provisor* cared for and defended the rights of conjugal couples. But justice—intended for the purpose of regulating, not ameliorating, the slave experience—came at a snail's pace in the conflict over rightful authority. People squandered short lives waiting for resolution. Slaves knew this better anyone, and Gracía learned it firsthand when Antonío Martín left Mexico. Her fate paled in comparison to Antonío Martín's fortunes in Oaxaca. Suddenly, sixteen years of service represented little to her master.

In taking on Antonío Martín, Pedro Coquete relied, of course, on his attorney. Steeped in the intricacies of the law, Pedro Gómez mounted an effective defense on his client's behalf. Though the outcome was still pending, Pedro Gómez had complicated the contest to such an extent that the *provisor* could not rule hastily or solely on the basis of canon law. Gracía and Lorenzo were entitled to a married life, but under what circumstances? Could Lorenzo be removed from Pedro Coquete simply because Antonío Martín represented the owner with seniority? How did Lorenzo's petition, an explicit declaration that he wanted to remain in Mexico with Pedro Coquete, affect the deliberations? Civil law complicated these questions. Could a master be forced to sell his slave to comply with matrimonial law when such an act threatened his welfare? Antonío Martín questioned Pedro Coquete's claim about Lorenzo's worth on the basis that "any other slave" could acquire the required skills to run a bakery. Even though he dismissed Pedro Coquete's assertion about the worth of his slave, Antonío still acknowledged that value should play a role. Antonío Martín pointed to Gracía's value and her indispensability as his governess. How would the *provisor* view matters? In the last analysis, could he, as the defender of canon law, be the final arbiter in a case that also touched on civil matters? In trying to delay the proceedings, Pedro Gómez performed an invaluable service for his client. In the end, Antonío Martín had little patience for a protracted legal battle.

Pedro Coquete's behavior mirrored that of other masters confronted with the loss of chattel. Such efforts depended on a master's tenacity and resources. Powerful masters had the ability to defend their interests against peers. In the absence of parity, arrogance—born of wealth, status, or occupation—persuaded a number of masters to prey on less-fortunate owners. In exposing a master's predatory behavior, the following example also illustrates how an attitude of modesty led judges to temper the arrogance of power. As the purported defenders of the meek, the moral sentiments of the authorities often resided with the humble, which in the Indies included numerous slave masters.

On September 24, 1648, the tribunal of the Holy Office sat in session as a scribe read a notarized letter from Hernando de Utrera in which the Spaniard defended his property rights.[59] This case involved Margarita, the slave of handicapped street vendor Hernando de Utrera. Margarita was married to Joseph, a slave of Don Juan de Suaznabar y Aguirre, the *alguacil mayor* of the Inquisition in Mexico City. Joseph had recently exhibited many behaviors of a slave in resistance to his master, including prolonged absences, theft, and attempts to take his master's life. In a last-ditch effort to control his unruly slave, Juan de Suaznabar had attempted to purchase Margarita from Utrera. It was at this point that Utrera approached inquisition officials to enlist their help.

On the basis of the position he held, Juan de Suaznabar was accustomed to having his way. He knew the awe that the Inquisition invoked and felt confidant that his superiors would close ranks against a plebeian who derived his sustenance from the stall he ran in the *plaza mayor*. Juan assumed that if he initiated the case with the tribunal, though it was properly the domain of the ecclesiastical court, his superiors would rule in his favor.[60] Intent on protecting their institution, corporate officials often transgressed jurisdiction when situations involved their members. Juan, in fact, was the *alguacil mayor* and more. He occupied the position that had previously belonged to his father, Capítan Tomás de Suaznabar y Aguirre. In defending his property rights against the son of the *alguacil mayor* and now that position's occupant, Hernando confronted a family tradition within New Spain's most feared corporate body.

Hernando seemed undaunted by the task. Four days after he lost Margarita's services due to her arrest by inquisition officials, Hernando pleaded his case. The inquisitors had acted, of course, on a petition from Don Juan. Despite institutional loyalty, the tribunal listened to Hernando de Utrera's claims. In his communiqué, Hernando observed how Margarita had been born in his house and from their births had nurtured his children. Now this loyal slave assisted him in the stall, which he maintained "without having other means to sustain me and my family." Hernando knew that Don Juan alleged that Margarita had helped Joseph in his recent unruly behavior, and he denied Margarita's responsibility for Joseph's misdeeds. According to Hernando, the *alguacil* had had his sights on Margarita for years. He alleged that when he refused to sell Margarita, the *alguacil* "threatened to take her from me, leaving me with a broken hand and sequestering her more than ten months." Hernando also declared that Don Juan had employed "very rigorous tactics, with the purpose of getting his way and I as a poor invalid, cannot aid in stopping him." Hernando also questioned Juan de Suaznabar's moral claims. The street vendor recalled how the *alguacil* had on more than one occasion taken Joseph from Mexico. After confining the slave in a textile mill in Atusco, the *alguacil* removed him to a distant sugar estate. Hernando pointed out that as owner of these enterprises, the *alguacil*'s motives for wanting Margarita were informed by his need for labor. Hernando finally implored the inquisitors not to acquiesce to Juan de Suaznabar's demand. Margarita represented more than a slave and member of his family, for "she sustains us through God and her diligence." According to Hernando, Margarita's financial contribution was of such importance that he and his family could ill afford to lose her while the inquisitors sat in deliberation.

Moved by the letter, the inquisitors remanded Margarita into Hernando's custody until the resolution of the case. For Hernando, this constituted a notable victory. In persuading the inquisitors to override their earlier order, Hernando inspired the tribunal to break ranks with one of their own. In a society that valued institutional loyalty, the actions of the inquisitors represented a setback for Juan de Suaznabar and an insinuation that the *alguacil* had not been forthright.

Anxious to build on his moral momentum, Hernando appeared in person before the tribunal to address Juan de Suaznabar's allegations. Hernando carefully pointed out that even though the *alguacil* said he wanted to buy Margarita because he believed that as Joseph's wife she bore responsibility for "the calamity committed by the said his slave," Juan de Suaznabar "wants to purchase the said black woman in order to sell her beyond this city with the said negro." Hernando reminded the inquisitors that, "as I have professed in my letter," Margarita represented a relative, "having been born in my family and raised my kids." Then Hernando added that due to his ill state of health "my sustenance and that of my family" depends on Margarita, who toils in the stall "where I assist but . . . negotiates all the business." In contrast to his dire straits, Hernando depicted Juan de Suaznabar as an affluent man who had easily dispensed with Joseph's labor by placing him on the "water-powered mill that produces sugar where he confined him to working with prisoners." A man of such means, Hernando implied, could resolve the truculence of a slave without depriving a less fortunate person of his sole source of sustenance. For Hernando, the *alguacil* intended to "give me neither security nor congruent means." With this carefully crafted observation, Hernando ended his statement.

On October 17th, Juan de Suaznabar y Aguirre responded. Nearly three weeks after he initiated the proceedings, the *alguacil mayor* now found himself on the defensive in front of his superiors. Initially, he claimed that Joseph had been the source of unending trouble that included prolonged absences, theft, and attempts on his life. Juan acknowledged having repeatedly punished Joseph in trying to gain mastery of his slave, even confining Joseph on his water-powered mill. But Joseph remained obstinate and a physical threat. Juan acknowledged that he had stopped giving Joseph arms—a radical step, because it was the custom among *alguaciles* to arm their slaves since they assisted them in the performance of their duties. Juan de Suaznabar y Aguirre had hoped to end Joseph's rebelliousness by purchasing Margarita. Margarita represented Joseph's wife but, more important, his accomplice. Despite the fact that his rebuttal focused on Joseph's behavior, the *alguacil's* tone highlights his defensive posture.

Juan alleged that Margarita was the key to controlling Joseph. Thus he asked his superiors to demand that Hernando name an assessor. In making this request, Juan did not simply rely on the inquisitors' goodwill. He invoked the law "and in the present case military rules of law demand that a master of any married slave having cause that the husband not remain in the kingdom be commanded to sell her." According to Juan, this law called for an appraisal so that the rights of the contending parties would be protected. Juan derided Hernando de Utrera's assertion that Margarita had been born in his household and now sustained him and his family. "He has no basis to allege what his says," asserted the *alguacil*. "He wants to avoid the sale," declared Juan, noting "that he would be able to buy another and apply her to the same job."

Defensive but far from contrite, Juan congratulated his adversary for his efforts to remedy Joseph's unruly behavior. He then proclaimed emphatically "I am a person able to punish my slaves without his advice." Finally, Don Juan declared that "I would also be justified by the force of the law even in the event he sells me the said negra who in a manner was complicit in all the said negro committed." The *alguacil*'s tone revealed his frustration and the arrogance he wielded vis-à-vis the humble street vendor. Though the *alguacil* still had to convince his superiors, he would not brook a challenge to his masterly authority and manhood. In the eyes of Juan de Suaznabar y Aguirre, Hernando de Utrera lacked both a firm legal basis and the stature to stand in his way. As was often the case, adversaries quickly turned legal contests into questions of honor.

Rights over slaves and dependents invariably invoked masculine codes of honor. The powerful demanded respect for their position even when the courts placed the adversaries on a par with each other. Powerful men bowed to the law and the equality it bestowed on the contestants, but when events favored persons of lesser status, they quickly resorted to elite posturing. Unfortunately, we do not know how the inquisitors responded to the *alguacil*'s tone. After Juan Suaznabar y Aguirre's rebuttal, the document abruptly ended. In an effort to avoid ruling unfavorably against their *alguacil,* the inquisitors may have remanded the case to another court. But which court would the tribunal have selected to adjudicate over a matter involving an official of the Inquisition? In the proceedings, both masters focused on their rights to property. Hernando defended his right to own Margarita since this industrious slave woman sustained him and his family. In turn, Juan insisted that as an owner he could sell the slave couple. Until such time, he could punish Joseph as he saw fit.

Though civil matters rose to the fore, this case also touched on canon law—a slave couple's entitlement to a conjugal existence. The contest over authority and livelihood overshadowed the matter of a married life. Joseph and Margarita, however, had conjugal rights. In the context of these rights, the couple navigated the demands of bondage to secure a marital existence. Though enslaved, the couple saw themselves like other married couples. Juan Suaznabar acknowledged as much when he informed the inquisitors that in his absence Joseph and Margarita had on numerous occasions entered his bedroom and even slept in his conjugal bed. The symbolism speaks volumes and sheds light on the couple's efforts to steal comfort as they attended to the marital debt. Undaunted by Juan Suaznabar's heavy hand, Joseph and Margarita insisted that the *alguacil* respect their marital status. When she was concerned about Joseph's absence, Margarita even approached the *alguacil* demanding to know her husband's whereabouts. Juan recalled how Margarita "came to my residence as if she were a person of importance demanding to know where I hid her husband." In lieu of their own testimony, the couple's behavior signaled an understanding of their entitlements. Unable to alter their legal status, Joseph and Margarita clung to their rights as husband and wife. Any ruling in this case needed to accord preeminence to their married life.

Though judicial conflicts involving slaves often pitted owners as adversaries, masters did not monopolize agency. As we have seen, slaves and dependents often emerged as agents in cases touching on their conjugal existence. In such cases, the enslaved displayed a keen awareness of their rights. Of course, they relied on the protection of the Church, but ecclesiastical authorities had to be notified and mobilized. In acting as protector and advocate, the Church reacted to pleas from masters and the enslaved. Among the enslaved, this awareness emerged over time and through the creolization process. All Christians had the right to a married life, yet only the most astute knew to initiate proceedings on their behalf.

Though canon law and the ecclesiastical court—like all Spanish courts— privileged men, a number of enslaved females claimed their rights to a conjugal existence. As the following examples reveal, enslaved women, like male slaves, used their rights as Christians, restricting in the process the masters' authority to define them and their husbands solely as labor. This juridical act, intent on expanding their cultural autonomy, was by definition also a political act. Time inextricably linked to control constituted a political phenomenon for masters, but among slaves it delineated the boundaries of their cultural domain. Yet in the struggle for time, the cultural phenomenon of being a husband, wife, parent, and child became political.

In 1674, the enslaved black woman Antonía de la Natividad petitioned the *provisor* for an order that would enable her husband to leave his master "at least one time a week to have a married life with her." If this demand represented an onerous burden that would persuade Jerónimo del Pozo to sell Miguel, Antonía demanded that her husband's master be required to sell him to a resident of Mexico. Antonía's petition represented an audacious demand.[61] Here a slave woman insisted on determining how a master should regulate his property. Even as a slave and a woman, Antonía believed she had a right, as wife, to define how her husband's master could regiment Miguel de la Cruz's time. Antonía shared a conviction manifest among many of the enslaved that she as a wife had an entitlement to a married life and on these grounds sought to circumscribe the extent to which the master could define her husband as property and a laborer. In a slave society, such expectations—sanctioned by canon law—challenged the masters' authority and the very definition of slavery.

The *provisor* acquiesced to Antonía's demand and ordered Jerónimo del Pozo to allow Miguel to "leave in order to have a married life with his wife every Saturday and another day of the week." In addition, the ecclesiastical judge warned Jerónimo not to abuse Miguel with "words or with work and if he should sell him than do so to a resident of Mexico." By imposing such elaborate restrictions on the master, the *provisor* in effect limited Miguel's slave status, during two days of the week, to a juridical category. At most, Jerónimo had five days each week to determine how best to employ his slave. In his response, Jerónimo questioned the judiciousness of the *provisor's* order yet tacitly acknowledged the Church's power to restrict his authority over his slave. Jerónimo implored the ecclesiastical judge "not to allow Miguel de la Cruz to leave for he is a rebel and a fugitive which is why I bought him." Instead Jerónimo proposed that Antonía be granted unlimited access to his *obraje* "to have a married life." Jerónimo added that he would gladly comply with the *provisor's* ruling if the judge was willing to insure his slave.[62]

Antonía opposed Jerónimo's proposal and implored the judge to enforce his initial order.[63] Jerónimo countered that the *provisor* should revoke his order allowing Miguel to leave in pursuit of a conjugal life. As master, Jerónimo exclaimed, he could not risk losing the slave or the money he had paid for him. He then observed that granting Miguel freedom of movement was unwise "because his character is malevolent and accustomed to flight." Not wanting to appear indifferent to Antonía's concerns, Jerónimo reiterated "that his house is open for the woman of his to come there and have a married life with her husband." In closing, Jerónimo concluded that Antonía's objections to his proposal, based on distance and the need to serve her master, simply represented excuses.[64] With this stalemate, the record ended. We can only imagine in whose favor the *provisor* ruled. The case, however, magnifies Antonía's sense of entitlement, which led her to request that Jerónimo give up significant control over his slave.

In voicing her demands, Antonía attempted to define the very nature of Miguel's, and by implication her, slave experience. In a slave society, Antonía's terms constituted a fundamental breach of order and a challenge to the master's authority. In New Spain, however, such demands gradually represented the norm instead of the exception. As the enslaved acquired an understanding of their rights to a married life, they constantly struggled to expand the scope and definition of a conjugal existence. Though tenuously reconciled to a life of slavery, the enslaved actively tried to configure bondage in ways that gave them more time and control over their lives. This vision, in this instance articulated by an enslaved woman, highlights the slave's moral vision with which they tried to limit the demands masters placed on their time and bodies. In the ensuing contests with masters, slaves invariably enlisted the clergy as legal aides. Antonía, for example, simply voiced her desire to have a more fulfilling life with her husband, Miguel. For the *provisor,* this request was enough for him to intervene on the couple's behalf with the might of the Church and canon law.

On October 27, 1674, another enslaved woman utilized her rights as a Christian to effect a change in her slave experience. Identifying herself as Gracía de la Cruz "from the land of Congo," she declared, "I am married to José de la Cruz, a negro from the land of Angola and the slave of Jacome Chirini according to the dictates of our holy mother church." Gracía then reported that Jacome had sent her husband to a water-powered mill, as a result of which "we have been separated from marriage, cohabitation, and the ability to have a married life as obligated." Gracía proposed that "in order that we cohabit and have a married life . . . your mercy should order the said Jacome Chirini" to transfer his slave to Mexico. "If Jacome opted to sell José," Gracía added, "then it should be a resident of this city." Finally, Gracía requested that José be promptly brought to Mexico. In the event that Jacome refused, the *provisor* should "send a person at his [Jacome Chirini's] expense in order to deliver him [José]." [65]

Gracía's petition bore the hallmarks of careful and Christian construction. She was, of course, a Christian but also a *bozal* slave from the Kongo region of West Central Africa. In other words, Gracía had recently become a Christian, yet she could already construct a narrative that enabled her to make personal demands that had political implications. Gracía observed that her husband's master had acted callously in sending José to a water-powered mill and beyond her presence. Jacome's indifference impeded the couples' "obligations" to have a marital existence. This resourceful woman, however, had a simple solution— return José to Mexico. Gracía's request was both skillfully crafted and daring. Her proposal offered nothing less than a challenge to slavery. [66] After all, García stated that Jacome should regulate his slave in consideration of "their obligations." If slavery accorded masters absolute control over the slave, then Gracía's demands—voiced publicly and duly recorded in the ecclesiastical court —questioned the very essence of bondage.

In bestowing on Christians the right to a married life, canon law did not stipulate the nature of this conjugal existence. Similarly, the canons never envisioned that the enslaved would employ ecclesiastical law, which was ostensibly crafted to regulate Christians, to define the nature of the duties with which they would make claims on their rights. Gracía determined that the law obligated her and José to have a married life, an abstraction that called for cohabitation. To effect cohabitation, José needed to reside in proximity to Gracía. By elaborating on "their obligations" in the way the medieval canon lawyers never intended, Gracía attempted to expand her rights and those of her husband as members of a Christian couple.

As many of the aforementioned examples illustrate and this case makes explicit, the language of duty and privilege provided slaves with a strategy that they exploited to their advantage. In the hands of the enslaved, married life became more than legally sanctioned marriage. For those held in bondage, it represented a meaningful conjugal existence that above all else involved time—time for cohabitation, for fulfilling the marital debt, and even to be parents. In specifying the content of conjugality, the enslaved relied on their developing legal consciousness to exploit the law's ambiguity to their advantage. Their choice to do so provides us a glimpse of the effects of the legal system on the formation of culture.

The *provisor* thought García's proposal sounded both reasonable and legitimate. He issued an order that effectively repeated all of Gracía's demands. In an understated yet important way, he also followed Gracía's lead in delimiting slavery. As the ecclesiastical judged instructed Jacome Chirini to allow José "to cohabit and to have a married life," he specified a designated amount of time. "If he [Jacome Chirini] should take his slave from this city," the *provisor* stipulated "he should return him to her within six days." In decreeing a specific amount of time, the judged allotted more than a day of visitation. On the day set aside, the *provisor* granted preeminence to José's identity as a Christian person over his status as a slave, and he sanctioned that identity under the threat of excommunication of that master who tried to thwart it. Suddenly, married life constituted more than a legally recognized abstraction—it acquired substance.[67]

On being notified of the ecclesiastical proceedings, Jacome Chirini manifested no interest in the *provisor*'s decree restricting him to his slave six out of seven days. Capitán Chirini was more concerned with José's insolence and the slave's proclivity to flee. Jacome also felt that the *provisor* needed to know that Gracía had instigated most of the incidents he was about to reveal. According to Jacome, José de la Cruz had entered his household because Gracía had persuaded him to take custody of the slave on the grounds that they were married. Rather than allowing José to languish in a textile mill—in which Juan López Godinez, his master, had placed him—Jacome took possession of the slave. The capitán alleged that Gracía "came to my house many times asking me to take the said negro from the obraje saying he was her husband." Only later did he learn that Gracía had deceived him.[68]

Once José resided with his new custodian, he allegedly became insolent, eventually fleeing for more than a month. For Jacome Chirini, Gracía represented the culprit, and he immediately resolved to return José to his master. The couple also acted quickly. Intent on remaining together, Gracía and José opted for a legal marriage as the most judicious tactic. Jacome learned of Gracía's initial deception through the announcement of their banns. These ecclesiastical formalities also alerted him to José's future presence. As Jose left the cathedral with his new bride, a constable accompanying Jacome Chirini detained the slave and returned him to the textile mill. Fearful of José's pending return to his master's distant sugar estate, Gracía searched frantically for a buyer. In trying to secure a new owner for José that would enable them to have a married life, even the constable came to the couples' aid. Neither Gracía nor the constable were effective. Crown officials eventually shipped José to his owner even though that action impeded the couple's conjugal existence.

As he concluded his statement, Jacome Chirini acknowledged the couple's right to married life. He asked that the *provisor* tell Gracía to locate a buyer for José. Jacome Chirini stated that in the event she could not do so, "I am charged in name of the said Juan López Godinez to buy the said black woman if she is a slave in order to take her to the said sugar estate so as to assist her husband." With this offer, Jacome Chirini left Gracía de la Cruz in a quandary. She had married José to prevent his return to the sugar estate, but now bondage—in a legal and matrimonial sense—threatened to reunite her and her husband on the feared sugar estate.

Gracía was not, however, easily outwitted. Three weeks later, she informed the *provisor* that she was in compliance with his ruling. She had searched actively for a buyer. Yet José's absence presented her with an impossible task. Buyers, Gracía exclaimed, wanted to see the slave. Thus, the *provisor* should compel Jacome Chirini to bring José to Mexico. Finding her appeal convincing, the judge acceded to her request. After five months and repeated orders, Jacome Chirini finally responded. Instead of acquiescing to the *provisor*'s order, the capitán asked that the matter be taken up with Juan López Godinez, José's master. As the administrator of Juan López Godinez's sugar estate, Jacome saw no reason why the judge should make "me go against my judgment or obligate me the turn over the slave." "Don't induce in me an action beyond my duties," pleaded the capitán, especially "when the deed ought to be handled by the slave's legitimate owner."[69] However, the *provisor* did not relent, and Jacome Chirini eventually acquiesced to the order by placing José in a Mexico City textile mill.

Suddenly, Gracía felt pressured to find a buyer. After nearly two months, she still had no definitive prospect. She attributed her lack of success to an illness that until lately had confined her to the chapel of Santa Cruz. She simply needed more time and permission to have a constable escort José "to the homes of persons who wanted to buy him." With this petition, Gracía's active involvement in the case ends.[70] In the course of the proceedings, which lasted another year, Gracía's master, Juan de Cespedes, defended his slave and insisted that she should not be obligated to find a buyer. Juan de Cespedes saw this as an undue burden on Gracía that ironically—in light of her demand that José be granted cohabitation time—would detract from her labor obligations to him.[71] We do not know how the *provisor* resolved the matter. Gracía's tenacity, bolstered by her master's support and the might of ecclesiastical law, probably ensured the couple a conjugal existence in Mexico City.

In New Spain, numerous slaves like Gracía de la Cruz emerged. As astute observers of the legal landscape, they mobilized the weapons at their disposal. Some resorted to civil courts in pressing for their freedom and that of their children. Others claimed in the same courts that abusive and sadistic masters had forfeited their ownership rights. In some instances, slaves and free persons prevailed in civil courts, but most successful cases emerged from ecclesiastical proceedings. The *provisor,* sanctioned in his actions by canon law, offered slaves and dependents the most dependable weapon to change their life circumstances. The language of obligation bestowed rights that persons of African descent sought to exploit to their advantage. In the process of doing so, Africans and their descendants used the regulatory sites in ways the designers never intended. The instruments of rule sought to master the experiences of Guinea's children. For these reasons, the regulatory agencies recorded the innumerable encounters with Africans and their various descendants that began in Guinea and continued indefinitely in the Indies.

6 Creoles and Christian Narratives

The contemporary state of race relations almost always affects what blacks are willing to tell whites.[1]

I read these documents with the hope of gaining a glimpse of black life during slavery and the postbellum period while remaining aware of the impossibility of fully reconstituting the experience of the enslaved.[2]

After mass on March 6, 1575, inquisition officials in Mexico City escorted thirty-one penitents—wearing *sanbenitos*, with candles in hand, nooses around their necks, and paper coronets on their heads—from the Franciscan chapel of San José.[3] Outside, the tribunal's *alguacil* and his deputies stripped the twenty-four men and seven women of their shirts and then placed them on pack animals. They then led the penitents through the principal streets while the newly appointed inquisitor general, Licenciado Don Alonso Hernández de Bonilla, presided over a separate but related procession.[4] Like before, a motley gathering observed the auto-de-fé's somber spectacle. In the *plaza mayor*, the two processions united and the officials proclaimed the penitents' "crimes" to a throng of onlookers. At the culmination of this spectacle, the *alguacil* dragged the Irishman William Cornelius, another survivor of the Hawkins expedition, from the scaffold and led him to the San Hipólito marketplace. There the executioner administered several fatal blows and tied the dying man to the stake before setting him ablaze. The following day, executioners administered, on average, 200 lashes to twenty-nine of the penitents. Among the thirty-one were the mulattos Isabel Díaz, Francisco Granados, Juan de Perales, and Beatriz Ramírez. The executioners applied 100 lashes to Isabel Díaz's "dark and stocky" back, administered 200 strokes to Beatriz Ramírez's "short and fat" body and that of Francisco Granados while reserving the lion's share, 300 lashes, for Juan de Perales.[5] Afterward, exile and seclusion awaited all four victims.[6] Even with the ultimate display of power—the taking of life—modesty in size, pomp, and the social status of the penitents characterized this two-day ritualized display.

With New Spain's second auto-de-fé, the tribunal shifted its gaze to members of the República de los Españoles. In so doing, the tribunal attempted to impose orthodoxy on the commonwealth. The inquisitors specifically aimed their offensive against the amorphous population defined as "people of reason." As was customary in the Old World, the tribunal directed considerable energy at regional problems. "Each Inquisition," Solange Alberro, a noted authority, has observed, "proceeded according to its 'style,'" but in line with regional practices and local concepts of justice.[7] In short, the inquisitors modified their strategy in accordance with a region's cultural topography. In sixteenth-century New Spain, particularly in the viceregal epicenter, the African majority and the rapidly growing hybrid population represented a specific concern that prompted numerous inquisition proceedings against *bozales,* black creoles, and particularly mulattos. For the tribunal, the lack of conformity to Christian practice among *bozales* and black creoles, a phenomenon equally manifest among the growing hybrid population, threatened the dominion of the *república* and the Catholic sovereign. The specter of sedition exacerbated the tribunal's concerns about heresy.[8]

The numerous inquisition proceedings involving Africans and their various descendants underscore official anxieties about that population's growth and its purported defiance of Christianity. Mastering the República de los Españoles necessitated control over its African majority and the proliferating population of African descent. In their regulatory efforts, Spaniards did not restrict themselves to corporal punishment and an armed presence. Despite the pillory's ubiquity, authority generally assumed a cultural and legal character. Physical violence represented a measure of last resort. By subjecting Africans and their descendants to its jurisdiction—a legal as well as a cultural act—the tribunal attempted to shore up orthodoxy, which they inextricably linked to Christian gender and familial and kinship norms employed in the service of the Spanish state. But in defining Christian obligations, the inquisitors also granted the king's subjects rights as Christians.[9] As the descendants of Africans —slave and free—grappled with Christian customs, they manifested a Christian subjectivity that emerged from the lexicon of rights and obligations. *Bozales* grasped their subjective sense of self as Christians soon after landing in the Indies, and they rapidly assimilated the dominant moral discourse and its corresponding rituals in practice, if not in content.

As a result of their creole consciousness, persons of African descent represented themselves and their experiences at inquisition proceedings in conformance with Christian norms. These representations, filtered by Christianity's moral discourse, offer a unique glimpse of the lives of Africans and their descendants in the New World.[10] As the accused and witnesses discussed family members, friends, and foes, the events and experiences they described transcend the historical narrative with its incessant focus on the linear, the symmetrical, and analytical coherence. Though disjointed, ambiguous, and produced within the context of an interrogation, the anecdotes constitute the earliest and richest sources pertaining to the African and Afromestizo past.[11] Like all representations, they derived from a regulatory process yet embodied conformance and contest.[12] Evidence of Christian compliance surfaced as often as did indifference to Christian morality. While the trial proceedings highlight human folly and foibles, they also underscore the expectations of the inquisitors. In regulating the social practices of Africans and their descendants, the tribunal held *bozales,* black creoles, and mulattos to the highest Christian standards. For enslaved persons of African descent, such standards implicitly limited the masters' ability to define human chattel solely as property. But these moral standards—often configured around the use of the body—also shaped existing representations of New World African identities and those of their descendants, since Christianity encompassed ethics and more. Despite the contest over morality, the enslaved and the colonized occupied a disadvantaged position that required them to modify at least the external manifestation of their beliefs, cultural practices, and behavior in accordance with Christian orthodoxy. Discerning the implications of Christian regulation for persons of African descent represents a significant part of this chapter.

Marital Transgressions

As Beatriz Ramírez lingered near death, friends and familiars expressed mixed emotions. Few, if any, rejoiced at her suffering. Even Beatriz's legitimate husband, Diego López, known as "el Indio," whose honor she had besmirched, probably did not entertain festive thoughts as his wife suffered the executioner's excruciating blows. Though he may have seen the auto-de-fé and Beatriz's flogging as retribution, el Indio had little cause to celebrate. He had been unsuccessful at controlling Beatriz, and the trial and the dramatic spectacle also represented a public indictment against his masculinity.[13] On the other hand, Beatriz's second husband, Diego López—a forty-year-old black creole known as "el Negro"—probably manifested both remorse for having reported his wife to the tribunal and relief that he had avoided punishment. He too felt the executioner's strokes, since they dismantled the social network that he, Diego López, and Beatriz had painstakingly created. The trial testimony, though a product of regulation, offers a rare glimpse of their social network.

In the late 1550s, Antonío de Savedra, a Spaniard employed on Don Luís de Castillo's hacienda in Taxco's mining center, hired the young free mulatto Beatriz Ramirez as a domestic servant.[14] Evidently, Don Luís employed one or both of her parents, since Beatriz recalled being reared in his household. Beatriz probably first entered the labor market as Antonío de Savedra's employee while she was still in her early teens. In 1558, soon after he acquired Beatriz's services, Antonío de Savedra left Taxco for the newly formed bishopric of Michoácan with his mulatto servant in tow.[15] Near the ever-shifting "Chichimeca" frontier, Antonío de Savedra found employment for himself and his servant with the rancher Gaspar de Salvago, owner of several ranches four

leagues from the pueblo of San Miguel.[16] Beatriz eventually developed a romantic attachment to one of the cowboys, known as el Indio, with whom
she subsequently cohabited. Unsatisfied with this arrangement, the couple requested Antonío de Savedra's permission to be married.[17] Within days, Father
Pinto married Beatriz and el Indio in the presence of a large contingent of "Indians, blacks, mestizos and Spaniards" from the Salvago estate and the pueblo
of San Miguel.[18] Afterward, the newlyweds returned to the ranch. The relationship soon soured; years later, Beatriz informed the inquisitors that Diego "gave
me a bad life . . . beating me where and whenever he wanted."[19] The insufferable abuse prompted Beatriz to flee for Guanajuato, ending their 2-year marriage.

On April 20, 1574, the day that the other Diego López, known as el Negro,
appeared unsolicited before the Inquisition so as to "discharge his conscience,"
he had been married to the mulatto for six years.[20] El Negro met Beatriz in
Guanajuato soon after she left her abusive husband. After a brief period in the
mining center, Beatriz and her new companion headed south for Oaxaca, where
el Negro had been the archdeacon's slave before securing his freedom. The
couple formalized their relationship in Oaxaca, but they eventually departed
for Mexico City, where they settled in the barrio of Santa María la Redonda.[21]
Unfortunately, Beatriz's former neighbor and coworker on the Salvago estate,
the mestizo Juan de Medina, also resided there.

During an encounter with Beatriz, Juan asked about el Indio, only to be told
"he was dead."[22] Juan evidently knew otherwise and informed Gaspar de Salvago, now residing in Mexico City, of this meeting.[23] Don Gaspar, in turn,
notified el Indio of his wife's whereabouts and sent word about Beatriz's previous marriage to el Negro. On learning of Beatriz's previous relationship, el
Negro allegedly confronted her; she assured him that "they had never married."[24] Beatriz evidently assuaged Diego's concerns, since a month later don
Gaspar sent another envoy with the other Diego in tow to confront el Negro in
the plaza where he sold fruit. Finally, convinced of Beatriz's guilt or simply
fearful of recriminations, el Negro proceeded to the Inquisition.

Initially, Beatriz denied any wrongdoing, claiming that the proceedings with
el Indio had not been binding. Though she acknowledged having had a relationship with Diego López which included sex, Beatriz insisted that she had
the moral authority to abandon him since "he gave me a bad life." During intense cross-examination, Beatriz maintained her innocence, but six months
later, after surviving a life-threatening illness, she confessed to the first marriage.[25] According to Beatriz, "fear of justice" prompted her previous denials.
The inquisitors, however, ruled unanimously against Beatriz Ramirez; they had
little patience with deception and even less with bigamists.[26] If the inquisitors
hoped to mend the tear in the moral fabric, they had to make examples of in-

dividuals such as Beatriz Ramírez. As mulattos, Beatriz Ramírez, Isabel Díaz, and Francisco Granados constituted part of a visible population and a perceived threat that the tribunal actively tried to curb.

As the *alguaciles* paraded Isabel Díaz and Francisco Granados through Mexico City on a pack animal, "naked from the waist up," the two mulattos seemed unlikely threats to the moral order. But, the inquisitors saw matters differently. As some of Mexico City's residents peered at Isabel Díaz and Francisco Granados's familiar but harried faces, they probably questioned the judgment of the inquisitors. Even though the inquisitors had convicted Isabel and Francisco of bigamy, some residents of Tacuba, San Agustín, San Sebastian, Santa Ana, and San Juan, among other Mexico City neighborhoods in which Isabel and Francisco had resided, entertained competing views about the guilt of their sibling, friend, employee, workmate, and neighbor.[27] After all, the couple had been publicly involved with each other for many years prior to their bigamous marriage.

The relationship between the lifelong residents of Mexico City began years after the Indian shoemaker Pedro García left his black wife, Isabel Díaz, and their infant mulatto daughter.[28] According to Isabel, "he left this city, never to return and some said that he was dead and others that he was alive."[29] At the time of the trial, Pedro had been absent from Mexico City for nearly fifteen years. In his absence, Isabel and the mulatto shoemaker, Francisco Granados, became lovers and initially seemed content with cohabiting. According to Isabel's employer Juan de Cintra, Francisco "frequented my house looking for her, taking her coming and going."[30] Although Juan and his wife, María Ramos, allegedly counseled for separation, Isabel and Francisco maintained their relationship. Undeterred, Francisco approached Juan de Cintra, stating that "some tell me that Isabel Díaz is married, others say no, some say her husband is dead.... I come to your mercy so that you may tell me the truth because I want to marry her."[31] Juan de Cintra, in turn, encouraged Francisco to ascertain if Pedro still lived. Juan advised Francisco that if Pedro was dead, he should "marry her at once, I will spend twenty or thirty pesos of good earnings on the fiesta and will be your patron helping . . . you establish a shop." But if Pedro still lived, Juan counseled Francisco to "separate yourself from her, since there are plenty of women."[32] Francisco did not act on Juan's advice. After killing a mestizo, he simply fled to Puebla with Isabel in tow.

From their arrival in Puebla, Francisco and Isabel acted married until Francisco fell seriously ill.[33] Fearful and "not wanting to die in mortal sin," Francisco implored Isabel to marry him, which she did, claiming that he had convinced her of Diego's death.[34] A few days after the hastily arranged wedding, Francisco recovered, and after two years the newlyweds returned to Mexico City. Four months after their return, the secular authorities arrested Francisco for murder, but Isabel soon arranged for his release. Thereafter, they lived together for several more months in the neighborhood of San Sebastian but separated when Isabel returned to her former employers, Juan de Cintra and María Ramos.

Isabel evidently hid her second marriage from her employers and relatives. Francisco instructed Isabel "not to say that he was her husband," but she also perceived it imprudent to circulate news about their marriage.[35] Paradoxically, Francisco, without being solicited, denounced Isabel to the inquisitors. This represented a calculated decision on Francisco's part to place all blame on Isabel. But, Francisco's strategy backfired, since far too many individuals knew of his relationship with Isabel. Gossip and rumors—the intangible manifestations of community boundaries—had circulated for years. It was only a matter of time before someone denounced Isabel and Francisco. The inquisitors ruled unanimously against Isabel Díaz and Francisco Granados but quibbled over the sentence. While one judge favored reducing the 100-peso fine by half, two inquisitors insisted on 100 additional lashes in light of the offense and the magnitude of Isabel and Francisco's deception. According to these two judges, the couple's crimes called for draconian measures since they undermined New Spain's moral fabric.[36]

In the case of Juan de Perales, the fourth person of African descent tried, convicted, and finally punished in the auto-de-fé of 1575, the tribunal also acted on hearsay but not injudiciously or with haste. In fact, it took nearly four years and two separate trial proceedings before the inquisitors found Juan guilty. In the final analysis, Juan's cunning offered no match for the tribunal's formidable arsenal. The young mulatto experienced the inquisitors' stinging wrath as an executioner dutifully administered 300 lashes.[37] Aside from courting the tribunal's attention, Juan's behavior also invited the ire of acquaintances whose disparaging prattle led to his conviction. In fact, the *fiscal* simply acted on information circulating freely among Juan's two wives and his in-laws, workmates, neighbors, and friends.[38] Juana, the mother of Juan's first wife Luísa, brought the bigamous marriage to the *fiscal*'s attention. Juan had borrowed money from Juana which he had never repaid and then shamed her daughter. In Juana, Juan made a relentless enemy. But Juan had numerous other adversaries, including his second wife (also named Juana), whom he attempted to control with frequent beatings.

In 1569, Juana, a 23-year-old mulatto servant and lifelong resident of Mexico, married mulatto Juan, who was a dung-cart driver. Many of her relatives, including her father, Francisco Suarez, and mother, María Hernández, witnessed the ceremony in Mexico's cathedral.[39] Despite this auspicious beginning, insinuations about Juana's infidelity wracked the marriage from the beginning. Rumors about Juana and Nicolás, the Portuguese-born slave of Don Luís de

Velasco, circulated freely. Pascual Nuñez, a black slave and resident of Mexico who had known Nicolás over ten years, noted that they "interacted as if they were good friends."[40] Mateo Díaz recalled seeing Nicolas and Juana "whispering secretly" with great frequency.[41] Even María Hernández, Juana's mother, testified that "eight years ago . . . Nicolas . . . informed me that 'Juana was his friend' and in spite of me . . . he had availed himself of her."[42]

Juan knew of these rumors and repeatedly chided Juana about ending her relationship with Nicolás. His efforts came to no avail, since María Hernández informed the inquisitors that Juan continually scolded Juana for conversing with Nicolás. Unable to dissuade his wife from seeing her alleged lover, a distraught Juan—with his masculine honor publicly scorned—resorted to physical abuse when he found Juana pregnant after his five-month absence from Mexico City. As his rage mounted Juan beat Juana mercilessly until he left the viceregal capital. Embittered by this abuse, Juana "wanted badly to kill" her husband.

In the end, she simply testified that Juan was previously married. Yet Juana's marital indiscretion and Nicolás's reputation as a drunk and philanderer cast doubts on her testimony.[43] In fact, the ecclesiastics acquitted Juan, who remained at large until January 1575, when the inquisitors, armed with additional testimony, had inconvertible proof of his guilt.[44] Though Juan's second wife had cause to indict her husband, his first wife Luísa's mother was instrumental in bringing his moral infraction to the inquisitors' attention. Juan had deeply offended her, and she relentlessly pursued justice. For his mother-in-law Juana, justice was served when the tribunal subjected Juan to the proceeding of faith.

Although the auto-de-fé linked the fate of the four mulattos, the cases—with the exception of the case of Isabel Díaz and Francisco Granados—were unrelated. Conceivably, Isabel Díaz and Francisco Granados knew Juan de Perales or Beatriz Ramírez prior to their encounter with the Inquisition. If so, they probably glimpsed one another strolling through the *traza* or the neighborhoods while pursuing daily chores or while traveling in search of work on New Spain's dusty commercial routes. To assume familiarity among them, however, belittles Mexico City's population density, underestimates New Spain's magnitude, and trivializes racial consciousness. Distinct social networks divided the shared social space that Isabel, Francisco, Juan, and Beatriz inhabited. The trial proceedings and, especially, the depositions provide a rare glimpse of this space and its contours. Simply put, in the second half of the sixteenth century, persons of African descent led much more ambiguous lives than heretofore imagined. This complexity manifested itself in their networks of relationships, the fluidity of their social relations, their mobility (irrespective of legal status), and their interaction with Spanish elite, ecclesiastical, and secular officials.

While these disparate narratives constitute important sources for reconstructing fragments of the African and Afromestizo past, they also delineate the parameters of New Spain's sixteenth-century moral terrain. From the inception of colonial rule, the Spaniards sought to insinuate Christian norms and practices among Amerindians, Africans, and their descendants. Although the brown and black majorities manifested distinct ideas about gender, sexuality, and kinship norms, their status as the colonized and the enslaved limited their ability to openly practice preexisting or newly constructed non-Christian mores. Yet it is unclear whether Africans and their descendants actually embraced Christian norms. If persons of African descent adhered to Christian norms, to what extent did these beliefs permeate their lives and consciousness? A closer examination of the trial narratives sheds light on their observance of Christianity, which in form, at least, reflected a highly sophisticated understanding of the dominant moral discourse. By means of this understanding, Africans and their descendants demonstrated the acumen that enabled them to navigate New Spain's sixteenth-century cultural landscape.

Sinners in the Community

Moments after Diego López known as el Negro came face to face with Diego López known as el Indio, he scurried in the direction of the barrio of Santo Domingo in order to "discharge his conscience." As the 40-year-old black fruit vendor sped toward the Inquisition's headquarters, he probably rehearsed his recent conversation. Nervous and possibly angry, Diego López recalled the encounter in the plaza where he usually plied his craft. After several blocks, Diego stood before an inquisitor recounting the exchange that prompted him to denounce his wife Beatriz Ramirez. Diego related how "today . . . selling fruit in the plaza . . . a small black servant with a black beard who walked in a clerical habit" approached him to ask what had he "done" about his wife's marriage. At first Diego took offense, informing the black man that "he lived with her as his wife." He then told his antagonist that "if someone knew anything they should come to express it." The strangely robed man, in turn, pointed and exclaimed "there was the said Indian her first husband and he had proof of such." The stranger warned Diego that el Indio had come "to give notice of her." Diego knew full well what the black man implied and made a beeline for the Inquisition.[45]

Diego clearly wished to avoid the fate of the Inquisition's most recent victims. As a cleric's former slave, Diego had a rudimentary understanding of Christianity and had probably experienced ecclesiastical wrath first hand. While Diego's motives remain shrouded in obscurity, his actions highlight an awareness of Christian orthodoxy. This awareness shaped the content of his confession.[46] As Diego described his life with Beatriz, he claimed ignorance about her previous marriage. Diego recounted how a month previously Gaspar Salvago had informed him that "his wife [Beatriz] was initially married with an Indian from his ranch."[47] Diego claimed to have confronted his wife on this matter. While Beatriz conceded that banns had been published, she maintained that "they had not married." Satisfied with this explanation, Diego did not pursue the matter until his encounter "today . . . in the plaza." Diego López concluded his testimony by insisting on his innocence.

At the conclusion of Diego's denunciation, the inquisitor asked a number of routine questions to substantiate the bigamy allegations. The interrogator wanted to know if there was anyone who could testify that he, Diego, had contracted marriage with Beatriz. Diego responded by naming Father Diego de Frías and Juan Díaz, both of whom had been in Oaxaca at the time of the wedding. Father Frías, a former resident of Oaxaca but now assigned to the Colegio de Mestizas in Mexico, had in fact granted the couple their marriage license, while Juan Díaz, the scribe of the lower court and now resident of Mexico, was present during the ceremony.[48] Next, the inquisitor asked Diego if he knew anyone who had knowledge of Beatriz's marriage "with the said indio." Diego declared that "he knew no more than what he had said." He thus denied knowing the whereabouts of Beatriz's alleged husband. Finally, the inquisitor asked Diego if he had come to testify out of malice. "No," responded Diego, stating that "to lose my wife would feel if I had lost an eye." At the conclusion of this remark, the inquisitor dismissed Diego with instructions "to guard the secret" or risk severe punishment.

On April 27th, a week later, Beatriz's reputed husband, Diego López alias el Indio, appeared unsolicited before the tribunal. His motives probably differed from those of el Negro. Beatriz, after all, had publicly shamed his masculine honor. As a result, Diego used the Holy Office to exorcise the personal dishonor his workmates had witnessed on the Salvago estate. But the 30-year-old indio ladino also knew that the Church frowned on malice; therefore he shaped his denunciation in a manner to appear as the aggrieved. El Indio noted how his employer Gaspar Salvago had recently "written him that the said Beatriz, his wife, was in Mexico married to a black man that they call Diego who sells fruit in the plaza [and] lives in Santa María la Redonda." The inquisitor responded by asking Diego if he harbored malice against Beatriz. "No," replied Diego, "she is my wife," noting that he came forward "to salvage his soul." Through such sentiments, Diego signified his conformance to Christian orthodoxy.

Diego subsequently declared that after the publication of the banns, Padre Pinto had united them in the presence of witnesses. He testified that he had married Beatriz in the pueblo of (San Miguel) Apaceo twelve years before while Gaspar Salvago, Antonío de Savedra, Rodrigo Quesada, "and some blacks" belonging to the mulatto Miguel Sánchez stood in attendance. Diego insisted on the legality of their actions, citing the banns, the exchange of hands, and "being together two years eating and sleeping together and having intercourse like husband and wife." At the end of those two years, Beatriz fled. Diego offered no explanation for her sudden departure. He only noted that Gaspar Salvago had recently informed him of Beatriz's whereabouts and her second marriage. As Diego recounted his interaction with Beatriz, he layered his confession with a Christian texture. Although some combination of piety, revenge, and self-portrayal as a victim informed Diego's narrative, the narrative also highlights his awareness of Christian moral discourse. Irrespective of his motives, Diego knew that the inquisitors defined Beatriz's behavior as sinful and thus he felt compelled to "give account to this Holy Office." Diego's confession manifested a Christian sensibility just three years after the Holy Office was established in Mexico City. The Inquisition insinuated itself among New Spain's inhabitants with great speed.

On the same day that Diego López, el Indio, leveled his denunciation, the inquisitors questioned a Spanish creole from the city of Santo Domingo, Antonío de Savedra. Asked if he knew why "he had been called," Antonío replied "yes." As a resident and employee on Gaspar Salvago's estates, Antonío knew both Beatriz and her first husband. In fact, sixteen years previously, Antonío had brought Beatriz to the Gaspar Salvago cattle estates. Beatriz subsequently informed him that "she wanted to marry an Indian named Diego." Antonío took the couple to the pueblo of San Miguel, where Beatriz and Diego López petitioned Padre Pinto for a marriage license. On receiving this request, the vicar, Antonío observed, issued the required banns. Antonío recalled how the vicar took Diego's and Beatriz's hands, "declaring them husband and wife" in accordance to the Holy Mother Church."[49]

Antonío testified that after the wedding, the newlyweds "returned to the ranch where they were together for a long time eating and sleeping together alone in their house like husband and wife." But two years after the ceremony, Beatriz fled for Guanajuato "without returning to her husband the said Indian Diego's dominion." Antonío recalled seeing Beatriz four years previously yet always in the company of the "black man who sells fruit in the plaza." Antonío had "heard it said," that Beatriz had married el Negro, who regularly observed how "she is his wife." On being told of Beatriz's previous marriage, el Negro, according to Antonío, manifested little concern about his marriage to a bigamist. "If she was married to the said Indian," Diego allegedly informed Antonío, "they would punish her but I will not be guilty." With this insinuation of Diego López's complicity, Antonío de Savedra concluded his testimony.

After the audience with Antonío de Savedra, the inquisitor ordered Beatriz's arrest.[50] Four days later, Beatriz had the first of three interviews with the tribunal. After she identified herself as a 25- or 26-year-old mulatto and native of Tasco's mines, Beatriz, as was customary, gave "the discourse of her life." She noted her birthplace on the hacienda of Don Luís de Castilla, where "she was reared having being born free from an Indian and a black father."[51] Beatriz testified that she lived near the "Chichimecas" frontier in Michóacan, Tasco, Guanajuato, Puebla, and Oaxaca before settling in Mexico. When asked why she had been incarcerated, Beatriz acknowledged knowing "the reason." Beatriz recalled having petitioned for banns "in a church on the said ranch." At the time she wanted to marry Diego López and he wanted "the same." Beatriz claimed that though they had their banns read, they "did nothing else." She thus denied having wed "the said Indian." Beatriz insisted that "the said cleric told them they should go to San Miguel that there he would marry them. They never went and as such it remained." Adamant that she had never married Diego, Beatriz testified that "he gave her a bad life . . . and would hit her where he wanted when he found her."[52] Finding the abuse insufferable, Beatriz acknowledged "fleeing to Guanajuato," where she eventually married Diego López, el Negro.[53]

During the initial warning, which followed "the discourse of her life," Beatriz observed that "I have already said what I have to say there is no more." But the inquisitor questioned Beatriz about the length of her marriage to Diego López, el Negro. She responded that they had been married five years. Then the inquisitor asked who was present during the wedding and whether any of those persons now resided in Mexico. Following Beatriz's response, the inquisitor raised the same question about the banns with Diego, el Indio. The event, Beatriz noted, had taken place fifteen years before "in the presence of indios and mulatos whose names she did not know."

Now the inquisitor asked why "did the marriage with the said Diego not go into effect?" "Because he gave me a bad life," responded Beatriz. The inquisitor wanted to know "if she had a married life with the said Indio and treated each other like husband and wife after the banns?" Beatriz acknowledged residing together "calling each other husband and wife and treating each other as such." The inquisitor then asked "where did the marriage take place since she was together with him calling him husband and living together like husband and wife?" Since they were engaged, Beatriz responded, "she was entitled to be together and to call him husband." But she insisted that they were only engaged. Next the inquisitor wanted to know if after the banns the cleric had taken their hands, proclaiming them husband and wife. "No, we never exchanged hands," responded Beatriz. "Did she believe that the banns constituted a promise to the said indio that she would marry him?" "No," replied Beatriz. The inquisitor then wondered if she "promised the said Diego, indio to marry him and he to marry her?" "This was the case," responded Beatriz. Asked if they had had carnal intercourse, Beatriz noted that "after the banns we were together and had carnal intercourse, thinking that he was her husband and treating him as such."

Next, the inquisitor asked Beatriz if the said Indian was dead or alive. Beatriz responded that "she had never seen him again, but her husband el Negro told her that some men had informed him that Diego was on the Salvago haciendas." The inquisitor asked Beatriz "Why did she marry a second time if she thought of the said Diego, indio, as her husband?" Beatriz recalled how "Father Pinto told her that she was not married to Diego and she could marry another person and not be lost." At this point, the inquisitor asked Beatriz for the truth, promising mercy if it were quickly revealed. On May 4th, Beatriz ratified her confession. Two days later, another interrogation took place. Afterward, the prosecutor formally charged Beatriz with bigamy and assigned her a lawyer. On the same day, the *fiscal* also presented Beatriz with the depositions without revealing the identities of the authors. Beatriz concurred with the content of the depositions except to contest the allegations that she had legally married "Diego el indio." A day later, the inquisitors again asked Beatriz to ratify her statements, and she complied.

Two weeks later, the inquisitors heard further testimony from Juan Díaz, the 16-year-old scribe of the "lower court" who knew Diego López, "the black fruit vendor," in Oaxaca. He simply asserted that "five years ago more or less" Diego the free black "having been the slave of the archdeacon" married Beatriz whom he identified as a "short and fat mulatto."[54] That same day, the inquisitors received additional information from the mestizo Juan de Medina. A "native of Mexico" and resident of Santa María la Redonda, Medina recalled that "sixteen years ago more or less" Gaspar Salvago had sent him to Mexico "with letters" and that by the time he returned to the ranch, Padre Pinto "had married" Diego and Beatriz, who until that time had cohabited. Although Medina missed the ceremony, Gaspar Salvago, Antonío Savedra, and "all the Indians, blacks, mestizos and Spaniards" who had witnessed the event told him about it afterward. Medina noted that for a while Beatriz and Diego enjoyed conjugality. He stated that Beatriz habitually identified el Indio as her "husband." Juan Medina concluded his testimony by detailing his recent encounter with Beatriz in the viceregal capital. When asked about "Diego el Indio her husband," Beatriz simply observed that "he was now dead."

Two weeks later, Dr. de la Fuente, the tribunal's physician, informed the inquisitors that Beatriz had fallen ill and "was in need of bleeding and purging." He requested permission to transfer Beatriz to a hospital. The inquisitor granted this request but ordered the steward not to permit Beatriz to leave "without license from this Holy Office." The brush with death evidently encouraged Beatriz to rethink her previous declarations. After her recovery, Beatriz requested an audience, during which she implored God and the Holy Office for "mercy" for having lied about her relationship with "Diego the Indian cowboy." Beatriz admitted having married Diego, something she had previously denied "out of fear that justice would be blind." After this dramatic confession, the inquisitors convicted Beatriz, but instead of mercy she received a stiff sentence.

After six months and intense cross-examination, Beatriz Ramirez finally acknowledged having lied. She, of course, did so "out of fear." Despite the utilitarian motives behind her actions, the ability to construct and maintain a deception of this magnitude highlights Beatriz's understanding of the dominant moral discourse. Beatriz's awareness of Christian morality enabled her to fabricate a credible narrative. Aside from depicting herself as a virtuous Christian female who left an abusive spouse, Beatriz displayed remarkable poise during the interrogations.[55] Following the reading of the banns, Beatriz acknowledged having "had carnal copulation" with Diego. Again, Beatriz wanted the inquisitors to know that she was cognizant of when the Church permitted sexual intercourse. Although Beatriz initially denied "that they gave hands" she knew that engagement condoned sex. Beatriz willing conceded that, "thinking that he [el Indio] was her husband . . . they had carnal copulation" as a part of her female obligation. Yet when Diego "gave her a bad life," Beatriz ended the relationship. Attempting to tap the judges' moral sensibilities Beatriz stated that "he beat her wherever he wanted when he encountered her." Beatriz knew that Diego's behavior violated Christian norms and that she could elicit the inquisitors' masculine sympathy. Beatriz's rhetorical strategy, with its Christian allusions, reveals a sophisticated awareness of Catholic morality and masculine honor.[56]

Beatriz's responses and the persistent ways in which she lied underscore her immersion in the dominant culture of New Spain—a phenomenon rarely associated with the enslaved and freedpersons of African descent—which temporarily allowed her to impede the judicial proceedings headed by literate and learned Spaniards. This tactical use of Christianity should not be a surprise. Spanish ecclesiastics held Africans and their descendants to Christian moral standards. Christian morality invariably prescribed gendered behavior, gendered social and ceremonial practices, and an elaborate system of domestic norms. Although this awareness enabled Beatriz to momentarily engage inquisition officials on their terms, her actual beliefs remain obscured. Beatriz may have adhered to the Christian beliefs and practices that informed her trial narrative. But it was not necessary to practice orthodoxy to construct a Christian narrative. A rudimentary understanding of Christianity was all that Beatriz required.[57]

Individuals did not fabricate lies simply for the inquisitors. Persons who tried to deceive the inquisitors invariably concocted similar fictions for neighbors, workmates, and kin.[58] Fear prompted individuals to lie to family and friends, a fact that highlights the ambiguous role of acquaintances as accomplices and informants. Driven by a mix that included self-interest, vengeance, and a Christian conscience, family and friends invariably helped the Church and the Inquisition to police public morality. Suspicious that neighbors, kin, employers, and co-workers would report them to the authorities, individuals often lied to their nearest and dearest. Lies, as the following example illustrates, did not just flow vertically between sinners and the inquisitors. Like rumors and gossip, they also circulated horizontally among family and peers. In fact, the circuit of a lie magnifies community boundaries; it includes deception, secrets, and misrepresentation under the guise of belonging.

In the early morning of July 19, 1574, a 26-year-old mulatto clog maker, a resident of the viceregal capital, appeared unsolicited before Inquisitor Bonilla. After identifying himself as Francisco Granados, the Mexico native proceeded "to make known" his 6-year relationship with the free mulatto Isabel Díaz, who was employed by Juan de Cintra.[59] Four of those years, Francisco confessed, were spent in concubinage. But two years previously he had fallen ill while residing in Puebla with Isabel, at which time a priest had married them.[60] After he recovered, Francisco acknowledged fulfilling his marital obligations, which included having "copulated as with his wife." Eventually, the couple moved to Mexico. A year into his marriage with Isabel, Francisco learned from a shoemaker on Tacuba Street named Parrales that Isabel Díaz was already married to Pedro, an Indian who had worked for the cobbler. As proof, Parrales offered Juan de Cintra and María Ramos. Francisco ended his testimony by ascribing sole responsibility for the bigamy to Isabel Díaz.

Following this denunciation, the inquisitor asked Francisco if he knew whether Pedro was "alive or dead." Francisco deflected the question, noting that it was only after his marriage to Isabel that Parrales had informed him that Pedro "was alive in Aguascalientes." Inquisitor Bonilla then asked Francisco about the wedding proceedings, in particular whether the banns had been publicized in Puebla. Francisco replied affirmatively, "because the silk weavers . . . told me that about the banns since I was sick in the house." Finally, the inquisitor asked Francisco about Isabel's whereabouts. Though he insisted he had not seen Isabel in a month, Francisco revealed that "every day she comes to Juan de Cintra's house, where she has a daughter whom they say is from her first husband." As the inquisitor ended his cross-examination, he inquired whether Francisco harbored malice toward Isabel Díaz. "No," replied Francisco.

On July 20, 1574, the day after Francisco Granados made his denunciation, the inquisitor heard corroborating evidence from Spaniards Juan de Cintra and his wife, María Ramos, Isabel's lifelong employers and alleged godparents.

When asked why he had been called, the 50-year-old blacksmith replied he did not know the reason for his appearance before the tribunal. The inquisitor then asked the Madrid native and resident of Tacuba Street about the composition of his household staff. Juan stated that his household included a black woman, an Indian woman from the northern frontier, and a mulatto of fourteen years, who was the daughter of Isabel Díaz and Pedro García. Alerted by the inquisitor's interest in Isabel Díaz, Juan identified Pedro García as the person the black woman had married, the cathedral as the wedding site, and his role as godfather.[61] Juan noted that the wedding had taken place nearly fourteen years before, but recalled that their "married life" had lasted only two or three years. Afterward, "Pedro García, an Indian, left this city and never again has returned." According to Juan, however, Pedro was still alive since his brother-in-law, Francisco Carranza, had seen him in the vicinity of Guanajuato. Subsequently, the inquisitor asked for a description of Isabel Díaz and Pedro García. Juan described Isabel as "a mulatto approximately thirty-five-years old, very black, ugly, with a good stature and very large breast." He characterized Pedro as a 30-year-old Indian who was "crazed as if he were much beyond reason." According to Juan, Pedro's mental state explained his sudden departure and long absence from Mexico. This absence convinced Juan that Isabel did not know "if he [Pedro García] was alive or dead." In fact, Juan assured the inquisitor that if Isabel Díaz had any information about Pedro's death "she would have come to his house to tell him."[62]

Next, the inquisitors interviewed 55-year-old María Ramos, who also claimed not to know "why she had been called." As was customary, the inquisitor asked María if "she knew of any persons who have done or said some thing that ought to be manifest in this Holy Office." María stated that she had nothing to report. Still, the inquisitor pursued this line of inquiry, asking María if she knew anyone who had violated "the seven sacraments . . . and particularly . . . marriage."[63] Again María responded, "No." At this point, the inquisitor opted for a more direct approach. He questioned María about the composition of her servant staff. María identified two enslaved black women and the free mulatto Isabel Díaz, who came "to serve when they called her."[64] María began testifying about her servant's marriage to Pedro, her role as godmother, and Pedro's subsequent departure. María remarked that despite Pedro's lengthy absence, Isabel "always" believed that her husband was alive "because she never has heard that . . . he was dead." Indeed, "a year ago" María's relatives, Pedro Carranza and his son Juan, informed Isabel "that they have seen the said Pedro guarding livestock." Armed with this information, the inquisitor asked María "if she knew" whether Isabel remarried. "No," replied María.[65] Like her husband, Juan de Cintra, María insisted that Isabel would have informed her of a marriage.

For the punctilious inquisitors, the conclusion of María Ramos's testimony did not signal the end of that day's investigation. Juan de Cintra and María Ramos mentioned that their kin, Carranza, who was the treasurer of Mexico's royal court, and his son, Juan, had recently sighted Pedro García. If the tribunal wished to pursue bigamy allegations against Isabel Díaz, they needed assurance that Pedro was, in fact, alive. With the 40-year-old Spaniard Diego de Carranza, the inquisitors forsook the vague introductory questions with which they hoped to learn of suspicious behavior. They asked Diego directly "if he knew Isabel Díaz, Juan de Cintra's mulatto servant, ugly, very black, with good stature and ugly breast." Diego responded that "he knew her well." He observed that Isabel was married to the Indian Pedro García, "a ladino, tall of stature [and] somewhat crazed" with whom she had a 14-year-old daughter. Though he had not attended the wedding, Diego recalled the event. He did, however, see Isabel and Pedro together referring to each other as husband and wife.[66] After a few years, Pedro departed and "he [Diego] never saw him again in the city [Mexico]."

But Diego did see Pedro again. Over a year before, on the road from Guadalajara, he had encountered Pedro "near the village of Lagos." According to Diego, Pedro García was guarding pigs belonging to his Spanish brother-in-law Salazar. "That night and the following day," Diego spoke to Pedro. Pedro even gave Diego a message and some money for Isabel Díaz, which the latter promptly delivered. Since then, Diego claimed he had never seen Pedro again.[67] With Diego's testimony and the identical statement from Juan de Carranza, Diego's son, the inquisitors had sufficient evidence for a formal indictment. On July 20th, the presiding official ordered Isabel's arrest. That same day, he wrote the archdeacon of Puebla's cathedral requesting assistance in ascertaining the circumstances of Francisco Granados and Isabel Díaz's wedding.[68]

On Wednesday July 21, 1574—two days after Francisco Granados leveled his denunciation and a day after the inquisitors interrogated the first battery of witnesses—the tribunal's *alguacil* escorted Isabel Díaz up from the Inquisition's dank cellar. Isabel identified herself as a 35-year-old mulatto and native of Mexico, the daughter of the mulatto Francisco Díaz and "an india whose name I do not know."[69] Asked for "the discourse of her life," Isabel recalled her birth in Mexico, where "she has always resided" with the exception of three years in Puebla. She said that she knew the reason for her arrest. She then described her marriage to Pedro García eighteen years before in Mexico's cathedral. Isabel could not remember the curate's name but observed that he had returned to Spain. Isabel spent several months with Pedro before learning of her pregnancy. Isabel recalled that Pedro, "who was very crazed," soon left Mexico, never to return. Isabel then remarked that "some said he was dead" but others believed he lived. She, however, never knew for sure.

Introducing the subject of Francisco Granados, Isabel acknowledged an 8-

year relationship with the mulatto clog maker that had begun in Mexico but had carried over to Puebla after he "killed a man."[70] In Puebla, Francisco informed Isabel that "Pedro, her husband, was dead." And when Francisco Granados fell ill, he implored Isabel to marry him. Isabel insisted that, uncertain about Pedro's death, she had initially refused. Francisco had countered that "he knew in Mexico that he [Pedro García] was dead because a negro had told him." Isabel finally relented and married the ailing Francisco. But then Francisco recovered. Though "never veiled," Isabel confessed that they had lived like husband and wife.[71] Eventually the couple moved back to Mexico City. There they experienced a brief separation when the civil authorities apprehended Francisco for murder. Isabel soon secured Francisco's freedom. For a while they resided in Juan de Cintra's house on Tacuba Street. Isabel recalled that she hid the marriage from her employers. The relationship finally ended when Francisco informed Isabel that "she should not say that he was her husband." Isabel concluded her testimony, noting "she has no more to say."

As the inquisitor cross-examined Isabel, he focused on procedural matters. Did she, for instance, inform Puebla's ecclesiastical officials of her previous marriage? "No," answered Isabel, but noted "Nor did they ask." The inquisitor wanted to know why she believed Francisco's story about Pedro's death. He also asked if anyone else had been present at the moment of persuasion. Isabel responded that they had been alone when Francisco informed her. In any case, she wanted to believe him. The inquisitor asked Isabel when she had learned that Pedro was alive. Isabel recalled being in the Cintra house when Francisco declared "Sister, don't you realize that what we have done has no value because they tell me that your husband is here." Finally, the inquisitor wanted to know if her employers, Juan de Cintra and María Ramos, knew whether Pedro was alive. Isabel could not respond with certainty but recalled that María Ramos questioned her interaction with Francisco. Isabel simply told her mistress that she wanted to marry Francisco. María Ramos advised Isabel not to act "without investigating . . . Pedro García's death." With this response, the inquisitor ended the initial cross-examination, assayed Isabel's property, issued a stern warning calling for "the truth," and ordered a cleansing of "the conscience." Only then could Isabel expect the Holy Office's customary clemency.

Isabel Díaz, however, had no more to say. In subsequent interrogations, Isabel observed "it is true that I am a baptized Christian and it is true that I married the said indio Pedro García and the said mulatto Francisco Granados as I confessed. Therefore I request a merciful penitence and that is the truth and I do not have any more to say." Following Isabel's third interview, the inquisitors formally charged her with bigamy, assigned her a lawyer, and initiated their deliberations. At the same time, Puebla's archdeacon began interrogating witnesses about Isabel and Francisco's wedding. This testimony underscores how the geographical scope of Francisco and Isabel's deception extended from Mexico to Puebla. In both locations the couple maintained the appearance of being good Christians. This appearance, as the Puebla testimony underscored, rested on lies and omissions.

On July 29th, the archdeacon heard evidence from a Granadian, Juan de Molina, a resident of Puebla. Juan testified that he had known Francisco Granados "more or less three years and eight months," since they lived in the same house.[72] Juan vividly recalled that Francisco fell ill and "being in danger of dying" called for a curate in order to confess. In the presence of other household residents, Francisco implored the priest to marry him to Isabel. Juan de Molina claimed that this request had come as a surprise since he thought that Isabel was already his wife. The priest acquiesced to the request and united Francisco and Isabel. Juan identified the marital witnesses as his wife, Isabel Romera, Francisco Ruíz, and Francisco's "Indian" wife Magdalena. Juan acknowledged that he had not been present "at the giving of the hands" but met the priest on the "other road" shortly after the service. Juan recalled that before leaving Puebla, Isabel and Francisco "lived together as husband and wife." In Mexico, he learned from Francisco "that he no longer has a life with the woman Isabel Díaz . . . [since] a man from afar came to Mexico and said that the said Isabel Díaz was his wife." Juan was worried that he might be implicated for not revealing what he knew and claimed that Francisco had assured him that "the *provisor* knew . . . and they have ordered that [I] not be with her." Since "the said Granados told him that the matter was before the *provisor*," Juan sought to deflect his guilt for not having denounced Isabel Díaz.[73]

Juan de Molina's wife, Isabel Romera, testified similarly. On learning that Isabel Díaz and Francisco Granados were not married, Isabel Romera also registered surprise since the couple arrived in Puebla referring to each other as husband and wife. Isabel Romero allegedly learned of the deception when Francisco Granados fell ill. She stated that the couple exchanged vows during Francisco's bout with death. Afterward, Isabel Romero and Isabel Díaz talked about mistaken perceptions. Isabel Romero recalled that Isabel Díaz finally "told her . . . that they have lived together eight years . . . and he wanted to marry her in order not to die in mortal sin."[74]

A day after providing their testimony, Isabel Romero and Juan de Molina reappeared before Puebla's archdeacon to ratify their depositions. The next day, Puebla's archdeacon heard testimony from Francisco Ruíz and his wife, Magdalena Ruíz. Magdalena defined herself as a 30-year-old "native of Mexico City" and resident of Puebla who had known Francisco Granados, the mulatto shoemaker, for five years. Francisco, who worked in Puebla, evidently frequented Mexico with regularity. Magdalena Ruíz recalled that after one of his trips, Francisco returned with "a mulatto servant called Isabel Díaz." "Until the said Granados fell ill of a dangerous sickness," Magdalena assumed that Isabel was his wife. Magdalena ended her testimony by noting that she had been present at the hastily arranged wedding.

Next, Francisco Ruíz presented his testimony. Like his wife, the 43-year-old Francisco identified himself as a native of Mexico City and a resident of Puebla. He claimed to have known Francisco Granados for five years "because they lived together in a house of the master school of the Holy Church." Asked "if he knew" of Francisco Granados's marriage and "with whom," Francisco Ruíz recalled the circumstances under which his housemate and workmate introduced Isabel Díaz. Francisco Ruíz informed the archdeacon that as a clog maker Francisco Granados made frequent trips to Mexico "to carry certain goods for his occupation." On one of these trips he returned with Isabel Díaz. But then Francisco Granados fell ill. During a bout with death lasting "all night and into the morning," Francisco pleaded "for the love of God" that a priest be called who would wed him to Isabel Díaz "because he did not want to die in mortal sin." With the curate's arrival, a hastily arranged marriage took place, at which many people were present. Shortly thereafter, Francisco recovered, but "three or four months" later left for Mexico with Isabel. Francisco Ruíz recalled seeing his former housemate in Mexico City and asked him about Isabel Díaz. Francisco Granados responded that "he no longer had a life with her since it is said that the said Isabel Díaz was married to an indio."[75]

On the following day, Magdalena and Francisco Ruíz ratified their depositions. A day later, the archdeacon wrote the tribunal to report his findings.[76] In Mexico City on the same day, the inquisitors heard further evidence from María Ramos, who brought additional information pertaining to Francisco Granados. Inquisitor Bonilla asked María Ramos pointedly "if she knew" whether Francisco Granados "has had interaction and communication with the said Isabel Díaz." María replied that after Pedro García left Mexico, Isabel Díaz and Francisco Granados started cohabiting. The inquisitor then asked María Ramos if Francisco Granados knew of Isabel Díaz's marriage to Pedro García. María informed the inquisitor that seven or eight years previously, Francisco Granados had confessed to her husband his desire to marry Isabel Díaz. Since Isabel was already married, Juan de Cintra denied the possibility of Francisco Granados's request. Juan de Cintra, however, encouraged Francisco "to investigate and to know if the said Pedro García was alive or dead." María Ramos noted that Juan de Cintra had even offered to defray the expenses involved. María Ramos remembered that afterward Francisco still insisted on coming to "her house with this demand," although he did nothing to ascertain Pedro García's status. María Ramos testified that she did not know if Francisco Granados had pursued this matter. Nonetheless, Isabel Díaz and Francisco Granados "dealt and had dealings" in her house. Convinced that

Francisco Granados knew of Isabel Díaz's marriage, Inquisitor Bonilla asked María "if there are other persons" who could testify about the mulattos' awareness that her servant "was married." María denied knowing any such persons and with derision noted that these "are the matters of mulattos."

María Ramos's additional testimony directed a serious indictment against Francisco Granados. Clearly, María Ramos wanted the inquisitors to know that Francisco Granados also bore some guilt. Indeed, María Ramos insinuated that Francisco Granados had masterminded the entire affair. By doing so, María Ramos relied on existing gender conventions, whereby males allegedly manipulated females. In any event, her testimony raised the specter of intentional malice toward Francisco. In their efforts to regulate the moral domain, the inquisitors directed just as much attention on intent as they did on heresy. As a result, they subjected Francisco Granados to greater scrutiny, especially once the dossier from Puebla arrived. On August 7th, the inquisitors received and examined the depositions from Puebla. On the same day, they released Isabel Díaz into the custody of Juan de Cintra, who had posted her bail.[77] As the inquisitors deliberated over Isabel Díaz's case, they focused increasingly on the involvement of Francisco Granados. María Ramos's deposition, the evidence from Puebla, and the additional testimony from Juan de Cintra encouraged the inquisitors to proceed against Francisco Granados for willful intent.

On the evening of September 1st, Juan de Cintra also reappeared before Inquisitor Bonilla. He too had come to provide additional testimony in the matter of Isabel Díaz and Francisco Granados. Juan recalled that "seven or eight years ago more or less" Francisco Granados and Isabel Díaz had cohabited. Juan stated that Francisco "frequented his house" in search of Isabel Díaz, from which he "took, carried and returned her." Alarmed by this interaction, Juan de Cintra repeatedly called on Francisco to end his relationship with Isabel. But Francisco, according to Juan, simply responded that "he wanted to marry her." Juan replied that this was impossible. Undeterred, Francisco eventually approached Juan, saying that "some tell me that Isabel Díaz is married, others no, others that her husband is dead. . . . I come to your mercy that you tell me the truth because I want to marry her." Juan responded that "I have already said many times that she is married to Pedro García, the Indian but what you should do is go where they say her husband is and if he is dead marry her and I will spend good money, twenty or thirty pesos, on the fiesta and will be your padrino and also will assist and favor you by establishing you in a shop. If he is alive, separate from her since you will not lack women." Juan de Cintra testified that after this melodramatic exchange "nothing happened because later he [Francisco] killed a mestizo and left for Puebla, where he took the said Isabel Díaz."[78] Though Juan stated that "nothing happened," the inquisitor repeated the question. This time, Juan replied that "he did not know what he

[Francisco] had done" in order to determine if Pedro García still lived. But Juan de Cintra doubted that Francisco Granados had pursued the matter and "since the said Isabel and her siblings frequented [his house] because they saw him as a father they would have told him." Instead, "because the said Granados killed the said mestizo," Juan concluded that he left for Puebla, eventually taking Isabel Díaz with him.

On August 2nd, Francisco returned to the Inquisition and in the presence of Pedro de los Ríos ratified his initial statement. The proceedings began with Francisco Granados noting that he had married Isabel Díaz four years before and "not two as he has said."[79] Following this correction, the inquisitor proceeded to ask Francisco a series of questions about Isabel Díaz's initial marriage. The inquisitor wondered if Francisco Granados had tried to ascertain if Pedro García "was dead or alive." "I did not try anything of the sort," replied Francisco. The inquisitor asked if while cohabiting with Isabel Díaz he had realized that she was a married woman. Francisco claimed that "she did not say that she was married nor did I know anything." The inquisitor challenged Francisco Granados about his response. Pedro de los Ríos remarked that "in this Holy Office there is information that the said Isabel Díaz told you that she was married and that you persuaded her to marry you telling her that you had been informed that Pedro García, indio, her first husband, was dead." Francisco denied these allegations, insisting that "there is no more that I have to say, she never told me that she was married."[80]

In October, a month later, the inquisitor finally proceeded against Francisco Granados. Sixteen days later, the *alguacil* of the Holy Office arrested Francisco, impressed his earthly possessions, and placed him in the Inquisition's goal.[81] The next day, the inquisitors interrogated the self-identified mulatto and "native of Mexico." Asked why he had been incarcerated, Francisco Granados insisted that it had to do with Isabel Díaz, whom "he came to denounce." In response an order to repeat his initial testimony, Francisco Granados declared that "he would tell the truth as if he stood before God." Francisco then revised his earlier testimony. He acknowledged having known Isabel ten as opposed to six years, which included a lengthy period of concubinage "with the said Isabel Díaz, knowing she was married to Pedro García. Francisco alleged that Isabel had informed him a year after they met that "her husband was dead." Implying that his interaction with Isabel was platonic at that time, Francisco recalled that she "left for the Chichimeca frontier since she longed for another person but returned, nearly a year later, at what point they started cohabiting until . . . I killed a mestizo for which reason I went to Puebla to live carrying the said Isabel Díaz with me."

In fabricating his narrative, Francisco Granados contradicted more than Isabel's version; he also questioned the corroborating testimony of interested and disinterested witnesses. Francisco clearly understood the nature of his moral transgression and desperately pointed blame at Isabel. He recalled speaking to Isabel about marriage, who "always responded that he [Pedro García] was dead." As a result, Francisco admitted, they initiated proceedings in Puebla. Careful to depict himself as a moral being, Francisco recalled how lingering doubts had led him to question Isabel's employer about his lover's marital status. He asked Juan de Cintra "to tell the truth if the said Isabel Díaz was married . . . and if he the husband was alive or dead since he wanted to marry her." Cintra's response, according to Francisco, was inconclusive. After falling ill in Puebla, Francisco, who was fearful of dying in sin for cohabiting with Isabel, asked to be married with his long-standing mistress. Francisco testified that when he subsequently learned that Pedro was alive, "I tried to separate from her . . . although a cleric who confessed me . . . told me that I was obligated to be with the said Isabel Díaz until I knew for certain if the said Pedro García her husband was truly alive, and I ought to go and find out. I did not go due to my poverty but more than two years ago I learned from a cowboy that the said Pedro García was alive in Aguascalientes." From that moment, he remarked that "I have not been together with her."

Francisco Granadas carefully crafted his testimony in order to appear as innocent. In his version, Isabel was the bigamist who willfully led him into a state of sin. Dubious that Pedro García was dead, though Isabel allegedly told him that he was, Francisco asked Juan de Cintra "to tell him the truth." Only a near-fatal illness and mortal sin prompted Francisco to dispense with the customary marriage proceedings. Even after unwittingly committing a sin, Francisco abided by the advice of his confessor, though it troubled his conscience. Wracked by moral pangs, Francisco left Isabel, eventually denouncing her to the Inquisition. In structuring this latest version of his narrative, Francisco insisted that "now I have told the truth without missing a point." Francisco acknowledged his earlier omissions, which he neglected to report "out of fear of being arrested." But the inquisitors had sufficient proof of Francisco's complicity in Isabel's bigamous marriage and his willful deception. Shortly thereafter, the inquisitors convicted Francisco Granados for facilitating a bigamous marriage. As this elaborate case underscores, deceivers did more than lie (both by commission and omission) to the inquisitors. Sinners invariably lied to a community comprised of kin, patrons, workmates, and neighbors. After the Inquisition began, it was advisable to lie to acquaintances and intimates since the tribunal thrived on placing a community of familiars on trial.

As familiars of an accused person stood before the inquisitors, it was often difficult to discern who was under investigation. The tribunal routinely initiated its proceedings by questioning witnesses whether they knew of any practices that violated the Church's teachings. Through this ritual the inquisitors elicited demonstrations of conformity whereby the witnesses manifested their identities as Christians. But the inquisitors' gesture also signified the tribunal's reliance on family members and neighbors, both friends and foes, to provide them with cultural intelligence. Even the formidable arsenal of the early modern state existed in a symbiotic relationship with the communities under its dominion.[82] Familiarity with the disciplinary regime that this relationship engendered enabled some individuals to navigate the regulatory maze to their advantage and to the disadvantage of others. The Inquisition thrived on this dynamic, and the symbiosis underscores the ways in which absolutism rested on the complex interaction between familiars, the aggrieved, and those who transgressed.

By means of this process Spanish absolutism emerged and insinuated its presence among the sovereign's disparate subjects. As the following case illustrates, rumors and gossip—which one lawyer referred to as the "inventions of his [client's] enemies"—spread the state's presence over a community and sustained the institutional memory so vital to defining the early modern state.

On January 21, 1575, the inquisitors received a letter from the criminal court's *alcalde* informing them of a free mulatto prisoner named Juan de Perales. The *alcalde* observed that Juan had been cleared of criminal wrongdoings but that a petition had arrived accusing him of being a bigamist and in flight from the Holy Office. On the basis of this accusation, the presiding inquisitor ordered Juan de Perales's transfer from the royal prison to the "secret cells of the Holy Office." The next day, a 30-year-old mulatto slave who was Juan's purported wife, Luísa Hernández, appeared before the tribunal as instructed. Asked by the inquisitor why she had been called, Luísa Hernández responded that it involved her husband, who had formerly been called Juan de Quesada but who was then identifying himself as Juan de Perales. Luísa testified that they had exchanged vows fifteen years earlier in the cathedral, but that as a result of her master's opposition, she had never been veiled. Luísa told the inquisitors that she and Juan had enlisted the ecclesiastical court's assistance to overcome Gaspar de Miranda's objections to their union. The *provisor* and his staff sequestered Luísa from her master's authority because she was entitled to conjugality even if he objected. A few days after having placed Luísa in *depósito*, the *provisor* granted the couple a marriage license and dispensed with the customary banns. Presented with a fait accompli, Gaspar de Miranda had shipped the newlyweds to his livestock estate in Tepozotlán. But after five months, Juan had abandoned Luísa, eventually taking another wife.

At the conclusion of Luísa's testimony, the inquisitors asked Juan for his version of the events. Initially, Juan insisted that he could not explain why the inquisitors held him captive. Then the *fiscal* questioned him about his marital status. He responded that he had been married for six years to the mulatto Juana Hernández. Following this interrogation, the *fiscal* advised Juan to clear his conscience. Prompted by this ritualized threat, Juan observed that four years before the *provisor* had initiated but then had dropped proceedings against him.

Five days later, following the customary second interrogation and the requisite warning, the turnkey of the Holy Office informed the inquisitors that he had narrowly averted Juan's escape. Alerted by Juan's soiled hands, he had uncovered a hole in the prisoner's cell. Though Juan acknowledged that he had dug the hole, he said that he had done so in order to see. The attempted escape raised even more suspicion about his guilt. After additional testimony and consultation of the proceedings of the ecclesiastical court, the tribunal convicted Juan of bigamy.

This case underscores the elaborate arsenal on which the inquisitors could draw. Despite its distinct jurisdiction, the criminal court brought Juan to the Inquisition's attention, and the ecclesiastical court granted the Holy Office access to its archives. Institutional memory, like history itself, represented a formidable weapon. Yet without the spark provided by personal animosity, a guilty conscience, or a desire for justice, institutional memory would have remained inert. As the proceedings against Juan de Perales reveal, individual denunciations mobilized the bureaucratic process.

The proceedings reveal that Juan had numerous enemies. For instance, Juan married Luísa despite her master's objections, thereby challenging Gaspar de Miranda's authority. Juan also borrowed money from Juana, Luísa's mother, which he never repaid. Then, after five months, he abandoned his bride, having enjoyed her virtue. Jealous and then angry about his second wife's affair with the enslaved black man from Portugal, Nicolás, Juan routinely beat Juana Hernández despite her pregnancy. Finally, a lawyer of the royal court denounced Juan after being informed about his past marriages days after he petitioned for another marriage license. A master, two mothers-in-law, a lover, and two wives all expressed deep-seated animosity against Juan de Perales. During the ecclesiastical proceedings, Pedro de Mora, Juan's court-appointed defender, convinced the *provisor* that the accusations simply represented the "inventions of his enemies." But the tenacity of Juan's foes and his blatant disregard for Christian conventions brought him before the tribunal of the Holy Office.

Juan's reckless abandon made him the subject of scrutiny. As regulatory instruments, the ecclesiastical court and the tribunal drew on the sentiments of the angered, the shamed, and the offended. Though the inquisitors always questioned witnesses about their beliefs and Christian conscience, revelations did not simply emanate as a result of this process. Grudges, personal vendettas, and an affront to an individual's sense of decency often prompted pointed testimony. Earlier we saw how Isabel Diaz's patrons, Juan de Cintra and María

Ramos, provided additional evidence highlighting Francisco Granados's complicity in transforming a member of their household into an adulteress and then a bigamist. Patrons were not the only persons to act in this manner. In the proceedings against Juan de Perales, Luísa's patrons represented the minority among those who testified. Most witnesses identified themselves as persons of African descent whose occupations were as servants and slaves. In transgressing their moral sensibilities, Juan violated the personal codes of individuals who shared a similar identity and status.

A group of plebeians such as this, in fact, may have expressed strong antipathy toward the representatives of church and state.[83] But Juan's behavior violated the norms of his own community and made it extremely unlikely that its members would collectively lie to help him. Juan had transgressed a localized moral economy, prompting those whom he offended or shamed to find justice in their revelations to the tribunal. Juana, a 50-year-old enslaved black woman and the mother of Juan's first wife, disliked her son-in-law. Mateo Diaz, a 40-year-old black slave, recalled that Juana had called Juan a rogue for not repaying the money she loaned him and for the way he treated her daughter.[84] Another witness, 30-year-old mulatto Juan Pérez, claimed that Juana "manifested hatred and anger against the said Juan . . . wanting badly to kill him."[85] By abandoning her daughter and refusing to honor his monetary debt, Juan had invited Juana's ire. In Juana, Juan confronted a tenacious opponent. As Juana spoke against Juan, she upheld the belief system that the Inquisition intended to uphold. Juana took offense that Juan had abandoned her daughter and refused to respect his financial debt. She lambasted Juan before all who would listen. Juana's anger stemmed not from Juan's violation of Christian morality but from his personal affront to her. The tribunal simply gave her the satisfaction of seeing him being punished. Though for different reasons, Juana saw Juan's trial and conviction as a matter of justice.

Though a person's sense of honor overlapped with Christian morality, his or her personal code of conduct flourished in relative autonomy from the dominant discourse. An alternate set of gender, sexual, and kinship practices competed with those of the Church. The mulatto Ana Caballero stated as much when she professed that it was "more important to cohabit happily than be unhappily married."

This widely shared view, of course, represented a blasphemous act. While the canons stipulated, in painstaking detail, which social practices conformed to Christian orthodoxy, the priests fought an endless battle against prevailing conventions. Ecclesiastical courts and the tribunal of the Holy Office brought a small fraction of cases of violators to trial and then only the most egregious ones. In his attempt to discredit the testimony of his second wife and that of her lover, Juan de Perales, for instance, informed the *provisor* of Juana's infidelity and the pending birth of her bastard.[86] By depicting Juana as an adulteress who, along with her lover, Nicolás, gave him a bad life, Juan cast suspicion over their testimony. Juan insinuated that adulterers, like all transgressors of Christian norms, could not be trusted. Characterizing himself as the aggrieved, Juan carefully crafted his testimony to deflect the judges' attention from the allegations leveled against him. But the *provisor* and the inquisitors manifested little interest in Juan's revelation, although several witnesses, including Juana's mother, substantiated the allegations. Conscious of their limitations, the ecclesiastical court and the Inquisition did not pursue all transgressions; they were only able to curtail, not eliminate, competing social norms.

As the ecclesiastical judge and the inquisitors questioned witnesses about Juan de Perales, the behavior of individuals whose lives intersected with his came under scrutiny. When asked by the Inquisition's *fiscal* about her daughter's relationship with Nicolás, María Hernández acknowledged the illicit affair. María noted that Nicolás had been present in her daughter's life long before Juan and that their relationship constituted a source of grave concern. María characterized Nicolás as a drunk, a "bad Christian and liar because though married he is publicly cohabiting with a black woman known as María 'the beautiful,' who bore him a child."

In contrast, María characterized Juan as a "good Christian, fearful of God and his conscience." Though Juan often scolded her daughter for interacting with Nicolás, María observed that this was to no avail. Once Juan learned, however, that Nicolás had impregnated Juana, his behavior turned violent. In María's eyes, Juana's behavior warranted Juan's aggression and did little to deflect from his Christian character. Despite the marked contrast in character and her daughter's illicit behavior, María had not denounced her daughter's affair with the seducer Nicolás. Yet as a witness in the proceedings against Juan de Perales, María finally found herself exposing her daughter Juana. The fact that she and a host of other witnesses had not denounced Juana and Nicolás implied a level of consent to the couple's illicit behavior, revealing ways in which their beliefs diverged from the Christian ideal.

But Juan's reckless behavior brought official scrutiny to their community. If the inquisitors did not find cause to act, the presiding *provisor* surely would. Dr. Moya, the former inquisitor general and newly appointed Archbishop of Mexico, was reforming the clergy with the intent of monitoring the behavior of the laity with greater vigor.[87] The *provisor* and the ecclesiastical court demonstrated Moya's zeal, which led to numerous proceedings in the last decades of the sixteenth century. Even before these reforms, the clergy, as we have seen, had attempted to impose orthodoxy among New Spain's inhabitants. Invariably, the clergy acted decisively against egregious infractions, and Juan's misdeeds certainly fit that category.

On February 23, 1575, the tribunal of the Holy Office of the Inquisition convicted and sentenced Juan de Perales to receive 300 lashes. Two weeks later, the secular authorities carried out their gruesome responsibility, again warning New Spain's inhabitants of the ominous scrutiny that was increasingly enveloping the *república*. As astute observers of the political landscape, some plebeians complied with Christian norms. But the majority maintained existing practices until forced by the authorities to change. In the event that their behavior attracted the official gaze, plebeians quickly mastered the language of contrition, which represented an invaluable but not foolproof strategy. In the closing decades of the sixteenth century, this rhetoric, with its Christian allusions, was widely manifest in New Spain's reformation.

Christian Self-Fashioning

In the waning decades of the sixteenth century, Africans, and especially their descendants, increasingly entered the historical record as their lives intersected with Spanish absolutism. As an unprecedented number of *bozales* arrived in New Spain, Spain's sovereign competed with the labor process as the most ominous influence to transform "Africans" into "slaves." While slavery harnessed the labor of *bozales*, the king stipulated which social categories their bodies and behavior could assume. By regulating the sumptuary, gender, and sexual customs of the new arrivals, the Spanish monarch prescribed the material forms of black personhood. Through the encounter with the regulatory institutions, the beliefs, customs, and bodies of Africans were steadily redefined in Christian terms. This eventually led to the emergence of cultural forms narrowly associated with blacks and blackness. Since ecclesiastical intervention was less attentive to ameliorating the plight of the enslaved than with regulating the behavior of Africans and their descendants in conformance with Christian orthodoxy, this transformation underscores absolutism and, by implication, the disruptive potential of Christianity.

For persons of African descent, acceptance of Christianity represented a departure. In the contest with Catholicism, the enslaved occupied a disadvantaged position, which led them to modify the public expression of their sexual norms and gendered assumptions to conform to Christian orthodoxy. As individuals stood before church and state authorities, spectacles of conformity to Christianity became ubiquitous.[88] In the drama of representation, only a Christian narrative would suffice. Even individuals who defied orthodoxy depicted themselves in a manner favorable to Christianity.

The tribunal routinely subjected persons of African descent to the proceedings of the Inquisition. This process, though indicative of the size and urban presence of the black population, highlights the sovereign's interest in defining the population of African descent as vassals. Spaniards perceived persons of African descent as different, yet as officials these same Spaniards treated them in practice and in custom like long-standing Christians. As a tangible manifestation of *mestizaje,* mulattos stood firmly in the jurisdictional vortex of the Inquisition. Mulattos did not share the Indians' liminal status, which offered the latter protection from the tribunal. In constituting Africans, particularly mulattos, as subjects with defined Christian obligations, the tribunal bestowed rights that individuals manifested in the narratives they created for the inquisitors.

Obligations fostered rights that subjects employed in their defense and desire to modify their life circumstances. In the closing decades of the sixteenth century, mulattos in particular displayed this acquired acumen, a hallmark of their creole consciousness. As the following example illustrates, the deft manner in which persons of African descent handled the tribunal's proceedings underscores a legal acumen usually associated with the most skillful cultural navigators. But this consciousness also reflects a degree of cultural immersion among persons of African descent that has been overlooked.

In 1580, Spanish merchant and Mexico City resident Cristóbal de Pastrana sent an unsolicited letter to inquisition officials. In his communiqué, Cristóbal accused Diego de Hojeda of being a bigamist noting that

> this mulatto is the son of Francisco de Hojeda, resident of Puebla and the grandson of Juan de Hojeda, a silkmaker and resident of this city. And they say that the mulatto is married to an Indian woman who is in the house of the said his father and he is also married . . . with a black woman called Ana who . . . now is mine. . . . After it came to my notice that he was married previously in Puebla . . . I wrote to two persons in Puebla so as to know the truth. . . . They informed me that they spoke to the father of the mulatto and he said it was the truth, that he [Diego] was married there [in Puebla] and for added satisfaction they spoke to Diego del Castillo, silkmaker, Spaniard and resident of the said city of the Angeles who was his [Diego's] godfather and who told them that it was as such.[89]

This letter brought a serious indictment. But the specific motives behind Cristóbal's denunciation remain unclear. Cristóbal's Christian conscience may have prompted the bigamy charges, but his desire to control Ana probably played a part as well. Fearing that he would forfeit Ana's services if the tribunal learned about her putative marriage from different sources, Cristóbal probably denounced Diego for self-interested reasons. On the other hand, Cristóbal may have leveled the bigamy charges to eliminate a potential rival for Ana's attention. After the death of Martín Alonso Contreras, Ana's previous owner, Cristóbal had acquired the young black woman, who at the time was already "married with this mulatto."[90] For Cristóbal, Ana's marriage represented a liability. In sixteenth-century New Spain, neither secular nor ecclesiastical officials accorded slave-owners precedence over the sanctity of marriage. Thus, any juridical conflict that ensued over Ana—Cristóbal's slave and Diego's wife—risked ecclesiastical intervention on the couple's behalf.

Irrespective of his motives, Cristóbal's denunciation alerted the authorities to a breach of the moral code. After deliberating over Cristóbal's letter, the tribunal initiated a preliminary investigation, eventually charging Diego de Hojeda with bigamy.[91] On November 21, 1581, two days after being apprehended and charged with bigamy, Diego de Hojeda provided the inquisitors with a lengthy deposition.[92] "I was married to Catalina . . . by the hand of a curate" in 1575 at the age of 21, noted Diego.[93] He recalled having "had a married life with her like husband and wife," but after several months he had left for Mexico, where he initiated an amorous affair with a "black woman named Ana."[94] Since Diego regularly frequented Zacatecas and Veracruz on behalf of his employer, his relationship with Ana initially remained informal. This changed when a mestizo muleteer, another Cristóbal, informed Diego in Veracruz that his wife was gravely ill and was in all likelihood dead.[95] "I believed this," Diego reported.

Now an alleged widower, Diego returned to Mexico "ill from the road" and married Ana "in order to be at peace with God and not to die in a bad state." The couple spent several months together, until Diego learned that Catalina was alive. On learning that Catalina still lived, Diego abandoned Ana. As he stood before the tribunal, Diego insisted that he had not intentionally contracted a bigamous marriage. He implored the inquisitors "for penance with mercy, because I did not do it with malice, nor in order to deride holy marriage and in payment for my sin I want to be placed in a monastery practicing my silk-making profession which I know how to do very well."[96] Despite the eloquence of Diego's plea, the inquisitors imposed the standard punishment for a bigamist.[97] Soon after the tribunal decreed its sentence, secular officials led Diego de Hojeda in a solemn procession through Mexico's "public streets" with a noose around his neck, a candle in hand, and the sinner's crown precariously balanced on his head. Afterward, if he survived the application of 200 lashes, Diego spent five excruciating years on the king's galley, a ship on which the oarsmen were convicts.

Aside from punishing Diego, the decision of the inquisitors underscores the moral precepts that governed Africans and their descendants. Spaniards expected all Christians, including Africans and their descendants, to adhere to Christian orthodoxy and severely punished those who failed to do so. Both creoles and Africans understood the risks involved for the slightest breach in the moral code. As the accused structured their narratives, they manifested this awareness and their command of orthodoxy. Versed in Christian ethics, individuals such as Diego acquired the acumen that enabled them to construct a moral monologue for the inquisitors' edification.

After a cursory introduction, during which the inquisitors questioned Diego about "the cause" of his arrest, the presiding official asked the 27-year-old mulatto about his "genealogy and discourse of his life." Diego noted that his grandfather, Juan de Hojeda, was a Spanish silkmaker residing in Mexico. Diego's father, Francisco de Ojeda, was also of Spanish birth and a silkmaker, while Elvira, his mother, was a free mulatto. Diego testified that his parents lived in Puebla with their "other legitimate children." As a youth, Diego apprenticed as a silkmaker with his father and grandfather. As a journeyman, he returned to Puebla to work for another Spanish silkmaker, Diego del Castillo. In Puebla, Diego met Catalina, and the two were quickly married. Yet soon after this marriage, over which father and son came to blows, Diego departed for Mexico, where he became a muleteer.[98]

On his hearing this biographical sketch, the prosecutor asked Diego to signify his exposure to Christianity. Diego recited the Paternoster, Ave María, Credo, and Salve Regina, after which an inquisitor noted "he knows no more." Asked if he was a "baptized Christian," Diego responded that his baptism took place in Mexico's cathedral and that the confirmation was held in Puebla. Diego also insisted that he confessed and received the sacraments every Lent. After outlining his Christian upbringing, Diego proceeded to "tell the truth." In constructing his narrative, Diego privileged details that depicted him in a favorable light. He claimed, for instance, that "a curate from the cathedral" presided over both weddings. After his marriage to Catalina, they led a conjugal life, with Diego as provider. But then he abandoned Catalina. Diego claimed that his involvement with Ana began after he learned of Catalina's death. Diego observed that he married Ana "to be in peace with God and not wanting to die in a bad state." Diego insisted that after he learned that Catalina still lived, moral considerations persuaded him not to maintain his relationship with Ana. "I could not be together with one or the other," declared Diego.[99]

Diego's narrative represents the epitome of careful construction. He emphasized two generations of familial connections—a distinct feat for persons of African descent customarily seen as genealogical isolates and, therefore, a disruptive social influence.[100] Diego realized the futility of pleading innocence and knew the consequences of his behavior. Yet he wanted some say in his punishment and crafted his narrative accordingly. Realizing that intentional "malice" constituted a grave offense, Diego insisted that he contracted a bigamous marriage without wanting "to deride holy marriage." Diego could distinguish among sins and tried to depict his behavior in the most favorable manner. Strategically minded throughout the proceedings, Diego realized that doubt about intent could work in his favor.

Aside from highlighting Diego's awareness of Christianity, the trial underscores a critical facet of New Spain's sixteenth-century moral terrain. The tribunal did not address the abandonment of a spouse or adultery. But the inquisitors deemed willful bigamy to be a dire sin. For the inquisitors, intent also constituted a matter of concern and posed a larger challenge. Royal and ecclesiastical authorities realized that Castilian sovereignty relied on awed and obedient vassals. Keenly aware of their limitations, New Spain's officials attempted to quell all manifestations of autonomy, and their investigation of sinful behavior focused on intent and willful malice. Willful intent involved a deeper level of deception aimed at both officials and affines. Deception of this magnitude often encouraged the aggrieved and their sympathizers to act in concert with the inquisitors, highlighting absolutism's diffusion into the lives of the diverse subjects of the sovereign. A creole consciousness did more than enable peoples of African descent to elude and navigate justice. In Leonor Sarmiento's case, as we shall see, creolization enabled persons of African descent to use absolutist institutions in a quest for justice. Creolized persons were aware of existing regulations and were able to use them to their own advantage.

In the late afternoon on Saturday, November 21, 1592, a 40-year-old mulatto "appearing on his own" entered the tribunal austere chambers.[101] After swearing a brief oath, Lázaro de Estrada invoked the Inquisition's formalist language and insisted he came to "discharge his conscience." As Inquisitor Sancho García listened intently, Lázaro accused Francisco Robledo of being a bigamist. Lázaro had known Francisco and his first wife, Leonor de Sarmiento, for "more or less twenty years." He dated their relationship to a time when all three were slaves in Gaspar Pérez de Monterrey's household.[102] It was then that Francisco and Leonor had exchanged marital vows, but afterward Gaspar Pérez had sold the couple. Lázaro recalled that Francisco and Leonor's new owner promptly took them to Chiametla, the alluvial mining region in northwestern New Spain. Despite the great distance involved, Francisco and Leonor initially maintained contact with members of their former household in Mexico City.[103] One day Francisco returned to Mexico City, however, "saying that Leonor was dead." Afterward, Francisco acquired his freedom and departed for Oaxaca, where, according to Lázaro, he married "a black woman."[104] Lázaro last saw Francisco in 1585 when he and his new wife visited Mexico City.[105] Lázaro claimed that at the time, he was still unaware of Francisco's deception. Finally, in 1591, Lázaro learned the truth when he sighted Leonor, who "came to this city . . . in search of Francisco."[106] At the conclusion of his deposition, Lázaro again used the formulaic language of the tribunal as he maintained that his confession was not born of malice.[107]

The inquisitor was not, however, concerned with Lázaro's motives or with the timing of his confession. Instead, he hastily issued an order transferring Francisco from the royal penitentiary, where he languished for outstanding debts, to the Inquisition's goal.[108] Francisco spent the weekend in the Inquisition's cellar pondering his fate. The following Monday, Inquisitor García began questioning Francisco Robledo about the allegations without revealing the identity of his informant. As Francisco Robledo stood before Sancho García he sounded weary but undaunted. He provided the inquisitor with a biographical sketch, identifying himself as Juan Francisco Robledo, a 48-year-old free black man who was initially enslaved to Gaspar Pérez de Monterrey.[109] Juan Francisco testified that his mother, Andrea, "a black woman from tierra nueva," had given birth to him in Mexico City. He still claimed to be a resident of Mexico, though he lived in Puebla.[110] Questioned about his Christian heritage, Juan Francisco acknowledged having been baptized in Mexico's cathedral but could not recall being confirmed. Evidently, Juan Francisco had received extensive Christian instruction since he could easily recite the Paternoster, the Ave María, the Credo, the Salve Regina, the Ten Commandments, and the standard confession. Afterward, the inquisitor remarked that "he said them all very well."[111] Queried about his adult life, Juan Francisco simply noted that he had acquired his freedom ten years before and that since that time "with some small mules I have walked searching for an existence in Oaxaca, Veracruz and other parts of New Spain."[112]

After these preliminary remarks, Inquisitor García asked Juan Francisco if he knew the cause for his incarceration. "Because it is said that I married twice," Juan Francisco responded. But he informed the inquisitor that the charges were misleading. In his defense, Juan Francisco chronicled his marriage to Leonor and related events that had mistakenly, as he claimed, led to his arrest. He recalled that after marrying Leonor in Zacatecas, the couple had moved to Mexico, where they lived in Gaspar Pérez de Monterrey's household. After a while, they returned to Chiametla, where Juan Francisco claimed to have left Leonor "more than fifteen years ago."[113] Juan Francisco returned to Mexico, acquired his freedom, and subsequently left the viceregal capital in search of a livelihood. Years later, he resurfaced in Mexico but this time with María de Vergara in tow. Although Juan Francisco conceded that he had cohabited with María, he also insisted "that I am not married to her."[114]

Evidently, the inquisitor believed Juan Francisco and ordered his return to the royal penitentiary. But as a precautionary measure, he instructed the secular authorities not to release Juan Francisco without his consent.[115] Despite the apparent veracity of the narrative, Inquisitor García needed incontrovertible proof of Juan Francisco's innocence. As the tribunal's *alcalde* carted Juan Francisco back to the royal prison, Sancho García instructed Puebla's commissary, Licenciado Alonso de Santiago, to question María de Vergara about her relationship with Juan Francisco.[116] Two weeks later, María appeared before the tribunal's representative in Puebla.

María de Vergara identified herself as a 20-year-old black woman and native of Antequera, where she was born and raised in the house of Nicolás de Vergara, who was the former canon of the cathedral and from whom she had acquired her surname.[117] She informed her inquisitor of her free status and residence in Puebla, where she lived in the house of Francisco de Torres Dávila—Juan Francisco's employer and the person who had had him imprisoned in Mexico "for a debt of two hundred pesos." María knew why she had been called, claiming that "some neighbors of mine have told me that he [Juan Francisco]" had been incarcerated for bigamy.[118] María was neither surprised nor concerned about "Juan Robledo who there [in Mexico City] is called Francisco Robledo." María declared that "he brought me to this city from Antequera deceitfully saying that he would marry me and so we have been together in this city several years and have lived in a house as if we were married and I bore him two children."[119] While María acknowledged that she had heard of Juan's marriage, she maintained that she had learned of it only when an unknown free black from Mexico and Catalina, a woman servant in Francisco de Torres's household, finally informed her.[120] As María concluded her testimony, she told the inquisitor "it is alright . . . because I wanted to be separated from him because he was a ill-tempered black man."[121]

On the basis of María's deposition, the inquisitor ordered Juan Francisco's release on Christmas Eve 1592.[122] Though he was free, Juan Francisco's ordeal did not end. Eight months later, on September 6, 1593, Licenciado Alonso de Santiago wrote his superiors in Mexico informing them that the *fiscal* of Tlaxcala's bisphoric had apprehended Juan Francisco in Puebla, where he was being held "for the reason that his denouncer gave."[123] Despite his familiarity with this case, Alonso Santiago requested instructions from his superiors. In the interim, however, he had ordered the *fiscal* to retain Juan Francisco in custody.[124] As it turns out, Leonor Sarmiento—Juan Francisco's legally recognized wife—had orchestrated the arrest. For years, the 30-year-old free black woman had been plotting to bring her philandering husband to justice.

In her deposition, Leonor recalled arriving in Mexico "more or less three years ago," knowing that Juan Francisco had married for a second time. Leonor had informed the tribunal of that fact, "which took note of this transaction," but she ruefully noted that "until today there have been no proceedings for this cause nor have I been called."[125] Now, years later, Leonor was obliged to initiate judicial proceeding against her husband for the second time. On August 23rd, after years of separation and rumors that he had married a second time, Juan Francisco had approached Leonor, "saying that he came for me in order to take me to the mines of Cuautla." Leonor had expressed no interested in reconciliation. Instead, she "ran to the *provisor* of this city in order to give notice of what happened." The *provisor* ordered Juan Francisco's arrested but demanded that Leonor "present information" in support of her allegations, warning her that "we will have to free him" if she failed to comply. Leonor suddenly found herself in a quandary. How could she prove her allegations? On the verge of despair, Leonor had a chance encounter with a carpenter named Gutiérrez. He advised her to seek assistance from the commissary of the Holy Office, Canon Alonso de Santiago.[126] On the basis of Gutiérrez's advice, Leonor confided in Licenciado de Santiago, who ordered that Juan Francisco be held until he issued further instructions.[127] Several days later, Leonor returned to the commissary's house in great haste, declaring that "some muleteers have come to this city who know that . . . Francisco de Robledo was married in Oaxaca."[128] For the next two days, the commissary and his notary heard testimony from Leonor Sarmiento, Andrés de Mota, Juan Rodriguez, Francisco Hernándes, Beatriz de Ansurez, and Francisco Hernández.[129]

As the principal accuser, Leonor Sarmiento appeared first. She identified herself as a creolized free black who, as a slave, had been born and reared in Juan Sarmiento's household in Puebla. Leonor claimed that "because I was very young," she did not recall the exact date of her marriage. She remembered that Father Espinosa had presided over the wedding in Zacatecas while an unknown Spanish male and an enslaved black woman had served as godparents.[130] Leonor noted that several enslaved black women, including Francisca Montes, María Caballos, and a woman named Isabel, stood in attendance. Years later, Leonor knew their whereabouts, which implies that she had periodic contact with them.[131] As she left the proceedings, Leonor surely pondered whether the inquisitors would render justice in her case. Nearly four years had passed since she had brought charges against Juan Francisco. Now, close to two decades after Juan Francisco had abandoned her and their son, Andrés, Leonor still hoped that justice would be served. Despite Leonor's testimony, however, Juan Francisco's guilt was still in doubt. As the inquisitors pondered the allegations against Juan Francisco Robledo, the depositions of the witnesses, including that of the three muleteers, carried greater weight.

As Leonor departed, Canon Santiago called on the enslaved muleteer Andrés de Mota. The 38-year-old Andrés stated that he was both a "ladino and creole" from Antequera who belonged to Gabriel de Mota.[132] He acknowledged that he knew why "he had been called," since Beatriz, "an old black woman," had badgered him about Juan Francisco in the plaza where she sold fruit. Andrés recalled that "eleven years ago," on his return from Guatemala, he stopped in a pueblo named Guelocingo, "seventy leagues" south of Oaxaca. There he met a free black couple, Francisco and María, who asked him if he knew Francisco de Robledo and María, "a creole from Oaxaca." Andrés acknowledged that he knew María but was unfamiliar with Francisco. Then in the distance Andrés sighted María and at once turned to the couple, asking "Why did you ask me if I knew them?" Francisco and María proceeded to inform Andrés of María's wedding "in that pueblo." As Andrés related these details, he informed Licenciado Alonso de Santiago that "in the province" Francisco's and María's wedding was "very public and talked about." María, moreover, had personally informed Andrés of her marriage "a year and a half later" during an encounter in Antequera. Andrés recalled asking María if she was indeed married to Francisco, to which she had replied that "it was the truth." Thus, Andrés was not at all surprised to see "them living together as husband and wife in a house in Oaxaca."[133]

Juan Rodriguez, one of two muleteers who had accompanied Andrés to Puebla and to the proceedings, also recalled seeing Francisco and María "living together in Oaxaca." But unlike Andrés, Juan—a mulatto born in Oaxaca who had been free for twenty years—had known Juan Francisco personally for over a decade. He recounted how Juan Francisco took María, nicknamed "María Cuchara," to the province where he had heard they were married. As Juan Rodriguez was transporting goods to Guatemala, he found confirmation of the hearsay. In Guelocingo, several residents, including a mulatto named Juan and two others "whose names I cannot remember," informed him of Juan Francisco and María's wedding. Thus when "a black woman named Beatriz" told Juan that the inquisitors would question him about Juan Francisco, the fearful young mulatto had acquiesced.[134]

Francisco Hernándes also noted that a woman "they say was Francisco de Robledo's wife" approached him in the plaza.[135] "Born in Guinea of the Biafra caste," the 40-year-old Francisco testified having known "Francisco de Robledo" for seven years. Francisco Hernándes knew of Juan Francisco's relationship with María, stating that he "saw them together in the pueblo of Guelocingo" on his frequent trips between Oaxaca and Guatemala. Like his workmates, Francisco perceived Francisco and María as a married couple since "they interacted as if they were." The couple's behavior was not limited to the provinces. Francisco informed Licenciado Alonso de Santiago that he had seen Juan Francisco and María in Oaxaca "[living] together in a house, having and raising children like husband and wife."[136]

At the conclusion of Francisco Hernándes's testimony, Alonso de Santiago adjourned the proceedings. But two days later, the hearings continued when the 60-year-old Beatriz de Ansurez, calling herself a "native of Guinea from the Berbesies caste who sold fruit in the plaza," appeared. She identified herself as a former slave who was now free and a resident of Puebla. Beatriz informed the canon that she was quite aware of why she had been called and noted that she had a lifelong relationship with Leonor; in fact, she had been present when Leonor was born. Beatriz's interaction with Juan Francisco and María was considerably shorter. But Beatriz had more than a passing relationship with María's mother. Beatriz recalled that "the mother of María Cuchara is from my land," and that for a time they had lived together in Oaxaca.

Beatriz testified that she heard that Francisco had come to Oaxaca and had taken María with him to the adjacent province. On a visit to Oaxaca, Beatriz invited the couple to stay with her. It was then that María notified her mother's compatriot that she "had married" Juan Francisco. Afterward, Beatriz moved to Puebla but maintained contact with various Oaxaqueños, including María. María, in fact, came to Puebla "in search of Francisco Robledo" and temporarily resided with her. María disclosed that the confessor had declined "to absolve her" because she and Juan Francisco were not "veiled." María noted that Francisco steadfastly refused to marry her, insisting "that he wanted to confess with the priests but not with the monks." Beatriz concluded her testimony by remarking that they always "interact[ed] as if they were husband and wife."

Licenciado Alonso de Santiago finally interrogated Francisco Hernándes, an Hispanicized Indian born in Antequera, Oaxaca's provincial capital, who now resided in Puebla. When asked if he knew the cause he had been called, Francisco responded that Beatriz "who brought me from Oaxaca" had informed him that it pertained to Juan Francisco. Francisco recalled that twelve years before, when he was an employee on a pack train, he had stopped at Gueguetlán, a village situated between Oaxaca and Guatemala, where he heard an enslaved African woman named Victoria say "I don't know why María Cuchara, the free black from Oaxaca[,] married an African freedman." Francisco entered the fray by informing Victoria that "she [María] is married with a free black." Francisco recalled seeing Juan Francisco and María in Puebla "living in a house as husband and wife . . . raising children."[137] With Francisco Hernández's testimony, Licenciado Alonso de Santiago ended the hearings. Two days later, on September 6th, he notified his superiors of the charges, forwarded the depositions, and informed them that Juan Francisco awaited judgment and would be transferred to Mexico.[138]

As an *alcalde* escorted Juan Francisco Robledo to Mexico City, the free black once again pondered his fate. Juan Francisco knew that Leonor was responsible for his current predicament. She had, after all, informed the authorities of his presence in Puebla. Yet it is unlikely that Juan fathomed the formidable arsenal of evidence that friends, neighbors, and even passing acquaintances had mounted against him. Despite the circumstantial and contradictory nature of the depositions, the inquisitors relied on accumulated hearsay, rumors, fleeting conversations, sightings, and chance encounters as evidence—evidence on which a defendant's fate would be decided. In the nine months since Juan Francisco's initial release from the royal jail, the case against him had grown significantly stronger. But until the inquisitors heard from Antonío Pérez, Ana de Zárate, and Antón de Paz, no one actually claimed having been present at Juan Francisco Robledo and María de Vergara's wedding.[139]

On October 6, 1593, three Oaxaqueños residing in different Mexico City households testified in the matter related to Juan Francisco Robledo. Antonío Pérez, Ana de Zárate, and Antón de Paz respectively claimed to be a free mulatto and enslaved black creoles. Despite the burdens of work and the size of the city they lived in, these Oaxaqueños interacted with some regularity. It is probably within their Oaxaqueño network that they learned about the plight of their compatriot, María de Vergara. Independently, all three revealed their familiarity with María and her family. Perhaps this familiarity informed their concerns and persuaded Antonío, Ana, and Antón to level incriminating evidence against Juan Francisco.[140] Antonío was well acquainted with María's family, informing the inquisitors that she "lived in the company of her mother" and an unnamed sister who is "married with Morales a free black." According to Antonío, "the three women all had a small house" beneath San Sebastian. It was in this "the same small house" that Antonío saw María and Juan Francisco raise "three or four children."[141] Antonío observed that María was still in her early teens when she bore her children. Along similar lines, Ana focused on María's genealogical identity. She initially identified María as a free mulatto but later recanted, stating that "Juana María Cuchara, Catalina's daughter[,] is not mulatto but black."[142]

The inquisitors were not concerned with such details, however. The fact that Antonío, Ana, and Antón had witnessed Juan Francisco and María's wedding was their paramount concern. The Oaxqueños independently recalled seeing Juan Francisco marrying María "twelve years ago . . . in the main church of this city [Oaxaca]."[143] During Sunday mass with "many white and black people" in attendance, including Antonío and Ana, Father Franco had unwittingly presided over Juan Francisco's second and bigamous marriage.[144] Antonío maintained that Juan Francisco publicly denied afterward that this wedding took place, claiming that "[María] was not his wife but his friend." Antonío, who had heard "a fat black woman named Leonor Sarimento" insist that Juan Francisco was "her husband," knew why Juan Francisco would want to deny his marriage.[145] This testimony finally offered the inquisitors conclusive proof of Juan Francisco's guilt.

Even though they were established for the express purpose of curbing the Protestant presence, the activities of the Holy Office of the Inquisition underscored a local concern that allegedly threatened the Christian commonwealth: persons of African descent. By routinely including the descendants of Africans, the tribunal manifested its desire to discipline those local persons who offered a challenge to the Christian *república*. If order and the Catholic sovereign's dominion were to prevail, the inquisitors had to subordinate the *república*'s inhabitants to Christian orthodoxy. In theory, there could be no exceptions. But there were. In obligating baptized Africans and their descendants to abide by Christian norms, the inquisitors treated them like an Old World population. In its juridical manifestations, the Holy Office differentiated blacks from Indians, since the Crown exempted the latter from the tribunal's jurisdiction. Subject to the Inquisition, persons of African descent displayed a keen understanding of the norms governing their lives and identities. Yet understanding these norms and conforming to them were two very different things. As the various depositions illustrate, many individuals utilized their acumen about Christian norms to circumvent existing customs. Those caught and prosecuted bestowed remarkable and unrivaled glimpses of their lives to posterity. The disparate portraits, though structured in the context of an interrogation, reveal a social complexity not usually associated with enslaved Africans and their creole descendants. In New Spain, however, the charter generations manifested this social complexity from their arrival.

Postscript

A different historical perspective emerges when we acknowledge that Christian absolutism shaped New Spain's African presence. Slavery—as a juridical status and way to discipline labor—simply did not constitute the full extent of the African experience. At the height of the slave trade in Mexico, Africans and their New World progeny wielded diverse identities juridically based in the Kingdom of New Spain and the Christian commonwealth. Africans—including slaves—constituted vassals of the king, while those who converted represented Christian subjects with defined obligations and particular rights. In availing themselves of their Christian rights, Africans and creoles did more than restrict their master's dominion over them. As we have seen, Africans and creoles utilized Christian regulatory practices, especially the marriage petition, to affirm identities meaningful to them. The selection of spouses and marriage sponsors underscores the multiple ways that Africans and their descendants constituted themselves ethnically and culturally within Christianity's boundaries. While the sources underscore a widely disseminated Christian identity or performance thereof among New Spain's African and creole population, the records also reveal several other phenomenon as well.

Absolutism concerned itself with Africans and their descendants in a manner that historians have yet to explore. This should be apparent from the tantalizing glimpses that this study offers. Intent on asserting absolutism over the fledgling realm, Spain's sovereign did not give masters complete dominion over their chattel. Such behavior typified the contest over authority—not just property—that characterized Christian expansion in the course of the reconquest, an era in which sovereigns steadily curtailed the nobles' feudal rights and the municipalities' rights. Following the discovery and conquest of the Indies, the Spanish monarchy similarly extended its authority at the expense of the conquistadors' feudal ambitions.

By the second half of the sixteenth century, however, the conquistadors and their descendants did not represent absolutism's principal threat. In the aftermath of the Protestant Reformation—the central threat to Catholic absolutism —heresy became tantamount to treason. Anxious to curtail its spread, Spain's Catholic stalwarts deployed various instruments. For this reason, the Inquisition arrived in 1571 and ecclesiastical reforms followed soon thereafter. The growing African and creole population, though not the explicit focus of this institutional process, became an object of scrutiny. Converted Africans and black creoles increasingly found themselves before the Inquisition's tribunal accused of crimes. Mounting clerical vigilance also resulted in numerous ecclesiastical proceedings involving persons of African descent, highlighting the manner in which Africans encountered Catholicism—an encounter that explicitly defined Christian behavior.

For the growing African and creole populations, Christian conversion brought both obligations and rights. It entitled all Christians to a married life, a right that in practice restricted the master's authority over chattel. This practice was most pronounced in Mexico City, since in the capital patricians confronted the full manifestation of absolutist authority. In this sense, *Africans in Colonial Mexico* situates the African experience in an imperial vortex that featured patricians, paterfamilias, and masters on one side and the absolutist sovereign and the Catholic Church on the other.

A focus on the various regulatory sites—colonial legislation, inquisition proceedings, and parish life—delineates the reach and limits of absolutism while underscoring how the grand narrative touched and was shaped by Africans and their descendants. Though subjects of regulation and discipline, Africans also utilized the competing laws and institutions to ends never imagined. The picture that emerges is atypical. Africans appear as slaves and yet much more. Still, we need to remind ourselves that this very portrayal underscores the ambiguity characterizing the African experience in the earliest phase of the Spanish imperial expansion.

In the aftermath of the Spanish conquest, most Africans arrived as slaves. But as we have seen, in the era of Spanish imperial expansion and consolidation, the absolutist sovereign challenged competing claims to dominion. Even as opposing interests vied for jurisdictional authority, they concurred that Africans needed to be regulated. Ameliorating slavery was never the intent. Still, the jurisdictional breach provided Africans and their descendants with opportunities to navigate the households, institutions, and imposed practices that were intent on defining them as chattel, vassals, and Christians. With the most heightened strategic consciousness—a symptom of the creolization process—Africans and creoles learned how to deploy the institutional practices and discourses to their advantage, even though this practice insinuated Christian absolutism even further into their lives.

The stories at the heart of this project show both how slave-owners attempted to structure the lives of Africans and their progeny and how members of this group structured their own lives. But since these stories were produced within a Christian narrative structure they also accentuate the regulatory process that informed the lives of Africans and their descendants—and the contours in which, officially at least, they could define themselves. The histories conveyed in the preceding pages only offer a fragmentary perspective. Far from being an exhaustive study, *Africans in Colonial Mexico* points to richer possibility than even the pioneer historians of the African experience in Mexico imagined.

As this book suggests, there are countless histories of the African experience still to be written. Such histories will assume many forms, ultimately situating persons of African descent in a past that centers them and their experiences. By tapping into these richly textured sources, future scholars may do more than track the relationship between absolutism and the African presence. The existing records underscore the possibilities of recovering a deeply neglected past yet one that does not confine the African experience to conventional depictions of slavery.

Of course, the sources address life under slavery. They also shed light on why and how the free black population was the largest group of people of African descent at the height of the Mexican slave trade and slavery. The strategic consciousness of the enslaved surely limited bondage to a generation at most. In short, freedom emerged as a birthright for many urban creoles. Still, there is much more that can be gleaned from the records. The stories represent, without question, the richest repository for the African and black experience in the New World. Indeed by centering their stories, gossip, and utterances, it may be possible to render an even richer understanding of the African encounter with Christianity.

Glossary

aguacil mayor	magistrate
asiento	monopoly contract
audiencia	administrative court
auto-de-fé	literally "proceedings of faith"; the Inquisition's punitive processional
barrio	neighborhood
bozal	African directly from Guinea who was unable to speak Castilian
cabildo	municipal (town) council
Castile	Iberian kingdom often synonymous with Spain
chino/a	term for people from the Spanish Philippines
converso	descendants of Jews who converted to Christianity
conviviencia	literally "coexistence"; refers to Christian, Jewish, and Muslim coexistence on the Iberian Peninsula
coyote	literally "coyote"; offspring of an African and Indian
criollo	creole; a native of the Americas; term initially used to refer to descendants of Africans
depósito	female sanctuary
engenhos	Portuguese term for landed estate or plantation
entrada	expedition
extra ecclesiam	Christian designation for all people who did not accept the Catholic (Universal) faith
fiscal	prosecutor
fueros	juridical privileges granted to towns or members of specific corporations
gente de razón	literally "people of reason"; term for allegedly rational subjects
Guinea	term for sub-Saharan Africa, especially the area from south of the Senegal River to southern Angola
hacienda	landed estate
indio/a	Indian
Indies	synonymous with the Americas
información matrimonial	marriage petition
ladino	an African culturally conversant in Castilian
mestizaje	biological and cultural mixing

mestizo	offspring of a Spaniard and Indian
morisco	a Christian of Moorish descent
Nahua	the largest indigenous group in central colonial Mexico
New Spain	Castilian designation for colonial Mexico
pardo	term for the offspring of African-Indian unions
pieza de India	unit representing a prime slave
plaza mayor	town square representing the juridical epicenter of a Spanish settlement
portero	doorman
provisor	ecclesiastical judge
reconquista	Christian conquest of the Muslim-occupied Iberian Peninsula
relación	legal brief
República de los Españoles	Spanish commonwealth; a juridical domain metaphorically occupied by Spaniards
República de los Indios	Indian commonwealth; a juridical domain ideally restricted to the indigenous inhabitants of the Indies
Siete Partidas	thirteenth-century Castilian legal code
solar	an urban plot of land
traza	the thirteen blocks surrounding the plaza mayor ideally restricted to Spaniards
vecino/a	resident

Notes

Introduction

1. R. G. Collingwood, *The Idea of History*, ed. and intro. Jan Van Der Dussen (Oxford: Oxford University Press, 1994), 247.

2. I use the terms "African" and "free blacks" advisedly since the colonial authorities usually referred to direct arrivals from "Guinea," the early modern Spanish and Portuguese referent for West and subsequently West Central Africa, as "*bozales.*" While the Spaniards employed the term "*negro libre*" (free black), they avoided it in describing a population segment. Nomenclature occupies an important role in the history of racial formation and thus in the meanings of categories, terms, and concepts that emerged during particular administrative and historical moments. In New Spain and throughout the Americas, naming practices reflected the fluctuations of the slave trade. As African and European slave traders drew their victims from different areas and imposed cultural specificity on generic territorial points of origin, the survivors of the middle passage assigned multiple and contradictory meanings to being from the land of "Angola," "Bran," "Congo," and "Terra Nova." Though slavers bestowed the name of the port of embarkation on the enslaved, such territorial referents thrived because the structures of dominion privileged the African elite and the European merchants. "Angola" is a case in point. People from the "land of Angola" constituted the majority of arrivals in seventeenth-century New Spain. As the symbol of political rule, "Ngola" defined the port and subsequently became the name ascribed to the enslaved people who passed through that region. In its commercial/political specificity, the term overshadowed the unstable meanings embedded in the use of "Angola." Philip D. Curtin, *The Atlantic Slave Trade: A Census* (Madison: University of Wisconsin Press, 1969), 104–105.

    Recently, Joseph C. Miller wrote that "northern Europeans knew the entire coastline of Central Africa south of Cape Lopez as 'Angola,' and they designated slaves they purchased there as 'Angolas,' employing the term in a sense entirely different from, and considerably less distinct than, Portuguese and Brazilian uses of it. For the Portuguese, the 'Kingdom of Angola' had referred in the 1570s to the region subject to the ngola a kiluanje, the African ruler along the middle Kwanza; after government officials established their principal slaving port at Luanda in the early seventeenth century, they designated the inland regions subject to their military control as the 'reino e conquista d' Angola.' 'Angola' thereafter served in Brazil as cognate to 'Luanda' in distinguishing slaves embarked through government formalities executed at the designated port of embarkation. However, the 'Angolas' reaching the Caribbean and North America aboard the ships of the French, Dutch, and English from 1670s onward had begun their Middle Passages at any of the bays north of the Zaire—Mayumba nearest Cape Lopez, then Loango, Malimbo, Cabinda, and the 'Congo' River (as the Zaire was known) mouth itself." "Central Africa during the Era of the Slave

Trade, c. 1490s–1850s," in *Central Africans and Cultural Transformation in the American Diaspora*, ed. Linda M. Heywood (New York: Cambridge University Press, 2002), 28–29.

Instability also characterized the term "black," since it referred to creoles born in the Indies, to ladinos who had spent considerable time on the Iberian peninsula and the Caribbean or simply could converse in Spanish or Portuguese, and, finally, to *bozales*, persons directly from Africa, when the term was used to classify race rather than ethnicity. The usage of "mulatto" underscores the complexity informing corporate labels, as it carried no intrinsic social or cultural meaning. In urban areas, "mulatto" often referred to persons of both black and white origins, while in the countryside the term usually referred to the offspring of a creole (and in some cases an ethnic African) and an indigenous parent. Among the proliferating population of freedpersons, a complex and elusive cultural dynamic was at work that precluded the emergence of a coherent and self-conscious mulatto population. Indeed, all that mulattos shared was a notion that usually one parent (and in many situations a distant grandparent) was of African descent. In the definition of "mulatto," this real or imagined relative of African descent represented the only constant. Thus, the complexity of the kinship ties, the memory of kin, and the range of relationships that could produce a mulatto rendered the category culturally unstable, if not useless. For many individuals, especially secular and ecclesiastical authorities, mulatto simply constituted a descriptive and juridical referent to transgression and impurity. In an effort to regulate the population, such terms acquired meaning—for authorities and for those who wielded the terms as identities. Often manifest in regulatory moments, the terms became symbolic markers that flourished despite the ways in which they obscured the nuances of experience and diverse meanings. Throughout this study, I attend to the shifting specificity of terms. In doing so, I draw on (among others) Joan Wallach Scott, "Gender as a Category of Analysis," in *Gender and the Politics of History* (New York: Columbia University Press, 1988), 28–31; and Benedict Anderson, *Imagined Communities: Reflections on the Origin and Spread of Nationalism*, rev. ed. (New York: Verso), 53. For demographics on the slave and free colored population see Gonzalo Aguirre Beltrán, *La población negra de México: Estudio etnohistorico*, 2nd ed. (México: Fondo de Cultura Económica, 1972), 214–219; Sherburne F. Cook and Woodrow Borah, *Essays in Population History: Mexico and the Caribbean* (Berkeley: University of California Press, 1974), 2:197; Colin A. Palmer, *Slaves of the White God: Blacks in Mexico, 1570–1650* (Cambridge, Mass.: Harvard University Press, 1976), 27–28; Frederick P. Bowser, *The African Slave in Colonial Peru, 1524–1650* (Stanford, Calif.: Stanford University Press, 1974), 337–341 and "Colonial Spanish America," in *Neither Slave nor Free: The Freedmen of African Descent in the Slave Societies of the New World*, ed. and intro. David W. Cohen and Jack P. Greene (Baltimore: Johns Hopkins University Press, 1972), 19, 37; Herbert S. Klein, *African Slavery in Latin America and the Caribbean* (New York: Oxford University Press, 1986), 28–36, 296 and "Blacks," in *The Countryside in Colonial Latin America*, ed. Louisa Schell Hoberman and Susan Migden Socolow (Albuquerque: University of New Mexico Press, 1996), 169–173. Scholars generally concur on the size and relative importance of the slave populations in Peru and New Spain but seem reluctant to draw conclusions about the free colored population. The ambiguity of classification may explain this aversion, since the authorities also defined some free coloreds as *castas*, who, according to R. Douglas Cope, were "products of miscegenation." *Plebeian Society in Colonial Mexico City, 1660–1720* (Madison: University of Wisconsin Press, 1994), 4. See also Patricia Seed, *To Love, Honor, and Obey in Colonial Mexico: Conflicts over Marriage Choice, 1574–1821* (Stanford, Calif.: Stanford University Press, 1988), 24; and Magnus Mörner, *Race Mixture in the History of Latin America* (Boston: Little, Brown and Company, 1967), 53.

3.   Palmer, *Slaves of the White God*, 27–28; Aguirre Beltrán, *La población negra de México*, 206, 217. Though the CD-ROM database *The Trans-Atlantic Slave Trade* (David Eltis, Stephen D. Behrendt, David Richardson, and Herbert S. Klein, eds., *The Trans-Atlantic Slave Trade: A Database on CD-ROM* [New York: Cambridge University Press, 1999]) brings considerable refinement to our understanding of the slave trade, Colin Palmer's assessment of the sixteenth- and seventeenth-century slave trade to Spanish America still stands. Palmer revised the initial estimates offered by Aguirre Beltrán, which Philip D. Curtin registered as realistic suppositions in *The Atlantic Slave Trade: A Census* (Madison: University of Wisconsin Press, 1969). For a listing of slave ships that left Iberian ports for Africa and then landed in the Americas before 1640, see Enriqueta Vila Vilar, *Hispano-America y el comercia de Esclavos: Los Asientos Portugueses* (Sevilla: Escuela de Estudios Hispano-Americanos de Sevilla, 1977), 200, 206–207.

4.   Aguirre Beltrán, *La población negra de México*, 214–219; Cook and Borah, *Essays in Population History*, 197.

5.   Aguirre Beltrán, *La población negra de México*, 232, 234.

6.   Anthony Pagden, ed. and trans., *Hernán Cortés: Letters from Mexico*, intro. by J. H. Elliott (New Haven, Conn.: Yale University Press, 1986), xii–xxvi.

7.   Richard L. Kagan has traced the history of this contest in Castile from the medieval to the early modern periods. *Lawsuits and Litigants in Castile, 1500–1700* (Chapel Hill: University of North Carolina Press, 1981), xix, 24, 211.

8.   In making this claim, I question the assertion that "initially, slaves were sent to rural areas such as plantations or to mines located on coastal areas where, since the beginning of the frontier years, the indigenous population had either died or moved away, escaping Iberian encroachment." Christine Hünefeldt, *Paying the Price of Freedom: Family and Labor among Lima's Slaves, 1800–1854*, trans. Alexandra Stern (Berkeley: University of California Press, 1994), 1.

9.   Frederick P. Bowser made a similar claim thirty years ago in "The African in Colonial Spanish America: Reflections on Research Achievements and Priorities," *Latin American Research Review* 7, no. 1 (1972): 77–94. James Lockhart drew a prescient conclusion about persons of African descent in early Peru which held true for New Spain but whose implications have yet to be explored. "Africans . . . were a factor of absolutely first importance in Peru in the conquest period. They were an organic part of the enterprise of occupying Peru from its inception. The dominance of Spanish language and culture was never threatened, but in terms of ethnic or racial groups, the conquest of Peru was carried out by an equal partnership. . . . Far from their own roots . . . the Negroes assimilated Spanish culture with amazing speed, and were for the main part the Spaniards' willing allies. . . . And this willingness is understandable. Though Negroes were subordinated to

Spaniards, they were not exploited in the plantation manner; except for mining gangs, Negroes in Peru counted as individuals." *Spanish Peru 1532–1560: A Colonial Society* (Madison: University of Wisconsin Press, 1968), 198.

10. Sally Engle Merry, *Getting Justice and Getting Even: Legal Consciousness among Working-Class Americans* (Chicago: University of Chicago Press, 1990), 5; Susan F. Hirsch and Mindie Lazarus-Black, "Introduction: Performance and Paradox: Exploring Law's Role in Hegemony and Resistance," in *Contested States: Law, Hegemony, and Resistance,* ed. Susan F. Hirsch and Mindie Lazarus-Black (New York: Routledge, 1994), 13–20; Mindie Lazarus-Black, "Slaves, Masters, and Magistrates: Law and the Politics of Resistance in the British Caribbean, 1736–1834," in *Contested States,* 253.

11. Seed, *To Love, Honor, and Obey in Colonial Mexico,* 32–46.

12. Ibid., 75–91.

13. Dennis Nodin Valdés, "The Decline of the Sociedad de Castas in Mexico City" (Ph.D. dissertation, University of Michigan, 1978), 139, 146.

14. Lockhart, *Spanish Peru,* 175.

15. This formulation of creolization should not be restricted to the urban landscape. Edward Brathwaite noted how creolization in a "colonial plantation polity" represented "a way of seeing the society, not in terms of white and black, master and slave, in separate nuclear units, but as contributory parts of a whole." *The Development of Creole Society in Jamaica, 1770–1820* (Oxford: Clarendon Press, 1971), 307.

16. In sustaining this assertion we need only to revisit existing narratives—with what might arguably be termed as a subaltern perspective—that have been offered for different analytical purposes. In a memorable anecdote, Patricia Seed introduces an unnamed but "huge black slave" who assisted his master in locking up the latter's son, Gerónimo Valverde, to prevent him from marrying a competitor's daughter, Juana Herrera. Though Seed pursued the case from the vantage point of the Spaniards, we should not forget that the "huge black slave" participated in the father-son conflict and subsequently was ordered to move aside when the church prosecutor and royal constable sought to free Gerónimo from custody. The fact that he was privy to this conflict and ultimately witnessed officials overrule the father in a matter concerning free will allows us to imagine that the slave could utilize such cultural intelligence in an unrelated scenario where a fellow slave insisted on having a married life. Seed, *To Love, Honor, and Obey in Colonial Mexico,* 1–4.

17. According to Cope, "*plebe*" emerges in the early seventeenth century as a social designation for "*castas.*" *The Limits of Racial Domination,* 22.

18. David Eltis observed how "one implication of the more rapid evolution of possessive individualism in northwestern Europe was that the English government exercised far less control than its Spanish counterpart over the way colonists treated non-Europeans." *The Rise of African Slavery in the Americas* (New York: Cambridge University Press, 2000), 26.

19. Robert Bartlett, *The Making of Europe: Conquest, Colonization, and Cultural Change, 950–1350* (Princeton, N.J.: Princeton University Press, 1993).

20. David Brion Davis, *The Problem of Slavery in Western Culture* (Ithaca, N.Y.: Cornell University Press, 1966); Winthrop D. Jordan, *White over Black: American Attitudes toward the Negro, 1550–1812* (Chapel Hill: University of North Carolina Press, 1968); Edmund S. Morgan, *American Slavery, American Freedom: The Ordeal of Colonial Virginia* (New York: W. W. Norton & Company, 1975); Orlando Patterson, *Slavery and Social Death: A Comparative Study* (Cambridge, Mass.: Harvard University Press, 1982).

21. Joan W. Scott, "The Evidence of Experience," *Critical Inquiry* 17 (Summer 1991): 776.

22. Most of the evidence for the African presence resides in records created in attempts to regulate. The slave-trade records chronicle *asientos* (monopoly contracts) and list the number of *pieza de India* (a measurement unit designed to categorize a primary slave and against which individual slaves were assessed) and *bozales* that were allowed to enter the Indies. Such records usually confine the African past to ports of embarkation. Africans also emerge in notary records, bills of sale, estate inventories, census records, municipal proceedings, and the occasional royal ordinances. But here they usually emerge as commodities or property acted upon by others. Municipal proceedings (*actas de cabildos*) represent a far richer source, since they describe infractions, unruly behavior, and concerns of the local elite, which included the growing presence of Africans and the existence of black brotherhoods (*cofradias*), their nocturnal gatherings, and their social occasions—funerals and processionals. These proceedings also record evidence of fugitive flight, marronage, conspiracies, and rebellions. For the most part, these sources portray Africans and their descendants as abstracted categories, as a problem, or as a population in need of regulation. Among the records dealing with the possession of land and land conflicts—Tierras (land), Mercedes (property), and Indios (Indians)—Africans remain largely invisible until the late seventeenth century. Rarely are the sentiments or concerns of Africans and their descendants recorded. For such records, scholars need to turn to court records—civil, criminal, ecclesiastical, and inquisition proceedings. To date, criminal records have been neglected by scholars interested in examining the experiences of Africans. This is rather peculiar, given their demonstrated potential. As this study shows, ecclesiastical and inquisition records remain underutilized as a source. Their potential is enormous.

23. Ranajit Guha, *Dominance without Hegemony: History and Power in Colonial India* (Cambridge, Mass.: Harvard University Press, 1997). Guha, among others, offers a powerful corrective to those who subscribe to the belief that an autonomous history and historiography divorced from an analysis of power represents a possibility.

24. Franz Fanon, *Black Skin, White Masks*, trans. Charles Lam Markmann (New York: Grove Press, 1967), 14.

25. Kathleen Canning, "Feminist History after the Linguistic Turn: Historicizing Discourse and Experience," *Signs* 19 (Winter 1994): 368–403.

26. Scott, "Gender: A Useful Category of Historical Analysis," 28–31.

27. My understanding of "discursive domain" draws on Michel Foucault, *The Archaeology of Knowledge and the Discourse on Language,* trans. A. M. Sheridan Smith

(New York: Pantheon Books, 1972), 21–39; Edward W. Said, *Orientalism* (New York: Penguin Books, 1978), 1–28; and Peter Hulme, *Colonial Encounters: Europe and the Native Caribbean, 1492–1797* (New York: Routledge, 1986), 1–12. But most important, I am indebted to the work of Bernard Cohn, including *An Anthropologist among Historians and Other Essays* (New York: Oxford University Press, 1987) and *Colonialism and Its Forms of Knowledge: The British in India* (Princeton, N.J.: Princeton University Press, 1996). See also Nicholas B. Dirks, *The Hollow Crown: Ethnohistory of an Indian Kingdom* (Ann Arbor: University of Michigan Press, 1993); and Mahdavi Kale, *The Fragments of Empire: Capital, Slavery, and Indian Indentured Labor in the British Caribbean* (Philadelphia: University of Pennsylvania Press, 1998).

28. Aguirre Beltrán, *La población negra de México*; Palmer, *Slaves of the White God* and *Human Cargoes: The British Slave Trade to Spanish America, 1700–1739* (Urbana: University of Illinois Press, 1981); Adriana Naveda Chávez-Hita, *Esclavos negros en las haciendas azucareras de Cordóba, Veracruz, 1690–1830* (México: Universidad Veracruzana, 1987); Lolita Gutiérrez Brockington, *The Leverage of Labor: Managing the Cortés Haciendas in Tehuantepec, 1588–1688* (Durham, N.C.: Duke University Press, 1989); Patrick J. Carroll, *Blacks in Colonial Veracruz: Race, Ethnicity and Regional Development* (Austin: University of Texas Press, 1991); Vincent V. Mayer, Jr., "The Black Slave on New Spain's Northern Frontier: San Jose de Parral 1632–1676" (Ph.D. dissertation, University of Utah, 1975); Frederick P. Bowser, "Colonial Spanish America," 19–58; John K. Chance, *Race and Class in Colonial Oaxaca* (Stanford, Calif.: Stanford University Press, 1978); Solange Alberro, "Juan de Morga and Gertrudis de Escobar: Rebellious Slaves," in *Struggle and Survival in Colonial America,* ed. David G. Sweet and Gary B. Nash (Berkeley: University of California Press, 1981), 165–188; Cope, *The Limits of Racial Domination*; Klein, *African Slavery in Latin America and the Caribbean*; Ben Vinson, III, *Bearing Arms for His Majesty: The Free-Colored Militia in Colonial Mexico* (Stanford, Calif.: Stanford University Press, 2001); María de Lourdes Villafuerte García, "Relaciones entre los groupos socials a traves de la informacion matrimonial Ciudad de Mexico, 1628–1634" (tesis de licenciada: Universidad Nacional Autonoma de México, 1991); and *Presencia africana en México*, comp. Luz María Martínez Montiel (México: Consejo Nacional para la Cultura y las Artes, 1994).

29. Laird W. Bergad's study on Minas Gerais, Brazil, underscores the magnitude of the problem characterizing the study of slavery. Until Bergad discovered that the nineteenth-century slave population of Minas Gerais reproduced itself—the only "large-scale Latin American and Caribbean slave society where this was the case"—the assumption was that a natural rate of reproduction among slaves was unique to British North America. *Slavery and the Demographic and Economic History of Minas Gerais, Brazil, 1720–1888* (New York: Cambridge University Press, 1999), xvii. Similar assumptions, akin to myths, are still pervasive in the study of slavery. This is particularly so for Latin America, given the paucity of work on early modern Latin American slavery.

30. Ira Berlin and Philip D. Morgan, "Introduction: Labor and the Shaping of Slave Life in the Americas," in *Cultivation and Culture: Labor and the Shaping of Slave*

Life in the Americas, ed. Ira Berlin and Philip D. Morgan (Charlottesville: University Press of Virginia, 1993), 1–45.

31. Ecclesiastical and especially inquisition testimonies offer far more depth and range of expression than do slave narratives crafted in the 1930s by the WPA. See John W. Blassingame, ed., *Slave Testimony: Two Centuries of Letters, Speeches, Interviews, and Autobiographies* (Baton Rouge: Louisiana State University Press, 1977), xvii–lxv.

32. Gonzalo Aguirre Beltrán, *Medicina y Magia: el proceso de aculturación en la estructura colonial* (México: Fondo de Cultura Económica, 1963); Richard Boyer, *Lives of the Bigamists: Marriage, Family, and Community in Colonial Mexico* (Albuquerque: University of New Mexico Press, 1995); and Solange Alberro, *Inquisición y Sociedad en México, 1571–1700* (México: Fondo de Cultura Económica, 1988).

33. The romance with slave testimonies resulted in the corpus of Afro-American History created in the aftermath of the U.S. Civil Rights Movement. Soon thereafter a critique emerged, which suggested that social history had lost its symbiotic relationship to power. While I share the concerns about the role of power in the analysis of the post–Civil Rights portrayals of black life and culture under slavery, I continue to marvel at that scholarship.

34. Gabrielle Spiegel, *The Past as Text: The Theory and Practice of Medieval Historiography* (Baltimore: Johns Hopkins University Press, 1997), 3–28.

35. My focus on the Church and on clerical intervention on behalf of slaves and servants facilitates an exploration of the ways power operated in colonial New Spain. Ecclesiastical authorities policed the bodies of persons of African descent in Mexico City just as thoroughly as the slave-owners who bought and sold them, broke up their families, and used violent physical force to control their labor and behavior. The methods of the officials of the Inquisition were just as effective, if not more so, because they invaded the consciousness of the residents of New Spain by parading periodic spectacles of violence and by marshalling the memories of friends, relatives, and acquaintances to police the behavior of individuals. A study that focused on legal practice and physical treatment alone would miss the insidious power of the Holy Inquisition in the lives of its subaltern subjects. Power over consciousness is power indeed.

1. Soiled Gods and the Formation of a Slave Society

1. Eugene D. Genovese, *The World the Slaveholders Made: Two Essays in Interpretation* (New York: Vintage Books, 1971), 63.

2. Edgar T. Thompson, "The Plantation: Background and Definition," in *Plantation Societies, Race Relations, and the South: The Regimentation of Populations: Selected Papers of Edgar T. Thompson* (Durham, N.C.: Duke University Press, 1975), 3–40.

3. Joseph P. Reidy, "Obligation and Right: Patterns of Labor, Subsistence, and Exchange in the Cotton Belt of Georgia, 1790–1860," in *Cultivation and Culture: Labor and the Shaping of Slave Life in the Americas,* ed. Ira Berlin and Philip D. Morgan (Charlottesville: University Press of Virginia, 1993), 138–154; Woodville K. Marshall, "Provision Ground and Plantation Labor in Four Windward Islands:

Competition for Resources during Slavery," in *Cultivation and Culture*, 203–220; Dale Tomich, "*Une Petite Guinée:* Provision Ground and Plantation in Martinique, 1830–1848," in *Cultivation and Culture*, 221–242; John Campbell, "As 'A Kind of Freeman'?: Slaves' Market-Related Activities in the South Carolina Upcountry, 1800–1860," in *Cultivation and Culture*, 243–274; Roderick A. McDonald, "Independent Economic Production by Slaves on Antebellum Louisiana Sugar Plantations," in *Cultivation and Culture*, 275–299; Richard B. Sheridan, "Strategies of Slave Subsistence: The Jamaican Case Reconsidered," in *From Chattel Slaves to Wage Slaves: The Dynamics of Labour Bargaining in the Americas*, ed. Mary Turner (Bloomington: Indiana University Press, 1995), 48–67; Michael Mullin, "Slave Economic Strategies: Food, Markets and Property," in *From Chattel Slaves to Wage Slaves*, 68–78; Betty Wood, " 'Never on a Sunday'?: Slavery and the Sabbath in Lowcountry Georgia 1750–1830," in *From Chattel Slaves to Wage Slaves*, 79–96.

4.   This perspective invariably appears in works of synthesis. In Robin Blackburn's majestic study of New World slavery, the dominance of the plantation complex as the unit of analysis is continually reasserted, most notably in describing the shift from baroque to creole slavery. *The Making of New World Slavery: From the Baroque to the Modern, 1492–1800* (New York: Verso, 1997), 20–24.

5.   Ira Berlin, "Time, Space, and the Evolution of Afro-American Society on British Mainland North America," *American Historical Review* 85 (February 1980): 44–78.

6.   The exceptions of Salvador, Rio de Janiero, Havana, and Charlestown (Charleston) are instructive since they are located in the heart of the quintessential New World slave societies. See Mary C. Karasch, *Slave Life in Rio de Janiero, 1808–1850* (Princeton, N.J.: Princeton University Press, 1987); Sandra Lauderdale Graham, *House and Street: The Domestic World of Servants and Masters in Nineteenth-Century Rio de Janiero* (Austin: University of Texas, 1988); João José Reis, *Slave Rebellion in Brazil: The Muslim Uprising of 1835 in Bahia*, translated by Arthur Brakel (Baltimore: Johns Hopkins University Press, 1993); Rebecca J. Scott, *Slave Emancipation in Cuba: The Transition to Free Labor, 1860–1899* (Princeton, N.J.: Princeton University Press, 1985); and Peter H. Wood, *Black Majority: Negroes in Colonial South Carolina from 1670 through the Stono Rebellion* (New York: W. W. Norton & Company, 1974).

7.   For an earlier but still powerful historiographical perspective, see Richard M. Morse, "The Heritage of Latin America," in *The Founding of New Societies: Studies in the History of the United States, Latin America, South Africa, Canada, and Australia*, ed. Louis Hartz (New York: Harcourt Brace Jovanovich, Publishers, 1964), 123–177.

8.   This perspective is often most discernible in conference proceedings and edited collections. See Turner, ed., *From Chattel Slaves to Wage Slaves*; Berlin and Morgan, eds., *Cultivation and Culture*; and Heywood, ed., *Central Africans and Cultural Transformations in the African Diaspora*.

9.   Ira Berlin, *Many Thousands Gone: The First Two Centuries of Slavery in North America* (Cambridge, Mass.: The Belknap Press of Harvard University Press, 1998), 8.

10.   Genovese, *The World the Slaveholders Made*, 63.

11.   Cope, *The Limits of Racial Domination*; Mörner, *Race Mixture in the History of Latin America*; and Seed, *To Love, Honor, and Obey in Colonial Mexico*.

12.   Emphasis added. Frank Tannenbaum, *Slave and Citizen: The Negro in the Americas* (New York: Vintage Books), 40.

13.   Thomas Holt's very perceptive rereading of Tannenbaum has been instrumental in shaping this project from its inception. Holt reads Tannenbaum as "suggesting not simply that Africans were major contributors to New World cultures, but that the system of slavery and its corollary institutions formed the essential template upon which those cultures were built." In revisiting this aspect of *Slave and Citizen,* Holt aids in rescuing the Africans' cultural importance without reinscribing the argument about the benign forms of Latin American slavery. In the intellectual fray that followed the Tannenbaum thesis, the contribution of Africans was one of the central casualties. Thomas C. Holt, "Slavery and Freedom in the Atlantic World: Reflections on the Diasporan Framework," in *Crossing Boundaries: Comparative History of Black People in Diaspora,* ed. Darlene Clark Hine and Jacqueline McLeod (Bloomington: Indiana University Press, 1999), 34.

14.   *We People Here: Nahuatl Accounts of the Conquest of Mexico,* ed. and trans. James Lockhart (Berkeley: University of California Press, 1993), 82–83.

15.   By the sixteenth century, a significant African and creole population flourished on the Iberian Peninsula. In fact, the conquest generation included many ladinos. Vicenta Cortés, *La eslavitud en Valencia durante el reinado de los Reyes Católicos, 1479–1516* (Valencia: Archivo Municipal de Valencia, 1964); Jose Luis Cortés Lopez, *Los origenes de la eslavitud negra en España* (Madrid: Mundo Negro, 1896) and *La esclavitud negra en la España peninsular del Siglo XVI* (Salamanca: Universidad de Salamanca, 1989); Alfonso Franco Silva, *La esclavitud en Sevilla y su tierra a fines de la edad media* (Sevilla: Excma. Diputacion Provincial de Sevilla, 1979) and *Regesto Documental sobre la Esclavitud Sevillana, 1453–1513* (Sevilla: Universidad de Sevilla, 1979); Vicente Graullera Sanz, *La esclavitud en Valencia en los Siglos XVI y XVII* (Valencia: Instituto Valenciano de Estudios Históricos, 1978); and Manuel Lobo Cabrera, *La esclavitud en las Canarias Orientales en el Siglo XVI: negros, moros y moriscos* (Tenerife: Excmo. Cabildo Insular de Gran Canaria, 1982).

16.   It is possible that Juan Garrido used "Castile" in a metaphorical sense as opposed to a strictly geographical sense. Pedro Garrido, for instance, was a *vecino* of Badajoz in the Extremadura province. It is conceivable that Domingo Garrido, a *vecino* of Huelva, was actually Juan's master since he too was in Cuba in 1519 and joined Cortés's *entrada.* Peter Boyd-Bowman, *Indice geobiográfico de cuarenta mil pobladores españoles de América en el siglo XVI,* 2 vols. (Bogotá: Instituto Caro y Cuervo, 1964), 1:15, 63.

17.   Archivo General de la Nación Mexico City (hereafter AGN), Inquisición 103, expediente 5, 1575; AGN, Inquisición 103, expediente 6, 1575. See also Aguirre Beltrán, *La población negra de Mexico,* 19–20 and Boyd-Bowman, *Indice geobiográfico de cuarenta mil pobladores españoles de América en el siglo XVI.*

18.   *Diccionario autobiografico de conquistadores y pobladores de Nueva España,* ed. Francisco A. de Icaza. 2 vols. (Madrid, 1923), 1:98.

19. Mörner, *Race Mixture in the History of Latin America.*

20. Evidently, Juan arrived in Santo Domingo the same year that Pedro Garrido, a Spaniard, landed. The relationship between the two men remains a mystery, though it may have begun in 1503 in Castile when Pedro purchased Juan after his arrival from Lisbon. Pedro arrived in Santo Domingo in 1510. In 1518, he resettled in Cuba, where he joined the Cortés expedition. Boyd-Bowman, *Indice geobiográfico de cuarenta mil pobladores españoles de América en el siglo XVI,* 1:15. For a slightly different perspective, see Jane Landers, *Black Society in Spanish Florida* (Urbana: University of Illinois Press, 1999), 10–12.

21. Although Juan Garrido's name is absent from a list of prominent individuals who laid siege to Tenochitlán, he was in all likelihood a member of the conquest generation. See Aguirre Beltrán, *La población negra de México,* 19; and Peter Gerhard, "A Black Conquistador in Mexico," *Hispanic American Historical Review* 58 (August 1978): 452–453.

22. Bernal Díaz del Castillo, *The Discovery and Conquest of Mexico, 1517–1521,* trans. A. P. Maudslay, intro. Irving A. Leonard (New York: Farrar, Straus and Cudahy, 1956), 312–323.

23. Lucas Alaman, *Disertaciones sobre la historia de la republica megicana desde la época de la conquista que los españoles hicieron a fines del siglo XV y principios del XVI de las islas y continente americano hasta la independencia,* 3 vols. (México, 1844–1849), cited in Gerhard, "A Black Conquistador in Mexico," 453–454.

24. This lends support to the theory that Garrido was a member of the conquest generation, since it was customary for persons defined as First Conqueror, Conqueror, *Poblador antiguo* (first settler), and *Poblador* (settler) to be granted the status of *vecinos,* often of several cities, and given a plot on which they established their residence. Robert Himmerich y Valencia, *The Encomenderos of New Spain, 1521–1555* (Austin: University of Texas Press, 1991), 6–9.

25. *Actas de cabildo de ciudad de México,* August 12, 1524; January 13, February 28, June 2, and December 15, 1525; and August 17 and December 10, 1526, cited in Gerhard, "A Black Conquistador in Mexico," 456–457.

26. In the two decades that followed the defeat of the Triple Alliance, the Spaniards searched desperately but in vain for treasures of gold and silver. As they scoured the provinces, they took note of the regional resources on which the colonial economy and settlements were eventually built. The Africans who accompanied these missions were often among the first to become provincial settlers. Throughout the colonial period, as we shall see, Africans and their descendants—usually freedpersons but also the enslaved—traveled widely in search of or because of their livelihood. On their voyages, they extended or simply reinforced the African presence throughout New Spain. The African presence was initially linked to the Spanish commercial networks that dotted the landscape. In time, the African and the Afromestizo presence acquired a momentum largely independent of the colonial economy.

27. *Diccionario autobiografico de conquistadores y pobladores de Nueva España,* 1:98.

28. Aguirre Beltrán, *La población negra de México,* 19–20.

29. According to Hubert Howe Bancroft, Cortés's expedition in lower California (the

Baja peninsula) involved 700 persons, of which the descendants of Africans accounted for 300. *The Works of Hubert Howe Bancroft,* vol. 10, *The History of Mexico,* 2nd vol., 1521–1600 (San Francisco: A. L. Bancroft & Co., 1883), 423n44. See also Bowser, *The African Slave in Colonial Peru,* 5–10; Lockhart, *Spanish Peru,* 171–172; and Alvar Nuñez Cabeza de Vaca, *The Account: Alvar Nuñez Cabeza de Vaca's Relación,* trans. Martin A. Favata y Jose B. Fernandez (Houston: Arte Publico Press, 1993).

30.   The 1537 conspiracy in Mexico City highlights the growing tension between Africans and Spaniards. This pattern also manifested itself in Hispañiola when the *bozales* staged a rebellion in 1512. Though in Mexico City the enslaved *bozales* masterminded the conspiracy, ladinos, like Juan Garrido, may have been sympathetic to the conspirators, given the decline in their own status. In the aftermath of this aborted conspiracy, the authorities acted swiftly to reinforce racial boundaries by imposing greater restrictions on *bozales* and ladinos and their respective descendants. David M. Davidson, "Negro Slave Control and Resistance in Colonial Mexico, 1519–1650," *Hispanic American Historical Review* 46 (1966): 235–253. See also Aguirre Beltrán, *La población negra de Mexico,* 23.

31.   Mark A. Brukholder, "Honor and Honors in Colonial Spanish America," in *The Faces of Honor: Sex, Shame, and Violence in Colonial Latin America,* ed. Lyman L. Johnson and Sonya Lipsett-Rivera (Albuquerque: University of New Mexico Press, 1998).

32.   *Thomas Gage's Travels in the New World,* ed. with intro. by J. Eric S. Thompson (Norman: University of Oklahoma Press, 1958), 73.

33.   David Eltis, drawing on Peter Bakewell's scholarship, asserts as much in his recent study of labor, slavery, and freedom in the early modern Atlantic world. *The Rise of African Slavery in the Americas,* 25.

34.   Richard Boyer, "Mexico in the Seventeenth Century: Transition of a Colonial Society," *Hispanic American Historical Review* 57 (August 1977): 463–464. The conceptual implications of Boyer's argument have yet to be fully explored.

35.   Aguirre Beltrán, *La población negra de México,* 219.

36.   Gibson, *The Aztecs under Spanish Rule: A History of the Indians of the Valley of Mexico, 1519–1810* (Stanford, Calif.: Stanford University Press, 1964), 58–62.

37.   Horacio Crespo, Sergio Reyes Retana, Enrique Vega Villanueva, Arnulto Embriz, Carolos Zolla, Carlos González Herrera, Alejandro Pinet, and Beatriz Scharrer, eds., *Historia del azucar en México* (México: Fondo de Cultura Económica, 1988), 1:36; Fernando B. Sandoval, *La industria del Azucar en Nueva España* (México: UNAM, 1951), 24.

38.   With these ships, Cortés hoped to transport his livestock and their by-products to the Spanish settlements on the Pacific coast. Woodrow Borah, *Early Colonial Trade and Navigation between Mexico and Peru* (Berkeley: University of California Press, 1954), 23; Lolita Gutiérrez Brockington, *The Leverage of Labor: Managing the Cortés Haciendas in Tehuantepec, 1588–1688* (Durham, N.C.: Duke University Press, 1989), 6.

39.   Crespo et al., eds., *Historia del azucar en México,* 1:40–41, 50.

40.   Ibid., 1:50; Sandoval, *La industria del Azucar en Nueva España,* 31–32.

41. Crespo et al., eds., *Historia del azucar en México*, 2:605; James Lockhart, *The Nahuas after the Conquest: A Social and Cultural History of the Indians of Central Mexico, Sixteenth through Eighteenth Centuries* (Stanford, Calif.: Stanford University Press, 1993) and *Nahuas and Spaniards: Postconquest Central Mexican History and Philology* (Stanford, Calif.: Stanford University Press, 1991), 202–242; Rebecca Horn, *Postconquest Coyoacan: Nahua-Spanish Relations in Central Mexico, 1519–1650* (Stanford, Calif.: Stanford University Press, 1997).

42. Lockhart, *Nahuas and Spaniards*, 202–242; Ida Altman and James Lockhart, eds., *Provinces of Early Mexico: Variants of Spanish American Regional Evolution* (Los Angeles: UCLA Latin American Center Publications, 1976).

43. Altman and Lockhart, eds., *Provinces of Early Mexico*, passim.

44. Klein, *African Slavery in Latin America and the Caribbean*, 30.

45. The indigenous peoples invariably accused Africans and their descendants of assaulting them on behalf of Spanish employers. The frequency of these accusations in the 1530s and 1540s suggest that Africans were a permanent yet growing fixture in the postconquest countryside. Gibson, *The Aztecs under Spanish Rule*, 147; S. L. Cline, *Colonial Culhuacan: A Social History of an Aztec Town* (Albuquerque: University of New Mexico, 1986), 43.

46. Palmer, *Slaves of the White God*, 27.

47. *Documentos inéditos relativos a Hernan Cortes y su Familia* (Mexico: Archivo General de la Nacíon, 1935), 254–266.

48. "Carta de Don Luis de Velasco, El Primero, A Felipe II-México, February 7, 1554," in *Documentos inéditos del siglo xvi para la historia de México*, ed. Mariano Cuevas (México: Jose Porrua e Hijos, 1914), 183–218.

49. Huguette and Pierre Chanu estimate that prior to 1550, 15,000 African slaves entered the Americas and that 36,500 arrived between 1551 and 1595. Based on these figures, it was initially estimated that New Spain's *bozal* population numbered 20,000 in 1553 and 18,569 in 1570, to which Gonzalo Aguirre Beltrán added 2,000 maroons, thus bringing the total to 20,569. Colin Palmer has noted, however, that "these population estimates raise an important question. If prior to 1553 only 15,000 slaves entered all of Spanish America, it seems unlikely that there would have been 20,00 blacks in New Spain alone in 1553 in view of their high mortality rates and the sexual imbalance of the slaves." Palmer consequently revises the estimates for the annual importation of slaves for all of the Americas upward from 810 to 1,000 for the period 1521 to 1594. "Thus the Indies would have received approximately 73,000 slaves during this period, and Mexico about 36,500 of the total." Palmer's upward revisions seem very appropriate, but he may be overlooking the importation of individuals from Spain, Portugal, and the Atlantic provinces. *Slaves of the White God*, 27.

50. "Census de la población del Virreinato de Nueva España en el siglo XVI," *Boletín del Centro de Estudios Americanistas de Sevilla de Indias* (February–March 1919): 44–62.

51. Gibson, *The Aztecs under Spanish Rule*, 136–138, 460–462, 499–500.

52. "Census de la población del Virreinato de Nueva España," 44–62.

53. Various contributors to *Provinces of Early Mexico* note the presence of isolated Africans, black creoles, and mulattos. See also Lockhart, *Nahuas and Spaniards,* 202–242. Yet even in the countryside, most descendants of Africans seem to have resided in pueblos or on large estates where their living conditions had an urban quality. Some Mexicanists highlight distinctive rural and urban African experiences. Such a perspective is misleading, however, since the rural African presence was primarily confined to estates that resembled villages and offered the amenities of smaller urban settlements. More important, Spanish urban centers were symbiotically linked to the hinterlands. The Hispanic population, including Africans and their descendants, moved freely and frequently from the countryside to nearby Spanish settlements and urban markets. Legal status was not an impediment to mobility, since enslaved cowboys, muleteers, and auxiliaries on roundups, drives, and treks in search of work and even urban slaves traveled widely throughout this period. Mobility, residential patterns, and the urban-hinterland continuum are factors that mitigate against an analysis that makes rigid distinctions between urban and rural experience. Such categories were simply not that meaningful in sixteenth-century New Spain.

54. "Census de la población del Virreinato de Nueva España," 44–62.

55. Horn, *Postconquest Coyoacan,* 144–225.

56. Other groups represented in the marriage records include individuals from the "land of Biojo," "the land of Zape," and persons from Cape Verde and Banoles. But unlike Biafarans, Brans, Terra Novas, and, to a lesser extent, Gelofes and Mandingas, these groups only appear sporadically in archival sources. See AGN, Matrimonios. Scholars concur that "tierra nueva" in Spanish and "terra nova" in Portuguese probably referred to a region in Guinea which today is associated with Nigeria. Person taken from this region are often characterized as Lucumis or Yoruba. The presence of a person who identified and was identified as being from "tierra nueva" is consistent with the slave-trading patterns of the sixteenth century. See, for example, Palmer, *Slaves of the White God,* 21.

57. Curtin referred to "Guinea de Cabo Verde" as the region from Senegal to Sierra Leone. According to Curtin, this region provided the bulk of slaves until the sixteenth century. "We have little more than a general impression that these slaves came dominantly from a region stretching south of the Senegal River to the vicinity of present-day Sierra Leone, with only a scattering exported from other parts of West or Central Africa." Curtin also cites a study on Bolivia that documents the dominance of the Wolofs in the middle decades of the sixteenth century, "followed by the Bight of Biafara in the second half of the century, and then by a sharp shift to Angola in 1594." *The Atlantic Slave Trade,* 18, 96, 110; See also Rodney's "Portuguese Attempts at Monopoly," *Journal of African History* 6 (1965): 307. According to the patterns identified by Lockhart, 74.4 percent of the African-born population came from the Senegambia, or present-day Guinea-Bissau. In that sample of 256 blacks, 80 percent were actually born in Africa, while creoles only accounted for 20 percent. In the sample taken from Aguirre Beltrán, who, in turn, cites Hernan Cortés ("Documentos ineditos," 242–278), 88 percent were from "Guinea of Cape Verde." *Spanish Peru,* 173–174.

58. Aguirre Beltran, *La población negra de México,* 217; Curtin, *The Atlantic Slave*

Trade, 95–126; and Palmer, *Slaves of the White God*, 30. Though impressive, the CD-ROM database *The Trans-Atlantic Slave Trade* relies on the foundational work of Vila Vilar in *Hispano-America y el comercio de Esclavos*, 200.

59. Palmer, *Slaves of the White God*, 16; Vila Vilar, *Hispano-America y el comercio de Esclavos*, 200. As scholars of the slave trade have noted, an active contraband trade existed, and in some years more slaves were introduced illegally than legally.

60. This figure is based on shipping records and import figures for the years 1595 to 1622. Between 1623 and 1639, the Spaniards imported an estimated 47,000 enslaved Africans into the Americas, but the records do not reveal how many arrived in New Spain. Palmer, *Slaves of the White God*, 16; Vila Vilar, *Hispano-America y el comercio de Esclavos*, 200.

61. Aguirre Beltrán, *La población negra de México*, 219.

62. Brockington, *The Leverage of Labor*, 3–22.

63. Ibid., 146.

64. Ibid.

65. Ibid., 116, 147.

66. Ibid., 133.

67. Among the 1,000 nonindigenous people who lived in Morelos in 1570, 900 were persons of African descent. "Ovando Reports (ca. 1570)," cited in Peter Gerhard, "Continuity and Change in Morelos, Mexico," *The Geographical Review* 65 (July 1975): 344. For a comparative perspective, see Bowser, *The African Slave in Colonial Peru*, 337–341; Klein, *African Slavery in Latin America and the Caribbean*, 28–36; and Stuart B. Schwartz, *Sugar Plantations in the Formation of Brazilian Society, 1550–1835* (New York: Cambridge University Press, 1985), 65–72.

68. Martin, *Rural Society in Colonial Morelos*, 23–45, 38–40; Ward J. Barrett, *The Sugar Hacienda of the Marqueses del Valle* (Minneapolis: University of Minnesota Press, 1970), 78.

69. Martin, *Rural Society in Colonial Morelos*, 38.

70. Ibid., 38–39.

71. Ibid., 124, 130.

72. Ibid., 128; Barrett, *The Sugar Hacienda of the Marqueses del Valle*, 79.

73. Martin, *Rural Society in Colonial Morelos*, 129.

74. Ibid., 128.

75. Ibid., 122.

76. María Guadalupe Chávez Carbajal, "El negro esclavo en la jurisdicción de Valladolid 1600–1650," *Tzintzun* 9 (January–December 1988): 10.

77. Chávez Carbajal, "El negro esclavo en la jurisdiccion de Valladolid 1600–1650," 8–9. Morin notes that until 1600, eleven of New Spain's forty water- and animal-powered mills were in Michoácan. *Michoácan en la Nueva España del Siglo XVIII: Crecimiento y desigualdad en una economía colonial* (México: Fondo de Cultura Económica, 1979), 33.

78. Chávez Carbajal, "El negro esclavo en la jurisdiccion de Valladolid 1600–1650,"

5–6, 8–9, 11–13, 15, 17–18; Claude Morin, *Michoácan en la Nueva España del Siglo XVIII*, 33.

79.   Crespo et al., eds., *Historia del azucar en México*, 1: 90–93.

80.   Chávez Carbajal, "El negro esclavo en la jurisdiccion de Valladolid 1600–1650," 15.

81.   Ibid., 17–18.

82.   Ibid., 11–13.

83.   Morin calls this period "the century of the blacks"; *Michoácan en la Nueva España del Siglo XVIII*, 33–35.

84.   Carroll, *Blacks in Colonial Veracruz*, 30.

85.   Ibid., 70–71, 167.

86.   Ibid., 65.

87.   Chávez-Hita, *Esclavos negros en las haciendas azucareras de Cordóba*.

88.   Carroll, *Blacks in Colonial Veracruz*, 172.

89.   Ibid., 166.

90.   Aguirre Beltrán, *La población negra de México*, 197–264; Palmer, *Slaves of the White God*, 31–35; Klein, *African Slavery in Latin America and the Caribbean*, 36–37; Dennis N. Valdés "The Decline of Slavery in Mexico," *The Americas* 44 (1987): 177; Claudio Esteva-Fabregat, *Mestizaje in Ibero-America*, trans. John Wheat (Tucson: University of Arizona Press, 1995), 161, 176–179, 199–243; Richard Konetzke, ed., *Colección de documentos para la historia de la formación social de Hispanoamérica, 1493–1810* (hereafter cited as *CFS*), 3 vols. (Madrid: Consejo Superior de Investigaciones Científicas, 1953–1962), 1:206, 210, 140, 237–240, 427; Gibson, *The Aztecs under Spanish Rule*, 147, 502n39; Lockhart, *The Nahuas After the Conquest*, 191; Horn, *Postconquest Coyoacan*, 166–167, 171–193, 219–225; James Lockhart, *Nahuas and Spaniards*, 202–242; Asunción Lavrín, ed., *Sexuality and Marriage in Colonial Latin America* (Lincoln: University of Nebraska Press, 1989), 43; Seed, *To Love, Honor, and Obey in Colonial Mexico*, 97–98; John K. Chance, *Race and Class in Colonial Oaxaca*, 122–123, 170.

91.   Valdes, "The Decline of the Sociedad de Castas," 139, 142.

92.   Lockhart, *Spanish Peru*, 181.

93.   Boyer, "Mexico in the Seventeenth Century," 455–456.

94.   As creatures of habit, sixteenth-century Spaniards associated certain skilled and menial occupations with enslaved Africans. Centuries of accumulated experiences on the Iberian Peninsula, the Atlantic Provinces, and, most recently, in the Caribbean had shaped the Spanish preference for African labor. Once in a position to act on their preference, they willingly consumed a familiar human commodity. Contrary to prevailing views that link the African presence to the declining indigenous population, Spaniards clamored for Africans because of their familiarity with them and because they perceived them to be reliable.

95.   Lockhart observed that "the second reason why Negroes were desired as servants was that they were one essential part of the general pattern of Spanish ambitions. No encomendero felt happy until he owned a large house, land, livestock and—most to the point here—Negro servants. Most Spaniards could not hope to

achieve this goal in its entirety, but they aimed at least for two essentials, a house and Negroes." *Spanish Peru*, 181.

96. Lyman L. Johnson, "Dangerous Words, Provocative Gestures, and Violent Acts: The Disputed Hierarchies of Plebeian Life in Colonial Buenos Aires," in *The Faces of Honor*, 141–144. Scholars of comparative slavery have noted how displays of violence and an indifference to African lives underscores the African's value as labor and the master's power to be indifferent to the economic dimension of the slave. This process again serves to remind us of the multiple slave identities. The existing historiography often acknowledges this dynamic but then neglects it in favor of exploring the economic imperatives informing slave regimes. Analysis of white supremacy, for instance, remains deeply in tune to the ways in which the control over the black body through this process is not always concerned with regulating labor since it correctly demonstrates that the economic was inextricably linked to the symbolic. Carolyn E. Fick, *The Making of Haiti: The Saint Domingue Revolution from Below* (Knoxville: University of Tennessee Press, 1990); Kim F. Hall, *Things of Darkness: Economies of Race and Gender in Early Modern England* (Ithaca, N.Y.: Cornell University Press, 1995), 211–253.

97. Juan Pedro Viqueira Albán, *Relajados o reprimidos?: diversiones públicas y vida social en la Ciudad de México durante el Siglo de las Luces* (México: Fondo de Cultura Económica, 1987). A masterful English translation has been recently released as *Propriety and Permissiveness in Bourbon Mexico*, trans. Sonya Lipsett-Rivera and Sergio Rivera Ayala (1987; reprint, Wilmington, Del.: Scholarly Resources, 1999), 1–26.

98. *Thomas Gage's Travel in the New World*, 65.

99. Ibid., 67.

100. Ibid., 68.

101. Ibid., 70.

102. In this respect Gage was not unusual. Richard Dunn has observed that "one of the more telling points about these first English impressions of the Caribbean is their silence on the subject of African slavery. The Elizabethan sea dogs met plenty of slave ships and saw plenty of blacks in the Spanish settlements. Although their narratives sometimes mention 'Negroes' or 'slaves' in passing, these men showed no curiosity about the blacks, their African culture, their bondage, or their treatment by the Spaniards." *Sugar and Slaves: The Rise of the Planter Class in the English West Indies, 1624–1713* (New York: W. W. Norton, 1973), 13.

103. Berlin, *Many Thousands Gone*, 8; Seed, *To Love, Honor, and Obey in Colonial Mexico*; and Cope, *The Limits of Racial Domination*.

104. James Lockhart, *Of Things of the Indies: Essays Old and New in Early Latin American History* (Stanford, Calif.: Stanford University Press, 1999), x–xin3.

2. "The Grand Remedy"

1. Karl Marx, *Wage Labour and Capital* (1891; reprint, Peking: Foreign Languages Press, 1978), 29.

2. The Siete Partidas (Seven Parts) is a legal code compiled in 1248 during the reign

of Ferdinand III (1217–1252) but associated with his son and successor Alfonso X (1251–1284), named the "wise" king. While most scholars place the genesis of the Siete Partidas in Roman law, Gwendolyn Midlo Hall insists that Islamic law had greater influence. *Social Control in Slave Plantation Societies: A Comparison of St. Domingue and Cuba* (Baltimore: Johns Hopkins University Press, 1971; reprint, Baton Rouge: Louisiana State University Press, 1996), 1. Frank Tannenbaum was one of the most prominent scholars to draw attention to the rights of the enslaved that he saw rooted in the Siete Partidas. Scholars have criticized Tannenbaum on the basis that his conclusions reflect a preoccupation with the rhetoric of the law as opposed to its actual practice. Yet most of Tannenbaum's detractors have ignored his insistence that the Siete Partidas "was framed in . . . Christian doctrine." Even those who appreciated this observation have generally limited themselves to the early modern incarnation of Christianity and then focused on theology, largely forsaking medieval Christianity and the all-important canon law tradition. Tannenbaum, *Slave and Citizen*, 48–55; Davis, *The Problem of Slavery in Western Culture*, 29–121, 165–261; Genovese, *The World the Slaveholders Made*, 3–113; Eugene D. Genovese, *In Red and Black: Marxian Explorations in Southern and Afro-American History* (New York: Pantheon Books, 1971; reprint, Knoxville: University of Tennessee Press, 1984), 23–52; Eugene D. Genovese, *Roll, Jordan, Roll: The World the Slaves Made* (New York: Vintage Books, 1974), 178–179, 168–183; William McKee Evans, "From the Land of Canaan to the Land of Guinea: The Strange Odyssey of the Sons of Ham," *The American Historical Review* 85 (February 1980): 15–43; Palmer, *Slaves of the White God*, 84–118. Despite legal developments and their importance, transformations in Christianity during Europe's high Middle Ages played, as we shall see, a determining role in shaping the formative experiences of enslaved Africans who were married and resided in Castile or its provinces. Kagan, *Lawsuits and Litigants in Castile*; Seed, *To Love, Honor, and Obey in Colonial Mexico*.

3.   Orlando Patterson, *Slavery and Social Death: A Comparative Study* (Cambridge, Mass.: Harvard University Press, 1982), 17–32; John W. Baldwin, *The Language of Sex: Five Voices from Northern France around 1200* (Chicago: University of Chicago Press, 1994), 6; James A. Brundage, *Law, Sex, and Christian Society in Medieval Europe* (Chicago: University of Chicago Press, 1987); Kenneth Pennington, *The Prince and the Law 1200–1600: Sovereignty and Rights in the Western Legal Tradition* (Berkeley: University of California Press, 1993), 96–98, 202–237; Bowser, *The African Slave in Colonial Peru*, 233–267; and Tannenbaum, *Slave and Citizen*, 5–65.

4.   James Muldoon, ed., *Popes, Lawyers, and Infidels: The Church and the Non-Christian World, 1250–1550* (Philadelphia: University of Pennsylvania Press, 1979), 6.

5.   Ibid., 7.

6.   Ibid., 8–9.

7.   Ibid., 10.

8.   Ibid., 15–16.

9.   Ibid., 8, 156; Kenneth Pennington, *Popes, Canonists, and Texts, 1150–1550*

(Brookfield, Vt.: Variorum, 1993), 6; Pennington, *The Prince and the Law*; Brundage, *Law, Sex, and Christian Society.*

10. Woodrow Borah, *Justice by Insurance: The General Indian Court of Colonial Mexico and the Legal Aides of the Half-Real* (Berkeley: University of California Press, 1983), 10.

11. David Nirenberg, *Communities of Violence: Persecution of Minorities in the Middle Ages* (Princeton, N.J.: Princeton University Press, 1996); R. I. Moore, *The Formation of a Persecuting Society: Power and Deviance in Western Europe, 950–1250* (Cambridge, Mass.: Blackwell, 1987); John Boswell, *Christianity, Social Tolerance, and Homosexuality: Gay People in Western Europe from the Beginning of the Christian Era to the Fourteenth Century* (Chicago: University of Chicago Press, 1980); Joseph F. O'Callaghan, *A History of Medieval Spain* (Ithaca, N.Y.: Cornell University Press, 1975), 185; Kagan, *Lawsuits and Litigants*, 22–32; Deborah Root, "Speaking Christian: Orthodoxy and Difference in Sixteenth-Century Spain," *Representations* 23 (Summer 1988): 118–134.

12. Frances Gardiner Davenport, ed., *European Treaties Bearing on the History of the United States and Its Dependencies to 1648* (Washington, D.C.: Carnegie Institution, 1917); Anthony Pagden, *The Fall of Natural Man: The American Indian and the Origins of Comparative Ethnology* (New York: Cambridge University Press, 1982), 57–108; Pennington, *The Prince and the Law*; Pennington, *Popes, Canonists, and Texts*; Muldoon, *Popes, Lawyers, and Infidels*; James Muldoon, *The Americas in the Spanish World Order: The Justification for Conquest in the Seventeenth Century* (Philadelphia: University of Pennsylvania Press, 1994). Although conciliar canons preceded the twelfth century, the systematic use of canon law started with the jurist Gratian. Brundage, *Law, Sex, and Christian Society*, 239–235, 229–416; Pennington, *The Prince and the Law*, 8–37; Brundage, *Law, Sex, and Christian Society*, 325–486. The Church sought both to benefit materially from colonization and to increase the number of Christian souls. The focus on the former process has obscured the importance of canon law and the ability of colonizers to be both the protector of the colonized and the beneficiary of colonialism. Seymour Phillips, "The Outer World of the European Middle Ages," in *Implicit Understandings: Observing, Reporting, and Reflecting on the Encounters between Europeans and Other Peoples in the Early Modern Era,* ed. Stuart B. Schwartz (New York: Cambridge University Press, 1994), 57; Miguel Angel Ladero Quesada, "Spain, circa 1492: Social Values and Structures," in *Implicit Understandings*, 100–104; Root, "Speaking Christian," 118–134.

13. Bartlett, *The Making of Europe*, 209; Ladero Quesada, "Spain, circa 1492," 100–104; Root, "Speaking Christian," 121, 131; Borah, *Justice by Insurance*, 11.

14. The term "secular church" refers to that part of the Christian Church not bound by monastic rules and orders.

15. *CFS*, 1:237–240; Bowser, *The African Slave in Colonial Peru*, 222–223; Palmer, *Slaves of the White God*, 119–144.

16. "Permission granted to the Governor of Bresa for four thousand slaves," in *Documents Illustrative of the History of the Slave Trade to America*, ed. Elizabeth Donnan (Washington, D.C.: Carnegie Institution of Washington, 1930), 1: 41–42.

17. Aguirre Beltrán, *La población negra de México*, 17–18; Charles Haring, *The Spanish Empire in America* (New York: Harcourt, Brace & World, 1947), 25, 204; Boyd-Bowman, *Indice geobiográfico de cuarenta mil pobladores españoles de América en siglo XVI*; Patricia Seed, *Ceremonies of Possession in Europe's Conquest of the New World, 1492–1640* (New York: Cambridge University Press, 1995), 69–99, 179; Roberto González-Echevarría, *Myth and Archive: A Theory of Latin American Narrative* (Durham, N.C.: Duke University Press, 1998), 43–92; John Lynch, *Spain 1516–1598: From Nation State to World Empire* (Cambridge, Mass.: Basil Blackwell, 1991), 211–218, 267–284.

18. "Permission granted to the Governor of Bresa," 41–42.

19. The conversion of Africans has not been a subject of concern among scholars of early modern Latin America. Colin A. Palmer's work represents an important exception but seems dated in light of recent studies on Christian conversion in the Indies. "Religion and Magic in Mexican Slave Society, 1570–1650," in *Race and Slavery in the Western Hemisphere: Quantitative Studies,* ed. Stanley L. Engerman and Eugene D. Genovese (Princeton, N.J.: Princeton University Press, 1975), 311–328 and *Slaves of the White God,* 84–118. The conversion experience in Protestant colonies still constitutes the prism through which we see the religious lives of enslaved Africans in the Americas. The standard works for early modern British America include Mechal Sobel, *Trabelin' On: The Slave Journey to an Afro-Baptist Faith* (1979; reprint, Princeton, N.J.: Princeton University Press, 1988) and *The World They Made Together: Black and White Values in Eighteenth-Century Virginia* (Princeton, N.J.: Princeton University Press, 1985); and Margaret Washington Creel, *"A Peculiar People": Religion and Community-Culture among the Gullahs* (New York: New York University Press, 1988). Recent works include Michael Mullin, *Africa in America: Slave Acculturation and Resistance in the American South and the British Caribbean, 1736–1831* (Urbana: University of Illinois Press, 1992), 62–74, 174–212, 241–267; Sylvia R. Frey and Betty Wood, *Come Shouting to Zion: African American Protestantism in the American South and British Caribbean to 1830* (Chapel Hill: University of North Carolina Press, 1998); Michael A. Gomez, *Exchanging Our Country Marks: The Transformation of African Identities in the Colonial and Antebellum South* (Chapel Hill: University of North Carolina Press, 1998); and Jon F. Sensbach, *A Separate Canaan: The Making of an Afro-Moravian World in North Carolina, 1763–1840* (Chapel Hill: University of North Carolina Press, 1988).

20. "Deposition of William Fowler of Ratcliffe, Merchant," in Elizabeth Donnan, ed., *Documents Illustrative of the History of the Slave Trade to America,* 1:72.

21. *CFS,* 1:80–81.

22. Ibid., 1:99–100.

23. Ibid., 1:400.

24. Although authorities believed that they used terms such as "ladino" and "ladina" with great precision, in actuality, the terms glossed over a variety of factors that the community of individuals of African descent used to distinguish among themselves, such as the depths of a person's cultural immersion and linguistic facility with Spanish. Louisa de Abrego, a ladina and native of Jérez de la Frontera (a port town southeast of Seville), had a distinctly different experience with

the customs and language of Iberia than a person transported from the Guinea coast to Portugal and then purchased by a Castilian buyer in Seville before departing abruptly for the Indies. Both, however, would be defined as ladinos. AGN, Inquisición 103, expediente 6, "Declaración de Luisa de Abrego," 28 February 1575, Mexico City. For a discussion of nomenclature and historical specificity, see Manuel Alvar, *Léxico del mestizaje en Hispanoamérica* (Madrid: Ediciones Cultura Hispánica, 1987); Thomas M. Stephens, *Dictionary of Latin American Racial and Ethnic Terminology* (Gainesville: University Press of Florida, 1999); Aguirre Beltrán, *La población negra de México,* 153–194; Mörner, *Race Mixture in the History of Latin America;* Jack D. Forbes, *Africans and Native Americans: The Language of Race and the Evolution of Red-Black Peoples,* 2nd ed. (Urbana: University of Illinois Press, 1993); and A. C. de C. M. Saunders, *A Social History of Black Slaves and Freedmen in Portugal, 1441–1555* (New York: Cambridge University Press, 1982), xii–xiii, 134–148. As an ideal type, ladinos represented what Homi Bhabha has called "the desire for a reformed, recognizable Other, *as a subject of a difference that is almost the same, but not quite*" (italics in original). But in their sameness, ladinos gained the facility to navigate the very instruments of colonial rule. Bhabha, "Of Mimicry and Man: The Ambivalence of Colonial Discourse," in *The Location of Culture* (New York: Routledge, 1994), 86. Ann Stoler makes similar observations and extends Bhabha's insights about the ways in which mimicry is simultaneously a strategy of containment and subversion in *Race and the Education of Desire: Foucault's History of Sexuality and the Colonial Order of Things* (Durham, N.C.: Duke University Press, 1995), 95–136 and "Deposition of William Fowler of Ratcliffe, Merchant," in *Documents Illustrative of the History of the Slave Trade to America,* 1:72. The relationship between language and social value has a long history that dates back to Aristotle, among others; it has played a very important role in Europe's early modern expansion and cross-cultural encounters. See Pagden, *The Fall of Natural Man,* 15–26; Hall, *Things of Darkness,* 144–145; and Henry L. Gates, Jr., *Figures in Black: Words, Signs, and the Racial Self* (New York: Oxford University Press, 1987), 3–25. Frank Moya Pons identifies at least three orders (29 March 1503, 15 September 1505, and 22 January 1510) in which Castile's monarch permitted the importation of enslaved Africans in *La Española en el siglo XVI, 1493–1520: Trabajo, Sociedad y Politica en la Economía del Oro* (Universidad Católica Madre y Maestra Santiago: República Dominicana, 1973), 70–71. See also Carl Ortwin Sauer, *The Early Spanish Main* (Berkeley: University of California Press, 1969), 206–207; and *CFS,* 1:80–81, 99–100, 427, 435, 444, 450; Aguirre Beltrán, *La población negra de México,* 187–188; Cope, *The Limits of Racial Domination,* 17–26; Moya Pons, *La Española en el siglo XVI,* 70–71; and Haring, *The Spanish Empire in America,* 206. R. Douglas Cope observed that "colonials perceived a biformity within the Hispanic república. On the one hand were the Spaniards; on the other, the castas. In theory, this racial principle should have neatly split Hispanic society into two groups. . . . Many elements of this division did persist in the Hispanic imagination. The official stereotype of castas as illegitimate, criminally inclined, and neophytes in the faith lasted into the seventeenth century and beyond." As Cope rightly observed, the language of blood, genealogy, and kinship marked the divide between Spaniards and *castas,* but it also marked differences between elite and plebeian whites. He noted how "Spaniards justified their domination of Mexico—and assigned rank within the Hispanic república—on the basis of lineage. Now the colonial elite found itself faced with the development of a permanent underclass of plebeian Spaniards whose behavior was no more 'rational' or 'moral' than that of the plebe's casta members." *The Limits of Racial Domination*, 19, 23. According to Benedict Anderson, "dreams of racism actually have their origin in ideologies of class, rather than in those of nation: above all in claims to divinity among rulers and to 'blue' or 'white' blood and 'breeding' among aristocracies." *Imagined Communities*, 149. In this formulation Anderson stands at odds with Michel Foucault, who identified class distinctions as a product of racism. Stoler, *Race and the Education of Desire*, 30.

25.   *CFS*, 1:81–82.

26.   Ibid.

27.   Palmer, *Slaves of the White God*, 120, 131; Cope, *The Limits of Racial Domination*, 25, 125–160; Seed, *To Love, Honor, and Obey in Colonial Mexico*, 32–46, 205–225; Ramon Gutiérrez, *When Jesus Came, the Corn Mothers Went Away: Marriage, Sexuality, and Power in New Mexico, 1500–1846* (Stanford, Calif.: Stanford University Press, 1991), 248–259. Various authorities contested the power of the prince over another man's property—a view that was far from hegemonic in the Middle Ages and the early modern period. Pennington, *The Prince and the Law*, 22–24, 114–116; Anthony Pagden, "Dispossessing the Barbarian: The Language of Spanish Thomism and the Debate over the Property Rights of the American Indians," in *The Languages of Political Theory in Early-Modern Europe*, ed. Anthony Pagden (Cambridge: Cambridge University Press, 1987), 79–98. In the Spanish Indies, as opposed to British North America, the sovereign's authority prevailed over a master's property, a policy that speaks to Spanish America's fragile civil domain. This is especially evident in laws where the state manifested an interest in the behavior of their Christian subjects. Watson, *Slave Law in the Americas*, 40–62; Hall, *Social Control in Slave Plantation Societies*, 81–84, 92–96; Verena Martinez-Alier, *Marriage, Class, and Colour in Nineteenth-Century Cuba: A Study of Racial Attitudes and Sexual Values in a Slave Society* (1974; reprint, Ann Arbor: University of Michigan Press, 1989), 11–12.

28.   *CFS*, 1:81–82.

29.   Ibid.

30.   As late as the 1680s, some individuals still believed that a Christian marriage would free an enslaved person. See AGN, Matrimonios, expediente 1, folios 1–35, 1688. In his discussion of the emergence of racism in the British North American colony of Virginia, Edmund S. Morgan observed that white patricians in 1667 decided that Christian conversion did not free either Africans or Indians. *American Slavery, American Freedom*, 329.

31.   AGN, Inquisición 103, expediente 6, "Declaración de Luisa de Abrego," 28 February 1575, Mexico City; Alonso de Sandoval, *Un tradado sobre la esclavitud (De Instauranda Aethiopum Salute)*, Introducción, transcripción y traducción de Enriqueta Vila Vilar (Madrid: Alianza Editorial, 1987), 382–401.

32.   "Memorial del obispo de Chiapa don fray Pedro de Feria para el Sínodo Provin-

cial que se celebra en México este presente año de 1585," in Llaguno, *La personalidad jurídica del indio y el III Concilio Provincial Mexicano (1585),* 183.

33. Robert Ricard, *The Spiritual Conquest of Mexico: An Essay on the Apostolate and
the Evangelizing Methods of the Mendicant Orders in New Spain, 1523–1572,* trans.
Lesley Byrd Simpson (Berkeley: University of California Press, 1996), 15, 17; Serge
Gruzinski, *The Conquest of Mexico: The Incorporation of Indian Societies into the
Western World, 16th–18th Centuries,* trans. Eileen Corrigan (Cambridge, Mass.:
Polity Press, 1993), 14–15; Gibson, *The Aztecs under Spanish Rule,* 98–99, 101; Bartlett, *The Making of Europe,* 5–7; *CFS,* 1:69–70; Llaguno, *La personalidad jurídica
del indio,* 1–39; R. Po-Chia Hsia, *The World of Catholic Renewal, 1540–1770* (Cambridge: Cambridge University Press, 1998), 1–7, 166, 170; Stafford Poole, C. M.,
*Pedro Moya de Contreras: Catholic Reform and Royal Power in New Spain, 1571–
1591* (Berkeley: University of California Press, 1991).

3. Policing Christians

1. Charles R. Cutter, *The Legal Culture of Northern New Spain, 1700–1810* (Albuquerque: University of New Mexico Press, 1995), 59.

2. Saidiya V. Hartman, *Scenes of Subjection: Terror, Slavery, and Self-Making in
Nineteenth-Century America* (New York: Oxford University Press, 1997), 7.

3. In response to the Protestant heresy, Catholic prelates from throughout Christendom met in Rome (the Vatican) from 1543 to 1565. Over the course of the Council, the Catholic clerics address various issues raised by Luther, among other Protestants. Aside from addressing the Protestant charges, the Catholic clerics focused
attention on how to reform and thereby make the Catholic clergy more efficient
in regulating their flocks. Consequently, the Council set out to define, stipulate,
and clarify what the role of the priest was and his responsibility to his parishioners. Also, the faithful were called upon to display greater conformity to Catholic
dogma, norms, and practices. The tridentine reforms, as the various rulings,
decrees, and exhortations were called, affected almost every aspect of Catholic
Christianity, including the institution of marriage, which, in contrast to Protestant marriage, was to reflect the free will of the lovers as opposed to the will of
the parents. These reforms were implemented with varying degrees of success
throughout areas in which Catholicism prevailed. In Spain, the reforms may
have had some of their greatest success, and this would also influence Spanish
America. After all, Pedro de Moya was a tridentine prelate.

4. J. H. Elliott, *Imperial Spain, 1469–1716* (New York: St. Martin's Press, 1964), 225–
227; John Lynch, *Spain 1516–1598: From Nation State to World Empire* (Cambridge:
Basil Blackwell, 1991), 243–249; Richard E. Greenleaf, *Zumárraga and the Mexican
Inquisition, 1536–1543* (Washington, D.C.: Academy of American Franciscan History, 1961), 3–25.

5. Elliott, *Imperial Spain, 1469–1716,* 226.

6. Greenleaf, *Zumárraga and the Mexican Inquisition,* 6.

7. Aguirre Beltrán, *La población negra de México,* 205–210.

8. *Books of the Brave: Being an Account of Books and of Men in the Spanish Conquest*

and Settlement of the Sixteenth-Century New World, intro. Rolena Adorno (Cambridge, Mass.: Harvard University Press, 1949; reprint, Berkeley: University of California Press, 1992), 185.

9. "A Discourse written by one Miles Philips Englishman, One of the Company put on shoare northward of Panuco, in the West Indies by M. John Hawkins," in Richard Hakluyt, ed., *The Principal Navigations, Voyages, Traffiques and Discoveries of the English Nation Made by Sea or Over-land to the Remote and Farthest Distant Quarters of the Earth at Any Time within the Compasse of These 1600 Yeeres* (Glasgow: James MacLehose and Sons, 1903–1905), 10:430.

10. *CFS,* 1:167–168, 290–291, 299–300, 420.

11. *CFS,* 1:502–503.

12. Alberro, *Inquisición y Sociedad en México,* 8–9, 455.

13. In his effort to historicize the concepts of "conquest" and "colonization," J. Jorge Klor de Alva questions the ease with which scholars lump the various subject populations into the category of the "colonized." Africans, Amerindians, and their descendants, he rightly notes, did not inhabit the same juridical location, nor were their experiences similar. "The Postcolonization of the (Latin) American Experience: A Reconsideration of 'Colonialism,' 'Postcolonialism,' and 'Mestizaje,'" in *After Colonialism: Imperial Histories and Postcolonial Displacements,* ed. Gyan Prakash (Princeton, N.J.: Princeton University Press, 1995), 261.

14. Alberro, *Inquisición y Sociedad en México,* 26.

15. "The Voyage of Robert Tomson Marchant, into Nova Hispania in the yeere 1555. with divers observations concerning the state of the Countrey: And certaine accidents touching himselfe," in Hakluyt, ed., *The Principal, Navigations, Voyages, Traffiques, and Discoveries of the English Nation,* 9:338–358.

16. Ibid., 339.

17. Ibid.

18. After spending twenty days on the Grand Canary Island in the company of the English factors, the entourage moved on and eventually joined a fleet headed for the Indies which include a ship "belonging to an Englishman married in the citie of Cadiz in Spaine, whose name was John Sweeting, and there came in the sayd ship for captain also an Englishman married in Cadiz, and sonne in law to the sayde John Sweeting, whose name was Leonard Chilton: there came also in the sayd ship another Englishman which had been a marchant of the citie of Exeter . . . whose name was Ralph Sarre." Ibid., 341.

19. In the town of Vera Cruz, the party "very naked and distressed of apparell, and all other things" encountered Gonzalo Ruíz de Cordova, "an olde friend of [Fields's] acquaintance in Spaine," who provided them with clothing, sustenance and transportation. Ibid., 346.

20. Ibid., 347.

21. Ibid., 351.

22. Ibid.

23. "Voyage of Robert Thomson."

24. Ibid., 353.

25. Ibid., 348.

26. Ibid.

27. Fearful that Spain's Supreme Inquisition would sentence him to burn at the stake, Boacio jumped ship off the Spanish coast. Tomson served his time and afterward worked for another English merchant in Spain until he married a wealthy widow.

28. The following reconstruction relies heavily on José Toribio Medina's account, which, in turn, draws extensively and nearly verbatim on Dr. Moya's letters to Philip II. Philip II issued his initial proclamation on January 25, 1569. On August 16, 1570, he instructed his viceroy, Martín Enríquez, on the tribunal's juridical function, jurisdiction, and composition. *História del tribunal del Santo Oficio de la Inquisición en México* (Santiago, Chile: Imprenta Elzeviriana, 1905; reprint, Mexico: Miguel Angel Porrua, 1987), 25. For the institutional background, see Alberro, *Inquisición y Sociedad en Mexico*; Richard E. Greenleaf, *The Mexican Inquisition of the Sixteenth Century* (Albuquerque: University of New Mexico Press, 1969) and *Zumárraga and the Mexican Inquisition*; Ricard, *The Spiritual Conquest of Mexico*; Yolanda Mariel de Ibáñez, *El tribunal de la Inquisición en México (Siglo XVI)*, 3rd ed. (México: Editorial Porrua, 1984), 115–186; and John Frederick Schwaller, *The Church and Clergy in Sixteenth-Century Mexico* (Albuquerque: University of New Mexico Press, 1987).

29. The retinue included the tribunal's *alguacil*, Francisco Verdugo de Bazán; the newly appointed notary Pedro de los Ríos; the Inquisition's treasurer Pedro de Arriarán; and Gaspar Salvago, Silvestre Espindola, and Juan de Savedra. Medina, *História del tribunal del Santo Oficio de la Inquisición en México*, 25.

30. Ibid.

31. Whether the 60,000 indigenous peoples who resided outside of the *traza* were required to attend remains unclear. Richard E. Greenleaf notes how "the perplexing problem of enforcing orthodoxy among the recently converted Indians was linked with the debate over whether or not the Indian was a rational human being who had the capacity to comprehend the Roman Catholic faith and enjoy the full sacramental system of the Church. As in the case of the rationality controversy, the position of the Indian vis-à-vis the Holy Office of the Inquisition was not resolved articulately, and after the first decades of the spiritual conquest the question took on added importance as the Mexican clergy discovered recurrent idolatry and religious syncretism among their flocks." "The Inquisition and the Indians of New Spain: A Study in Jurisdictional Confusion," *The Americas* 22 (October 1965): 138; Medina, *História del tribunal del Santo Oficio de la Inquisición en México*, 25.

32. Medina, *História del tribunal del Santo Oficio de la Inquisición en México*, 26.

33. On several occasions, Castile's sovereign issued orders that the descendants of relaxed and reconciled persons could not migrate to the Indies. ("Relaxed and reconciled" was a judicial formulation that meant that the person was no longer subject to the inquest and had been brought back into the Christian community.) Those who violated this order understood the significance of the tribunal's

arrival in New Spain. Relatives of the Inquisition's victims in Castile bore the burden of kinship in a manner akin to race; it was passed from one to another. From the official perspective, genealogy and race represented the same phenomenon; the crime of a relative marked a family indefinitely. *CFS*, 1:192–193.

34. Irving A. Leonard, *Baroque Times in Old Mexico: Seventeenth-Century Persons, Places, and Practices* (Ann Arbor: University of Michigan Press, 1959), 7–10. Useful comparative examples include Bernard S. Cohen, "Representing Authority in Victorian India," in *The Invention of Tradition*, ed. Eric Hobsbawm and Terrence Ranger (Cambridge: Cambridge University Press, 1983), 189–209; Michel Foucault, *Discipline and Punish: The Birth of the Prison*, trans. Alan Sheridan (New York: Vintage Books, 1979), 32–69; Douglas Hay, "Property, Authority and the Criminal Law," in *Albion's Fatal Tree: Crime and Society in Eighteenth-Century England*, ed. Douglas Hay, Peter Linebaugh, John G. Rule, E. P. Thompson, and Cal Winslow (New York: Pantheon Books, 1975), 17–63; Arthur S. Keller, Oliver J. Lissitzyn, and Frederick J. Mann, *Creation of Rights of Sovereignty through Symbolic Acts, 1400–1800* (New York: Columbia University Press, 1938), 23–48.

35. Medina, *História del tribunal del Santo Oficio de la Inquisición en México*, 26.

36. Although largely concerned with questions of the Catholic faith, the tribunal's relationship to Spain's monarch gave it a decidedly secular quality. As the inquisitor general, Dr. Moya occupied equal footing with New Spain's most illustrious corporate representatives: the viceroy, the *audiencia*'s president, and Mexico's archbishop. But he reigned supreme in all matters of the faith. Greenleaf, *The Mexican Inquisition of the Sixteenth Century*, 158–190; Haring, *The Spanish Empire in America*, 166–193; Medina, *História del tribunal del Santo Oficio de la Inquisición en México*, 26.

37. Medina, *História del tribunal del Santo Oficio de la Inquisición en México*, 26.

38. Ibid., 27.

39. Greenleaf notes that Dr. Moya sent letters to officials throughout New Spain, who he ordered to take a similar oath. Interestingly enough, only secular officials were required to swear this oath despite the jurisdictional conflicts that characterized corporate bodies within the Church (i.e., Franciscans, Jesuits, or secular clergy). Greenleaf, *The Mexican Inquisition of the Sixteenth Century*, 160; Medina, *História del tribunal del Santo Oficio de la Inquisición en México*, 27.

40. Medina, *História del tribunal del Santo Oficio de la Inquisición en México*, 29.

41. As we shall see, soon after Dr. Moya issued this admonishment, confessors throughout New Spain adhered to his strict guidelines. See, for example, AGN, Inquisición 103, expediente 6, "Declaración de Luisa de Abrego," 28 February 1575, Mexico City; and Medina, *História del tribunal del Santo Oficio de la Inquisición en México*, 29.

42. The Inquisition clearly sought to insinuate itself between confessors and penitents and within the social network of penitents. This practice has a lengthy history that dates back to earliest phases of Christianity. Ibáñez, *El tribunal de la Inquisición en México (Siglo XVI)*, 42.

43. By the end of 1572, the inquisitors had concluded thirty-nine cases and ordered the arrest of sixteen additional heretics and bigamists. This letter is dated Febru-

ary 8, 1572. Medina, *História del tribunal del Santo Oficio de la Inquisición en México*, 31.

44.   For an account of these events, see "Hawkins—Third Voyage: The Third Troublesome Voyage made with the Jesus of Lubeck, the Minion, and four other Ships, to the parts of Guinea and the West Indies, in the years 1567 and 1568," in *Voyages of the Elizabethan Seamen: Select Narratives from the "Principal Navigations" of Hakluyt*, ed. Edward John Payne, notes by C. Raymond Beazley (London: Oxford University Press, 1907), 69–81; "A Discourse written by one Miles Philips Englishman," 10:398–445 and "The travailes of Job Hortop, which Sir John Hawkins set on land within the Bay of Mexico, after his departure from the Haven of S. John de Ullua in Nueva Espana, the 8 of October 1568," 10:445–465, both in Hakluyt, ed., *The Principal Navigations, Voyages, Traffiques and Discoveries of the English Nation*; and Frank Aydelotte, "Elizabethan Seamen in Mexico and Ports of the Spanish Main," *The American Historical Review* 48 (October 1942): 1–19.

45.   Greenleaf, *The Mexican Inquisition of the Sixteenth Century*, 162–168.

46.   This reconstructed narrative relies largely on Miles Philips's account and Licenciado Bonilla and Dr. Moya's jointly authored letter addressed to their superiors in Spain, which Medina cited nearly verbatim. "A Discourse written by one Miles Philips Englishman," 426–429 and *História del tribunal del Santo Oficio de la Inquisición en México*, 35–48. See also Greenleaf, *The Mexican Inquisition*, 162–172.

47.   "A Discourse written by one Miles Philips Englishman," 427.

48.   Medina, *História del tribunal del Santo Oficio de la Inquisición en México*, 44–45.

49.   "A Discourse written by one Miles Philips Englishman," 428.

50.   Ibid., 428. There is some discrepancy about how many persons were subject to the auto-de-fé and how many people were burned at the stake that day.

51.   "A Discourse written by one Miles Philips Englishman," 428–429.

52.   The auto-de-fé juxtaposed the English as "enemies of God" against the heterogeneous mass of Catholics. On March 15, 1574, Dr. Moya described the proceeding of the first auto-de-fé in a letter to Philip II in which he invoked this juxtaposition, simultaneously acknowledging the plurality of the public, for whom, after all, this event was staged. According to Dr. Moya, "neither the indio, negro, mulato nor mestizo could understand or comprehend [*acordase*] that there were Christians who lived in accordance to a different law than we have taught them." Medina, *História del tribunal del Santo Oficio de la Inquisición en México*, 46. The 1574 auto-de-fé was, among other things, a performance in the plurality of whiteness—the victorious and powerful Spanish Catholics versus the defeated and effete English Lutherans.

53.   The Protestant presence enabled the elites and plebeians, the inquisitors and the public to see themselves united as Catholics and residents of New Spain. Town criers called on people to "behold these English dogs, Lutherans, enemies of God," while the inquisitors exhorted the executioners to "strike lay, on those English heretiks"; the auto-de-fé served to purge the incipient nation. The spectacle momentarily simplified the drama of belonging. The symbolic importance of ritual exorcism resides in the cohesiveness it provided for the Hispanic and

Hispanicized population—a cohesiveness that existed alongside stark and growing social disparities. "A discourse written by one Miles Philips Englishman," 428–429.

54. In response to the royal ban against arming slaves, Viceroy Enríquez petitioned the king to allow officials and the elite to staff their liveries with armed slaves. Despite his anxieties, the king granted the request but stipulated that armed blacks could traverse the viceregal capital only in the company of their masters. *CFS*, 1:427, 433.

55. Ibid., 513.

56. Ibid., 533.

57. Alberro, *Inquisición y Sociedad en México*, 75.

58. It is not clear why this case came to the attention of the Inquisition. Juan implied that his incarceration was the result of Juana's complaint "about me not having a life with her." Evidently the 1564 proceedings stemmed from Juan's efforts to separate from Juana. The Inquisition initiated the 1574 proceedings because Juana was an alleged bigamist. AGN, Inquisición (without reference) 1574, "Juan de Llanes," 26 April 1564, Mexico City.

59. Juan stated that they had "beseeched me not to complain about her." In light of past behavior, this may have amounted to physical threats by his wife's consorts.

60. AGN, Inquisición (without reference) 1574, "Juan de Llanes," 28 April 1564, Mexico City.

61. Ibid.

62. Pedro later observed that "while in my house [Juana] hated and despised Juan[,] often quarreling with him because he scolded her." AGN, Inquisición (without reference) 1574, "Pedro de Villalón," 29 April 1564, Mexico City.

63. AGN, Inquisición (without reference) 1574, "Pedro de Villalón," 29 April 1564, Mexico City.

64. Ibid.

65. AGN, Inquisición (without reference) 1574, "Francisca González," 29 April 1564, Mexico City.

66. Juana allegedly took the young man, from whom she wished to be separated, to a friend's house, where two men were waiting to assail the unsuspecting victim. As the assassination attempt unraveled, Juana was stabbed. Ibid.

67. Although this is a possible interpretation, it is not a probable scenario, since Juana failed to respond to the allegations of Juan and the witnesses. Juana's absence from the proceedings and her reluctance to respond to the accusations tacitly support Juan's claims. Two months after being informed of the charges, the inquisitors were still waiting for Juana's reply and defense. AGN, Inquisición (without reference) 1574, "Instancia de Juan de Llanes para que se vea la causa de su divorcio dado su mujer no ha respondido en la primera audiencia como tenia que haberlo hecho," 30 May 1564, Mexico City; AGN, Inquisición (without reference) 1574, "Instancia de Juan de LLanes para que se de por hecha la publicacion de testigos dado que su mujer aunque ha sido notificada no ha contestado y ya ha pasado el termino," 3 July 1564, Mexico City.

68. Despite Juana's silence, the allegations and testimony raise important issues about domestic relations and gender conventions. In light of their obvious age difference, what brought Juan, an older Spaniard, and Juana, a younger mulatto, together? Though there is no mention of her legal status, Juan may have purchased and freed and then married Juana as a security measure for old age. This would explain why Juana told Francisca González "I did not want to have a life with him." Yet the marriage may have been mutually convenient for both parties. In any event, Juan relied physically on Juana, a condition that may explain his tolerance for her sexual indiscretions. For instance, the divorce proceedings emphasized the physical threat that Juana posed to Juan over the reputed adulterous incidents. Juan repeatedly claimed that his "life will not be safe being with her." For her part, Juana did not abide by established gendered norms in her relationship with Juan. Yet she was not oblivious to social conventions. In her relationship with Morillas, Juana apparently conformed to New Spain's gender conventions, since she washed her lover's clothes and "had respect for all that he ordered and said." She also valued the ritual of marriage, since she contracted a second and bigamous marriage with Gaspar Pereira instead of maintaining a consensual union. AGN, Inquisición (without reference) 1574, "Francisca González," 29 April 1564, Mexico City; AGN, Inquisición (without reference) 1574, "Pedro de Villalón," 29 April 1564, Mexico City.

69. AGN, Bienes Nacionales 497, expediente 10, 1570, Mexico City.

70. Ibid.

71. *CFS*, 1:206–207, 210, 213, 290–291, 297, 321, 422, 504, 513–514, 527–528, 533–534, 566, 586.

72. AGN, Bienes Nacionales (without reference) 1570, "Proceso de Hernan Gutierrez de Bustamante, Fiscal de este Arzobispado de Mexico contra Francisco de Acevedo, español, y Juana, mulata, por Amancebados," Mexico City. See, for example, AGN, Bienes Nacionales 497, expediente 319, 1570, for a case in which one person denied the allegations while the other party confessed to the deed.

73. AGN, Bienes Nacionales 1087, expediente 12, 1574, Mexico City.

74. Juana's use of the term "knowing" remains unclear. It could refer to carnal knowledge or just personal familiarity. Juan, however, testified to having known Juana "by sight" for three months but carnally for only one night. AGN, Bienes Nacionales 497, expediente 29, 1571, Mexico City.

75. Poole, *Pedro Moya de Contreras*, 39, 127–162.

76. AGN, Bienes Nacionales 497, expediente 30, 1572, Mexico City.

77. Ibid.

78. Unfortunately, the case does not included Marcos Pérez's sentence. Ibid.

79. Alberro, *Inquisición y Sociedad en México*, 50.

80. See, for example, AGN, Inquisición 103, expediente 3, "Denuncia de Juan de Pinillos," 26 March 1574, Mexico City; AGN, Inquisición 134, expediente 3, "Denuncia de Diego López," 20 April 1574, Mexico City; AGN, Inquisición 101, expediente 8, "Denuncia de Francisco Granados," 19 July 1575, Mexico City; AGN, Inquisición 134, expediente 8, "Denuncia de Cristóbal de Pastrana," 15 March 1580, Mexico

City; AGN, Inquisición 134, expediente 8, "Ana, negra," 19 April 1580, Mexico City; AGN, Inquisición 185, expediente 3, "Denuncia de Leonor de Sarmiento," 2 September 1593, Puebla; and AGN, Inquisición 185, expediente 3, "Denuncia de Lázaro de Estrada," 21 November 1592, Mexico City. Richard Boyer, one of the most astute readers of inquisition cases, provides a brilliant discussion of this phenomenon in *Lives of the Bigamists.*

81. AGN, Inquisición 116, expediente 6, "Denuncia de Juan Bautista Gallegos," 26 February 1574, Mexico City.

82. Ana evidently made her comments in the presence of mixed company. Doña Luisa did not know the identity of either the man or the woman in Ana's store but noted that the woman was a *mulata.* AGN, Inquisición 116, expediente 6, "Doña Luisa de Villalobos," 10 March 1574, Mexico City; AGN, Inquisición 116, expediente 6, "Denuncia de Juan Bautista Gallegos," 26 February 1574, Mexico City.

83. Blinded by their zeal, the inquisitors initially underestimated the enormity of their task and therefore heard all and listened to everyone. The tribunal's unrealistic understanding of the size and scope of the Hispanic and Hispanicized population encouraged the patriarchal yet personal manner in which they held *audiencias.* Soon after the installation ceremony, accusers and the accused appeared before the ubiquitous and powerful Dr. Moya, Licenciado Bonilla, and Don de los Ríos, among others. When the inquisitors listened, interrogated, and deliberated, they assumed the guise of patriarchy as they judged, admonished, and punished their errant "children." As such, trial proceedings involved a stern "father" who cajoled, scolded, and administered corporal punishment to his "offspring," in the process alerting the "siblings" of the victims that they faced a similar fate if they misbehaved.

84. Such revelations eventually ensured that friends, familiars, and neighbors knew that they needed to tread carefully in Juan's presence. Thus, a sudden silence would envelop Ana's friends and associates when their neighbors, Juan and Doña Luisa, passed by.

85. As Ana crafted her petition and, subsequently, her confession, the recent auto-de-fé surely must have weighed on her mind. Even if she did not witness the spectacle, Ana undoubtedly overheard Mexico's inhabitants, including her friends and neighbors, describing the awe-inspiring events. Doña Luisa noted that Ana made the blasphemous remarks in the confines of her house, which doubled as a store in which friends and acquaintances surrounded her. Conceivably, the small gathering in Ana's store might have discussed, among other things, an acquaintance the inquisitors had convicted for bigamy. Ana probably voiced an opinion that was shared by members of her small audience. For Ana, the circumstances surrounding the "certain marriage" convinced her that cohabitation without marriage constituted a viable option.

86. AGN, Inquisición 116, expediente 6, "Instancia de Ana Caballero," 11 March 1574, Mexico City.

87. In this sense, the confession mirrored an unrehearsed command performance in which the Inquisition imposed the dialogue that Ana spontaneously performed.

88. Evidently Ana arrived alone, for neither her parents nor a spouse were listed as inhabitants of New Spain. She also did not have the usual labels associated with a freedperson.

89. AGN, Inquisición 116, expediente 6, "Confesion de Ana Caballero," 11 March 1574, Mexico City.

90. Ibid., AGN, Inquisición 116, expediente 6, "Auto del Provisor," 13 March 1574, Mexico City; AGN, Inquisición 116, expediente 6, "Poder de Ana Caballero a Juan Mendez para que actua en su nombre en esta causa y pleito," 15 March 1574, Mexico City.

91. For this insight, I am indebted to Carol F. Karlsen's *The Devil in the Shape of a Woman: Witchcraft in Colonial New England* (New York: Vintage Books, 1987).

92. AGN, Inquisición 116, expediente 6, "Repuesta de Ana Caballero a la acusación del fiscal," 14 May 1574, Mexico City.

93. AGN, Inquisición 116, expediente 6, "Audiencia con el Abogado," 22 May 1574, Mexico City.

94. AGN, Inquisición 103, expediente 6, "Votos de los Inquisidores," 17 February 1576, Mexico City; AGN, Inquisición 103, expediente 6, "Declaración de Luisa de Abrego," 28 February 1575, Mexico City.

95. AGN, Inquisición 103, expediente 6, "Declaración de Luisa de Abrego," 28 February 1575, Mexico City.

96. Nearly an entire year separated Luisa's initial confession and her self-indictment before the Inquisition. "Declaración de Luisa de Abrego," 28 February 1575, Mexico City; "Juan de Pinillos," 26 March 1574, Mexico City; "Juan de Vega," 27 March 1574, Mexico City; "Blas de Avila," 27 March 1574, Mexico City. All in AGN, Inquisición 103, expediente 6.

97. Two of the six judges voted to absolve Luisa, three called for an auto-de-fé, and one called for her to "hear mass in the chapel of the Holy Office" wearing the penitent garb of a bigamist. Lacking a consensus, the judges absolved Luisa. AGN, Inquisición 103, expediente 6, "Votos de los Inquisidores," 17 February 1576, Mexico City.

98. AGN, Inquisición 103, expediente 6, "Declaración de Luisa de Abrego," 28 February 1575, Mexico City. Although the *audiencia* with the Inquisition is dated 28 February 1575, it actually lasted two days.

99. The details about Jordan's unsuccessful encounter with Juan Luís were revealed on February 29, 1575. In her deposition before the Inquisition, Luisa stated "he did not take me since later [after the conversation with Juan Luís] he left the house on the account of anger and I never saw Jordan again." AGN, Inquisición 103, expediente 6, "Declaración de Luisa de Abrego," 28 February 1575, Mexico City.

100. Ibid.

101. Ibid.; AGN, Inquisición 103, expediente 6, "Miguel Rodriguez," 27 March 1574, Mexico City.

102. Evidently, the marriage between Luisa and Miguel took place in 1566. "Juan de Vega," 27 March 1574, Mexico City; "Blas de Avila," 27 March 1574, Mexico City;

"Miguel Rodriguez," 27 March 1574, Mexico City. All in AGN, Inquisición 103, expediente 6.

103. Luisa recalled telling Miguel about her doubts because he "revealed the case to various persons." It is conceivable that these persons included Juan de Vega and Blas de Avila. Juan de Pinillos testified before the Inquisition that Juan and Blas had informed him of the bigamous affair. In the Indies, Blas testified, he had only spent time in Mexico City and Florida. Yet this did not preclude his Segovian compatriots from maintaining contact over a great distance. "Juan de Pinillos," 26 March 1574, Mexico City; "Juan de Vega," 27 March 1574, Mexico City; "Declaración de Luisa de Abrego," 28 February 1575, Mexico City. All in AGN, Inquisición 103, expediente 6.

104. AGN, Inquisición 103, expediente 6, "Miguel Rodriguez," 27 March 1574, Mexico City.

105. Under interrogation Luisa claimed that her confessor, not "the Church," bore responsibility for her year-long separation from Miguel. According to Luisa, Miguel "went to complain to the *provisor*" about their separation. The ecclesiastical official ordered a reunification, since "the Church gave her as wife." Luisa testified that after they were reunited Miguel "slept with me one night." Afterward, Luisa returned to her confessor "to give account" of their "*carnal acesso.*" Miguel also alluded to the competing advice he received from the *provisor,* who "told me do not listen to the said Curiel." Curiel and the *provisor* were in all likelihood voicing the conflict manifest between the secular and regular clergy. "Declaración de Luisa de Abrego," 28 February 1575, Mexico City; "Miguel Rodriguez," 27 March 1574, Mexico City. Both in AGN, Inquisición 103, expediente 6.

106. AGN, Inquisición 103, expediente 6, "Juan de Pinillos," 26 March 1574, Mexico City.

107. AGN, Inquisición 103, expediente 6, "Juan de Vega," 27 March 1574, Mexico City.

108. AGN, Inquisición 103, expediente 6, "Blas de Avila," 27 March 1574, Mexico City.

109. Ibid.

110. Luisa frequented the Inquisition's premises in order to visit Miguel, who had been incarcerated for outstanding debts. "Juan de Pinillos," 26 March 1574, Mexico City; "Juan de Vega," 27 March 1574, Mexico City; "Blas de Avila," 27 March 1574, Mexico City; "Miguel Rodriguez," 10 December 1575, Mexico City. All in AGN, Inquisición 103, expediente 6.

111. Ruth Behar, "Sex and Sin, Witchcraft and the Devil in Late-Colonial Mexico," *American Ethnologist* 14 (1987): 33–54; Serge Gruzinski, "Individualization and Acculturation: Confession among the Nahuas of Mexico from the Sixteenth to the Eighteenth Century," in *Sexuality and Marriage in Colonial Latin America,* ed. Lavrín, 96–115.

112. AGN, Inquisición 103, expediente 6, "Declaración de Luisa de Abrego," 28 February 1575, Mexico City.

113. This interrogation took place on February 28, 1575, immediately after Luisa confessed before the Inquisition. She was asked "Do you know the reason why you have been called?" a standard procedure that enabled the accused or witnesses to reveal matters that went against the faith. A significant part of the confession

and testimony involved biographical details of oneself or others, including ages, race, occupation, mobility, and patterns of interaction with friends, neighbors, and kin. In contrast, the cross-examinations were narrowly focused on the chronology and evidence of sinful behavior. AGN, Inquisición 103, expediente 6, "Declaración de Luisa de Abrego," 28 February 1575, Mexico City.

114. Ibid.

115. Ibid.

116. By the end of the sixteenth century and during the first part of the seventeenth century, the tribunal's zealousness faded. As result, the critical task of record-keeping, whereby the tribunal kept track of suspicious persons over the course of years, suffered enormously. The absence of institutional memory meant that the tribunal cases began to lack the accustomed depth of information with which they prosecuted individuals. Alberro, *Inquisición y Sociedad en México*, 34–39.

4. Christian Matrimony and the Boundaries of African Self-Fashioning

1. Thomas Mann, *The Magic Mountain*, trans. John E. Woods (1924; reprint, New York: Vintage International, 1996), 242.

2. AGN, Matrimonios 65, expediente 53, folios 193–194, 1584.

3. Daisy Rípodas Ardanaz, *El Matrimonio en Indias: realidad social y regulación jurídica* (Buenos Aires: Fundación para la Educción, la Ciencia y la Cultura, 1977), 84–96.

4. Ibid., 215–222.

5. Ibid., 223–257.

6. For a discussion of Pedro Moya de Contreras, see Stafford Poole's impressive intellectual biography, *Pedro Moya de Contreras*, 148–203.

7. AGN, Matrimonios 63, expediente 24, folios 92–93, 1628. Francisco may have been one of the "Angolan" paterfamilias of Mexico City, given that he was 50 years old in 1628. It is critical to remember that the notion of age reflected in the marriage petitions is strictly a Christian formulation. From Luis and Francisco's testimony, we glean that Manuel arrived in New Spain in the period between 1598–1601. Catalina may have arrived from Guinea in 1608.

8. AGN, Matrimonios 64, expediente 65, folios 206–207, 1628.

9. AGN, Matrimonios 10, expediente 9, folio 17, 1629.

10. AGN, Matrimonios 64, expediente 86, folios 270–271, 1628.

11. AGN, Matrimonios 10, expediente 164, folio 375, 1629.

12. AGN, Matrimonios 19, expediente 20–26, folios 60–74, 1645.

13. AGN, Matrimonios 19, expediente 29–30, folios 79–82, 1645.

14. AGN, Matrimonios 29, expediente 89, folios 214–215, 1631.

15. AGN, Matrimonios 12, expediente 21, folios 84–88, 1635.

16. AGN, Matrimonios 126, expediente 27, folio 81, 1640. Don Antonío de Almaras

evidently objected to the prospective marriage during the period after the banns had been published on the ground that María was already married. María in reply testified that seven years previously she and the negro Bartolo had requested and received a license to marry in the pueblo of San [Juan?] Toliucan, but that his master had obstructed the process and Bartolo had died one year later. The authorities permitted the marriage after contacting María's previous owner, who stated that he had so many slaves in so many different places that he couldn't remember María or Bartolo and that he could not recall having placed any impediment in the way of the marriage of his slaves.

17. AGN, Matrimonios 19, expediente 87, folios 227–228, 1644.

18. AGN, Matrimonios 19, expediente 20–26, folios 60–74, 1645.

19. AGN, Matrimonios 75, expediente 73, folios 280–281, 1620.

20. AGN, Matrimonios 19, expediente 73–74, folios 185–188, 1644. The scribes' respective use of "Don" and "Doña" implies that Alonso Gonzalez de Villalba and Magdalena de Orduna were seen as Spaniards of honorable, if not noble, status.

21. AGN, Matrimonios 27, expediente 47, folios 160–161, 1631.

22. AGN, Matrimonios 19, expediente 20–26, folios 60–74, 1645.

23. Ibid.

24. AGN, Matrimonios 5, expediente 101, folios 278, 1633.

25. AGN, Matrimonios 126, expediente 33, folios 105, 1640.

26. AGN, Matrimonios 28, expediente 131, folios 352–353, 1628.

27. AGN, Matrimonios 10, expediente 11, folio 21, 1629.

28. AGN, Matrimonios 10, expediente 176, folio 399, 1629.

29. AGN, Matrimonios 65, expediente 46, folios 157–158, 1584.

30. AGN, Matrimonios 61, expediente 102, folios 374–374v, 1605.

31. See Richard Price, *First-Time: The Historical Vision of an Afro-American People* (Baltimore: Johns Hopkins University Press, 1983) and *Alabi's World* (Baltimore: Johns Hopkins University Press, 1990); and AGN, Tierras 3543.

32. AGN, Matrimonios 26, expediente 5–6, folios 293–296, 1633.

33. AGN, Matrimonios 28, expediente 161, folios 423–424, 1628. Mateo and Cristina's conjugal decision involved more than a matter of convenience. Since they belonged to different masters and resided in separate households, ethnicity played some role in the process of selecting a spouse.

34. AGN, Matrimonios 10, expediente 42, folio 98, 1629.

35. AGN, Matrimonios 10, expediente 69, folio 166, 1629.

36. AGN, Matrimonios 5, expediente 38, folio 132, 1633.

37. AGN, Matrimonios 27, expediente 48, folios 160–161, 1631; AGN, Matrimonios 27, expediente 57–59, folios 180–185.

38. AGN, Matrimonios 19, expediente 87, folios 227–228, 1644. For similar patterns, see AGN, Matrimonios 10, expediente 183, folio 414, 1629; AGN, Matrimonios 27, expediente 48, folios 160–161, 1631; AGN, Matrimonios 29, expediente 89, folios 214–215, 1631.

39. AGN, Matrimonios 10, expediente 183, folio 414, 1629.

40. AGN, Matrimonios 81, expediente 14, folios 52–53, 1621.

41. AGN, Matrimonios 81, expediente 38, folios 108–109, 1622.

42. AGN, Matrimonios 85, expediente 37, folios 68–69, 1621.

43. AGN, Matrimonios 81, expediente 44, folios 124–125, 1622. Catalina and Manuel, along with Manuel's deceased wife Catalina and Luis and Pedro, clearly interacted as Terra Novas prior to Catalina and Manuel's courtship. Indeed, the rapidity with which Manuel embraced Catalina highlights the intimacy and emotional depth this Terra Nova node had acquired.

44. AGN, Matrimonios 28, expediente 111, folios 297–298, 1628.

45. AGN, Matrimonios 10, expediente 80, folio 117, 1629.

46. AGN, Matrimonios 65, expediente 46, folios 157–158, 1584.

47. AGN, Matrimonios 61, expediente 71, folios 279–282, 1595.

48. AGN, Matrimonios 61, expediente 102, folios 374–375, 1605.

49. AGN, Matrimonios 63, expediente 68, folios 17–18, 1628.

50. AGN, Matrimonios 10, expediente 5, folio 9, 1629.

51. AGN, Matrimonios 10, expediente 102, folio 237, 1629.

52. AGN, Matrimonios 88, expediente 319, 1629. For an identical pattern, see AGN, Matrimonios, 5, expediente 65, folio 197, 1633.

53. AGN, Matrimonios 88, expediente 311(?), folio 311(?), 1629.

54. AGN, Matrimonios 113, expediente 53, folio 130, 1629.

55. AGN, Matrimonios 113, expediente 140, folio 355, 1629.

56. AGN, Matrimonios 10, expediente 153, folio 355, 1629.

57. AGN, Matrimonios 113, expediente 101, folio 258, 1629.

58. AGN, Matrimonios 29, expediente 95, folios 233–234, 1631.

59. AGN, Matrimonios 27, expediente 57–59, folios 180–181, 1631.

60. AGN, Matrimonios 19, expediente 3, folios 87–88, 1645.

61. AGN, Matrimonios 19, expediente 35–36, folios 93–96, 1645.

62. AGN, Matrimonios 19, expediente 29–30, folios 79–82, 1645.

63. AGN, Matrimonios 27, expediente 50, folios 165–166, 1631.

64. AGN, Matrimonios 27, expediente 48, folios 160–161, 1631.

65. AGN, Matrimonios 29, expediente 82, folios 200–201, 1631.

66. AGN, Matrimonios 26, expediente 5–6, folios 293–296, 1633.

67. AGN, Matrimonios 5, expediente 43, folio 151, 1633.

68. AGN, Matrimonios 5, expediente 89, folio 280, 1633.

69. AGN, Matrimonios 5, expediente 82, folio 235, 1633.

70. AGN, Matrimonios 47, expediente 3, folios 6–7, 1633.

71. AGN, Matrimonios 76, expediente 124, folios 438–439, 1637.

72. AGN, Matrimonios 126, expediente 17, folio 52, 1640.

73. AGN, Matrimonios 19, expediente 83–84, folios 216–219, 1644.

74. AGN, Matrimonios 19, expediente 35–36, folios 93–96, 1645.

75. AGN, Matrimonios 63, expediente 9, folios 41–42, 1628.

76. AGN, Inquisición 381, expediente 8, 1634–1635.

77. AGN, Matrimonios 63, expediente 64, folios 204–205, 1628. Based on the alleged age of these marriage witnesses in 1628, Pedro Ramírez, Ana María, and Isabel de la Cruz represented one of Mexico City's charter families whose creole identity tempered the differences in legal status and enabled them to created extended family ties across generations.

78. AGN, Matrimonios 10, expediente 26, folio 51, 1629.

79. AGN, Matrimonios 10, expediente 44, folio 102, 1629.

80. AGN, Matrimonios 10, expediente 194, folio 443, 1629.

81. AGN, Matrimonios 5, expediente 61, folio 188, 1633.

82. AGN, Matrimonios 5, expediente 126, folio 338, 1633.

83. AGN, Matrimonios 12, expediente 71, folios 225–226, 1635.

84. AGN, Matrimonios 126, expediente 6, folio 27, 1640.

85. AGN, Matrimonios 126, expediente 20, folio 63, 1640.

86. AGN, Matrimonios 126, expediente 32, folio 103, 1646.

87. AGN, Matrimonios 64, expediente 88, folios 276–277, 1628.

88. AGN, Matrimonios 64, expediente 122, folios 371–372, 1629.

89. AGN, Matrimonios 88, exp.(?), folio 353, 1629.

90. AGN, Matrimonios 113, expediente 115, folio 293, 1629.

91. AGN, Matrimonios 65, expediente 52, folios 185–186v, 1584.

92. AGN, Matrimonios 65, expediente 52, folios 185–186v, "Informacion de María," 1584.

93. AGN, Matrimonios 65, expediente 52, folios 185–186v, "Información de Francisca," 1584.

94. From the perspective of the Christian Church, the relevant past began the moment that the couple became "Duarte" and "Polonia." Existing impediments emerged from a person's existence as a Christian. Though *bozales* had lives that preceded their Christian selves and that constituted a part of their cultural memory, the Church focused on developments following their incarnation as Christians. Rípodas Ardanaz, *El Matrimonio en Indias,* 250–252. Much more work needs to done in this direction using examples such as that of Duarte and Polonia, who brought existing identities and ties forged in Guinea to the Indies. In fact, when they reached the Indies, the clergy already defined them as having reached the age of consent.

95. AGN, Matrimonios 65, expediente 54, folios 204–205v, 1584.

96. Ibid., "Información de Juan," 1584.

97. Ibid., "Informacion de Andrés," 1584.

98. Ibid., "Información de Juan," 1584.

99. María's sister's name was omitted in the *información*. Such omissions represented a truly rare occurrence. Even if they had separate fathers, it is interesting that María was labeled or characterized herself as a *mulata* while the sister is registered as an *india ladina*. If the mother was an *india* and María's father's identity was that of a person of African descent (negro or mulatto), the offspring, according to the standard typology, would not be a *mulata*. This case, in explicitly bringing genealogy and race together, underscores how arbitrary the categories were. AGN, Matrimonios 65, expediente 54, folios 204–205v, 1584.

100. AGN, Matrimonios 61, expediente 14, folios 68–70, 1591.

101. AGN, Matrimonios 29, expediente 66, folios 162–163, 1631.

102. AGN, Matrimonios 61, expediente 71, folios 279–282, 1595.

103. Richard Price, ed., "Introduction," in *Maroon Societies: Rebel Slave Communities in the Americas* (Baltimore: Johns Hopkins University Press, 1979), 27–28.

104. AGN, Matrimonios 61, expediente 28, folio 142, 1610.

105. AGN, Matrimonios 28, expediente 122, folios 331–332, 1628.

106. AGN, Matrimonios 10, expediente 106, folio 245, 1629.

107. AGN, Matrimonios 98, expediente 108, folio 287, 1612.

108. AGN, Matrimonios 88, expediente (?), folio 335, 1629.

109. AGN, Matrimonios 47, expediente 19, folios 45–46, 1633.

110. AGN, Matrimonios 75, expediente 85, folios 305–306, 1620.

111. AGN, Matrimonios 63, expediente 51, folios 169–170, 1628.

112. AGN, Matrimonios 10, expediente 3, folio 5, 1629.

113. AGN, Matrimonios 10, expediente 8, folio 15, 1629.

114. AGN, Matrimonios 10, expediente 196, folio 458, 1629.

115. AGN, Matrimonios 10, expediente 133, folio 301, 1629.

5. Between Property and Person

1. Hartman, *Scenes of Subjection*, 11.

2. AGN, Bienes Nacionales, legajo 131, expediente 1, "Antón, negro eslavo sobre que traigan a esta ciudad a su mujer que esta en la Puebla," 1579.

3. AGN, Bienes Nacionales, legajo 131, expediente 1, "Información de Lucas, negro esclavo," 1579.

4. AGN, Bienes Nacionales, legajo 131, expediente 1, "Información de Juan Alonso de Sosa," 1579.

5. Tannenbaum, *Slave and Citizen*, 99. For a dissenting view applicable to New Spain, see Palmer, *Slaves of the White God*, 107.

6. Brundage, *Law, Sex, and Christian Society in Medieval Europe*.

7. As has been evident throughout, social labels had an ambiguous quality. Though the sources often underscore a range of possibilities, these meanings never remained fixed nor were they employed beyond a given regulatory context. Again, "ladino" refers to African-born conversant in Spanish. "Creole" represented a

more ambiguous term that did not include Spaniards until the late sixteenth century, although it referred to "*negros*" (a term that referred to those born in Africa and blacks) from the conquest era. When they used "creole" as a noun and "*negro*" as the adjective, Spanish officials alluded to a black creole, or person of African descent born in the Indies. Social fluidity made it very difficult for clergy and royal officials to identify an alleged culprit. See, for instance, "Causa criminal a Matheo de la Cruz, mulato lobo, por casado dos veces," AGN, Inquisición 58b, expediente 8, folios 502–572, 1660–1667. In some instances, individuals contested the ways in which they had been defined. See AGN, Bienes Nacionales 1054, expediente 39, "Diligencias de Juan Antonío Zumayo sobre que se anote y pase al Libro de Espanoles su fe de bautismo que esta en el que no lo son en la parraquia de la catedral," 1697; and AGN, Bienes Nacionales 702, expediente 5, "Domingo Velazquez, Vecino de esta ciudad sobre que se pase su fe de baptismo a los libros de espanoles," 1699.

8.   For New Spain and Peru a rich historiography exists that examines how indigenous peoples quickly learned to utilize the Castilian judicial process in their defense. The abundance of this literature stands in stark contrast to the absence of a similarly rich historiographical tradition for persons of African descent. Steve J. Stern, *Peru's Indian Peoples and the Challenge of the Spanish Conquest* (Madison: University of Wisconsin Press, 1982); Borah, *Justice by Insurance*; Nancy M. Farriss, *Maya Society under Colonial Rule: The Collective Enterprise of Survival* (Princeton, N.J.: Princeton University Press, 1984); Karen Spalding, *Huarochiri: An Andean Society under Inca and Spanish Rule* (Stanford, Calif.: Stanford University Press, 1984); Susan Kellogg, *Law and the Transformation of Aztec Culture* (Albuquerque: University of New Mexico Press, 1995). Bowser's analysis represents a notable exception for the colonial period in *The African Slave in Colonial Peru*, 254–267. In *Lives of Bigamists*, Boyer also offers some fascinating examples of persons of African descent and the legal process but seems reluctant to theorize on the relationship between race and the use of the law. Of late, scholars of the mature colonial period have begun to address this lacuna. Hunefeldt, *Paying the Price of Freedom*; Carlos Aguirre, "Working the System: Black Slaves and the Courts in Lima, Peru, 1821–1854," in *Crossing Boundaries*, ed. Hine and McLeod, 202–222; Jane Landers, "'In Consideration of Her Enormous Crime': Rape and Infanticide in Spanish St. Augustine," in *The Devil's Lane: Sex and Race in the Early South*, ed. Catherine Clinton and Michele Gillespie (New York: Oxford University Press, 1997), 205–217; Kimberly S. Hanger, "Coping in a Complex World: Free Black Women in Colonial New Orleans," in *The Devil's Lane*, 218–231; Alberro, "Juan de Morga and Gertrudis de Escobar: Rebellious Slaves," in *Struggle and Survival in Colonial America*, ed. Sweet and Nash, 165–188. For comparative perspectives, see Schwartz, *Sugar Plantations in the Formation of Brazilian Society*, 379–412, especially 385–390; Silvia Hunold Lara, *Campos da Violencia: Escravos e Senhores na Capitania do Rio de Janeiro, 1750–1808* (Rio Janeiro: Editora Paz e Terra, 1988); A. J. R. Russell-Wood, "Acts of Grace: Portuguese Monarchs and their Subjects of African Descent in Eighteenth Century Brazil," *Journal of Latin American Studies* 32 (May 2000): 307–332; and Kristin Mann and Richard Roberts, eds., *Law in Colonial Africa* (Portsmouth, N.H.: Heinemann, 1991).

9.   For classic expressions of the relationship between family and cultural autonomy,

see E. Franklin Frazier, *The Negro Family in the United States* (Chicago: University of Chicago Press, 1939); Melville J. Herskovits, *The Myth of the Negro Past,* intro. Sidney W. Mintz (Boston: Beacon Press, 1990); Herbert G. Gutman, *The Black Family in Slavery and Freedom, 1750–1925* (New York: Vintage Press, 1976). Recent works have modified the initial conclusion about natal alienation and cultural anomie but not necessarily the conceptual assumption about the centrality of the family as an analytical category. See Allan Kulikoff, *Tobacco and Slaves: The Development of Southern Cultures in the Chesapeake, 1680–1800* (Chapel Hill: University of North Carolina Press, 1986); Brenda E. Stevenson, *Life in Black and White: Family and Community in the Slave South* (New York: Oxford University Press, 1996); and Larry E. Hudson, Jr., *To Have and to Hold: Slave Work and Family Life in Antebellum South Carolina* (Athens: University of Georgia Press, 1997).

10. AGN, Bienes Nacionales, legajo 131, expediente 1, "Antón negro esclavo de Alonso de Estrada," 1579.

11. As Patricia Seed makes clear, the 1680s played a pivotal role in the growth of patriarchy and the weakening of the Church vis-à-vis the state. After this period, the Church manifested greater reluctance to side with minors and wards against patricians and parents. *To Love, Honor, and Obey in Colonial Mexico,* 32–46; 75–91, 95–122. The essays in Lavrín, ed., *Sexuality and Marriage in Colonial Latin America* tend to substantiate Seed's observation. For contrasting views, see Gutiérrez, *When Jesus Came,* 248–259; and Hanger, "Coping in a Complex World," 220–222. These works have largely been inspired by Martinez-Alier's classic *Marriage, Class, and Colour in Nineteenth-Century Cuba.*

12. Tannenbaum, *Slave and Citizen;* Seed, *To Love, Honor, and Obey in Colonial Mexico;* Brundage, *Law, Sex, and Christian Society in Medieval Europe;* Jacqueline Murray and Konrad Eisenbichler, eds., *Desire and Discipline: Sex and Sexuality in the Premodern West* (Toronto: University of Toronto Press, 1996); Michel Foucault, *The History of Sexuality,* vol. 1, *An Introduction* (New York: Vintage Press, 1978); Jack Goody, *The Development of the Family and Marriage in Europe* (Cambridge: Cambridge University Press, 1983).

13. Tannenbaum, *Slave and Citizen,* 97–98.

14. Pennington, *The Prince and the Law;* James Muldoon, *The Americas in the Spanish World Order,* 127–142.

15. Muldoon, ed., *Popes, Lawyers, and Infidels* and *Varieties of Religious Conversion in the Middle Ages* (Gainesville: University Press of Florida, 1997); Pennington, *Popes, Canonists, and Texts;* J. E. Merdinger, *Rome and the African Church in the Time of Augustine* (New Haven, Conn.: Yale University Press, 1997).

16. A medievalist has observed that "by siding with consent to the exclusion of all other elements the popes attempted to free marriage from the influence of families and lords and to place it entirely within the partners' free choice guaranteed by ecclesiastical law." Baldwin, *The Language of Sex,* 7. See also Rípodas Ardanaz, *El Matrimonio en Indias,* 223–257; Seed, *To Love, Honor, and Obey in Colonial Mexico,* 32–46; and Lavrín, "Introduction," in *Sexuality and Marriage in Colonial Latin America,* ed. Lavrín.

17.	Baldwin, *The Language of Sex*, 7.

18.	Kagan, *Lawsuits and Litigants in Castile*, 10.

19.	AGN, Bienes Nacionales, legajo 1212, expediente 36, "Autos fechos contra los curas del Sagragio, por no haber querido casar a dos negros de Juan de Yepe," 1572.

20.	Ibid.

21.	"Instancia de Antón, negro esclavo al provisor del arzobispado de Mexico"; "Información de Pedro, negro de tierra bran"; "Información de Manuel de Silva, negro de tierra banguela." All in AGN, Matrimonios 5, expediente 66, folios 199–200v, 1633.

22.	"Instancia ante el provisor del arzobispado"; "Información de Francisco negro esclavo de doña Jerónima de Castro"; "Información de Sebastian negro angola esclavo de Diego de Vera." All in AGN, Matrimonios 7, expediente 81, folios 263–264v, 1634.

23.	See, for instance, AGN, Inquisición 101, expediente 8, 19 July 1574.

24.	AGN, Matrimonios 5, expediente 74, folios 218–219v, "Instancia de Catalina Gutiérrez, mestiza ante el provisor del arzobispado," 1633.

25.	"Información de Jacinto de Alfaro"; "Información de Diego de Esquivel"; "Información de Juan González." All in AGN, Matrimonios 5, expediente 74, folios 218–219v, 1633.

26.	AGN, Matrimonios 76, expediente 8, folios 38–51, "Instancia de Pedro González al provisor del arzobispado, Casamiento de Pedro González, español y María Brito, mulata esclava," 1612.

27.	"Información de Martín Velas Asensio (2 August 1612), Casamiento de Pedro González, español y María Brito, mulata esclava"; "Información de Alonso Navarro," 2 August 1612; "Información de Diego de Cobos," 2 August 1612; "Informacion de Cristóbal," 2 August 1612. All in AGN, Matrimonios 76, expediente 8, folios 38–51.

28.	"Francisco de Silva, Casamiento de Pedro González, español y María Brito, mulata esclava"; "Juan Pérez, Casamiento de Pedro González, español y María Brito, mulata esclava." Both in AGN, Matrimonios 76, expediente 8, folios 38–51.

29.	"Auto del provisor a los curas de la Catedral, Casamiento de Pedro González, español y María Brito, mulata esclava," and "Testimonio del notario." Both in AGN, Matrimonios 76, expediente 8, folios 38–51.

30.	AGN, Matrimonios 76, expediente 8, folios 38–51, "Notificación del cura de la catedral, Casamiento de Pedro González, español y María Brito, mulata esclava."

31.	AGN, Matrimonios 76, expediente 8, folios 38–51, "Instancia del procurador de García de Santillan, Casamiento de Pedro González, español y María Brito, mulata esclava."

32.	So far, I have not been able to locate María de Leonor's inquisition proceedings. The term "Angico" refers to a West Central African group with a presence in seventeenth-century New Spain. In the brief document comprised of two letters, María de Leonor's voice is muted, but her purported actions speak volumes. After being sold by her initial owner, Juan Antonío, María de Leonor eventually became the possession of Francisco Ansaldo. In the course of the civil transaction, María de Leonor played out her desires with another man whom she agreed to marry. As an adulteress, she in all likelihood would have avoided prosecution. But bigamy represented an egregious offense over which the tribunal of the Holy Office of the Inquisition had jurisdiction. AGN, Inquisición 317, expediente 56, "Carta de Juan de Matos, esclavo a la Inquisición de México, Juan Mateo negro, María de Leonor, Angico, pise se mande a su amo Francisco Ansaldo, se la mande," 1612.

33. Ibid.

34. The only explicit assistance that Juan received is a testimonial in his support from Pedro Alvárez. AGN, Inquisición 317, expediente 56, "Carta de Pedro Alváverez de Rosales apoyando la petición de Juan Matos, Juan Mateo negro, María de Leonor, Angico, pise se mande a su amo Francisco Ansaldo, se la mande," 1612.

35. Kagan, *Lawsuits and Litigants,* 10.

36. AGN, Matrimonios 5, expediente 103, folios 282-287, "Instancia al provisor del arzobispado de Nicolas de la Cruz," 1633.

37. AGN, Matrimonios 5, expediente 103, folios 282-287, "Información de Catalina de la Cruz," 1633.

38. AGN, Matrimonios 5, expediente 103, folios 282-287, "Auto del provisor dispensando las amonestaciones," 1633.

39. AGN, Matrimonios 5, expediente 103, folios 282-287, "Información de María de Barrios," 1633.

40. In the second half of the seventeenth century and beyond, parents of African descent demonstrated opposition to the spouses their children selected more frequently than they did during the first half of that century. See, for instance, AGN, Matrimonios 19, expediente 4, folios 1–9, 1673; and AGN, Matrimonios 2, expediente 10, folios 99–123, 1674.

41. The Colegio de las Niñas was an orphanage and a correctional facility.

42. AGN, Matrimonios 71, expediente 9, folios 54–67, 1612.

43. By taking a woman's virginity, a suitor could often persuade relatives and clergy to permit a marriage. During this time period, the Church sided with free will against parental control. It viewed desire as an expression of God acting through humans.

44. Ibid., "Información de Miguel López."

45. Don Antonío was, of course, right. According to Lavrín, the Church deemed that "a verbal promise was revocable, provided no sexual intercourse had taken place. The centrality of the physical union was paramount." "Introduction," in *Sexuality and Marriage in Colonial Latin America,* ed. Lavrín, 5. But in Francisco's declaration, we learn that Isabel had consummated her relationship and pledge with Rodrigo. AGN, Matrimonios 71, expediente 9, folios 54–67, "Información de Francisca de San Miguel," 1612.

46.   "Información de Francisca de San Miguel" and "Información de Inés Ana María." Both in AGN, Matrimonios 71, expediente 9, folios 54–67, 1612.

47.   AGN, Matrimonios 71, expediente 9, folios 54–67, 1612, "Declaración de Francisca," 10 November 1612.

48.   Fick, *The Making of Haiti*, 37–38; David Barry Gaspar, *Bondmen and Rebels: A Study of Master-Slave Relations in Antigua* (Baltimore: Johns Hopkins University Press, 1985), 43–62.

49.   Robert Olwell, *Masters, Slaves, and Subjects: The Culture of Power in the South Carolina Low Country, 1740–1790* (Ithaca, N.Y.: Cornell University Press, 1998).

50.   For ecclesiastical slave-owners, see Nicholas P. Cushner, *Lords of the Land: Sugar, Wine, and Jesuit Estates of Coastal Peru, 1600–1767* (Albany: State University of New York Press, 1980), 87–101; and Herman W. Konrad, *A Jesuit Hacienda in Colonial Mexico: Santa Lucía, 1567–1767* (Stanford, Calif.: Stanford University Press, 1980), 247–266.

51.   AGN, Bienes Nacionales 131, expediente 3, 1615, "Antonío Martín sobre que Pedro Coquete le venda un negro esclavo casado con una esclava suya por irse fuera y llevarse dicha esclava."

52.   AGN, Bienes Nacionales 131, expediente 3, "Auto del Provisor," 12 August 1615.

53.   AGN, Bienes Nacionales 131, expediente 3, "Poder de Pedro Coquete a Pedro Gómez, procurador de la Audiencia," 8 August 1615.

54.   AGN, Bienes Nacionales 131, expediente 3, 1615, "Instancia de Pedro Coquete en contra de la pretension de Antonío Martín," 21 August 1615.

55.   AGN, Bienes Nacionales 131, expediente 3, 1615, "Instancia de Antonío Martín en contra de la pretension de Pedro Coquete," 29 August 1615.

56.   AGN, Bienes Nacionales 131, expediente 3, 1615, "Instancia de Lorenzo, negro esclavo de Pedro Coquete," 3 September 1615.

57.   "Información de Francisco, negro esclavo de Francisco Duarte" and "Información de Antón García, esclavo de Pedro Coquete." Both in AGN, Bienes Nacionales 131, expediente 3, 1615.

58.   AGN, Bienes Nacionales 131, expediente 3, "Instancia de Antonío Martín," 5 September 1615.

59.   AGN, Inquisición 431, folios 466–473, 1648.

60.   For the most part, the trial proceedings involved testimony from the two contestants followed by the tribunal's order to sequester or release Margarita. The case lacked the customary structure of an ecclesiastical case. The tribunal did not hear testimony from witnesses. The inquisitors also did not examine the requisite documentation proving ownership and legal marriage. Of course, the rules for discerning heresy represented a distinct process from the process for a case touching on civil and canon law. Perhaps the structure of the proceedings underscores how, on behalf of their *alguacil mayor*, the members of the tribunal initially attempted to handle the matter as an internal affair.

61. AGN, Matrimonios (without reference), "Antonía de la Natividad, negra, sobre que el amo su marido le permita a este hacer vida maridable con ella," 1674.

62. AGN, Matrimonios (without reference), "Respues de Gregorio [sic] del Pozo," 1674.

63. AGN, Matrimonios (without reference), "Instancia de Antonía de la Natividad," 1674.

64. AGN, Matrimonios (without reference), "Instancia de Gregorio [sic] del Pozo," 1674.

65. AGN, Matrimonios 70, expediente 2, 1674–1676, "Instancia de Gracía de la Cruz, Pleito de Gracía de la Cruz, negra, esclava, mujer de José de la Cruz, negro, esclavo con el Capítan Jacome Chirini, vecino de Mexico sobre que traigan a ella al dicho José de la Cruz para que cohabiten y hagan vida maridable."

66. According to María Eugenia Chaves, "We have also seen that the agency of the slaves in intervening in the judicial process and influencing the arguments in favor of their freedom depended on the degree of knowledge they could acquire and on the extent to which they could mobilize a support network for their cause. The newly acquired confidence of the slaves in their legal pursuit of freedom—their 'judicial awakening'—was one among other factors by which the institution of slavery was slowly eroded." "Slave Women's Strategies for Freedom and the Late Spanish Colonial State," in *Hidden Histories of Gender and the State in Latin America,* ed. Elizabeth Dore and Maxine Molyneux (Durham, N.C.: Duke University Press, 2000), 119. A similar argument informs the essay by Stephen Gudeman and Stuart B. Schwartz in which they suggest how "baptism of slaves thus represented a threat to slavery. . . . The resolution to this incompatibility . . . was not to abolish slavery or baptism, although the contradiction eventually contributed to slavery's extinction." "Cleansing Original Sin: Godparenthood and the Baptism of Slaves in Eighteenth-Century Bahia," in *Kinship Ideology and Practice in Latin America,* ed. Raymond T. Smith (Chapel Hill: University of North Carolina Press, 1984), 42. Gracía's challenge, like Antonía's, brings into relief the paradox of slave society in seventeenth-century New Spain. At its pinnacle, slavery in New Spain largely was a single-generation phenomenon. Many, if not most, creoles held a distinct legal status from their parents. Perhaps the astuteness of slaves such as Gracía, which manifested itself in courts and their relations with masters, played a prominent role in slavery's brief legal legacy in any one family.

67. AGN, Matrimonios 70, expediente 2, 1674–1676, "Auto del Provisor," 27 December 1674.

68. "Notificación del auto al Capitán Jacome Chirini"; "Instancia de Jacome Chirini," 31 October 1674. Both in AGN, Matrimonios 70, expediente 2, 1674–1676.

69. AGN, Matrimonios 70, expediente 2, 1674–1676, "Instancia de Jacome Chirini," 10 May 1675.

70. AGN, Matrimonios 70, expediente 2, 1674–1676, "Instancia de Gracía de la Cruz," 17 July 1675.

71. AGN, Matrimonios 70, expediente 2, 1674–1676, "Instancia de Juan de Cespedes como amo de Gracía de la Cruz," 22 July 1675.

6. Creoles and Christian Narratives

1. "Introduction," in Blassingame, ed., *Slave Testimony*, xliv.

2. Hartman, *Scenes of Subjection*, 11.

3. AGN, Inquisición 134, expediente 3, "Publicación de la Sentencia," 6 March 1575, Mexico City; AGN, Inquisición 101, expediente 8, "Pronunciación de la Sentencia," 6 March 1575, Mexico City; AGN, Inquisición 102, expediente 2, "Sentencia contra Isabel Díaz y Francisco Granados," 6 March 1575, Mexico City; AGN, Inquisición 101, expediente 8, "Sentencia contra Juan de Perales," 6 March 1575, Mexico City; Medina, *História del tribunal del Santo Oficio de la Inquisición en México*, 50–51; Ibáñez, *El tribunal de la Inquisición en México (Siglo XVI)*, 155.

4. Medina, *História del tribunal del Santo Oficio de la Inquisición en México*, 49.

5. AGN, Inquisición 134, expediente 3, "Votos de los Inquisidores sobre el caso de Beatriz Ramírez," 9 January 1575, Mexico City; AGN, Inquisición 134, expediente 3, "Publicación de la Sentencia," 6 March 1575, Mexico City; AGN, Inquisición 101, expediente 8, "Votos de los Inquisidores," 23 December 1574, Mexico City; AGN, Inquisición 101, expediente 8, "Pronunciación de la Sentencia," 6 March 1575, Mexico City; AGN, Inquisición 102, expediente 2, "Sentencia contra Isabel Díaz y Francisco Granados," 6 March 1575, Mexico City; AGN, Inquisición 101, expediente 8, "Votos," 23 February 1575, Mexico City; AGN, Inquisición 101, expediente 8, "Sentencia contra Juan de Perales," 6 March 1575, Mexico City; Medina, *História del tribunal del Santo Oficio de la Inquisición en México*, 50–51.

6. Isabel Díaz was exiled for four years, whereas the others each received 5-year sentences. Moreover, the men were sentenced to spend their five years in the galleys of the king's Mediterranean navy. AGN, Inquisición 134, expediente 3, "Votos de los Inquisidores sobre el caso de Beatriz Ramírez," 9 January 1575, Mexico City; AGN, Inquisición 101, expediente 8, "Votos de los Inquisidores," 23 December 1574, Mexico City; AGN, Inquisición 102, expediente 2, "Sentencia contra Isabel Díaz y Francisco Granados," 6 March 1575, Mexico City; AGN, Inquisición 101, expediente 8, "Sentencia contra Juan de Perales," 6 March 1575, Mexico City; and Medina, *História del tribunal del Santo Oficio de la Inquisición en México*, 50–51.

7. Alberro, *Inquisición y Sociedad en México, 1571–1700*, 74–75.

8. Palmer, *Slaves of the White God*, 120–125.

9. Haring perceptively observed that "the government of Castile in the fifteenth and sixteenth centuries, therefore, was rapidly becoming an absolute, patrimonial monarchy. Like other growing nation-states of Europe as they were consolidated in the age of Renaissance, it escaped from the medieval limitations of Empire and Church and the feudal rights of the nobility—also from those acquired rights of municipal autonomy represented in Spain by the fueros of its principal cities. The superiority of the state over all long-standing customs, local privileges, and private jurisdictions was more and more accepted." *The Spanish Empire in America*, 3. As the early modern state, embodied in the absolutist sovereign, prevailed, the Church could not protect the rights of the *extra ecclesiam*.

10. In terms of sixteenth-century origins and biographical detail, the inquisition

records have no rival. For the enslaved outside of Spanish America, narratives began proliferating during the eighteenth century. But in scope, depth, and volume, they rarely approximate the inquisition records. For a critical introduction, see Blassingame's "Introduction," in *Slave Testimony*, xvii–lxv. Saidiya Hartman offers an invaluable critique of those scholars who approach slave narratives as if they represented transparent sources with which to reconstruct black past in *Scenes of Subjection*, 10–14. See also *Africa Remembered: Narratives by West Africans from the Era of the Slave Trade*, ed. Philip D. Curtin (Madison: University of Wisconsin Press, 1967); Lawrence W. Levine *Black Culture and Black Consciousness: Afro-American Folk Thought from Slavery to Freedom* (New York: Oxford University Press, 1977); William L. Andrews, *To Tell a Free Story: The First Century of Afro-American Autobiography, 1760–1865* (Urbana: University of Illinois Press, 1986); Carla L. Peterson, *"Doers of the Word": African-American Women Speakers and Writers in the North (1830–1880)* (New York: Oxford University Press, 1995); Hazel V. Carby, *Reconstructing Womanhood: The Emergence of the Afro-American Woman Novelist* (New York: Oxford University Press, 1987); and Gates, *Figures in Black*. For the Caribbean in particular and the Atlantic world in general, the brilliant work of Richard Price remains unrivalled. See *First-Time* and *Alabi's World*.

11. Despite the fact that it was driven by the bigamy proceedings, the trial testimony informing these disparate narratives is an important source with which to examine the genesis of the Afro-Mexican population. Because it is largely anecdotal, the testimony is an invaluable asset for reconstructing salient features of people's lives and lends volume to the voices of sixteenth-century New Spain's silent Hispanic majority. In the final analysis, the court depositions provide an indispensable glimpse of the earliest phase of the African diaspora.

12. Susan F. Hirsch and Mindie Lazarus-Black, "Performance and Paradox: Exploring Law's Role," in *Contested States*, ed. Hirsch and Lazarus-Black, 9–13; Mindie Lazarus-Black, "Slaves, Masters, and Magistrates: Law and the Politics of Resistance in the British Caribbean, 1736–1834," in *Contested States*, 260–267.

13. Antonío de Savedra refers to this explicitly when he states that "she [Beatriz] fled to the mines of Guanajuato without returning to the power of the said indio Diego." AGN, Inquisición 134, expediente 3, "Antonío de Savedra," 27 April 1574, Mexico City.

14. AGN, Inquisición 134, expediente 3, "Antonío de Savedra," 27 April 1574, Mexico City. Beatriz defined herself as a *mulata,* though she identified her mother as an *india* and her father as a *negro.*

15. Throughout the trial testimony, "Chichimeca"—a reference to nomadic Indians—served as a reference to the northern frontier to which the diocese of Michoácan still belonged in the second half of the sixteenth century. AGN, Inquisición 134, expediente 3, "Diego López," 20 April 1574, Mexico City; AGN, Inquisición 134, expediente 3, "Beatriz Ramirez," 30 April 1574, Mexico City.

16. AGN, Inquisición 134, expediente 3, "Antonío de Savedra," 27 April 1574, Mexico City; AGN, Inquisición 134, expediente 3, "Beatriz Ramirez," 30 April 1574, Mexico City.

17. AGN, Inquisición 134, expediente 3, "Antonío de Savedra," 27 April 1574, Mexico

City; AGN, Inquisición 134, expediente 3, "Juan de Medina," 21 May 1574, Mexico City.

18. AGN, Inquisición 134, expediente 3, "Diego López," 20 April 1574, Mexico City; AGN, Inquisición 134, expediente 3, "Antonío de Savedra," 27 April 1574, Mexico City; AGN, Inquisición 134, expediente 3, "Beatriz Ramirez," 30 April 1574; AGN, Inquisición 134, expediente 3, "Juan de Medina," 21 May 1574, Mexico City.

19. AGN, Inquisición 134, expediente 3, "Beatriz Ramirez," 30 April 1574, Mexico City.

20. AGN, Inquisición 134, expediente 3, "Diego López," 20 April 1574, Mexico City.

21. Evidently, they were married in Puebla and veiled in Oaxaca. AGN, Inquisición 134, expediente 3, "Diego López," 20 April 1574, Mexico City; AGN, Inquisición 134, expediente 3, "Juan Díaz," 21 May 1574, Mexico City.

22. AGN, Inquisición 134, expediente 3, "Juan de Medina," 21 May 1574, Mexico City.

23. Ibid. Antonío de Savedra also makes similar claims. Beatriz's former employer informed the inquisitors that he "saw her four years ago and since then has seen her with Diego . . . who sells fruit in the plaza." AGN, Inquisición 134, expediente 3, "Antonío de Savedra," 27 April 1574, Mexico City.

24. AGN, Inquisición 134, expediente 3, "Diego López," 20 April 1574, Mexico City.

25. Illness, especially the fear about what would happen in the afterlife, prompted individuals to address Christian immorality. Jacques Le Goff, *The Birth of Purgatory*, trans. Arthur Goldhammer (Chicago: University of Chicago Press, 1981).

26. AGN, Inquisición 134, expediente 3, "Beatriz Ramirez," 13 October 1574, Mexico City.

27. "Juan de Molina," 29 July 1574, Puebla; "Isabel Romera," 29 July 1574, Puebla; "Magdalena Ruíz," 30 July 1574, Puebla; "Juan de Cintra," 1 September 1574, Mexico City; "María Ramos," 2 August 1574, Mexico City. All in AGN, Inquisición 101, expediente 8. AGN, Inquisición 102, expediente 2, "Juana Velazquez," 12 November 1574, Mexico City.

28. "Juan de Cintra," 20 July 1574, Mexico City; "María Ramos," 20 July 1574, Mexico City; "Diego de Carranza," 20 July 1574, Mexico City; "Juan de Carranza," 20 July 1574, Mexico City. All in AGN, Inquisición 101, expediente 8.

29. AGN, Inquisición 101, expediente 8, "Isabel Díaz," 21 July 1574, Mexico City.

30. AGN, Inquisición 101, expediente 8, "Juan de Cintra," 1 September 1574, Mexico City; AGN, Inquisición 102, expediente 2, "María Ramos," 1 August 1574, Mexico City.

31. Ibid.

32. Ibid.

33. "Juan de Molina," 29 July 1574, Puebla; "Isabel Romera," 29 July 1574, Puebla; "Magdalena Ruíz," 30 July 1574, Puebla. All in AGN, Inquisición 101, expediente 8.

34. AGN, Inquisición 101, expediente 8, "Francisco Magdalena Ruíz," 30 July 1574, Puebla; AGN, Inquisición 102, expediente 2, "Isabel Díaz," 21 July 1574, Mexico City.

35. AGN, Inquisición 102, expediente 2, "Isabel Díaz," 21 July 1574, Mexico City.

36. AGN, Inquisición 102, expediente 2, "Votos de los Inquisidores," 9 February 1575, Mexico City.

37. AGN, Inquisición 103, expediente 5, "Sentencia contra Juan de Perales," 23 February 1575, Mexico City.

38. Though Juana Hernández, Luisa, Francisco Suarez, María Hernández, Elena, Cristobal Hernández, Juan Pérez, Mateo Díaz, and Pascual Nuñez (among others) eventually criticized Juan's "scandalous" behavior, they initially resisted leveling charges against him. Interestingly enough, Juan's network of familiars was extensively comprised of persons of African descent, most of whom were enslaved. "Juana Hernández," 9 October 1571, Mexico City; "Francisco Suarez," 9 October 1571, Mexico City; "Elena," 9 October 1571, Mexico City; "Cristobal Hernández," 10 October 1571, Mexico City; "Nicolas," 10 October 1571, Mexico City. All in AGN, Inquisición 103, expediente 5.

39. "Juana Hernández," 9 October 1571, Mexico City; "Francisco Suarez," 9 October 1571, Mexico City; "Elena," 9 October 1571, Mexico City; "María Hernández," 3 November 1571, Mexico City. All in AGN, Inquisición 103, expediente 5.

40. AGN, Inquisición 103, expediente 5, "Pascual Nuñez," 6 November 1571, Mexico City.

41. AGN, Inquisición 103, expediente 5, "Mateo Díaz," 5 November 1571, Mexico City.

42. AGN, Inquisición 103, expediente 5, "María Hernández," 3 November 1571, Mexico City.

43. Juan de Perales gathered a battery of witnesses who testified that Nicolas was a notorious drunkard and a well-known philanderer. "María Hernández," 3 November 1571, Mexico City; "Juan Pérez," 3 November 1571, Mexico City; "Mateo Díaz," 5 November 1571, Mexico City; "Pascual Nuñez," 6 November 1571, Mexico City. All in AGN, Inquisición 103, expediente 5.

44. "Luisa Hernández," 22 January 1575, Mexico City; "Arias de Valdes," 27 January 1575, Mexico City; "Gaspar de Miranda," 30 January 1575, Mexico City. All in AGN, Inquisición 103, expediente 5.

45. AGN, Inquisición 134, expediente 3, "Denunciación Diego López," 20 April 1574, Mexico City.

46. A number of important anthropological and historical works have examined the ways subaltern subjects appropriated the language of power in order to structure their narratives. Stern, *Peru's Indian Peoples*, 158–183; Kagan, *Lawsuits and Litigants*; David Warren Sabean, *Power in the Blood: Popular Culture and Village Discourse in Early Modern Germany* (Cambridge: Cambridge University Press, 1984); Price, *Alabi's World*, 67–68; James C. Scott, *Domination and the Arts of Resistance: Hidden Transcripts* (New Haven, Conn.: Yale University Press, 1990); Peter Burke, *The Art of Conversation* (Ithaca, N.Y.: Cornell University Press, 1993), 1–33; Mindie Lazarus-Black, *Legitimate Acts and Illegal Encounters: Law and Society and Antigua and Barbuda* (Washington, D.C.: Smithsonian Institution Press, 1994); and Kellogg, *Law and the Transformation of Aztec Culture*.

47. AGN, Inquisición 134, expediente 3, "Denunciación Diego López," 20 April 1574, Mexico City.

48. The Colegio de Mestizas was a tutorial school for mestizo children through which church and state hoped to regulate them and teach them the skills they would need in a European-dominated society.

49. AGN, Inquisición 134, expediente 3, "Antonío de Savedra," 27 April 1574, Mexico City.

50. AGN, Inquisición 134, expediente 3, "Orden de Prison Contra Beatriz Ramirez," 27 April 1574, Mexico City.

51. Beatriz's identification of herself as a mulatto underscores the ambiguity of ethnic labels. Despite the attempts of scholars to appropriate the official classification schemes, her definition carried greater valence, even in an official context. As Richard Price observed in reference to the Saramaka, "To reconstruct the meaning of . . . identity in the late eighteenth century—what it really meant to be a Matjau or a Nasi person—requires a complex effort of the imagination, holding simultaneously in mind a very large number of contemporaneously documented interactions and incidents while being constantly alert to the dangers of historical presentism or anachronistic inference." *Alabi's World*, 315.

52. Richard Boyer, "Women, *La Mala Vida*, and the Politics of Marriage," in *Sexuality and Marriage in Colonial Latin America*, ed. Lavrín, 252–286.

53. AGN, Inquisición 134, expediente 3, "Primera Audiencia de Beatriz Ramirez," 30 April 1574, Mexico City.

54. AGN, Inquisición 134, expediente 3, "Juan Díaz," 21 May 1574, Mexico City.

55. As the "25- or 26-year-old" *mulata* Beatriz Ramirez narrated her story and responded to questions, she demonstrated an acute understanding of Christian norms and morality. For instance, she chose not to mention having cohabited with "Diego el indio." Yet Juan de Medina recalled that Beatriz and Diego lived together before their marriage. Beatriz simply brings up the subject of her relationship with "Diego el indio" at the point that they wanted to contract a marriage. AGN, Inquisición 134, expediente 3, "Primera Audiencia de Beatriz Ramirez," 30 April 1574, Mexico City; AGN, Inquisición 134, expediente 3, "Antonío de Savedra," 27 April 1574, Mexico City; "Denunciación de Diego López," 27 April 1574.

56. The fact that Beatriz lied for strategic reasons does not undermine her entire testimony. Diego's abuse may have prompted Beatriz's flight. Her relationship and marriage to "Diego el negro" and general adherence to Christian precepts indicates in an inferential and minimal way that her allegations contained some truth.

57. This awareness underscores the degree to which sixteenth-century Africans and their descendants manifested a hybrid consciousness which, in turn, facilitated their cultural navigation in New Spain.

58. AGN, Inquisición 101, expediente 8, "Isabel Díaz," 1574; AGN, Inquisición 102, expediente 2, "Francisco Granados," 1574; AGN, Inquisición 185, expediente 3, "Juan Francisco Robledo," 1592.

59. AGN, Inquisición 101, expediente 8, "Denunciación de Francisco Granados," 19 July 1574, Mexico City.

60. Francisco identified Isabel Díaz as a free mulatto who had been reared in Juan

de Cintra's household and was the daughter of an Indian residing in San Juan—the Amerindian neighborhood adjacent to the *traza* where Spaniards and their household servants resided. As employed by Francisco, "mulatto" constituted a term with variable meanings that was not always linked to the Spanish-African binary with which the concept is usually associated.

61. AGN, Inquisición 101, expediente 8, "Juan de Cintra," 1574, Mexico City; Juan identified Pedro García as the husband and the cathedral as the site of the wedding.

62. With this last comment, Juan revealed his confidence about the relationship that he and Isabel Díaz shared. In subsequent testimony, Juan actually saw himself as a father of Isabel Díaz and her siblings. Juan noted how "Isabel Díaz and her siblings all come to me because they treat me as a father." Despite Juan's perception of their relationship, Isabel deceived her purported paterfamilias and fabricated an elaborate fiction for him.

63. The inquisitors did not always employ this open-ended questioning. It is interesting, therefore, that the inquisitors asked María Ramos, a Spanish woman, this question. Perhaps the inquisitors were reflecting their perceptions of gender. In other words, perhaps they felt that as a woman, María should be both more aware and more willing to divulge deviations from orthodox practices. The inquisitors clearly were operating from a confessional model in which individuals were expected to reveal their conscience. In the process, the inquisitors made witnesses feel as if they were on trial. The inquisitors understood that rumors and gossip often transcended ascribed boundaries.

64. Note the discrepancy between Juan de Cintra's testimony and that of María with regard to the size and composition of their household staff. María views Isabel's daughter as a *negra* even though she identified Isabel Díaz, her mother, as a mulatto. Juan, however, claiming to be an intimate of Isabel and her siblings, identified Isabel's daughter as a mulatto.

65. AGN, Inquisición 101, expediente 8, "María Ramos," 20 July 1574, Mexico City.

66. AGN, Inquisición 101, expediente 8. The marriage was public and Diego saw them together, but he also remembered not seeing Pedro again.

67. Diego de Carranza and his son, Juan, were quite familiar with the public portion of Isabel's life. They knew about her marriage and Pedro's departure. Their familiarity enabled them to recognize and then strike up a conversation with Pedro outside of a familiar context even though he had assumed a different name—perhaps even a distinct identity. (Diego de Carranza noted that Pedro García was known in the area of Lagos as Perrales; thus he assumed the name, if not the identity, of his former employer, in whose house he had been reared.) Encounters represented moments during which individuals exchanged and updated critical biographical information. Such information served to keep individuals abreast of faraway developments and of kin, familiars, and distant acquaintances. Biographical exchanges reveal the deep personal ties that united persons despite their mobility. Natalie Zemon Davis noted how in the sixteenth century Ponsett acquired information about and possibly from Martin Guerre in repeated conversations. Eventually, the biographical sketches and anecdotes enabled Ponsett to elicit further information about and from Martin Guerre's

familiars and former neighbors. *The Return of Martin Guerre* (Cambridge, Mass.: Harvard University Press, 1983).

68. AGN, Inquisición 101, expediente 8, "Carta del santo oficio de la inquisición al arcediano de la iglesia catedral de Puebla de los Angeles," 20 July 1574, Mexico City.

69. Evidently, Isabel had acquired the surname Díaz from her father. By identifying herself as a mulatto—though she described her father as a mulatto and her mother as an Indian—Isabel underscored her definition of mulatto.

70. The fact that Francisco and Isabel had been *amancebado* (in a state of concubinage) for four years suggests that on this matter of faith they were consciously indifferent to the teachings of the Church. Indeed, this was often the case, since numerous couples had been involved in such relationships for extended periods before extenuating circumstances, usually the fear of death, led to a legal marriage. Herman Bennett, "Lovers, Family and Friends: The Formation of Afro-Mexico, 1580–1810" (Ph.D. diss., Duke University, 1993), 16.

71. In early modern Catholic weddings there were two official steps—the actual ceremony of marriage followed by the veiling, another ceremony but usually not performed in the Church. During the veiling ceremony, the couple would celebrate or "come out" to their neighbors and friends. In Francisco's testimony, the emphasis on "*desposar*" (wedded) as opposed to "*velar*" (veiled) underscores his efforts to clarify that he did not contract marriage with Isabel while he was fully within reason. But once he recovered—which included the recovery of his reason—Francisco opted not to legitimize his union any further.

72. AGN, Inquisición 101, expediente 8, "Juan de Molina," 29 July 1574, Puebla.

73. This is a clear example that Juan knew what his Christian responsibility entailed. Perhaps this was an effect of the Edict of Faith or perhaps it was an effect of the auto-de-fé.

74. AGN, Inquisición 101, expediente 8, "Isabel Romero," 29 July 1574, Puebla.

75. AGN, Inquisición 101, expediente 8, "Francisco Ruíz," 30 July 1574, Puebla.

76. On August 6, 1574, six days later, the inquisitors received the dossier that confirmed what they already knew. AGN, Inquisición 101, expediente 8, "Carta del Arcediano de la catedral de Puebla al Santo oficio de México sobre que ha ordenado hacer la información de testigos sobre el matrimonio de Francisco Granados e Isabel Díaz," 1 August 1574, Puebla.

77. AGN, Inquisición 101, expediente 8, "Salida bajo fianza," 7 August 1574, Mexico City.

78. AGN, Inquisición 101, expediente 8, "Ampliación de la declaración de Juan de Cintra," 1 September 1574, Mexico City.

79. AGN, Inquisición 102, expediente 2, "Ratificación de Francisco Granados," 2 August 1574.

80. Ibid.

81. AGN, Inquisición 101, expediente 8, "Auto de Prison contra Francisco Granados," 9 October 1574; AGN, Inquisición 101, expediente 8, "Ingreso en las Carceles del Santo Oficio de Mexico de Francisco Granados," 25 October 1574.

82. William B. Taylor, building on the work of E. P. Thompson, who viewed the state as the "institutional expression of social relationships," insightfully observed that "the maintenance and exercise of systems of power through concrete personal mediations expands the concept of the state beyond the usual meaning of centralized institutions of the sovereign authority to encompass a larger field of institutional expressions of social relationship that have to do with the regulation of public life." "Between Global Process and Local Knowledge: An Inquiry into Early Latin American Social History, 1500–1900," in *Reliving the Past: The Worlds of Social History,* ed. Olivier Zunz (Chapel Hill: University of North Carolina Press, 1985), 147.

83. Cope, *The Limits of Racial Domination,* 27–48, 125–160.

84. AGN, Inquisición 103, expediente 5, "Mateo Díaz," 5 November 1571, Mexico City.

85. AGN, Inquisición 103, expediente 5, "Juan Pérez," 3 November 1571, Mexico City.

86. AGN, Inquisición 103, expediente 5, "Juan de Perrales," 30 October 1571, Mexico City.

87. Poole, *Pedro Moya de Contreras,* 38–117.

88. Susan Kellogg observed that, among the Nahuas, "the use of Catholic symbols and imagery . . . became increasingly pronounced after 1585. However, the earliest invocations of Christianity as an emblem of good character date from the early 1570s, when the litigants and witnesses began occasionally to describe themselves in their testimony as 'good Christians.'" *Law and the Transformation of Aztec Culture,* 74. Barbara Hanawalt and Kathryn Reyerson define "baptism, reading of the banns at the church doors, marriage and burials" as critical components of urban spectacles. But they view them as private rituals. "Introduction," in *City and Spectacle in Medieval Europe,* ed. Barbara Hanawalt and Kathryn Reyerson (Minneapolis: University of Minnesota Press, 1994), xviii.

89. AGN, Inquisición 134, expediente 8, "Denuncia por carta contra Diego de Ojeda de Cristóbal de Pastrana," 1580, Mexico City.

90. Ibid.; AGN, Inquisición 134, expediente 8, "Denuncia de Ana, Negra," 19 April 1580, Mexico City.

91. On May 2, 1580, the preliminary proceedings began when the Mexico City inquisition officials send a letter to the commissary of the Inquisition in Puebla. On October 19, 1580, the *fiscal* pressed formal charges against Diego, who was finally arrested on November 19, 1581. See "Carta del Santo Oficio al Comisario del Santo Oficio de Puebla para que haga las averiguaciones pertinentes al caso de Diego de Ojeda," 2 May 1580, Mexico City; "Carta del Comisario del Santo Oficio de Puebla al Santo Oficio de Mexico," 12 May 1580, Puebla; "Denunciación del fiscal de la Inquisición de México contra Diego de Ojeda, mulato por casado dos veces," 19 October 1580, Mexico City; and "Audiencia con Diego de Ojeda," 21 November 1581, Mexico City. All in AGN, Inquisición 134, expediente 8.

92. AGN, Inquisición 134, expediente 8, "Audiencia con Diego de Ojeda," 21 November 1581, Mexico City.

93. Br. Ribera performed the ceremony in the Chapel of Conception in Puebla's cathedral. Diego de Castillo and his wife, Mariana de Clavijo, served as *padrino* (godfather) and *madrina* (godmother). Diego de Ojeda's father, Francisco, did

not attend the wedding. Francisco testified before the Inquisition that upon hearing of the wedding he asked his son "Why did you marry?" Diego apparently
replied "Because it was my desire," at which point Francisco responded by administering "two or three strokes with his staff." Francisco defended his actions,
claiming "I was opposed to the said marriage until it was done." "Declaración de
Catalina," 29 December 1581, Puebla de los Angeles; "Diego de Castillo," 11 May
1580, Puebla de los Angeles; "Francisco de Ojeda," 11 May 1580, Puebla de los
Angeles. All in AGN, Inquisición 134, expediente 8.

94.　　Before his departure, Diego took Catalina to his father's house, where "he left
her," according to Francisco de Ojeda. Catalina remained in the Ojeda household until and possibly even after her husband's trial. "Declaración de Catalina,"
29 December 1581, Puebla de los Angeles; "Diego de Castillo," 11 May 1580, Puebla
de los Angeles; "Francisco de Ojeda," 11 May 1580, Puebla de los Angeles; "Audiencia con Diego de Ojeda," 21 November 1581, Mexico City. All in AGN, Inquisición
134, expediente 8.

95.　　Cristóbal allegedly acquired this information on his way to Soconusco, which
was south of Puebla and on the borders of the Kingdom of Guatemala. AGN,
Inquisición 134, expediente 8, "Audiencia con Diego de Ojeda," 21 November 1581,
Mexico City. Peter Gerhard, *A Guide to the Historical Geography of New Spain*
(Cambridge: Cambridge University Press, 1972), 140. Muleteers often relayed
information that they acquired as they crisscrossed New Spain. Bigamists often
credited muleteers and cowboys with providing them with news of faraway relatives and friends. See AGN, Inquisición 185, expediente 3, 1593.

96.　　AGN, Inquisición 134, expediente 8, "Audiencia con Diego de Ojeda," 21 November 1581, Mexico City.

97.　　AGN, Inquisición 134, expediente 8, "Votos de los Inquisidores," 2 March 1582,
Mexico City.　　　　　　　.

98.　　"Audiencia con Diego de Ojeda," 21 November 1581, Mexico City. Francisco de
Ojeda, Diego's father; Catalina, Diego's wife; and Diego de Castillo, the *padrino*
of the first marriage, provided similar evidence. "Declaración de Catalina,"
29 December, 1581, Puebla de los Angeles; "Diego de Castillo," 11 May 1580,
Puebla de los Angeles; "Francisco de Ojeda," 11 May 1580, Puebla de los Angeles.
All in AGN, Inquisición 134, expediente 8.

99.　　AGN, Inquisición 134, expediente 8, "Audiencia con Diego de Ojeda," 21 November 1581, Mexico City.

100.　　María Elena Cortés Jacome, "El Matrimonio y la Familia Negra en las Legis-
laciones Civil y Eclesiástical Coloniales. Siglos XVI–XIX," in *El placer de pecar y
el afán de Normar,* Seminario de Historia de las Mentalidades (México: Instituto
Nacional de Antropología e Historia, 1987), 217–248.

101.　　AGN, Inquisición 185, expediente 3, "Denunciación de Lázaro de Estrada," 21 November 1592, Mexico City.

102.　　Lázaro gave the impression that he, Leonor, and Francisco had been in Gaspar
Pérez de Monterrey's household for some time. While Francisco's deposition
confirms this impression, Leonor simply recalled being there for "more or less
a year and a half." "Denunciación de Lázaro de Estrada," 21 November 1592,

Mexico City; "Primera Audiencia con Juan Francisco Robledo," 23 November 1592, Mexico City; "Denunciación de Leonor de Sarmiento," 2 September 1593, Puebla de los Angeles. All in AGN, Inquisición 185, expediente 3. Such discrepancies vary in their importance but often reflect a person's familiarity with the accused (or lack thereof). Memory and familiarity, as we shall see, varied from person to person. Certain patterns seem to have prevailed. For one, individuals were rarely privy to biographical details that transpired outside their spatial orbit. Individuals usually relied on hearsay for transactions that occurred outside of their spheres of operation. In general, there was a relationship between level of familiarity, access, and relative accuracy of the biographical details a person provided in their depositions.

103.   Lázaro implied that this was the case for both Leonor and Francisco. Yet he mentioned only that Francisco returned to the household of his youth. AGN, Inquisición 185, expediente 3, "Denunciación de Lázaro de Estrada," 21 November 1592, Mexico City.

104.   While Leonor could have been Lázaro's source, it is plausible that he heard these rumors from members of the expatriate Poblano or Oaxaqueño community who resided in Mexico City. As slaves and servants in elite Spanish households, individuals could easily spread rumors from the provinces into the viceregal capital and then among households. See, for example, the depositions of Ana de Zárate and Antón de Paz, persons of African descent who had spent significant time in Oaxaca before their respective owners moved to Mexico City. In the viceregal capital, they and Antonío Pérez—a free mulatto who joined his employer in Mexico when the latter left Oaxaca—constituted an identifiable Oaxaqueño nucleus living in the *traza*. "Ana de Zárate," 6 October 1593, Mexico City; "Antonío Pérez," 6 October 1593, Mexico City; "Antón de Paz," 6 October 1593, Mexico City. All in AGN, Inquisición 185, expediente 3.

105.   Even though he had not seen Francisco for seven years, Lázaro kept partially abreast of Francisco's doings through hearsay. In an explicit reference to gossip, Lázaro noted that "now they saw that he [Francisco] has her in the City of the Angeles [Puebla]." AGN, Inquisición 185, expediente 3, "Denunciación de Lázaro de Estrada," 21 November 1592, Mexico City.

106.   According to Lázaro, Leonor was unsuccessful in tracking Francisco down and returned to her residence in Cuautla's mining center. Lázaro was clearly not well informed about Leonor's movements, since she actually lived in Puebla. Lázaro may have relied on hearsay to ascertain Leonor's whereabouts. Francisco tried, for instance, without success to take Leonor to Cuautla, alleging that a "Don Cristóbal de Oñate sent him for her." "Denunciación de Lázaro de Estrada," 21 November 1592, Mexico City; "Denunciación de Leonor de Sarmiento," 2 September 1593, Puebla de los Angeles. Both in AGN, Inquisición 185, expediente 3.

107.   AGN, Inquisición 185, expediente 3, "Denunciación de Lázaro de Estrada," 21 November 1592, Mexico City.

108.   AGN, Inquisición 185, expediente 3, "Auto para trasladar a Francisco de Robledo de la carcel publica a las del Santo Oficio," 21 November 1592, Mexico City.

109.   Until his interrogation, Juan Francisco was identified as "Francisco" by Lázaro de Estrado and Licenciado Sancho García. Throughout the case, the other wit-

nesses, with the exception of María de Vergara, identified Juan Francisco simply as "Francisco." AGN, Inquisición 185, expediente 3, "Primera Audiencia con Juan Francisco Robledo," 23 November 1592, Mexico City.

110. While he knew the purported identity and ethnicity of Andrea, his mother, Juan Francisco informed the inquisitor that "I do not know my father nor others of my lineage." AGN, Inquisición 185, expediente 3, "Primera Audiencia con Juan Francisco Robledo," 23 November 1592, Mexico City.

111. Although Andrea may have been the agent for this exposure to Christianity, setting may have also played some part. In all likelihood, Andrea was reared in Juan Francisco Gaspar Pérez de Monterrey's household. Juan Francisco noted that "first I was the slave of Gaspar Pérez de Monterrey." AGN, Inquisición 185, expediente 3, "Primera Audiencia con Juan Francisco Robledo," 23 November 1592, Mexico City.

112. Ibid.

113. Ibid.

114. Ibid.

115. "And with this the audiencia ended and it was ordered that the alcalde of this Holy Office return him [Juan Francisco] to the jail of the court from which he was transferred. While we investigate the said marriage the jailer and the alcalde of the jail are advised not to free him without an order from this Holy Office." Ibid.

116. AGN, Inquisición 185, expediente 3, "Carta del Santo Oficio de Mexico al Comisario de la Ciudad de los Angeles," 23 November 1592, Mexico City.

117. "María de Vergara," December 7, 1592, Puebla de los Angeles. See also "Andrés de Mota," September 2, 1593, Puebla de los Angeles; and "Juan Rodriguez," September 2, 1593, Puebla de los Angeles. All in AGN, Inquisición 185, expediente 3.

118. AGN, Inquisición 185, expediente 3, "María de Vergara," December 7, 1592, Puebla de los Angeles.

119. Ibid.

120. Ibid.

121. María stated that she "wanted to be separated from him because he was an ill-tempered black man." Ibid.

122. While the inquisitors lifted the allegation of bigamy, there was still the issue of a debt of 200 pesos. Conceivably, secular officials freed minor offenders as a display of magnitude, which could explain the fact that Juan Francisco was released at Christmas. His release is simply noted on the margins after his interrogation. AGN, Inquisición 185, expediente 3, "Primera Audiencia con Juan Francisco Robledo," 23 November 1592, Mexico City.

123. "Le prendió el fiscal del arzobispado por la razón que *la denunciadora* dio." Emphasis added. In Spanish, of course, the gender of the "denouncer" is immediately established. AGN, Inquisición 185, expediente 3, "Carta del Comisario del Santo Oficio de Puebla de los Angeles, Alonso Santiago, al Santo Oficio de México," 6 September 1593, Puebla de los Angeles.

124. Alonso Santiago recalled that his superior "ordered an investigation of a free black woman who lives in this city." Ibid.

125. AGN, Inquisición 185, expediente 3, "Denunciación de Leonor de Sarmiento," 2 September 1593, Puebla de los Angeles.

126. Leonor testified that Gutiérrez also passed judgment on this matter, stating that "he [Canon Santiago] will order that he not be freed because this was not a matter for which he [Juan Francisco] should not be allowed to be free." "Denunciación de Leonor de Sarmiento."

127. Ibid.

128. Ibid.

129. "Andrés de Mota," September 2, 1593, Puebla de los Angeles; "Juan Rodriguez," September 2, 1593, Puebla de los Angeles; "Francisco Hernándes," September 2, 1593, Puebla de los Angeles; "Beatríz de Ansurez," September 4, 1593, Puebla de los Angeles; "Francisco Hernández," September 4, 1593, Puebla de los Angeles. All in AGN, Inquisición 185, expediente 3.

130. The scribe noted that "many years have passed [since] the said wedding and the witness was very young and has no memory of their names." AGN, Inquisición 185, expediente 3, "Denunciación de Leonor de Sarmiento," 2 September 1593, Puebla de los Angeles.

131. Leonor noted that Juan Francisco left Zacatecas for Mexico but that subsequently he had returned to the mining center. Isabel and María were said to live in Fresnillo's mining center. AGN, Inquisición 185, expediente 3, "Denunciación de Leonor de Sarmiento," 2 September 1593, Puebla de los Angeles.

132. Racial labels took on meanings that were not necessarily shared throughout New Spain. The depositions from people who had been familiar with each for many years, if not a lifetime, suggests that there was much ambiguity in the meaning of racial and ethnic labels. Despite the contested meanings, the witnesses from Oaxaca and Puebla employed the term "black man" as a way to distinguish between the African-born and black creoles. André's use of "ladino" and "*criollo*" suggest that he was born and raised in Antequera but was also Hispanicized and culturally rooted. AGN, Inquisición 185, expediente 3, "Andrés de Mota," September 2, 1593, Puebla de los Angeles.

133. Ibid.

134. Juan recalled that while Beatriz sold fruit she engaged him in a conversation about "Francisco de Robledo." Realizing that the young mulatto had information about Juan Francisco's marriage in Oaxaca, Beatriz informed Juan that he would be called to testify. AGN, Inquisición 185, expediente 3, "Juan Rodriguez," September 2, 1593, Puebla de los Angeles.

135. Leonor Sarmiento accosted Francisco right after Gabriel de Mota's pack train arrived in Puebla. AGN, Inquisición 185, expediente 3, "Francisco Hernándes," September 2, 1593, Puebla de los Angeles.

136. Ibid.

137. AGN, Inquisición 185, expediente 3, "Francisco Hernández," September 4, 1593, Puebla de los Angeles.

138. Evidently, Alonso de Santiago had Juan Francisco transferred to the prison of the archdiocese in the viceregal capital. AGN, Inquisición 185, expediente 3, "Carta del Comisario del Santo Oficio de Puebla de los Angeles, Alonso Santiago, al Santo Oficio de México," 6 September 1593, Puebla de los Angeles.

139. It is an interesting commentary on the hierarchy of sins that while there was incontrovertible evidence of adultery, the inquisitors were not interested in prosecuting Juan Francisco for his common-law marriage with María de Vergara.

140. As Oaxaqueños residing in Mexico, Antonío testified that he and María had maintained contact and therefore he knew that María was "crippled with illness." In her testimony, Ana added that Juana María was again pregnant, suggesting that she, too, had recently seen her. Antón had not seen María, however, but noted that he had heard that she was in Mexico. "Antonío Pérez," 6 October 1593, Mexico City; "Ana de Zárate," 6 October 1593, Mexico City; "Antón de Paz," 6 October 1593, Mexico City. All in AGN, Inquisición 185, expediente 3.

141. AGN, Inquisición 185, expediente 3, "Antonío Pérez," 6 October 1593, Mexico City.

142. Ibid.

143. Ibid.; AGN, Inquisición 185, expediente 3, "Antón de Paz," 6 October 1593, Mexico City.

144. Despite the similarities of their testimony, each person's deposition also drew attention to distinct events. Ana recalled that the wedding was at eight o'clock in the morning. Antón, on the other hand, noted that the ceremony occurred "in the presence of many blacks." Antonío focused less on the timing of the ceremony or who was there than on María's physical characteristics, including her size and age. "Antonío Pérez," 6 October 1593, Mexico City; "Antón de Paz," 6 October 1593, Mexico City. Both in AGN, Inquisición 185, expediente 3.

145. "Antonío Pérez," 6 October 1593, Mexico City.

Selected Bibliography

Archival Sources

Archivo General de la Nación, Mexico City (AGN)
    Bienes Nacionales
    Edictos de la Santa y General Inquisición
    Inquisición
    Matrimonios
    Tierras

Published Primary and Secondary Sources

Abu-Lughod, Lila. *Veiled Sentiments: Honor and Poetry in a Bedouin Society.* Berkeley: University of California Press, 1986.

Adams, Julia. "The Familial State: Elite Family Practices and State-Making in the Early Modern Netherlands." *Theory and Society* 23 (Summer 1994): 505–539.

Adas, Michael. "The Reconstruction of 'Tradition' and the Defense of the Colonial Order: British West Africa in the Early Twentieth Century." In *Articulating Hidden Histories: Exploring the Influence of Eric R. Wolf,* ed. Jane Schneider and Rayna Rapp, 291–307. Berkeley: University of California Press, 1995.

Aguirre Beltrán, Gonzalo. *La población negra de México: Estudio etnohistórico.* México: Fondo de Cultura Económica, 1946.

———. *Medicina y magia.* Fondo de Cultura Económica, 1963.

Albán, Juan Pedro Viqueira. *Relajados o Reprimidos? Diversiones públicas y vida social en la ciudad de México durante el Siglo de las Luces.* México: Fondo de Cultura Económica, 1987.

———. *Propriety and Permissiveness in Bourbon Mexico.* Translated by Sonya Lipsett-Rivera and Sergio Rivera Ayala. Wilmington, Del.: Scholarly Resources, 1999.

Alberro, Solange. *Inquisición y Sociedad en México 1571–1700.* México: Fondo de Cultura Económica, 1988.

Altman, Ida. *Emigrants and Society: Extremadura and America in the Sixteenth Century.* Berkeley: University of California Press, 1989.

Anderson, Benedict. *Imagined Communities: Reflections on the Origin and Spread of Nationalism.* London: Verso, 1983.

Andrews, Kenneth R. *Trade, Plunder, and Settlement: Maritime Enterprise and the Genesis of the British Empire, 1480–1630.* Cambridge: Cambridge University Press, 1984.

Appadurai, Arjun, ed. *The Social Life of Things: Commodities in Cultural Perspective.* New York: Cambridge University Press, 1986.

Appiah, Kwame Anthony. *In My Father's House: Africa in the Philosophy of Culture.* New York: Oxford University Press, 1992.

Arrom, Silvia Marina. *The Women of Mexico City, 1790–1857.* Stanford, Calif.: Stanford University Press, 1985.

Asad, Talal. *Genealogies of Religion: Discipline and Reasons of Power in Christianity and Islam*. Baltimore: Johns Hopkins University Press, 1993.

Aufderheide, Patricia. "True Confessions: The Inquisition and Social Attitudes in Brazil at the Turn of the XVII Century." *Luso-Brazilian Review* X, no. 2 (1973): 208–240.

Bakewell, P. J. *Silver Mining and Society in Colonial Mexico: Zacatecas, 1546–1700*. Cambridge: Cambridge University Press, 1971.

Bakhtin, Mikhail. *Rabelais and His World*. Bloomington: Indiana University Press, 1984.

Baldwin, John W. *The Language of Sex: Five Voices from Northern France around 1200*. Chicago: University of Chicago Press, 1994.

Bartels, Emily C. "Imperialist Beginnings: Richard Hakluyt and the Construction of Africa." *Criticism* 34 (Fall 1992): 517–538.

Bartlett, Robert. *The Making of Europe: Conquest, Colonization and Cultural Change, 950–1350*. Princeton, N.J.: Princeton University Press, 1993.

Beezley, William H., Cheryl English Martin, and William E. French, eds. *Rituals of Rule, Rituals of Resistance: Public Celebrations and Popular Culture in Mexico*. Wilmington, Del.: Scholarly Resources, 1994.

Berlin, Ira. *Many Thousands Gone: The First Two Centuries of Slavery in North America*. Cambridge, Mass.: Harvard University Press, 1998.

Berlin, Ira, and Philip D. Morgan, eds. *Cultivation and Culture: Labor and the Shaping of Slave Life in the Americas*. Charlottesville: University of Virginia Press, 1993.

Bethell, Leslie, ed. *Colonial Brazil*. New York: Cambridge University Press, 1987.

Bhabha, Homi K. *The Location of Culture*. London and New York: Routledge, 1994.

Blackburn, Robin. *The Making of New World Slavery: From the Baroque to the Modern, 1492–1800*. New York: Verso, 1997.

Blake, John William, ed. *Europeans in West Africa, 1450–1560: Documents to Illustrate the Nature and Scope of Portuguese Enterprise in West Africa, the Abortive Attempt of Castilians to Create an Empire There, and the Early English Voyages to Barbary and Guinea*. London: Hakluyt Society, 1942.

Blanchard, Peter. *Slavery and Abolition in Early Republican Peru*. Wilmington, Del.: Scholarly Resources, 1992.

Blassingame, John W. *The Slave Community: Plantation Life in the Antebellum South*. New York: Oxford University Press, 1972.

Bolster, W. Jeffrey. *Black Jacks: African American Seamen in the Age of Sail*. Cambridge, Mass.: Harvard University Press, 1997.

Borah, Woodrow. *Justice by Insurance: The General Indian Court of Colonial Mexico*. Berkeley and Los Angeles: University of California Press, 1983.

Boswell, John. *Christianity, Social Tolerance, and Homosexuality: Gay People in Western Europe from the Beginning of the Christian Era to the Fourteenth Century*. Chicago: University of Chicago Press, 1980.

Bowser, Frederick P. "The African in Colonial Spanish America: Reflections on Research Achievements and Priorities." *Latin American Research Review* 7 (1972): 77–94.

——. *The African Slave in Colonial Peru, 1524–1650*. Stanford, Calif.: Stanford University Press, 1974.

——. "The Free Person of Color in Mexico City and Lima: Manumission and Opportunity, 1580–1650." In *Race and Slavery in the Western Hemisphere: Quanti-*

tative Studies, ed. Stanley L. Engerman and Eugene D. Genovese, 331–363. Princeton, N.J.: Princeton University Press, 1975.

Boxer, Charles R. *The Portuguese Seaborne Empire, 1415–1825.* New York: Alfred A. Knopf, 1969.

Boyer, Richard. "Mexico in the Seventeenth Century: Transition of a Colonial Society." *Hispanic American Historical Review* 57 (August 1977): 455–478.

———. *Lives of the Bigamists: Marriage, Family, and Community in Colonial Mexico.* Albuquerque: University of New Mexico Press, 1995.

Brading, David A. *The First America: The Spanish Monarchy, Creole Patriots, and the Liberal State, 1492–1867.* Cambridge: Cambridge University Press, 1991.

Brathwaite, Edward. *The Development of Creole Society in Jamaica, 1770–1820.* Oxford: Clarendon Press, 1971.

Brock, Lisa, and Digna Castaneda Fuertes, eds. *Between Race and Empire: African-Americans and Cubans before the Cuban Revolution.* Philadelphia: Temple University Press, 1998.

Brockington, Lolita Gutierrez. *The Leverage of Labor: Managing the Cortes Haciendas in Tehuantepec, 1588–1688.* Durham, N.C.: Duke University Press, 1989.

Brooks, George E. *Landlords and Strangers: Ecology, Society, and Trade in Western Africa, 1000–1630.* Boulder: Westview Press, 1993.

Brundage, James A. *Law, Sex, and Christian Society in Medieval Europe.* Chicago: University of Chicago Press, 1987.

———. "Playing by the Rules: Sexual Behavior and Legal Norms in Medieval Europe." In *Desire and Discipline in the Premodern West,* ed. Jacqueline Murray and Konrad Eisenbichler, 23–41. Toronto: University of Toronto Press, 1996.

Burke, Peter. *The Art of Conversation.* Ithaca, N.Y.: Cornell University Press, 1993.

———. "America and the Rewriting of World History." In *America in the European Consciousness, 1493–1750,* ed. Karen Ordhal Kupperman: 33–51. Chapel Hill: University of North Carolina Press, 1995.

Burke, Timothy. *Lifebuoy Men, Lux Women: Commodification, Consumption, and Cleanliness in Modern Zimbabwe.* Durham, N.C.: Duke University Press, 1996.

Burkhart, Louise M. *The Slippery Earth: Nahua-Christian Moral Dialogue in Sixteenth-Century Mexico.* Tucson: University of Arizona Press, 1989.

Burnham, Philip. *The Politics of Cultural Difference in Northern Cameroon.* Edinburgh: Edinburgh University Press for the International African Institute, 1996.

Burton, Antoinette. *Burdens of History: British Feminists, Indian Women, and Imperial Culture, 1865–1915.* Chapel Hill: University of North Carolina Press, 1994.

Burton, Antoinette, ed. *Gender, Sexuality, and Colonial Modernities.* New York: Routledge, 1999.

Butler, Judith. *Bodies that Matter: On the Discursive Limits of "Sex."* New York: Routledge, 1993.

Butler, Judith, and Joan W. Scott, eds. *Feminists Theorize the Political.* New York: Routledge, 1992.

Butler, Kim D. *Freedoms Given, Freedoms Won: Afro-Brazilians in Post-Abolition São Paulo and Salvador.* New Brunswick, N.J.: Rutgers University Press, 1998.

Campbell, Mary B. *The Witness and the Other World: Exotic European Travel Writing, 400–1600.* Ithaca, N.Y.: Cornell University Press, 1988.

Canny, Nicholas, and Anthony Pagden, eds. *Colonial Identity in the Atlantic World, 1500–1800.* Princeton, N.J.: Princeton University Press, 1987.

Carby, Hazel V. *Reconstructing Womanhood: The Emergence of the Afro-American Woman Novelist.* New York: Oxford University Press, 1987.

Carroll, Patrick J. *Blacks in Colonial Veracruz: Race, Ethnicity, and Regional Development.* Austin: University of Texas Press, 1991.

Castillo Mathieu, Nicolás del. *Esclavos Negros en Cartagena y sus Aportes Lexicos.* Bogota: Instituto Caro y Cuervo, 1982.

Certeau, Michel de. *The Practice of Everyday Life.* Berkeley: University of California Press, 1984.

Cervantes, Fernando. *The Devil in the New World: The Impact of Diabolism in New Spain.* New Haven, Conn.: Yale University Press, 1994.

Chance, John K. *Race and Class in Colonial Oaxaca.* Stanford, Calif.: Stanford University Press, 1978.

Chaves, Maria Eugenia. "Slave Women's Strategies for Freedom and the Late Spanish Colonial State." In *Hidden Histories of Gender and the State in Latin America,* ed. Elizabeth Dore and Maxine Molyneux, 108–126. Durham, N.C.: Duke University Press, 2000.

Clendinnen, Inga. *Ambivalent Conquests: Maya and Spaniard in Yucatan, 1517–1570.* New York: Cambridge University Press, 1987.

———. *Aztecs.* New York: Cambridge University Press, 1991.

Clifford, James. "Diasporas." *Cultural Anthropology* 9, no. 3 (1994): 302–338.

———. *Routes: Travel and Translation in the Late Twentieth Century.* Cambridge, Mass.: Harvard University Press, 1997.

Clifford, James, and George E. Marcus, eds. *Writing Culture: The Poetics and Politics of Ethnography.* Berkeley and Los Angeles: University of California Press, 1986.

Cline, S. L. *Colonial Culhuacan, 1580–1600.* Albuquerque: University of New Mexico Press, 1986.

Clinton, Catherine, and Michele Gillespie. "Introduction: Reflections on Sex, Race, and Region." In *The Devil's Lane: Sex and Race in the Early South,* ed. Catherine Clinton and Michele Gillespie, xiii–xx. New York: Oxford University Press, 1997.

Cohn, Bernard S. *An Anthropologist among the Historians and Other Essays.* New York: Oxford University Press, 1987.

———. *Colonialism and Its Forms of Knowledge: The British in India.* Princeton, N.J.: Princeton University Press, 1996.

Cohen, David William. *The Combing of History.* Chicago: University of Chicago Press, 1994.

Collingwood, R. G. *The Idea of History.* New York: Oxford University Press, 1946.

Cook, Alexandra Parma, and Noble David Cook. *Good Faith and Truthful Ignorance: A Case of Transatlantic Bigamy.* Durham, N.C.: Duke University Press, 1991.

Cope, R. Douglas. *The Limits of Racial Domination: Plebeian Society in Colonial Mexico, 1660–1720.* Madison: University of Wisconsin Press, 1994.

Cornwall, Andrea. "Gendered Identities and Gender Ambiguity among Travestis in Salvador, Brazil." In *Dislocating Masculinity: Comparative Ethnographies,* ed. Andrea Cornwell and Nancy Lindisfarne, 111–132. New York: Routledge Press, 1994.

Cornwall, Andrea, and Nancy Lindisfarne, eds. *Dislocating Masculinity: Comparative Ethnographies.* New York: Routledge, 1994.

Curtin, Philip D. *The Atlantic Slave Trade: A Census.* Madison: University of Wisconsin Press, 1969.

———. *Cross-Cultural Trade in World History.* New York: Cambridge University Press, 1984.

da Costa, Emilia Viotti. *Crowns of Glory, Tears of Blood: The Demerara Slave Rebellion of 1823.* New York: Oxford University Press, 1994.

Darnton, Robert. *The Great Cat Massacre and Other Episodes in French Cultural History.* New York: Vintage Books, 1985.

Davenport, Frances Gardiner, ed. *European Treaties Bearing on the History of the United States and Its Dependencies to 1648.* Washington, D.C.: Carnegie Institution of Washington, 1917.

Davis, Natalie Zemon. *Society and Culture in Early Modern France.* Stanford, Calif.: Stanford University Press, 1965.

———. *The Return of Martin Guerre.* Cambridge, Mass.: Harvard University Press, 1983.

Dening, Greg. *Mr. Bligh's Bad Language: Passion, Power, and Theatre on the Bounty.* New York: Cambridge University Press, 1992.

———. *Performances.* Chicago: University of Chicago Press, 1996.

Diaz, Maria Elena. *The Virgin, the King, and the Royal Slaves of El Cobre: Negotiating Freedom in Colonial Cuba, 1670–1780.* Stanford, Calif.: Stanford University Press, 2000.

Dirks, Nicholas B., ed. *Colonialism and Culture.* Ann Arbor: University of Michigan Press, 1992.

Dirlik, Arif. "The Postcolonial Aura: Third World Criticism in the Age of Global Capitalism." *Critical Inquiry* 20 (Winter 1994): 328–356.

Donnan, Elizabeth, ed. *Documents Illustrative of the History of the Slave Trade to America.* Washington, D.C.: Carnegie Institution of Washington, 1930.

Dore, Elizabeth, and Maxine Molyneux, eds. *Hidden Histories of Gender and the State in Latin America.* Durham, N.C.: Duke University Press, 2000.

Downs, Laura Lee. "If 'Woman' Is Just an Empty Category, Then Why Am I Afraid to Walk Alone at Night? Identity Politics Meets the Postmodern Subject." *Comparative Study in Society and History* 33, no. 2 (1993): 414–437.

Dussel, Enrique. *The Invention of the Americas: Eclipse of "the Other" and the Myth of Modernity.* Translated by Michael D. Barber. New York: Continuum, 1995.

Echevarría, Roberto Gonzalez. *Myth and Archive: A Theory of Latin American Narrative.* Durham, N.C.: Duke University Press, 1998.

Elbl, Ivana. "Cross-Cultural Trade and Diplomacy: Portuguese Relations with West Africa, 1441–1521." *Journal of World History* 3, no. 2 (1992): 165–204.

———. "'Men without Wives': Sexual Arrangements in the Early Portuguese Expansion in West Africa." In *Desire and Discipline: Sex and Sexuality in the Premodern West,* ed. Jacqueline Murray and Konrad Eisenbichler, 61–86. Toronto: University of Toronto Press, 1996.

Elliot, J. H. *Imperial Spain, 1469–1716.* New York: St. Martin's Press, 1963.

———. *The Old World and the New, 1492–1650.* New York: Cambridge University Press, 1970.

Eltis, David. *The Rise of African Slavery in the Americas.* New York: Cambridge University Press, 2000.

Esteva-Fabregat, Claudio. *Mestizaje in Ibero-America.* Translated by John Wheat. Tucson: University of Arizona Press, 1987.

Evans, William McKee. "From the Land of Canaan to the Land of Guinea: The Strange Odyssey of the 'Sons of Ham.'" *American Historical Review* 85 (February 1980): 15–43.

Fabian, Johannes. *Time and the Other: How Anthropology Makes Its Object.* New York: Columbia University Press, 1983.

———. *Language and Colonial Power: The Appropriation of Swahili in the Former Belgian Congo, 1880–1938.* Berkeley: University of California Press, 1986.

Fanon, Franz. *Black Skin, White Masks.* Translated by Charles Lam Markmann. New York: Grove Press, 1967.

Farriss, Nancy M. *Crown and Clergy in Colonial Mexico, 1759–1821.* New York: Oxford University Press, 1968.

———. *Maya Society under Colonial Rule: The Collective Enterprise of Survival.* Princeton, N.J.: Princeton University Press, 1984.

Ferrer, Ada. *Insurgent Cuba: Race, Nation, and Revolution, 1868–1898.* Chapel Hill: University of North Carolina Press, 1999.

Fick, Carolyn E. *The Making of Haiti: The Saint Domingue Revolution from Below.* Knoxville: University of Tennessee Press, 1990.

Florescano, Enrique. *Memory, Myth, and Time in Mexico: From the Aztecs to Independence.* Austin: University of Texas Press, 1994.

Foner, Philip S. *Antonio Maceo: The "Bronze Titan" of Cuba's Struggle for Independence.* New York: Monthly Review Press, 1977.

Forbes, Jack D. *Africans and Native Americans: The Language of Race and the Evolution of Red-Black Peoples.* Urbana: University of Illinois Press, 1993.

Foucault, Michel. *The Archaeology of Knowledge.* New York: Pantheon Books, 1972.

———. *The History of History: An Introduction.* New York: Vintage, 1978.

———. *Discipline and Punish: The Birth of the Prison.* Translated by Alan Sheridan. New York: Vintage Books, 1979.

Fradenburg, Louise, and Carla Freccero, eds. *Premodern Sexualities.* New York: Routledge, 1996.

Franklin, Julian H. *Jean Bodin and the Rise of Absolutist Theory.* Cambridge: Cambridge University Press, 1973.

Frey, Sylvia R., and Betty Wood. *Come Shouting to Zion: African American Protestantism in the American South and British Caribbean to 1830.* Chapel Hill: University of North Carolina Press, 1998.

Freyre, Gilberto. *The Masters and the Slaves: A Study in the Development of Brazilian Civilization.* Translated by Samuel Putnam. New York: Alfred A. Knopf, 1946.

Frye, David. *Indians into Mexicans: History and Identity in a Mexican Town.* Austin: University of Texas Press, 1996.

Frye, Northrop. *Anatomy of Criticism: Four Essays.* Princeton, N.J.: Princeton University Press, 1957.

Gaspar, David Barry. *Bondmen and Rebels: A Study of Master-Slave Relations in Antigua.* Durham, N.C.: Duke University Press, 1985.

Gates, Henry Louis, Jr. *Figures in Black: Words, Signs, and the "Racial" Self.* New York: Oxford University Press, 1987.

Genovese, Eugene D. *In Red and Black: Marxian Explorations in Southern and Afro-American History.* Knoxville, Tennessee: University of Tennessee Press, 1968.

———. *The World the Slaveholders Made: Two Essays in Interpretation.* New York: Vintage Books, 1971.

———. *Roll, Jordan, Roll: The World the Slaves Made.* New York: Vintage Press, 1972.

Georgia Writers' Project, Work Projects Administration. *Drums and Shadows: Survival Studies among the Georgia Coastal Negroes.* Garden City, N.Y.: Anchor Books, 1972.

Gilroy, Paul. *The Black Atlantic: Modernity and Double Consciousness.* Cambridge, Mass.: Harvard University Press, 1993.

Ginzburg, Carlo. *The Night Battles: Witchcraft and Agrarian Cults in the Sixteenth and Seventeenth Centuries.* Baltimore: Johns Hopkins University Press, 1992.

Given, James B. *Inquisition and Medieval Society: Power, Discipline, and Resistance in Languedoc.* Ithaca, N.Y.: Cornell University Press, 1997.

Gomez, Michael A. *Exchanging Our Country Marks: The Transformation of African Identities in the Colonial and Antebellum South.* Chapel Hill: University of North Carolina Press, 1998.

Gonzalez-Casanovas, Roberto J. "Gender Models in Alfonso X's Siete Partidas: The Sexual Politics of 'Nature' and 'Society.'" In *Desire and Discipline: Sex and Sexuality in the Premodern West,* ed. Jacqueline Murray and Konrad Eisenbichler, 42–60. Toronto: University of Toronto Press, 1996.

Goody, Jack. *The Development of the Family and Marriage in Europe.* Cambridge: Cambridge University Press, 1983.

Gordon, Colin, ed. *Power/Knowledge: Selected Interviews and Other Writings by Michel Foucault.* New York: Pantheon Books, 1980.

Gordon, Edmund T. *Disparate Diasporas: Identity and Politics in an African-Nicaraguan Community.* Austin: University of Texas, 1998.

Góngora, Mario. *Studies in the Colonial History of Spanish America.* Cambridge: Cambridge University Press, 1975.

Graham, Sandra Lauderdale. *House and Street: The Domestic World of Servants and Masters in Nineteenth-Century Rio de Janeiro.* Austin: University of Texas Press, 1988.

———. "Honor among Slaves." In *The Faces of Honor: Sex, Shame, and Violence in Colonial Latin America,* ed. Lyman L. Johnson and Sonya Lipsett-Rivera, 201–228. Albuquerque: University of New Mexico Press, 1998.

Greenblatt, Stephen. *Renaissance Self-Fashioning: From More to Shakespeare.* Chicago: University of Chicago Press, 1980.

———. *Marvelous Possessions: The Wonder of the New World.* Chicago: University of Chicago Press, 1991.

Greenblatt, Stephen, ed. *New World Encounters.* Berkeley: University of California Press, 1993.

Greene, Sandra E. *Gender, Ethnicity, and Social Change on the Upper Slave Coast: A History of the Anlo-Ewe.* Portsmouth, N.H.: Heinemann, 1996.

Greenleaf, Richard E. *The Mexican Inquisition of the Sixteenth Century.* Albuquerque: University of New Mexico Press, 1969.

Grunzinski, Serge. *The Conquest of Mexico: The Incorporation of Indian Societies into the Western World, 16th–18th Centuries.* Translated by Eileen Corrigan. Cambridge: Polity Press, 1993.

Gudeman, Stephen, and Stuart B. Schwartz. "Cleansing Original Sin: Godparenthood and the Baptism of Slaves in Eighteenth-Century Bahia." In *Kinship Ideology and Practice in Latin America,* ed. Raymond T. Smith, 35–58. Chapel Hill: University of North Carolina Press, 1984.

Guha, Ranajit. *Dominance without Hegemony: History and Power in Colonial India.* Cambridge, Mass.: Harvard University Press, 1997.

———. *Elementary Aspects of Peasant Insurgency in Colonial India.* Durham, N.C.: Duke University Press, 1999.

Gutiérrez, Ramón A. "From Honor to Love: Transformations of the Meaning of Sexuality in Colonial New Mexico." In *Kinship Practices in Latin America,* ed. Raymond T. Smith, 237–263. Chapel Hill: University of North Carolina Press, 1984.

———. *When Jesus Came, the Corn Mothers Went Away: Marriage, Sexuality, and Power in New Mexico, 1500–1846.* Stanford, Calif.: Stanford University Press, 1991.

Hall, Gwendolyn Midlo. *Social Control in Slave Plantation Societies: A Comparison of St. Domingue and Cuba.* Baltimore: Johns Hopkins University Press, 1971.

Hall, Kim F. *Things of Darkness: Economies of Race and Gender in Early Modern England.* Ithaca, N.Y.: Cornell University Press, 1995.

Hall, Stuart. "What Is This 'Black' in Black Popular Culture?" In *Black Popular Culture,* ed. Michele Wallace, 21–33. Seattle: Bay Press, 1992.

———. "Culture Studies: Two Paradigms." In *Culture/Power/History: A Reader in Contemporary Social Theory,* ed. Nicolas Dirks, Geoff Eley, and Sherry B. Ortner, 520–538. Princeton, N.J.: Princeton University Press, 1994.

Halter, Marilyn. *Between Race and Ethnicity: Cape Verdean American Immigrants, 1860–1965.* Urbana: University of Illinois Press, 1993.

Hanawalt, Barbara A., and Kathryn L. Reyerson, eds. *City and Spectacle in Medieval Europe.* Minneapolis: University of Minnesota Press, 1994.

Hanchard, Michael George. *Orpheus and Power: The Movimento Negro of Rio de Janeiro and Sao Paulo, Brazil, 1945–1988.* Princeton, N.J.: Princeton University Press, 1994.

Hanger, Kimberly S. *Bounded Lives, Bounded Places: Free Black Society in Colonial New Orleans, 1769–1803.* Durham, N.C.: Duke University Press, 1997.

———. "Coping in a Complex World: Free Black Women in Colonial New Orleans." In *The Devil's Lane: Sex and Race in the Early South,* ed. Catherine Clinton and Michele Gillespie, 218–231. New York: Oxford University Press, 1997.

———. "'Desiring Total Tranquility' and Not Getting It: Conflict Involving Free Black Women in Spanish New Orleans." *The Americas* 54, no. 4 (1998): 541–556.

Hanke, Lewis. *The Spanish Struggle for Justice in the Conquest of America.* Boston: Little, Brown and Company, 1965.

———. *All Mankind Is One: A Study of the Disputation between Bartolome de Las Casas and Juan Gines de Sepulveda in 1550 on the Intellectual and Religious Capacity of the American Indians.* DeKalb: Northern Illinois University Press, 1974.

Hannaford, Ivan. *Race: The History of an Idea in the West.* Baltimore: Johns Hopkins University Press, 1996.

Haring, Clarence H. *The Spanish Empire in America.* New York: Harcourt, Brace & World, 1947.

Hartman, Saidiya V. *Scenes of Subjection: Terror, Slavery, and Self-Making in Nineteenth-Century America.* New York: Oxford University Press, 1997.

Haskett, Robert. *Indigenous Rulers: An Ethnohistory of Town Government in Colonial Cuernavaca.* Albuquerque: University of New Mexico Press, 1991.

Heintze, Beatrix. "Der Portugiesisch-Afrikanische Vasallenvertrag in Angola im 17 Jahrhundert." *Paideuma* 25 (1979): 195–223.

——. "Das Ende des Unabhängigen Staates Ndongo (Angola): Neue Chronologie und Reinterpretation (1616–1630)." *Paideuma* 27 (1981): 197–273.

Herskovits, Frances S., ed. *The New World Negro: Selected Papers in Afroamerican Studies.* Bloomington: Indiana University Press, 1966.

Herskovits, Melville J. *The Myth of the Negro Past.* Boston: Beacon Press, 1941.

Heywood, Linda M., ed. *Central Africans and Cultural Transformations in the American Diaspora.* New York: Cambridge University Press, 2002.

Higginbotham, Evelyn Brooks. "African-American Women's History and the Metalanguage of Race." *Signs* 17, no. 2 (1992): 251–274.

Higgins, Kathleen J. *'Licentious Liberty' in a Brazilian Gold-Mining Region: Slavery, Gender, and Social Control in Eighteenth-Century Sabara, Minas Gerais.* University Park: Pennsylvania State University Press, 1999.

Higman, B. W. "Terms for Kin in the British West Indian Slave Community: Differing Perceptions of Masters and Slaves." In *Kinship Practices in Latin America,* ed. Raymond T. Smith, 59–81. Chapel Hill: University of North Carolina Press, 1984.

Hine, Darlene Clark, and Jacqueline McLeod, eds. *Crossing Boundaries: Comparative History of Black People in Diaspora.* Bloomington: Indiana University Press, 1999.

Hoberman, Louisa Schell, and Susan Migden Socolow, eds. *The Countryside in Colonial Latin America.* Albuquerque: University of New Mexico Press, 1996.

Hobsbawm, Eric, and Terence Ranger, eds. *The Invention of Tradition.* Cambridge: Cambridge University Press, 1983.

Hodgen, Margaret T. *Early Anthropology in the Sixteenth and Seventeenth Centuries.* Philadelphia: University of Pennsylvania Press, 1964.

Holt, Thomas C. "Marking, Race, Race-making, and the Writing of History." *American Historical Review* 100, no. 1 (1995): 1–20.

Horn, Rebecca. *Postconquest Coyoacan: Nahua-Spanish Relations in Central Mexico, 1519–1650.* Stanford, Calif.: Stanford University Press, 1997.

Horton, Robin. "African Conversion." *Africa* XLI, no. 2 (1971): 85–108.

Hsia, R. Po-Chia. *The World of Catholic Renewal, 1540–1770.* New York: Cambridge University Press, 1998.

Hulme, Peter. *Colonial Encounters: Europe and the Native Caribbean, 1492–1797.* New York: Routledge, 1986.

——. "Postcolonial Theory and the Representation of Culture in the Americas." *Ojo de buey: magazine cultural* II, no. 3 (1994): 15–25.

Hunefeldt, Christine. *Paying the Price of Freedom: Family and Labor among Lima's Slaves, 1800–1854.* Translated by Alexandra Stern. Berkeley: University of California Press, 1994.

Hunt, Lynn. "Introduction: History, Culture, and Text." In *The New Cultural History,* ed. Lynn Hunt, 1–22. Berkeley: University of California, 1989.

Hunt, Nancy Rose. *A Colonial Lexicon: Of Birth Ritual, Medicalization, and Mobility in the Congo.* Durham, N.C.: Duke University Press, 1999.

Hunter, Tera W. *To 'Joy My Freedom: Southern Black Women's Lives and Labors after the Civil War.* Cambridge, Mass.: Harvard University Press, 1997.

James, C. L. R. *The Black Jacobins: Toussaint L'Ouverture and the San Domingo Revolution.* New York: Vintage Books, 1938.

Jameson, Fredric. *The Political Unconscious: Narrative as a Socially Symbolic Act.* Ithaca, N.Y.: Cornell University Press, 1981.

Jeater, Diana. *Marriage, Perversion, and Power: The Construction of Moral Discourse in Southern Rhodesia, 1894–1930.* Oxford: Clarendon Press, 1993.

Jewsiewicki, Bogumil. "The Production of History and Social Conscience, or How to 'Civilize' the Other." *History in Africa* 8 (1981): 75–87.

Johnson, Lyman L., and Sonya Lipsett-Rivera, eds. *The Faces of Honor in Colonial Latin America: Sex, Shame, and Violence in Colonial Latin America.* Albuquerque: University of New Mexico Press, 1998.

Johnson, Walter. *Soul by Soul: Life Inside the Antebellum Slave Market.* Cambridge, Mass.: Harvard University Press, 1999.

Jones, Adam. *German Sources for West African History, 1599–1669.* Wiesbaden: Franz Steiner Verlag GMBH, 1983.

Jordan, Winthrop D. *White over Black: American Attitudes toward the Negro, 1550–1812.* Chapel Hill: University of North Carolina Press, 1969.

Kagan, Richard L. *Lawsuits and Litigants in Castile, 1500–1700.* Chapel Hill: University of North Carolina Press, 1981.

———. "A World without Walls: City and Town in Colonial Spanish America." In *Comparative and World History/Latin American Studies Program Seminar,* 1–49, ed. Richard Kagan. Baltimore: Johns Hopkins University Press, 1996.

Kale, Madhavi. *Fragments of Empire: Capital, Slavery, and Indian Indentured Labor in the British Caribbean.* Philadelphia: University of Pennsylvania Press, 1998.

Kamen, Henry. *Inquisition and Society in Spain in the Sixteenth and Seventeenth Centuries.* Bloomington: Indiana University Press, 1985.

———. *The Spanish Inquisition: A Historical Revision.* New Haven, Conn.: Yale University Press, 1997.

Kantorowicz, Ernst H. *The King's Two Bodies: A Study in Medieval Political Theology.* Princeton, N.J.: Princeton University Press, 1957.

Karasch, Mary C. *Slave Life in Rio de Janiero, 1808–1850.* Princeton, N.J.: Princeton University Press, 1987.

Karttunen, Frances. "After the Conquest: The Survival of Indigenous Patterns of Life and Belief." *Journal of World History* 3, no. 2 (1992): 239–256.

Kelley, Donald R. *The Human Measure: Social Thought in the Western Legal Tradition.* Cambridge, Mass.: Harvard University Press, 1990.

———. "New World, Old Historiography." In *Changing Identities in Early Modern France,* ed. Michael Wolfe, 275–293. Durham, N.C.: Duke University Press, 1997.

Kellogg, Susan. *Law and the Transformation of Aztec Culture, 1500–1700.* Norman: University of Oklahoma Press, 1995.

Kinsbruner, Jay. *Not of Pure Blood: The Free People of Color and Racial Prejudice in Nineteenth-Century Puerto Rico.* Durham, N.C.: Duke University Press, 1996.

Klein, Herbert S. *African Slavery in Latin America and the Caribbean.* New York: Oxford University Press, 1986.

———. "Blacks." In *The Countryside in Colonial Latin America,* ed. Lousa Schell Hoberman and Susan Migden Socolow, 167–186. Albuquerque: University of New Mexico Press, 1996.

Klor de Alva, J. Jorge. "The Postcolonization of the (Latin) American Experience: A Reconsideration of 'Colonialism,' 'Postcolonialism,' and 'Mestizaje.'" In *After*

Colonialism: Imperial Histories and Postcolonial Displacements, ed. Gyan Prakash, 241–275. Princeton, N.J.: Princeton University Press, 1995.

Kuehn, Thomas. *Law, Family, and Women: Toward a Legal Anthropology of Renaissance Italy.* Chicago: University of Chicago Press, 1991.

Kupperman, Karen Ordahl, ed. *America in European Consciousness, 1493–1750.* Chapel Hill: University of North Carolina Press, 1995.

Kutzinski, Vera M. *Sugar's Secrets: Race and the Erotics of Cuban Nationalism.* Charlottesville: University Press of Virginia, 1993.

Ladurie, Emmanuel LeRoy. *Montaillou: The Promised Land of Error.* Translated by Barbara Bray. New York: Vintage Books, 1979.

Landers, Jane. "'In Consideration of Her Enormous Crime': Rape and Infanticide in Spanish St. Augustine." In *The Devil's Lane: Sex and Race in the Early South,* ed. Catherine Clinton and Michele Gillespie, 205–217. New York: Oxford University Press, 1997.

———. "Female Conflict and Its Resolution in Eighteenth-Century St. Augustine." *The Americas* 54, no. 5 (1998): 557–574.

———. *Black Society in Spanish Florida.* Urbana: University of Illinois Press, 1999.

Lara, Silvia Hunold. *Campos da Violencia: Escravos e Senhores na Capitania do Rio de Janeiro, 1750–1808.* Rio de Janeiro: Paz E Terra, 1988.

Larson, Brooke. *Cochabamba, 1550–1900: Colonialism and Agrarian Transformation in Bolivia.* Princeton, N.J.: Princeton University Press, 1988.

Larson, Pier M. "'Capacities and Modes of Thinking': Intellectual Engagements and Subaltern Hegemony in the Early History of Malagasy Christianity." *The American Historical Review* 102, no. 4 (1997): 969–1002.

Lavrín, Asunción. "Introduction: The Scenario, the Actors, and the Issues." In *Sexuality and Marriage in Colonial Latin America,* ed. Asunción Lavrín, 1–43. Lincoln: University of Nebraska Press, 1989.

———. "Sexuality in Colonial Mexico: A Church Dilemma." In *Sexuality and Marriage in Colonial Latin America,* 47–95. Lincoln: University of Nebraska Press, 1989.

Lavrín, Asunción, ed. *Sexuality and Marriage in Colonial Latin America.* Lincoln: University of Nebraska Press, 1989.

Law, Robin, and Kristin Mann. "West Africa in the Atlantic Community: The Case of the Slave Coast." *William & Mary Quarterly* LVI (April 1999): 307–334.

Lazarus-Black, Mindie, and Susan F. Hirsch, eds. *Contested States: Law, Hegemony, and Resistance.* New York: Routledge, 1994.

Leonard, Irving A. *Books of the Brave: Being an Account of Books and of Men in the Spanish Conquest and Settlement of the Sixteenth Century New World.* 1949; reprint, Berkeley: University of California Press, 1992.

Levine, Lawrence W. *Black Culture and Black Consciousness: Afro-American Folk Thought from Slavery to Freedom.* New York: Oxford University Press, 1977.

Lewis, Earl. "To Turn as on a Pivot: Writing African Americans into a History of Overlapping Diasporas." *American Historical Review* 100, no. 3 (1995): 765–787.

Lewis, Laura A. "Colonialism and Its Contradictions: Indians, Blacks, and Social Power in Sixteenth and Seventeenth Century Mexico." *Journal of Historical Sociology* 9, no. 4 (1996): 410–431.

———. "The 'Weakness' of Women and the Feminization of the Indian in Colonial Mexico." *Colonial Latin American Review* 5, no. 1 (1996): 73–94.

Linebaugh, Peter, and Marcus Rediker. *The Many-Headed Hydra: Sailors, Slaves, Common-*

ers, and the Hidden History of the Revolutionary Atlantic. Boston: Beacon Press, 2000.

Littlefield, Daniel C. Rice and Slaves: Ethnicity and the Slave Trade in Colonial South Carolina. Urbana: University of Illinois Press, 1981.

Lockhart, James. Nahuas and Spaniards: Postconquest Central Mexican History and Philology. Stanford, Calif.: Stanford University Press, 1991.

———. The Nahuas after the Conquest: A Social and Cultural History of the Indians of Central Mexico, Sixteenth through Eighteenth Centuries. Stanford, Calif.: Stanford University Press, 1992.

———. Of Things of the Indies: Essays Old and New in Early Latin American History. Stanford, Calif.: Stanford University Press, 1999.

Lockhart, James, ed. We People Here: Nahuatl Accounts of the Conquest of Mexico. Bekeley: University of California Press, 1993.

Lockhart, James, and Stuart B. Schwartz. Early Latin America: A History of Colonial Spanish America and Brazil. New York: Cambridge University Press, 1983.

Lombardi, John V. The Decline and Abolition of Negro Slavery in Venezuela, 1820–1854. Westport, Conn.: Greenwood, 1971.

Lopez-Canete Quiles, Daniel, ed. El Descubrimiento de Guinea y las Islas Occidentales. Sevilla: Secretariado de Publicaciones de la Universidad de Sevilla, 1992.

Love, Edgar F. "Marriage Patterns of Persons of African Descent in a Colonial Mexico City Parish." Hispanic American Historical Review 51 (February 1971): 79–91.

Lovejoy, Paul E., ed. Identity in the Shadow of Slavery. New York: Continuum, 2000.

Lynch, John. Spain under the Habsburgs. Oxford: Basil Blackwell, 1965.

———. Spain 1516–1598: From Nation State to World Empire. Cambridge, Mass.: Basil Blackwell, 1991.

McAlister, Lyle N. Spain and Portugal in the New World, 1492–1700. Minneapolis: University of Minnesota Press, 1984.

MacCormack, Sabine. Religion in the Andes: Vision and Imagination in Early Colonial Peru. Princeton, N.J.: Princeton University Press, 1991.

MacLachlan, Colin M. Spain's Empire in the New World: The Role of Ideas in Institutional and Social Change. Berkeley: University of California Press, 1988.

Malkki, Liisa H. Purity and Exile: Violence, Memory, and National Cosmology among Hutu Refugees in Tanzania. Chicago: University of Chicago Press, 1995.

Mallon, Florencia E. "The Promise and Dilemma of Subaltern Studies: Perspectives from Latin American History." The American Historical Review 99, no. 5 (1994): 1491–1515.

Mamdani, Mahmood. Citizen and Subject: Contemporary Africa and the Legacy of Late Colonialism. Princeton, N.J.: Princeton University Press, 1996.

Mann, Kristin, and Richard Roberts, eds. Law in Colonial Africa. Portsmouth, N.H.: Heinemann, 1991.

Maravall, Jose Antonio. La cultura del Barroco: analisis de una estructura historica. Barcelona: Editorial Ariel, 1975.

Marcus, George E., and Michael M. J. Fischer, eds. Anthropology as Cultural Critique: An Experimental Moment in the Human Sciences. Chicago: University of Chicago Press, 1986.

Martin, Cheryl English. Rural Society in Colonial Morelos. Albuquerque: University of New Mexico Press, 1985.

———. *Governance and Society in Colonial Mexico: Chihuahua in the Eighteenth Century.* Stanford, Calif.: Stanford University Press, 1996.

Martinez-Alier, Verena. *Marriage, Class, and Colour in Nineteenth-Century Cuba: A Study of Racial Attitudes and Sexual Values in a Slave Society.* Cambridge: Cambridge University Press, 1974.

Marx, Karl. *Capital: A Critique of Political Economy.* New York: Vintage Press, 1977.

———. *Wage Labour and Capital.* Peking: Foreign Languages Press, 1978.

Maza, Sarah. *Private Lives and Public Affairs: The Causes Célèbres of Prerevolutionary France.* Berkeley: University of California Press, 1993.

Mbembe, Achille. *On the Postcolony.* Berkeley: University of California Press, 2001.

Mecham, J. Lloyd. *Church and State in Latin America.* Chapel Hill: University of North Carolina Press, 1934.

Mercer, Kobena. *Welcome to the Jungle: New Positions in Black Cultural Studies.* New York: Routledge, 1994.

Merdinger, J. E. *Rome and the African Church in the Time of Augustine.* New Haven, Conn.: Yale University Press, 1997.

Merry, Sally Engle. *Getting Justice and Getting Even: Legal Consciousness among Working-Class Americans.* Chicago: University of Chicago Press, 1990.

Miers, Suzanne, and Richard Roberts, eds. *The End of Slavery in Africa.* Madison: University of Wisconsin Press, 1988.

Mignolo, Walter D. *The Darker Side of the Renaissance: Literacy, Territoriality, and Colonization.* Ann Arbor: University of Michigan Press, 1995.

Miller, Christopher L. *Blank Darkness: Africanist Discourse in French.* Chicago: University of Chicago Press, 1985.

Miller, Joseph C. "Kings, Lists, and History in Kasanje." *History in Africa* 6 (1979): 51–96.

———. "The Significance of Drought, Disease and Famine in the Agriculturally Marginal Zones of West-Central Africa." *Journal of African History* 23, no. 1 (1982): 17–61.

———. *Way of Death: Merchant Capitalism and the Angolan Slave Trade, 1730–1830.* Madison: University of Wisconsin Press, 1988.

Miller, Joseph C., and John K. Thornton. "The Chronicle as Source, History and Hagiography: The Catalogo dos Governadores de Angola." *Paideuma* 33 (1987): 359–389.

Mills, Kenneth. *Idolatry and Its Enemies: Colonial Andean Religion and Extirpation, 1640–1750.* Princeton, N.J.: Princeton University Press, 1997.

Moore, Henrietta. *Feminism and Anthropology.* Minneapolis: University of Minnesota Press, 1988.

Moore, R. I. *The Formation of a Persecuting Society: Power and Deviance in Western Europe, 950–1250.* Cambridge: Basil Blackwell, 1987.

Moore, Sally Falk. *Social Facts and Fabrications: "Customary" Law on Kilimanjaro, 1880–1980.* New York: Cambridge University Press, 1986.

Morgan, Edmund S. *American Slavery, American Freedom: The Ordeal of Colonial Virginia.* New York: W. W. Norton & Company, Inc., 1975.

Morgan, Philip D. *Slave Counterpoint: Black Culture in the Eighteenth-Century Chesapeake and Lowcountry.* Chapel Hill: University of North Carolina Press, 1998.

Morner, Magnus. *Race Mixture in the History of Latin America.* Boston: Little, Brown and Company, 1967.

———. *Region and State in Latin America's Past.* Baltimore: Johns Hopkins University Press, 1993.

Morrison, Toni. *Playing in the Dark: Whiteness and the Literary Imagination.* Cambridge, Mass.: Harvard University Press, 1992.

Mudimbe, V. Y. *The Invention of Africa: Gnosis, Philosophy, and the Order of Knowledge.* Bloomington: Indiana University Press, 1988.

———. *The Idea of Africa.* Bloomington: Indiana University Press, 1994.

Muldoon, James. *Popes, Lawyers, and Infidels: The Church and the Non-Christian World, 1250–1550.* Philadelphia: University of Pennsylvania Press, 1979.

———. *The Americas in the Spanish World Order: The Justification for Conquest in the Seventeenth Century.* Philadelphia: University of Pennsylvania Press, 1994.

Muldoon, James, ed. *Varieties of Religious Conversion in the Middle Ages.* Gainesville: University Press of Florida, 1997.

Mulroy, Kevin. "Ethnogenesis and Ethnohistory of the Seminole Maroons." *Journal of World History* 4, no. 2 (1993): 287–305.

Mundy, Barbara E. *The Mapping of New Spain: Indigenous Cartography and the Maps of the Relaciones Geograficas.* Chicago: University of Chicago Press, 1996.

Murray, Jacqueline. "Introduction." In *Desire and Discipline: Sex and Sexuality in the Premodern West,* ed. Jacqueline Murray and Konrad Eisenbichler, ix–xxviii. Toronto: University of Toronto Press, 1996.

Murray, Jacqueline, and Konrad Eisenbichler, eds. *Desire and Discipline: Sex and Sexuality in the Premodern West.* Toronto: University of Toronto Press, 1996.

Nalle, Sara T. *God in La Mancha: Religious Reform and the People of Cuenca, 1500–1650.* Baltimore: Johns Hopkins University Press, 1992.

Nirenberg, David. *Communities of Violence: Persecution of Minorities in the Middle Ages.* Princeton, N.J.: Princeton University Press, 1996.

O'Callaghan, Joseph F. *A History of Medieval Spain.* Ithaca, N.Y.: Cornell University Press, 1975.

Olwell, Robert. *Masters, Slaves, and Subjects: The Culture of Power in the South Carolina Low Country, 1740–1790.* Ithaca, N.Y.: Cornell University Press, 1998.

Ortega, Sergio, ed. *De la Santidad a la Perversion o de porque no se cumplia la ley de Dios en la sociedad novohispana.* Mexico City: Editorial Grijalbo, 1985.

Ortner, Sherry B. "Theory in Anthropology Since the Sixties." In *Culture/Power/History: A Reader in Contemporary Social Theory,* ed. Nicolas Dirks, Geoff Eley, and Sherry B. Ortner, 372–411. Princeton, N.J.: Princeton University Press, 1994.

Ortner, Sherry B., and Harriet Whitehead, eds. *Sexual Meanings: The Cultural Construction of Gender and Sexuality.* Cambridge: Cambridge University Press, 1981.

Pagden, Anthony. *The Fall of Natural Man: The American Indian and the Origins of Comparative Ethnology.* Edited by P. E. Russell. Cambridge: Cambridge University Press, 1982.

———. "Identity Formation in Spanish America." In *Colonial Identity in the Atlantic World, 1500–1800,* ed. Nicholas Canny and Anthony Pagden, 51–93. Princeton, N.J.: Princeton University Press, 1987.

———. *Spanish Imperialism and the Political Imagination.* New Haven, Conn.: Yale University Press, 1990.

———. *European Encounters with the New World: From Renaissance to Romanticism.* New Haven, Conn.: Yale University Press, 1993.

――. *Lords of All the World: Ideologies of Empire in Spain, Britain, and France c. 1500–c. 1800.* New Haven, Conn.: Yale University Press, 1995.

Pagden, Anthony, ed. *Hernán Cortés: Letters from Mexico.* New Haven, Conn.: Yale University Press, 1986.

――. *The Languages of Political Theory in Early-Modern Europe.* New York: Cambridge University Press, 1987.

Palmer, Colin A. "Religion and Magic in Mexican Slave Society, 1570–1650." In *Race and Slavery in the Western Hemisphere: Quantitative Studies,* ed. Stanley L. Engerman and Eugene D. Genovese, 311–328. Princeton, N.J.: Princeton University Press, 1975.

――. *Slaves of the White God: Blacks in Mexico, 1570–1650.* Cambridge, Mass.: Harvard University Press, 1976.

――. *Human Cargoes: The British Slave Trade to Spanish America, 1700–1739.* Urbana: University of Illinois Press, 1981.

Paquette, Robert L. *Sugar Is Made with Blood: The Conspiracy of La Escalera and the Conflict between Empires over Slavery in Cuba.* Middletown, Conn.: Wesleyan University Press, 1988.

Patterson, Orlando. *Slavery and Social Death: A Comparative Study.* Cambridge, Mass.: Harvard University Press, 1982.

Paviot, Jacques, ed. *Chronique de Guinee (1453) de Gomes Eanes de Zurara.* Paris: Editions Chandeigne, 1994.

Pennington, Kenneth. *Popes, Canonists, and Texts, 1150–1550.* Norfolk, Great Britain: Variorum, 1993.

――. *The Prince and the Law, 1200–1600: Sovereignty and Rights in the Western Legal Tradition.* Berkeley: University of California Press, 1993.

Perry, Mary Elizabeth. *Gender and Disorder in Early Modern Seville.* Princeton, N.J.: Princeton University Press, 1990.

Pescador, Juan Javier. *De Bautizados A Fieles Difuntos: Familia y mentalidades en una parroquia urbana: Santa Catarina de México, 1568–1820.* México: El Colegio de México, 1992.

Peterson, Carla L. *"Doers of the Word": African-American Women Speakers and Writers in the North (1830–1880).* New York: Oxford University Press, 1995.

Phelan, John Leddy. *The Kingdom of Quito in the Seventeenth Century: Bureaucratic Politics in the Spanish Empire.* Madison: University of Wisconsin Press, 1967.

Pocock, J. G. A. *Politics, Language, and Time: Essays on Political Thought and History.* Chicago: University of Chicago Press, 1960.

Poovey, Mary. *Uneven Developments: The Ideological Work of Gender in Mid-Victorian England.* Chicago: University of Chicago Press, 1988.

――. *Making a Social Body: British Cultural Formation, 1830–1864.* Chicago: University of Chicago Press, 1995.

Prakash, Gyan. "Subaltern Studies as Postcolonial Criticism." *The American Historical Review* 99, no. 5 (1994): 1475–1490.

Prakash, Gyan, ed. *After Colonialism: Imperial Histories and Postcolonial Displacements.* Princeton, N.J.: Princeton University Press, 1995.

Price, Richard. *First-Time: The Historical Vision of an Afro-American People.* Baltimore: Johns Hopkins University Press, 1983.

――. *Alabi's World.* Baltimore: Johns Hopkins University Press, 1990.

Rabasa, Jose. *Writing Violence on the Northern Frontier: The Historiography of Sixteenth-*

Century New Mexico and Florida and the Legacy of the Conquest. Durham, N.C.: Duke University Press, 2000.

Raboteau, Albert J. *Slave Religion: The "Invisible Institution" in the Antebellum South.* New York: Oxford University Press, 1978.

Rafael, Vicente L. *Contracting Colonialism: Translation and Christian Conversion in Tagalog Society under Early Spanish Rule.* Ithaca, N.Y.: Cornell University Press, 1988.

Ragussis, Michael. "The Birth of a Nation in Victorian Culture: The Spanish Inquisition, the Converted Daughter, and the 'Secret Race.'" *Critical Inquiry* 20 (Winter 1994): 477–508.

Ravenstein, E. G., ed. *The Strange Adventures of Andrew Battell of Leigh, in Angola and the Adjoining Regions.* London: Hakluyt Society, 1901.

Rawley, James A. *The Transatlantic Slave Trade: A History.* New York: W. W. Norton & Company, 1981.

Reid-Pharr, Robert F. *Conjugal Union: The Body, the House, and the Black American.* New York: Oxford University Press, 1999.

Reis, João José. *Slave Rebellion in Brazil: The Muslim Uprising of 1835 in Bahia.* Translated by Arthur Brakel. Baltimore: Johns Hopkins University Press, 1993.

Ricard, Robert. *The Spiritual Conquest of Mexico: An Essay on the Apostolate and the Evangelizing Methods of the Mendicant Orders in New Spain, 1523–1572.* Translated by Lesley Byrd Simpson. Berkeley: University of California Press, 1966.

Richards, Jeffrey. *Sex, Dissidence, and Damnation: Minority Groups in the Middle Ages.* New York: Routledge, 1991.

Riley, Denise. *"Am I That Name?": Feminism and the Category of "Women" in History.* Minneapolis: University of Minnesota Press, 1988.

Rodney, Walter. *A History of the Upper Guinea Coast, 1545–1800.* Oxford: Clarendon Press, 1970.

Roediger, David R. *The Wages of Whiteness: Race and the Making of the American Working Class.* New York: Verso, 1991.

Root, Deborah. "Speaking Christian: Orthodoxy and Difference in Sixteenth-Century Spain." *Representations* 23 (Summer 1988): 118–134.

Ross, Dorothy. "Grand Narrative in American Historical Writing: From Romance to Uncertainty." *The American Historical Review* 100, no. 3 (1995): 651–677.

Rout, Leslie B., Jr. *The African Experience in Spanish America, 1502 to the Present Day.* New York: Cambridge University Press, 1976.

Russell-Wood, A. J. R. "'Acts of Grace': Portuguese Monarchs and Their Subjects of African Descent in Eighteenth-Century Brazil." *Journal of Latin American Studies* 32 (May 2000): 307–332.

Sabean, David Warren. *Power in the Blood: Popular Culture and Village Discourse in Early Modern Germany.* New York: Cambridge University Press, 1984.

Sahlins, Marshall. *Islands of History.* Chicago: University of Chicago Press, 1985.

Said, Edward W. *Orientalism.* New York: Penguin, 1978.

Sauer, Carl Ortwin. *The Early Spanish Main.* Berkeley: University of California Press, 1966.

———. *Sixteenth Century North America.* Berkeley: University of California Press, 1971.

Saunders, A. C. de C. M. *A Social History of Black Slaves and Freedmen in Portugal, 1441–1555.* London: Cambridge University Press, 1982.

Scheper-Hughes, Nancy. *Death without Weeping: The Violence of Everyday Life in Brazil.* Berkeley: University of California Press, 1992.
Schmidt, Elizabeth. *Peasants, Traders, and Wives: Shona Women in the History of Zimbabwe, 1870–1939.* Portsmouth, N.H.: Heinemann, 1992.
Schmidt-Nowara, Christopher. *Empire and Antislavery: Spain, Cuba, and Puerto Rico, 1833–1874.* Pittsburgh: University of Pittsburgh Press, 1999.
Schultz, Kirsten. *Tropical Versailles: Empire, Monarchy, and the Portuguese Royal Court in Rio de Janeiro, 1808–1821.* New York: Routledge, 2001.
Schwaller, John Frederick. *The Church and the Clergy in Sixteenth-Century Mexico.* Albuquerque: University of New Mexico Press, 1987.
Schwartz, Stuart B. *Sovereignty and Society in Colonial Brazil: The High Court of Bahia and Its Judges, 1609–1751.* Berkeley: University of California Press, 1973.
———. *Sugar Plantations in the Formation of Brazilian Society: Bahia, 1550–1835.* New York: Cambridge University Press, 1985.
Schwartz, Stuart B., ed. *Implicit Understandings: Observing, Reporting, and Reflecting on the Encounters between European and Other Peoples in the Early Modern Era.* New York: Cambridge University Press, 1994.
Scott, James C. *Domination and the Arts of Resistance.* New Haven, Conn.: Yale University Press, 1990.
Scott, Joan Wallach. *Gender and the Politics of History.* New York: Columbia University Press, 1988.
Scott, Rebecca J. *Slave Emancipation in Cuba: The Transition to Free Labor, 1860–1899.* Princeton, N.J.: Princeton University Press, 1985.
Seed, Patricia. *To Love, Honor, and Obey in Colonial Mexico: Conflicts over Marriage Choice, 1574–1821.* Stanford, Calif.: Stanford University Press, 1988.
———. *Ceremonies of Possession in Europe's Conquest of the New World, 1492–1640.* Cambridge: Cambridge University Press, 1995.
Seminario de Historia de las Mentalidades. *Familia y Sexualidad en Nueva Espana: Memoria del Primer Simposio de Historia de las Mentalidades.* Mexico City: Fondo de Cultura Economica, 1982.
———. *La memoria y el olvido: Segundo Simposio de Historia de las Mentalidades.* Mexico City: Instituto Nacional de Antropologia e Historia, 1985.
———. *El Placer de Pecas & el Afan de Normar.* Mexico City: Editorial Joaquin Mortiz, 1987.
———. *Familia y Poder en Nueva Espana: Memoria del Tercer Simposio de Historia de las Mentalidades.* Mexico City: Instituto Nacional de Antropologia e Historia, 1991.
Sensbach, Jon F. *A Separate Canaan: The Making of an Afro-Moravian World in North Carolina, 1763–1840.* Chapel Hill: University of North Carolina Press, 1998.
Sharp, William Frederick. *Slavery on the Spanish Frontier: The Colombian Choco, 1680–1810.* Norman: University of Oklahoma Press, 1976.
Shiels, W. Eugene. *King and Church: The Rise and Fall of the Patronato Real.* Chicago: Loyola University Press, 1961.
Silberblatt, Irene. *Moon, Sun, and Witches: Gender Ideologies and Class in Inca and Colonial Peru.* Princeton, N.J.: Princeton University Press, 1987.
———. "Becoming Indian in the Central Andres of Seventeenth-Century Peru." In *After Colonialism: Imperial Histories and Postcolonial Displacements,* ed. Gyan Prakash, 279–298. Princeton, N.J.: Princeton University Press, 1995.

Smith, Bonnie G. *The Gender of History: Men, Women, and Historical Practice.* Cambridge, Mass.: Harvard University Press, 1998.

Smith, Raymond T., ed. *Kinship Ideology and Practice in Latin America.* Chapel Hill: University of North Carolina Press, 1984.

Sobel, Mechal. *The World They Made Together: Black and White Values in Eighteenth-Century Virginia.* Princeton, N.J.: Princeton University Press, 1987.

———. *Trabelin' On: The Slave Journey to an Afro-Baptist Faith.* Princeton University Press, 1988.

Spalding, Karen. *Huarochirí: An Andean Society Under Inca and Spanish Rule.* Stanford, Calif.: Stanford University Press, 1984.

Spear, Jennifer M. "Whiteness and the Purity of Blood: Race, Sexuality, and Social Order in Colonial Louisiana." Ph.D. diss., University of Minnesota, 1999.

Spiegel, Gabrielle M. "History, Historicism, and the Social Logic of the Text in the Middle Ages." *Speculum* 65 (January 1990): 59–86.

———. *Romancing the Past: The Rise of Vernacular Prose Historiography in Thirteenth-Century France.* Berkeley: University of California Press, 1993.

———. *The Past as Text: The Theory and Practice of Medieval Historiography.* Baltimore: Johns Hopkins University Press, 1997.

Stern, Steve J. *Peru's Indian Peoples and the Challenge of Spanish Conquest: Huamanga to 1640.* Madison: University of Wisconsin Press, 1982.

———. *The Secret History of Gender: Women, Men, and Power in Late Colonial Mexico.* Chapel Hill: University of North Carolina Press, 1995.

Stoler, Ann. "Making Empire Respectable: The Politics of Race and Sexual Morality in 20th-Century Colonial Cultures." *American Ethnologist* 16, no. 4 (1989): 634–660.

———. "Rethinking Colonial Categories: European Communities and the Boundaries of Rule." *Comparative Study of Society and History* 31, no. 2 (1989): 134–161.

———. " 'In Cold Blood': Hierarchies of Credibility and the Politics of Colonial Narratives." *Representations* 37 (Winter 1992): 151–189.

———. *Race and the Education of Desire: Foucault's History of Sexuality and the Colonial Order of Things.* Durham, N.C.: Duke University Press, 1995.

Strathern, Marilyn. *The Gender of the Gift.* Berkeley: University of California Press, 1988.

Stuckey, Sterling. *Slave Culture: Nationalist Theory and the Foundations of Black America.* New York: Oxford University Press, 1988.

Summers, Carol. "Intimate Colonialism: The Imperial Production of Reproduction in Uganda, 1907–1925." *Signs* 16, no. 4 (1991): 787–807.

Sweet, David G., and Gary B. Nash, eds. *Struggle and Survival in Colonial America.* Berkeley and Los Angeles: University of California Press, 1981.

Tannenbaum, Frank. *Slave and Citizen: The Negro in the Americas.* New York: Vintage Books, 1946.

Taylor, William B. *Drinking, Homicide, and Rebellion in Colonial Mexican Villages.* Stanford, Calif.: Stanford University Press, 1979.

———. *Magistrates of the Sacred: Priests and Parishioners in Eighteenth-Century Mexico.* Stanford, Calif.: Stanford University Press, 1996.

Thompson, J. Eric S., ed. *Thomas Gage's Travels in the New World.* Norman: University of Oklahoma Press, 1958.

Thornton, John. "Demography and History in the Kingdom of Kongo, 1550–1750." *Journal of African History* 18, no. 4 (1977): 507–530.

———. "Early Kongo-Portuguese Relations: A New Interpretation." *History in Africa* 8 (1981): 183–204.

———. "The Kingdom of Kongo, ca. 1390–1678: The Development of an African Social Formation." *Cahiers d'Etudes Africaines* 22, no. 3–4 (1982): 325–342.

———. "The Development of an African Catholic Church in the Kingdom of Kongo, 1491–1750." *Journal of African History* 25 (1984): 147–167.

———. "On the Trail of Voodoo: African Christianity in Africa and the Americas." *The Americas* XLIV (January 1988): 261–278.

———. *Africa and Africans in the Making of the Atlantic World, 1400–1680.* New York: Cambridge University Press, 1992.

———. "'I Am the Subject of the King of Congo': African Political Ideology and the Haitian Revolution." *Journal of World History* 4, no. 2 (1993): 181–214.

———. *The Kongolese Saint Anthony: Dona Beatriz Kimpa Vita and the Antonian Movement, 1684–1706.* New York: Cambridge University Press, 1998.

Townsend, Camilla. "'Half My Body Free, the Other Half Enslaved': The Politics of the Slaves of Guayaquil at the End of the Colonial Era." *Colonial Latin America Review* 7, no. 1 (1998): 105–128.

Turner, Mary, ed. *From Chattel Slaves to Wage Slaves: The Dynamics of Labor Bargaining in the Americas.* Bloomington: Indiana University Press, 1995.

Turner, Victor W. *Schism and Continuity in an African Society: A Study of Ndembu Village Life.* Washington, D.C.: Berg, 1957.

———. *The Ritual Process: Structure and Anti-Structure.* Ithaca, N.Y.: Cornell University Press, 1969.

———. *Dramas, Fields, and Metaphors: Symbolic Action in Human Society.* Ithaca, N.Y.: Cornell University Press, 1974.

Twinam, Ann. *Public Lives, Private Secrets: Gender, Honor, Sexuality, and Illegitimacy in Colonial Spanish America.* Stanford, Calif.: Stanford University Press, 1999.

Valdés, Dennis Nodin. "The Decline of the Sociedad de Castas in Mexico City." Ph.D. diss., University of Michigan, 1978.

———. "The Decline of Slavery in Mexico." *The Americas* 44 (October 1987): 167–194.

van Dantzig, Albert, and Adam Jones, eds. *Pieter de Marees' Description and Historical Account of the Gold Kingdom of Guinea (1602).* New York: Oxford University Press, 1987.

Van Young, Eric. "The New Cultural History Comes to Old Mexico." *Hispanic American Historical Review* 79, no. 2 (1999): 211–247.

Verlinden, Charles. *The Beginnings of Modern Colonization.* Translated by Yvonne Freccero. Ithaca, N.Y.: Cornell University Press, 1970.

Vinson, Ben, III. *Bearing Arms for His Majesty.* Stanford, Calif.: Stanford University Press, 2001.

Wade, Peter. *Blackness and Race Mixture: The Dynamics of Racial Identity in Colombia.* Baltimore: Johns Hopkins University Press, 1993.

———. *Race and Ethnicity in Latin America.* Chicago: Pluto Press, 1997.

Wade, Richard C. *Slavery in the Cities: The South, 1820–1860.* New York. Oxford University Press, 1964.

Walkowitz, Judith R. *City of Dreadful Delight: Narratives of Sexual Danger in Late-Victorian London.* Chicago: University of Chicago Press, 1992.

Wallerstein, Immanuel. *The Modern World-System I: Capitalist Agriculture and the Origins of the European World-Economy in the Sixteenth Century.* New York: Academic Press, 1974.

Watson, Alan. *Slave Law in the Americas.* Athens: University of Georgia Press, 1989.

White, Hayden. *Tropics of Discourse: Essays in Cultural Criticism.* Baltimore: Johns Hopkins University Press, 1978.

White, Luise. *Speaking with Vampires: Rumor and History in Colonial Africa.* Berkeley: University of California Press, 2000.

Wiesner-Hanks, Merry E. *Christianity and Sexuality in the Early Modern World: Regulating Desire, Reforming Practice.* New York: Routledge, 2000.

Wightman, Ann M. *Indigenous Migration and Social Change: The Forasteros of Cuzco, 1570–1720.* Durham, N.C.: Duke University Press, 1990.

Williams, Brackette. *Stains on My Name, War in My Veins: Guyana and the Politics of Cultural Struggle.* Durham, N.C.: Duke University Press, 1991.

Williams, Eric. *Capitalism and Slavery.* Chapel Hill: University of North Carolina Press, 1944.

Williams, Raymond. *Culture and Society, 1780–1950.* New York: Columbia University Press, 1958.

———. *Keywords: A Vocabulary of Culture and Society.* New York: Oxford University Press, 1976.

———. *Marxism and Literature.* New York: Oxford University Press, 1977.

Wolf, Eric R. *Europe and the People without History.* Berkeley: University of California Press, 1982.

Wolf, Kenneth Baxter. "The 'Moors' of West Africa and the Beginnings of the Portuguese Slave Trade." *Journal of Medieval and Renaissance Studies* 24, no. 3 (1994): 449–469.

Wood, Peter H. *Black Majority: Negroes in Colonial South Carolina from 1670 through the Stono Rebellion.* New York: W. W. Norton & Company, 1974.

Wright, Donald R. *The World and a Very Small Place in Africa.* Armonk, N.Y.: M. E. Sharpe, 1997.

Young, Robert. *White Mythologies: Writing History and the West.* New York: Routledge, 1990.

Zurara, Gomes Eanes de, ed. *The Chronicle of the Discovery and Conquest of Guinea.* London: Hakluyt Society, 1896–1899.

Index

HERMAN L. BENNETT is Associate Professor of History at Rutgers University.

Lightning Source UK Ltd.
Milton Keynes UK
UKHW051620211221
395985UK00010B/325